BEST ENTRY-LEVEL JOBS

The
Princeton
Review

BEST ENTRY-LEVEL JOBS

RON LIEBER AND TOM MELTZER

Random House, Inc.
New York
www.PrincetonReview.com

The Princeton Review, Inc.
2315 Broadway
New York, NY 10024
Email: bookeditor@review.com

© 2006 by The Princeton Review, Inc.

ISBN 0-375-76560-3
ISBN-13 978-0-375-76560-5

Editorial Director: Robert Franek
Editor: Suzanne J. Podhurst
Production Manager and Designer: Scott Harris
Production Editor: Christine LaRubio

Manufactured in the United States of America.

9 8 7 6 5 4 3 2 1

ACKNOWLEDGMENTS

I had three first jobs. My day job was writing for *Lawyers Weekly USA*. At night and on weekends, I was a stringer for the Associated Press (turn to page 62 to read why it's valuable training for aspiring reporters). The third job was writing *Taking Time Off* with Colin Hall, who's still my all-time favorite coworker.

Taking Time Off would not have endured without the team at The Princeton Review. I remain indebted to John Katzman for hooking me up with Rob Franek and Erik Olson. They're not only accomplished idea men but also are exceptionally flexible coconspirators. I'm also grateful to Jeanne Krier, who makes publicity magic wherever she goes, and Tom Russell at Random House, for agreeing to take on both this book and *Taking Time Off*. Meanwhile, much of the credit for this particular enterprise ought to go to Tom Meltzer, Suzanne Podhurst, and Spencer Foxworth, who did almost all of the heavy lifting throughout this process. And finally, we should all have people as wise as my agent Christy Fletcher looking after our careers.

The idea for this book came to me in 1998, as my brother, David, and sister, Stephanie, were trying to make the best out of their first jobs. I tried to exorcise their particular demons in the form of a 1999 story for *Fast Company*. I'm grateful to Bill Taylor and Alan Webber for providing that forum. Although I'm not on the career beat full-time anymore, I'm so much better at everything I do thanks to intensive attention from the likes of Edward Felsenthal, Jesse Pesta, Neal Templin, and Eben Shapiro at the *Wall Street Journal*.

Finally, thanks go out to Liebers, Bramsons, Krimstons, and Kantors everywhere. Jodi, as much as I've tried (and failed) to cut down on the number of jobs I've taken on over the years, this new husband gig suits me pretty well, I think. I can't wait to see what new projects spring from it.

—Ron Lieber

Thanks to everyone who provided support on this project and without whose tireless efforts this book would have been impossible, especially Suzanne Podhurst, Chaitra Ramanathan, Andrew Baker, Erik Olson, and Spencer Foxworth; you all totally rock! Thanks to Ron for coming up with such a swell idea for a book, and finally, thanks to my wife Lisa for putting up with my grousing and for walking the dogs when it was my turn.

—Tom Meltzer

CONTENTS

INTRODUCTION

SO WHAT DO YOU WANT TO BE WHEN YOU GROW UP?

If you're about to graduate from college, the best way to answer this question is also the most honest way: I don't know because I'm not a grown-up yet.

Somewhere along the way, people got it into their heads that twenty-two-year-olds should finish school with a clear idea of what they want to do for a living. And nowadays, most parents become anxious if their children graduate and don't immediately find jobs, or find jobs that aren't lucrative, or find jobs that don't sound impressive.

But how on earth can you possibly know what you want to do with your life when all you've ever done is go to school? Sure, summer jobs help. Internships give you a sense of what the real world is like. But the vast majority of internships aren't substantive and don't last long enough to give you a true sense of what it would be like to work for a particular company or in a given industry for years, decades, or even through to retirement.

And consider this: In all likelihood, your first job will have little to do with your last job. Taking a job is not an irreversible trip down a one-way career path. In fact, for many twenty-two-year-olds, the function of a first job is merely to aid them in figuring out what they don't want to do. It's an experiment, almost like picking a major, but in some ways less important. After all, you have much longer than four years to figure out what you want to be when you grow up.

Now, about being a grown-up. You hear the word "adolescent" thrown around a lot when you're in high school. But many specialists in human development believe that adolescence extends long past the time when you're done growing into your own body. You're not truly a grown-up until you're done growing into your own head. And that can't possibly happen until you've been on your own for a while, living in your own place, fending for yourself financially, and working for a living.

So we've established that, at twenty-two, you have every reason in the world not to know what you want to be when you grow up. It turns out that college curriculum designers understand this. Many college graduates wrap up their undergraduate educations each year having majored in English, history, economics, and other courses of study that do not point to an obvious single first job. This is a perfectly good thing for students because they should be looking to shape their minds and not trying to scribble the first drafts of their resumes during their college years. Trade-specific study can come later.

At the end of the day, it is you who is responsible for finding your way into the world, and that is as it should be. Through absolutely no fault of your own, however, you probably lack some sense about what's possible beyond what older friends and parents' friends do all day. Even if you treat your trips to the career placement office as if they were part of an academic course, you still may not find the real-world stories and nitty-gritty details that tell you where the best first jobs are and, more importantly, what makes a first job great.

So that's where we come in. Some time ago, we came to the sad conclusion that most first jobs actually aren't very good and usually aren't fulfilling by design. The idea of the first job as a rite of passage is nothing new. In the old days, you had to apprentice yourself to a tradesman and work for free in return for an education in how to perform a set of tasks. Needless to say, the most grueling and menial tasks always fell to the apprentice.

Run-of-the-mill first jobs for twenty-two-year-olds in private companies, government offices, or nonprofit organizations are typically built on a philosophy of making workers pay their dues. This isn't bad in theory. Materials must be procured, goods must be counted, numbers must be crunched, facts must be checked, and research must be compiled. There are plenty of mind-numbing details within each of these tasks that are nevertheless vital to the functioning of any organization. During your first year, your mind may be numb most of the time. But it's important to know where the details come from. All too often in first jobs, you don't get to play a role in creating the report that contains your work, going to the meeting where it's discussed, or meeting with the customer who ends up using it. Your work has no sense of context for you.

Consider this, too: Bruce Tulgan, the preeminent consultant to companies who want to figure out how best to treat younger workers, notes that the whole culture of paying dues is partly based on the idea that there's a club you get to join once you're done shelling out. A generation or so ago, that club was the job-for-life club—the one for which you worked for forty years at one company and got a gold watch and a great pension at the end.

But nowadays few people want to work at the same company for their entire career. Any number of conditions keeps this from happening: Their closest colleagues move on, their spouses get jobs elsewhere, they get new bosses, they want to change careers, or recruiters come after them with great offers. Many potential employers are suspicious of people who stay in one place too long. And there exists the possibility that you'll eventually be laid off if you stick around one place for several decades.

The point of all this is only to state what's now plainly obvious to employees, but doesn't always get through to employers: What's the point of making people pay their dues if there isn't any club for them to join? A lousy first year or two in the workplace shouldn't be the price of admission for people who simply want to earn a living. In that time, you ought to be able to watch a few meetings, go to a conference, meet a few customers, tag along with your boss on a business trip, learn how to sell something, or learn how to create an Excel spreadsheet.

Consider this sobering observation that comes from Glen T. Meakem, an Internet entrepreneur who is also a Gulf War veteran: "We've won two wars while the current crop of graduates was in college. Both of those were won by platoons of eighteen- to twenty-two-year-olds on the ground being led by commanders who were often just a few years older. If we're capable of defending our country, isn't it insulting that we're shunted as a matter of course in most corporations to some isolated corner to do grunt work for a few years?"

It's ridiculous, of course, but nobody said you had to go work for companies that treat young people this way, either. You may have noticed by now that we haven't yet mentioned the name of a single good place to work. That's because in some ways, making sure that building blocks of a great first job are present in any position is just as important as who the company is that offers it and what the company does. So it's crucial to understand the current you're fighting against first—the tendency of most entry-level jobs to revert to mediocrity or worse.

Therefore, before we start naming the employers who offer entry-level jobs with opportunities for growth, we'd like to isolate all of the different ways in which many employers fail their entry-level hires. We hope that you'll use this list as an evaluation guide. Some of these considerations may be crucial for you depending on what you want to do, while others could be irrelevant for any number of reasons. For instance, advancement doesn't matter much for most investment bank analysts, since relatively few of them stay longer than two or three years at one place. And if you don't have any student loans, salary may not be that important if you're working for Newell Rubbermaid, since you're likely to be stationed in areas where the cost of living is relatively low. They better have a good expense reimbursement system, however, if you're going to be driving to stores all of the time. Still, if you're fortunate enough to get a few job offers, you'll want to consider your opportunities and the people and places they're coming from by using many of the following standards:

- **Are you entering a program or merely taking on a job?** Many big companies have turned the first job into something resembling a degree-granting institution. There's an admissions committee, fellow class members, course work, a dean who keeps track of all the new arrivals, and other such accoutrements. You may like structure like this, or you may find it stifling. Washington Mutual's PACE Program and GE's Corporate Leadership Development Programs, for example, prepare new hires for the challenges ahead with tons of formal training.

- **Will you be doing work that makes you excited (or makes other people excited when they hear that you're doing it)?** As a general rule, you have to like what you're doing all day if you expect to be truly successful. How will it sound when you explain it to others? Will you be proud of what you do? Occasionally, you may pull weeks of late nights because you know it will be worth it once a particular project gets done; you'll be able to say you worked on something really cool, even though you may not have gotten paid. Entry-level positions with the League of American Theatres and Producers or the Peace Corps may fall into this category for you.

- **How much responsibility will you have?** Some companies don't let twenty-two-year-olds near the big customers—or even near the boss's boss. Will they trust you to take trips on your own or to send e-mails without having them vetted? One of the best feelings of all as a young person in the workforce is to feel that you have a little piece of the business that belongs to you—a set of results that you're responsible for and actually have some control over. Will they trust you with something like this? They should. Teach for America, Newell Rubbermaid, and Boston Beer have entry-level positions that grant first jobbers an enormous amount of independence and shoulder them with a great deal of responsibility.

- **Who will your mentors be?** This is a tricky one, since you can't always figure this out in advance. In many companies, they'll try to assign someone to look after you before you even arrive. While the thought is nice, these relationships can sometimes feel forced. It's probably better for you to forge such relationships on your own after you arrive by approaching people who have something in common with you (say, an alma mater) or are in a part of the organization you hope ultimately to enter. While evaluating potential jobs, it's important to find out whether everyone who's already in an entry-level position has someone like this. As you'll note in their profiles, Ogilvy and KPMG both value mentor/coach relationships.

- **How will you get your feedback?** Whom will you get it from and how often? Are the bosses themselves evaluated on the basis of how well they give feedback to the people who work for them? The feedback process is a bit like being graded in college in that there will probably be some grading system to give you a sense of where you stand in comparison with your colleagues and against the expectations they have for you. Good feedback is given more than once a year. It happens every day or as often as possible, either on schedule or on demand, and it's thorough enough to cover every aspect of what you do and how you do it. Newbies at Katz Media and Wells Fargo learn as much (or more) through feedback from their seniors as they do in formal training.

- **How good are the bosses?** How well they give feedback is only one small part of what makes them effective. Are these people who have volunteered to help younger people along, or are they doing it because they have to? Once you enter the workforce, you'll probably recognize the unique psychological make-up of an entry-level employee in yourself. You have super-high expectations for this first job; you don't want to be disappointed. Yet in many ways, you have no earthly idea what you're doing or what you're supposed to be doing. Who's signed up for the privilege of keeping track of you and why? Did they start at this company themselves? Goldman Sachs' Big Buddy program, for example, pairs a new analyst with an experienced associate who helps him or her negotiate the new, sometimes alien, landscape that a high-pressure workplace presents to a recent college graduate.

- **Who will your peers be?** How many people tend to get hired each year, and where do they come from? Is it like college all over again, with happy hours and weekend get-togethers? Or is it not a particularly social enterprise? These are crucial and often overlooked questions for recent graduates. It can be extremely difficult to move to a new city without knowing anyone. So what does the company do to ease the transition? Once you've started, these people will become your colleagues, and if you stay at the organization or in that line of work, they'll become your network. So what kind of people does the place draw? Will you fit in? In Newell Rubbermaid's Phoenix Program, it won't matter; you won't see your peers on a day-to-day basis once you've completed your initial training because you'll be out on the road. And if you don't like happy hours, figuring out how to build a network at Booz Allen Hamilton may take some creative thinking.

- **How much will you learn about how the company works?** Some of the worst organizations put people like you to work without ever explaining to you what they do and how everything works.

Other good organizations take weeks to teach you everything. Entry-level jobs like those in Washington Mutual's PACE Program teach you the different aspects of how the total enterprise functions before you finally settle into one position within the business. This is to acknowledge an obvious fact that most first jobbers ignore: Most people graduate from college and have no idea whether they belong in sales or marketing or whether they function better as an editor or a Web developer.

- **Some of the best companies to work for will continue to give you exposure outside of your own area.** This may take the form of weekly lunch meetings for first jobbers at which different executives talk about what their group does or field trips on which you get to see other teams in action. If this sort of thing doesn't seem to go on at a place you're thinking about working for, ask if you can put it together yourself. That shows initiative and curiosity, two traits for which all hiring managers look. Members of the Green Corps spend two months out on their own in the field organizing campaigns and events, but every two months or so, corps members come together to debrief one another on their most recent events, receive more training, and prepare for their next campaigns out in the field.

- **How much money do you want to make? How much money do you need to make?** These are two different, but equally important, questions. There's no shame in wanting to make a lot of money as fast as possible. If you're a trader or a really good salesman, you can make a lot of money fast (and lose it just as fast, too). Moreover, big bucks often require working long hours; some supposedly high-paying jobs actually pay less per hour than do other jobs at which the annual salary is much lower. Engineers do well, as you'll see in the profiles for Raytheon and Schlumberger; bankers also do well, as the numbers for Goldman Sachs show. However, one job requires you to be out on an oil rig, far from friends and family, while the other job will keep you in the office until past midnight on some nights. Are you prepared to give up weeknights out and weekends away to make your desired salary? For many, it's the "need to make" part they have to reckon with before facing down their inner materialists. Although interest rates are still low, the average student loan balance just keeps going up, so you may be facing a payment of several hundred dollars a month. Combine that with a job in a low-paying creative industry in a big expensive city, and you could be looking at an impossible financial situation. Will your family help you out the first year? You should be calculating your loan payments and talking to your family before you even begin to look for work. Places like Random House don't pay starting salaries that compare favorably with those at big technology companies and investment banks; but if you stick around for a while and show some aptitude for and commitment to the publishing industry, you could become one of those legendary publishers in a corner office working with the great authors of our age. Know this before you sign on.

- **Perks are out there.** Northrop Grumman offers employees pet insurance, Electronic Arts gives its video-gaming geeks $100 toward a gaming console, and the League of American Theatres and Producers gives the president's assistant free tickets to just about every show on (and off) Broadway.

While you may not be worried about child care benefits and health care right now, you should pay careful attention to the retirement plan, which may seem like it should be the last thing on your mind. The fact is, the more you put away in your first couple of years on the job, the better off you'll be at age sixty-seven. That's because the sooner you set money aside, the more time it has to earn interest. If you care at all about retiring comfortably, do not scrimp on this now. And ask tough questions of some of the companies that don't let you participate in their 401(k) plans right away and instead make you wait a year before putting money aside. What kind of welcome message does that send?

- **Advancement.** You may not want to stick around for a long time at a company. Some entry-level workers at Deloitte want to get a few years of experience and then leave to work for a client company or to go back to business school. Then again, you may be like those rare people who like their entry-level jobs so much, they won't want to leave for a long time. In that case, talk to people who started working straight out of college and have been at the same company for years. Have there been enough opportunities for change and advancement to keep them interested and engaged? It's good to keep in mind that the chairman and chief executive officer of Caterpillar started as an entry-level trainee with the company more than thirty years ago; today, he runs an enterprise valued at more than $26 billion.

- **Industry leaders: Many organizations have reputations as not only great places to work but also as great places to have worked for.** In many respects, it's like having gone to a really good college. Not having gone there won't shut you out from later success in life, but it'll be easier to get your foot in the door if you're coming from the right place. If you want to build a career as an accountant, for example, experience with KPMG is simply going to get you further than experience with a smaller, lesser-known firm. Try to figure out where alumni of the first jobs you're considering end up. If it's a program that ends after two years, where did last year's "graduates" go next? What kinds of jobs did they get? What graduate schools did they get into?

We had a few rules for choosing the jobs that we feature in this book. There were no minimum salaries or geographical requirements or quotas. Our goal was to profile jobs in both the for-profit and nonprofit sectors, as well as across numerous industries. We wanted to find places at which people were happy, engaged with their work, nicely compensated, well positioned for advancement, getting great preparation for graduate school, doing really interesting stuff, or benefitting from any combination of these things. To profile these organizations, we interviewed not only their official representatives, but also—and more importantly—hundreds of the people who were currently holding (or formerly held) the positions we describe. They're the ones who know the most about what having one of these jobs is like, so we contacted as many of them as we could.

For this third edition, we contacted the organizations already featured directly to update the hard data in their profiles, particularly changes in salary, benefits offered, and other substantive details of the entry-level jobs themselves. Most of the changes involved salary and benefits, and they tended to be for the better. We also added thirty-nine companies to the mix. These included a significant number of nonprofit companies that offer wonderful opportunities for you to produce significant, positive change in the world around you.

Finally, a word about hiring prospects: As we're going to print, they're looking brighter for this year's college graduates than those faced by students who graduated in the 2004–2005 academic year. The National Association of Colleges and Employers (NACE, www.naceweb.org) regularly releases reports of employer responses to its *Job Outlook* survey, and one such report said that employers planned on hiring 14.5 percent more college graduates in 2005–2006 than they had hired in 2004–2005. That means you're entering a better hiring environment than the one experienced by your predecessors. It means you'll likely get more in return for your job-hunting efforts than they got. It means you could be offered a higher starting salary than those offered last year to people with similar skills and knowledge as you.

Of course the job market is still very competitive for newly minted college graduates. So the better your grades, the more internship experience you have, and the earlier you start your job search, the better. Early fall of your senior year isn't too soon to start sending out letters and resumes to prospective employers. If you don't have any internship or co-op experience in the industry in which you are interested in working, get some now—freshman year isn't too early, and senior year isn't too late. And network like crazy. Every family gathering, every career fair, and every mixer with faculty and administrators is a chance to get onto people's radar screens. Most people want to help young, energetic people just starting out in their careers. Adjunct professors (part-time professors who have other jobs outside of the university) are especially valuable in this regard. Impress them; they usually have more immediate "real-world" connections than do tenured, full-time faculty.

We consider this book a work in progress. We plan to release further editions, continually adding new companies and dropping those at which the quality of the experience has declined. You may have worked at a place you think is even better than the places we've profiled here. If so, drop us a line at bookeditor@review.com, and let us know about it.

SURVIVAL SKILLS
FOR YOUR JOB HUNT

Knowing about all of the awesome entry-level positions in the world won't help if you blunder when it counts in the job-hunting jungle. We thought it may help if we provided you with a list of essential job-searching tools: networking, perfecting your resume and cover letters, and acing the all-important interview.

Part One: Networking

You have a beautiful new interview outfit and a killer resume. You've worked hard to investigate possible contact organizations in this book, online, at the library, and at your college career center; you've spent hours sifting through job listings in your field of interest. You've sent out scores of resumes without so much as a nibble from prospective employers. Worse yet, you're running out of ideas and enthusiasm. What's wrong? Many people become so intent on their job searches that they end up conducting them in a vacuum. Networking is one of the most important components of career research and of the job search. The more people you know, the more information you gather, and the more you're out there, the better equipped you will be to find employment.

Who Are Your Contacts?

Even if you're starting with very few connections, you can network successfully. Most people focus their networking on those people immediately surrounding them. "Well, my mother or uncle or cousin doesn't know anyone in my field, so I'm sunk." The trick is to delve beyond that first layer of contacts and to use your imagination. Say you're pursuing a career in the music industry. You may know someone who works at your college's radio station. Although this person probably won't be your contact with the president of Sony BMG, he or she may know someone at an independent label who has been in contact with him or her to promote local bands. Or in checking out your college alumni directory, you may discover an alumnus who's an entertainment lawyer. Although he doesn't work at a record label, he may very well have contacts in the field. If you think creatively, networking contacts can be found in a bunch of places. Just learn to think outside the usual box—and ask anyone you come in contact with in your daily routine! Here's a list of possible resources to start your networking.

Family/extended family

Use your parents, guardians, siblings, grandparents, aunts, uncles, or cousins as possible resources. Remember: Look beyond the obvious.

Friends/acquaintances

This includes friends of friends, parents of friends, and people in your apartment building or neighborhood.

Coworkers and employers, past and present

Past and present colleagues can be good sources of networking information, even if they are in a seemingly unrelated field.

Teachers and professors, past and present

Educators can be excellent sources for contacts, particularly if you have had a good rapport with them.

College alumni

In addition to keeping individual listings for alumni, many schools organize alumni/ae receptions throughout the year, so it's always wise to inquire about such opportunities when contacting your alma mater. Most schools have their graduates categorized by career area and geographic location, so if you're considering moving to another city or state, find out if there are other alums in that area.

College counselors

This could include career counselors, deans, and college activities officers. Make nice with these people if you're still in school!

Clubs or organizations

People who have common interests...

Health clubs or sports teams

...and participate in common activities often have great information to share with one another.

Religious organizations

Churches, temples, or other religious organizations can be rich resources that offer a wide array of contacts in a variety of career fields.

Your doctor, dentist, banker, and anyone else who works with you

You may also want to contact the local chamber of commerce for a list of employers in your geographic area of interest.

People you don't know but who do work that interests you

Maybe you read an article about a successful civil engineer in your area, and you're interested in entering that field. Write that person a letter. Whether people enjoy the attention and recognition or are simply interested in helping out, you could benefit from initiating contact.

Professional organizations

Organizations such as the American Medical Association, the American Association of University Women, the NAACP, or the Asian American Journalists Association often keep lists of members divided up by geographic location.

Telephone books

The local phone book for your desired destination is still an excellent source of information related to your career field. Phone books for most major American cities can be found at branches of the public library or at your career development center.

Newspapers

Check out local papers to get acquainted with key players and organizations, career fair listings, and local job listings.

Online

In addition to the obvious sites like Yahoo, HotJobs, and Monster.com, don't overlook bulletin boards, newsgroups, and chat rooms.

Career/job fairs

With nonprofit fairs, business/financial service fairs, and minority career fairs making up but a few of the career fairs out there, these offer frequent opportunities to network with a large number of people without a lot of running around.

THE INFORMATIONAL INTERVIEW

The most effective way to network, with respect to time and money, is by conducting informational interviews. Usually no more than thirty minutes in duration, they're meant to do just that—help you gather information for career research and the job search. Through interviews or meetings with people, you can find out what a particular job involves and how best to prepare yourself for your job search. Informational interviews are usually limited to one meeting; they're not job interviews and shouldn't be used to ask for a job (though you hope they may lead to one). Rather, they're a way to discover pathways to particular jobs or careers. Research the person, the organization, and the career field ahead of time whenever possible.

INITIATING CONTACT

Once you've acquired your network of names, initiate contact with either a phone call or letter of inquiry. Don't overlook the importance of phone strategies when seeking out contacts. Since it's often the first communication you'll have with a networking contact, your phone tactics are just as important as your other networking strategies and thus deserve as much attention.

GETTING BEYOND THE GATEKEEPERS

You have to establish rapport not only with your contact, but also with the people (such as administrative assistants or receptionists) who can connect you with your contact. Your interaction with these people can determine your success in ultimately reaching your contact, so be professional and courteous at all times. If you're making an unsolicited or "cold" call and your contact isn't able to take your call, don't leave your name with the receptionist. Instead, ask when a convenient time would be to call back. If you leave a lengthy message, it may be recorded incorrectly, and you lose the power to call back. Simply leaving your name may put you at the bottom of the priority list for returned phone messages. If you're returning a call to a potential contact with whom you've already spoken, however, it's fine to leave your name, phone number, and a time when you can be reached.

VOICE MAIL

What happens when you keep getting your contact's voice mail? If you've made several attempts to phone, hanging up each time you hear, "Please leave a message," you should leave a message. Just make sure it's short and concise. If you're calling contacts with whom you've previously had contact and they're not available, leave a time you'll be available. Nobody likes playing phone tag.

And a word about *your* voice mail: Now's the time to have a clear, professional outgoing message. Your name and number will suffice.

MAKING CONTACT

When you speak with your contact, you won't have a lot of time to get your point across, so you want to be sure that you cover some important details. Be clear about your reason for making contact.

Identify yourself

Speak slowly and clearly. You also want to be alert, enthusiastic, confident, and poised.

Identify your purpose for calling

Be clear about why you've made contact. You need to set the groundwork for what's to follow.

Give specifics about what you want from your contact

Be concise. Convey that you're interested in information, not (necessarily) a job. Carefully consider what you want to say and, as potentially cheesy as it sounds, do a practice run before initiating your call.

LETTERS OF INQUIRY

An alternative to phoning your contact directly is first to send out a letter of inquiry for an informational interview and then to follow up with a phone call. Some people prefer this more formal method; the letter serves as an introduction before the phone contact. There are no surprises, and your networking contact will be expecting your call.

Get the correct spelling of your contact's name when sending the letter; if you're unsure for whatever reason, call first to verify. If you found your contact's name in trade publications or from what appear to be outdated job ads or organizational materials, call the organization to verify your contact's name and job title.

Use a standard business layout. It should be single-spaced and have a double-space between paragraphs. No grammatical errors, misspellings, or typos in your inquiry letter! Don't just spell-check it; have several people proofread your letter before you send it out.

Opening paragraph

Identify why you're writing. Be clear about how you've come to write to your networking contact; mention your referral source—whether it is another person, professional organization, or article in which your contact was cited.

Middle section

This is usually one to two paragraphs in length. Include some personal information. Briefly mention the school you'll be graduating from or your present position of employment as well as your (tentative, in some cases) future career plans. Be clear that you're in the process of gathering information about a particular career field—and that you're not, at this point, looking for a job. Here, you can propose an informational interview. Do so politely, and indicate that such a meeting would be at your networking contact's convenience.

Concluding paragraph

Thank your contact for his or her time and consideration and have a specific follow-up plan at the conclusion of the letter. You may want to suggest an informational interview via telephone; this can be scheduled over the phone or by e-mail.

PART TWO: TIPS FOR MAKING YOUR RESUME BEAUTIFUL

Submitting a resume that looks unprofessional is one of the surest ways to eliminate yourself from contention for a job, regardless of how impressive your qualifications may be. You would be amazed at the resumes we've seen with ketchup stains, chewed-off corners, handwritten updates, and illegible print. Fortunately, designing an attractive, eye-catching resume is very doable.

GETTING MARGINALIZED

Margins act like a frame, providing a welcome border of white space around your text, and they serve as a built-in memo pad for employers, many of whom like to make notes directly on your resume. Set your margins at one inch on all four sides to start. If space becomes an issue, you can shrink them down to as little as a half inch, but any smaller and your page will start looking extremely cramped.

TYPEFACES

When choosing a typeface, consider its readability, attractiveness, and appropriateness. It's best to use no more than two typefaces on your resume—one serif typeface for the body of your resume and, if you wish, one sans-serif typeface for your name and category headings. Traditional favorites for the body text include:

Times

Palatino

Garamond

Good choices for your name and category headings are

Arial

Helvetica

Tahoma

Stay away from fancy scripts, decorative typefaces, or any other type that strains the eyes. After all, you're sending out a resume, not a wedding invitation. Size-wise, you'll generally want to go with a ten- to twelve-point type for the body of your text, twelve- to fourteen-point type for your category headings, and sixteen- to eighteen-point type for your name:

This is Times 18 point.

This is Times 14 point.

This is Times 12 point.

This is Times 10 point.

LAYOUT

While there are literally dozens of ways to lay out a resume, there are certain basic rules you should follow. Your layout should always be clear, logical, and easy to follow, and there should be plenty of white space. Make sure you're consistent in your layout. Place key information—such as category headings, titles, names, and dates—in a logical order.

FINISHING YOUR STROKES

There are five main text embellishment techniques to consider: **bolding,** CAPITALIZING, • bulleting, *italicizing,* and ruled lines. CAPS should be used sparingly, as capital letters take up significantly more space than lowercase letters and will leave you severely pressed for room. **Bolding** works especially well for items that require the most emphasis, such as your name and category headings. Avoid the use of dingbats and graphics that tend to appear too gimmicky.

PROOFREADING

This is perhaps the most crucial—yet most overlooked—component of the entire resume-writing process. Never send out a resume before you've had it carefully reviewed by at least a couple sets of trusted eyes for typos, poor grammar, awkward or repetitive language, a misaligned layout, and other mistakes. There's no margin for error (pun intended, sorry). A single misspelled word could cost you an important opportunity.

PAPER AND PRINTING

Use paper that's 8.5″ x 11″ in size and with a weight of at least twenty-four pounds (sometimes referred to as seventy lb. text). Stick with neutral colors—white or a subtle off-white is best. The advantage of white is that it reproduces well when being either faxed or photocopied. Stay away from loud colors.

Laser printing is the only way to go. Never print more resumes than you're ready to send out at one time. Fifteen is a reasonable number unless you're attending a mega-career fair or other special event at which you expect to visit with a large number of prospective employers at one time.

ENVELOPES

Using envelopes that match your resume paper is a nice professional touch, but white envelopes will always do in a pinch. If you really want to impress your prospective employer, send your resume and cover letter in a large envelope (9″ x 12″ is a perfect size). By doing so, your resume will arrive flat, a definite advantage if it's going to be scanned into a database.

The downside of using a larger envelope is purely economic: They require additional postage compared with standard business envelopes. Whatever type of envelope you use, it's important that you print the recipient's address legibly and correctly, otherwise your resume may never reach its destination. The address can be typed, laser-printed, or handwritten (provided you have good penmanship). And don't forget to include your return address on the envelope!

GETTING YOUR RESUME INTO THEIR HANDS

The only thing left to do is make sure your resume (and accompanying cover letter) reaches your prospective employer in a timely fashion. There are several ways to do this—traditional mail, e-mail, fax, courier, and hand delivery. The method you select should be contingent on a) how badly you want the job, b) how long the job was posted before you heard about it, c) how much of a rush the employer is in to fill the job, and d) the personality type of the prospective employer.

In most cases, if the position was advertised, the ad will state the preferred method of resume submission. Follow the directions. Usually employers will ask that you reply by regular mail; faxing or e-mailing is fast, but you should always send a hard copy through the mail, just in case. If the organization won't accept a fax or e-mail submission and time is of the essence, you always have the option of sending your package via FedEx, UPS, USPS, or some other courier service. Overnighting a package is an expensive proposition, but in addition to getting your resume into your employer's hands quickly, you'll be sending a message that you want the job badly enough to spare no expense.

Another alternative, provided the employer is within close proximity, is delivering your package by hand. This approach has the added benefit of enabling you to get a peek at your potential place of employment, as well as providing an opportunity to see some of your prospective colleagues in action.

SAMPLE RESUME

Feel free to borrow from this resume to help create your own: Pay careful attention to format, layout, design, and phrasing.

Nada Kendra

1011 Oak Street • Rochester, NY 11111 • (716) 555-5555

Objective   Position as a counselor in a group home for emotionally disturbed adolescents.

Education

BS, Child and Family Studies

Syracuse University, *May 2005*

- Coursework included education, psychology, and family dynamics.

Counseling and Teaching Experience

Child and Family Counselor

Community Medical Center, Syracuse, NY, *Spring 2004*

- Interacted with children and parents while children waited for medical treatment.
- Modeled effective childcare techniques and provided feedback to parents regarding parenting behavior.
- Established ongoing relationships with families.

Student Teacher

Syracuse University Early Education Center, Syracuse, NY, *Spring 2003*

- Designed and implemented instructional activities for children ages 3–6.
- Researched learning styles and cognitive development of children.
- Organized and supervised educational field trips.

Student Teacher

Elizabeth M. Wall Nursery School, Syracuse, NY, *Fall 2002*

- Coordinated and led educational activities for groups of 4-year-olds.
- Planned new activities daily to teach group interaction skills.

Additional Experience

Assistant to Director, Creative Services, *2004 to present*

Cosmetics 'R Us, Rochester, NY

- Assist art director in coordinating photo shoots.
- Create and organize filing system for directors.
- Identify new products and displays by speaking with vendors.

Sales Clerk

Leigh Barrett Boutique, Rochester, NY, *Summer 1999*

- Created window displays and performed in-store merchandising.
- Assisted customers in selection of merchandise; maintained inventory.

United Jewish Appeal and American Red Cross, Volunteer

International Experience

Have lived in Australia and London; traveled extensively throughout Europe.

Part Three: Power Tools for Killer Cover Letters

The trick to writing an effective cover letter is to take some essential steps before you put pen to paper or fingers to keyboard. Once you've completed these five steps, you'll have all the basic components of your cover letter in place.

Power Tool #1: Identify the Reader's Needs

Far too many job seekers focus on what *they* want from the people who will read their cover letters, when the more strategic approach is to focus on their *readers'* needs and objectives. While employers recognize that they may need to train you and that they can offer an environment in which your interests may flourish, they can only justify hiring you if you can add some value to their organization, either right away or down the road. This isn't to say that you can't express some needs, interests, and goals in your cover letters; it's just that there must be a balance between what you ask for and what you can offer, and the scales should tip in favor of what you can offer.

Most readers' concerns fall into five categories:

- Are you the type of person they want in this job and this organization? Do you have the proper educational background and work experience? The right personal qualities?

- Do you have—or can you learn—the skills it takes to perform the day-to-day functions of this job?

- Have you demonstrated a commitment to and familiarity with this career field or industry?

- Have you chosen to contact their organization for a clearly identifiable reason?

- Can you organize your thoughts, express them clearly, and write well?

If you've done your homework at the start of your job search, you'll have plenty of information on the nature of career fields, specific types of jobs, and specific organizations or companies. Through library, bookstore, and online research, as well as by talking with people, you can learn a great deal about what employers are looking for. You can also find the qualities that a specific private-sector company or nonprofit organization is seeking out. Learning about an organization's culture, management style, products and services, areas of expansion, problems, and financial status can give you an edge when addressing your reader's needs. It's all right not to mention a specific job title in your letter, but you should at least define a functional area or division in which you'd like to work. You may say something like, "I would like to discuss any entry-level positions available in your marketing department," or "Given my skills and experience, I believe I could make the greatest contribution in your editorial department." These statements show much more focus and maturity than do general statements of interest in any entry-level position in the company.

POWER TOOL #2: IDENTIFY YOUR OBJECTIVES

Be clear about what you want and what action you'd like the reader to take. Your objectives will typically fall into two categories: career goals and immediate actions.

As far as career goals are concerned, you should let your reader know what type of position you're looking for on a spectrum of specific to broad. If you have a definite career objective in mind, then it's okay to mention a specific type of job, as long as you aren't so narrow that you miss out on any related opportunities the employer may have. Stating your career or job objective is especially important when sending an unsolicited resume because this is how you can direct the reader to particular jobs in which you'd be interested. If you're answering an ad, the job objective is obvious because you're applying for a specific position.

Your immediate-action objective is concerned with letting your reader know that you'd either like a call from him or her or that you'll initiate contact soon. Also, let him or her know if your goal is a phone appointment, an exploratory or office interview, or—if he or she is a network contact—merely obtaining some advice.

POWER TOOL #3: PREPARE YOUR JOB-SEARCH SOUND BITE

One way to construct a powerful cover letter is to be concise, and using a job-search sound bite is how you can achieve that end. A sound bite can serve as the thirty- or sixty-second pitch you give over the phone when you make cold calls to prospective employers or network contacts. It can also be the answer to that dreaded wide-open interview question, "Tell me about yourself." And with a little restructuring, it can be the profile or summary statement that appears at the top of your resume. So if you prepare your sound bite for your cover-letter writing, you'll also have it ready to use in other parts of your job search.

Who You Are

Give basic information about yourself that is the most impressive and relevant to the reader or the job you're seeking. This may include your educational status, school(s) attended, major or specialized program of study, and a brief reference to work experience (including volunteer work, internships, summer jobs, and paid employment).

What You Have to Offer

Include specific experience, specific skills, knowledge areas, and personal qualities.

POWER TOOL #4: DEVELOP YOUR REPERTOIRE

Now it's time to back up the claims you have made in your sound bite and expand on what you have to offer and what you're seeking. Your repertoire is a collection of specific examples that provide evidence of your skills, experience, and accomplishments; every job seeker should have a versatile repertoire to help him or her navigate each twist and turn of the job search.

To develop a repertoire, pick the key points that your target reader is looking for in you: personal qualities, specific skills, field or industry knowledge and/or commitment, and anything else. Then think of concrete examples from your work, academic, or extracurricular experiences that demonstrate these points.

POWER TOOL #5: ASK YOURSELF, "WHY THEM?"

The final step is to define for yourself and for your reader why you've chosen to write this letter. Employers want to know that you've chosen them for a reason, so flatter them a bit. Doing so also shows something about your character. If you've taken the time and initiative to gather information about a company, you're also displaying all sorts of positive characteristics, from attention to detail to good time management, research skills, and intellectual curiosity. And you won't come across as someone who's totally desperate for a job because you appear to be approaching your job search thoughtfully, rather than just writing to anybody and everybody.

Your reasons may include something about the company's products or services, and its corporate culture, philosophy, ethics, style, success rate, reputation, or growth and expansion.

Sample Cover Letter for an Exploratory Interview

Here's a cover letter requesting an exploratory, rather than informational, interview. The writer has already made her career decision and is ready to be considered as an actual applicant for a job. To keep the door open should no jobs be available, she asks simply for the opportunity to speak to the reader.

Eva Jackson

34 University Avenue, Apt. 4A

Columbus, OH 11111

(614) 555-5555

Ms. Margaret Ransom

Director, Special Education

The Sterling School

22 East State Street

Akron, OH 11111

March 18, 2005

Dear Ms. Ransom:

I am a senior at Ohio State University majoring in Speech Pathology, and I would like to speak with you about the special education curriculum and possible employment opportunities at the Sterling School. I have taken the liberty of enclosing my resume for your review.

Through a recent internship at the Columbus Speech and Hearing Center, I have put my education to practical use in a professional environment and demonstrated my ability to work effectively with both children and adults. The experience also strengthened my commitment to a career in speech therapy with young children.

I plan to pursue a master's degree in speech pathology, most likely on a part-time basis, so that I can make a long-term commitment to a school. I read about the outstanding program at Sterling as recently profiled in *Speech Therapy* journal and would welcome the opportunity to be a part of such a progressive, professional team.

Whether or not you know of your staffing needs for the upcoming summer or fall terms, I would appreciate the opportunity to speak with you by phone or in person to discuss your department. I will be in Akron in early April, so I will call you soon to see if we may be able to meet. Thank you for your time and consideration.

Sincerely yours,

Eva Jackson

Eva Jackson

PART FOUR: THE INTERVIEW—THEME QUESTIONS

There are really only a limited number of core questions that an interviewer can ask you—and an unlimited number of ways in which they can phrase these questions. Here's a list of some typical core questions, grouped by category, that you can expect.

College Experience Questions

- Why did you choose your major?

- Which classes in college have you liked best/least? Why?

- Why did you select your college? How have you liked it?

- Has your college experience prepared you well for a career?

- Describe your most rewarding college experience.

- If you could do it over, how would you plan your education differently?

- To which teaching styles do you react best?

- Do you plan to go to graduate school?

- Are your grades a good indicator of your potential?

- What have you learned from your extracurricular activities?

- Tell me about one of your papers or your thesis.

Questions About You

- Tell me about yourself.

- How did you choose this career direction?

- What are your strengths and weaknesses?

- How would you describe yourself? How would a friend or your last boss describe you?

- What motivates you to work hard?

- What does success mean to you?

- Of what are you most proud?

- In which kind of environment do you work best?

- How do you handle pressure?

- What's important to you in a job?

- Do you have a geographical preference? Would you relocate? Travel?

- Describe a major obstacle you've encountered and how you dealt with it.

- What have you learned from mistakes you've made?

- What would you do if you won the lottery?

- What else should I know about you?

Questions About Your Experience

- Tell me about your jobs/internships.

- How has your background prepared you for this job?

- What work-related skills do you have?

- What was the toughest job challenge you faced, and how did you deal with it?

Questions About Your Goals

- What do you see yourself doing five years from now? Ten? Fifteen?

- What do you really want out of life?

- Why do you want to work for us?

- Why do you want to work in this industry?

Questions to See If You Know What You're Getting into

- What do you know about this organization?

- What do you think it takes to be successful in this organization?

- Why do you want to work for us?

- What do you look for in a job?

- How can you make a contribution to our organization?

- Where do you think this industry is headed?

Sell Yourself, Gather Info, and Evaluate a Job by Asking Great Questions

Asking good questions throughout an interview helps you sell yourself. In this way, you demonstrate your interest in the organization and position as well as your professional curiosity. Also, you gather key information about the job and organization that will enable you to refine your sales pitch as you go. The more you understand about the interviewer's priorities, the more you can tailor what you have to offer to the employer's needs. Finally, the input you get from the interviewer will help you evaluate the job and decide whether or not you want to pursue a potential job offer. Here are some questions you can ask to get your creative juices flowing.

About the Organization

- How does your organization differ from its competitors?

- What are your company's plans for future growth?

- Is your organization facing any problems?

- What do you like most about working here?

- How would you describe the corporate culture (or work environment) here?

About the Job Itself

- Where does this position fit into the structure of the department and the organization as a whole?

- What are the future plans for this department?

- How much contact is there between departments or areas (if it is a large organization)?

- To whom will I report?

- What percentage of my time will be spent in the various functions that this job involves?

- Does the organization tend to promote from within?

- What is a typical career path for people in this position?

- Why is this position available?

- What personal qualities make someone successful in this job?

- May I speak with someone who currently holds or recently held this position? (Note that this question is only appropriate if an offer has been extended or seems imminent.)

How This Book Is Organized

The main body of this book is divided into two sections: "Jobs Within Organizations" and "Jobs Without Organizations." The primary difference is that jobs in the former (and larger) chapter are offered by specific companies or nonprofit organizations, while jobs in the latter section are either widely available at many companies and organizations or are freelance/independent in nature. The jobs in the first chapter appear in alphabetical order according to the name of the company or nonprofit organization. The jobs in the second chapter appear in alphabetical order according to the job title.

Each of the jobs listed in this book has its own profile. To make it easier to find information about the jobs in which you are interested, we have used the same format for each job. (If you are interested in learning more about jobs in a specific industry, please refer to the "Index by Industry" on p. 427.)

The name of the organization at the beginning of each profile is followed by the name of the position(s) or program(s) described. (For the jobs in the "Jobs Without Organizations" chapter, the name of an organization will not appear, obviously.) The body of each profile may have as many as ten fields of information. Not every field will appear for every job, as the information driving that field may not have been reported to us, or such information may not be applicable to a particular job. Some companies and nonprofits, for example, do not have data on how many entry-level employees are still with the company after three, five, and ten years simply because they haven't been operating for that long. In a profile that has complete information, however, you can expect to see the following:

THE BIG PICTURE

This is a short description of what the company or nonprofit organization does, and, if appropriate, how entry-level employees fit into the picture.

STATS

This section provides a snapshot of the facts that most job seekers want to know right away: where the job is located; how many applications are received each year and the number of available job openings; the titles of the available positions and the average number of hours worked each week by the people holding these positions; the percentage of entry-level hires who are still with the company after three, five, and ten years; the average starting salaries; the medical and additional benefits offered; and the contact information for those interested in applying for a job or in seeking additional information.

GETTING HIRED

Some organizations recruit on college campuses, and other organizations don't. Some only recruit new hires from select colleges with certain undergraduate majors, while others are looking for people with specific internship or cooperative work experience. Some will only want to interview you over the phone, and others will want to fly you to their headquarters for a battery of interviews; they may even ask you to take a test to boot. This is the admissions process for the organization, and as with colleges and graduate schools, it's different for every place. Compiled using information provided by employees and the organizations themselves, this section tells what you need to know about a company or nonprofit when you're trying to land the job.

MONEY AND PERKS

Let's face it, remuneration is at the top of almost every worker's mind, young *and* old. Some jobs offer low salaries, while others offer low salaries with the possibility of making much more in overtime hours. Jobs in finance and a few other industries often offer good salaries and the possibility of large bonuses, but these very same jobs also usually require employees to put in very long hours. Perks are the things that improve the quality of life, or at least make life a little easier, at no cost (or a reduced cost) to the employee. Some jobs offer laundry lists of perks, while other jobs offer none. Some of the most popular perks include 401(k) or similar retirement savings plans, paid time off, and flexible spending accounts (in which you get to use pre-tax dollars to pay for things like transportation and uncovered medical expenses). Additional perks may include gym memberships, tuition reimbursements, and matching donations to charitable causes.

THE ROPES

No matter where you go to work, you will receive training, whether it's an hour or two spent with a human resources representative talking about benefits and company policies or weeks of off-site classes on the different software technologies in which you will have to become an expert. In this section, we explain the structure and length of the training you can expect to receive before you actually start doing real work.

DAY IN THE LIFE

Once properly trained, employees are expected to work. Here, mostly in their own words, is what first jobbers do all day.

PEERS

What are the people in the position or program like? Are they similar to you in age and background? Do entry-level workers form close friendships with one another, or are they pretty much on their own because the employees with whom they spend most of their time are a little older? Is there a big after-hours social scene, or do people keep to themselves? Does the company do anything—such as sponsor corporate sports teams—to encourage fraternizing? This is where you'll find answers to all of these questions.

Moving on

When people have drawn all they can from a given entry-level position, what do they do next? Do they head to graduate school, get promoted into positions of greater responsibility within the organization, leave for more lucrative or better positions within the same industry, or launch new careers in completely different lines of work? Many people don't think about what comes after an entry-level job, but they should. This section tries to answer these questions and get you thinking about what your long-term plans may include.

Attrition

We asked employers how many entry-level employees leave their organizations within a year of being hired. In some cases, we've provided actual percentages, and in most cases, we've provided an explanation of *why* people depart from their jobs so early in their tenure.

Best and Worst

We asked employers to tell us who their best and worst entry-level employees were. Some responded with general descriptions of what makes a good or bad employee, while others gave us specific cases. For the jobs in the "Jobs Without Organizations" chapter, the best and worst employees descriptions were based on our own research and opinions.

JOBS WITHIN ORGANIZATIONS

ABBOTT
Professional Development Program

THE BIG PICTURE

A global health care company, Abbott is "devoted to the discovery, development, manufacture, and marketing of pharmaceuticals, nutritionals, and medical products, including devices and diagnostics." Abbott offers a wide assortment of entry-level jobs, including positions in science, information technology, finance/accounting, engineering, and sales/marketing. Many employees enter the company through its rotational Professional Development Program; this allows them to gain valuable industry experience in a number of areas before deciding which one best suits their interests and talents.

STATS

LOCATION(S) WHERE ENTRY-LEVEL EMPLOYEES WORK

"Entry-level employees work at Abbott's corporate headquarters in Lake County, Illinois and at most of Abbott's domestic and international sites."

AVERAGE NUMBER OF APPLICATIONS EACH YEAR

About 125,000 applications are received each year. There is no specific figure available for entry-level positions.

AVERAGE NUMBER HIRED PER YEAR OVER THE LAST TEN YEARS

"More than 5,000 new hires have come on board directly out of college over the last ten years."

ENTRY-LEVEL POSITION(S) AVAILABLE

"They can be grouped into functional areas, including science, engineering, sales/marketing, manufacturing/operations, quality, finance, information technology, and corporate administration (i.e., groups like human resources, public affairs, and purchasing). Specialized opportunities in environmental health and purchasing also exist."

AVERAGE HOURS WORKED PER WEEK

"Employees work around forty to fifty hours per week."

PERCENTAGE OF ENTRY-LEVEL HIRES STILL WITH THE COMPANY AFTER THREE, FIVE, AND TEN YEARS

Ninety percent, 85 percent, and 75 percent, respectively. "Abbott has an 84 percent conversion rate for the Professional Development Program, [and] Abbott's voluntary turnover is just 8 percent."

AVERAGE STARTING SALARY

"It is hard to generalize. We have so many hires per year. Abbott is known to have a competitive salary within the top quartile of the industry for base pay and benefits packages. The average base pay for the

Professional Development Program is determined by approximating the median in the external market, with total cash compensation exceeding this amount when the company performs well."

Benefits Offered

"Every employee starts with three weeks [of] paid vacation, plus medical, dental, and disability insurance; [and] pension plan, 401(k) plan, and profit sharing. *Money* magazine rated Abbott number three nationally in their 'Best Benefits' ranking [in 2002]."

Contact Information

Visit the career center at www.abbott.com.

Getting Hired

If you want to apply for a job at Abbott, you must do so through its website. "Post your resume [for a] job of interest; recruiters who have open jobs go through our files every day and fill over 90 percent of [available] jobs through Internet postings. This is a primary intake point for Abbott." The other gateway into entry-level jobs at Abbott is through their "five-star, nationally-ranked Internship Program" in which they "convert high-performing interns who are graduating within the next twelve months into entry-level hires." The company also has a robust College Relations strategy and presence on campus; it targets top schools and top talent for all functions throughout the year. "[Abbott] also [has] alumni networks working for [them]; for example, the University of Illinois [at Urbana-Champaign] produces forty entry-level hires per year, many of them referred by the 1,100 alumni working at Abbott." One entry-level employee says, "[Interviews are] mostly behavioral based, and the tone is very relaxed. I was able to ask a lot of questions about the interviewers' career paths and current jobs at Abbott." In all the interview sessions, "Abbott's core competencies (adaptability, initiative, innovation, integrity, and teamwork) were stressed, and questions were geared toward getting candidates [who] showed aptitude in those areas."

Money and Perks

The Professional Development Program is rotational. To be equitable to all participants, all first jobbers start out making the same money as their peers, so "starting salary is not very negotiable." Program participants want you to know, however, that "entry-level salaries are competitive" within the industry and that "Abbott is a meritocracy. High-performing people get ahead quickly here," earning solid raises and development opportunities to advance their careers in the process. Workers enjoy "a ton of special perks," including "flexible work scheduling, telecommuting, 100 percent tuition reimbursement, a relocation package, a sports and activities program [that has] 8,000 employees in leagues and clubs [who] meet outside the workplace, a mentoring program, an employee assistance program, and the Clara Abbott Foundation (scholarship program)."

The Ropes

The specific training Abbott's entry-level employees receive is relevant to their positions. One first jobber in information technology recalls, "I started with our diagnostics division, which has a dedicated training coordinator for each department. Through her, I was able to complete the training requirements (document reviews, computer-based training, and classroom training)." Some workers start with a two-day orientation: "The first day is the regular new employee orientation that all new employees go through, where you learn about benefits, payroll, etc. The second day focuses solely on the on-boarding process of your specific Professional Development Program, giving information on people involved with the program, [the company's] expectations, future training [opportunities], important phone numbers, and [relevant] websites." After that, "most of the training you receive is hands-on from members of your department— learning how basic business functions there. Other training consists of soft-skill training through Abbott Training Services." Many new hires are "assigned a mentor, whom [they] regularly meet with to discuss Abbott's business model and the general business of business. This is one of the program's biggest strengths and one of the best learning experiences at Abbott." Abbott also encourages diversity and inclusion through formal employee networks so that employees are able to grow in areas of personal and professional development and build relationships by creating an internal network.

DAY IN THE LIFE

Newbies at Abbott work in all areas of the company's core business units. A company representative says, "*All* of our new hires jump into meaningful work assignments. Responsibilities are directly related to the success of business. New hires meet periodically with their management team to make sure [they] are properly trained and [are] delivering results. Several areas have structured development programs— rotating assignments that are six to twelve months in duration." Many of our respondents participated in these rotations, and all of them enjoyed the experience. One writes, "I liked the rotational aspect of [my program]. It's great for college graduates who are not set on what they want their career paths to be because it gives them the opportunity to experience several different options within their field[s] while [still] being a part of the company." Another person adds, "As a member of the Professional Development Program, the job is constantly changing, and we are constantly being challenged and pulled to grow in arenas that make us well-rounded and skilled in several job sets around the company." A third employee adds, "I learned more in each of my six month rotations from my bosses than I could have learned in two years' worth of classes at college."

PEERS

Because Abbott's Professional Development Programs are geared toward recent college graduates, there is "a lot of contact with first jobbers at Abbott." One newbie in the finance department writes, "Because of my current assignment, I have three other first jobbers around me who are in their first rotation as well. There are often a lot of invitations to after-hours events, which allow us to socialize and get to know [one another] better." First jobbers also see one another at "monthly staff meetings, bimonthly luncheons, [and] quarterly social events." As mentioned above, Abbott actively encourages employees to participate in intracompany sports and networking groups to build a sense of community throughout the company.

MOVING ON

Those who leave Abbott are relatively few in number. "Over 80 percent will stay long-term," says one company representative. People who do leave often "go back to school for further education. [They] come to Abbott with expectations of working for a few years, then getting their [graduate or professional] degree. For example, I had two young human resources professionals [whom] I mentored, and both decided to go to law school. Both are now halfway through law degrees. Both want to return to Abbott. That is desirable turnover that we encourage, as we believe in investing in our employees with the intent of future return on investment."

BEST AND WORST

A company spokesperson describes one of the best first jobbers this way: "He joined the company about twenty-five years ago as an entry-level employee and second-generation Abbott employee. His father worked at Abbott. He performed well and was promoted through many functional roles. Today, he is president of one of Abbott's global divisions. That's not a unique story. Our Professional Development Programs have a great track record for producing corporate officers."

ABC News
Desk Assistant

THE BIG PICTURE

To get to the top of any skyscraper, you have to enter through the ground floor. In network news, the job of desk assistant is the ground floor; it's where everyone who wants a career in broadcast journalism begins. It's a low-paying, extremely demanding, and sometimes tedious job, but if your dream is to make it in the news biz, well, this is the way to go. The good news is that if you impress your bosses, you will eventually be promoted to a better position.

STATS

LOCATION(S) WHERE ENTRY-LEVEL EMPLOYEES WORK

The news organization has major office hubs in Los Angeles, California; New York, New York (most of the jobs are available in New York City); and Washington, DC.

AVERAGE NUMBER OF APPLICATIONS EACH YEAR

ABC News receives from 700–1,000 applications per year.

AVERAGE NUMBER HIRED PER YEAR OVER THE LAST TEN YEARS

ABC News has hired 150–200 people per year over the last ten years.

ENTRY-LEVEL POSITION(S) AVAILABLE

Entry-level hires work as desk assistants.

AVERAGE HOURS WORKED PER WEEK

Employees work from fifty to sixty hours per week.

PERCENTAGE OF ENTRY-LEVEL HIRES STILL WITH COMPANY AFTER THREE, FIVE, AND TEN YEARS

50 percent, 40 percent, and 30 percent, respectively.

AVERAGE STARTING SALARY

Entry-level hires earn $26,000 base pay, plus overtime.

BENEFITS OFFERED

The company provides medical, dental, life, and disability insurance.

CONTACT INFORMATION

Nissa W. Booker
ABC News Recruitment Coordinator
47 West 66th Street, 6th Floor
New York, NY 10023

GETTING HIRED

The job of desk assistant is among the most competitive low-paying positions to obtain, so finding some way to distinguish yourself from the pack is crucial. One desk assistant writes, "Once I knew that I wanted to pursue a network job, getting one was quite the challenge. Every desk assistant has become one through a different channel and brings with them different experiences. I believe what got me an interview was that I had a good producer resume tape that showed I had a decent amount of experience writing and editing. Plus, my resume demonstrated my other journalism experiences through internships, summer jobs, etc. I do believe, however, that you must bring something different to the position other than journalism skills. I was a Spanish and journalism double major and had completed a semester abroad. I think traveling and knowing another language helped me in that I could bring a wide variety of knowledge and passion for another subject other than broadcasting to ABC." A passion for the news is also crucial, of course. ABC is on constant lookout for good candidates, "even when there are no positions available." Network representatives tell us that "resumes are screened and interviews are conducted on a regular basis. If certain qualifications are met after an initial review of the resume, the candidate is invited to set up an exploratory interview. Resumes of interest are kept on file for one year. Resumes from the strongest candidates are flagged and reviewed again when a position becomes available. A hire is then made from that select group." ABC also holds "several job fairs" that "specific[ally] focus on minority recruitment."

MONEY AND PERKS

Desk assistants earn a pretty poor salary, especially considering the big-city location of the jobs. The best desk assistants, however, can earn much more (yet, still at a poor hourly rate), since they "make [a great deal] of their money in overtime earnings, which are largely dependant upon how good they are at the job. The best desk assistants are asked to work more and therefore make more money." Regardless of the pay, all desk assistants are happy to have the job because "in journalism the supply [of qualified candidates] is much greater than the demand [for such candidates]." The biggest perk, according to one desk assistant, "is that every day you are witness to and involved in the incredible process of making the news. It is very gratifying to know that you contributed in some way to a product that millions of people see. This is only amplified when major news breaks. I was a desk assistant during Election 2000, and even though the work wasn't that challenging, I had a front row seat to how this historic event was reported to the public. You are also exposed to a talented array of news professionals and news stars. Simply observing them is an education."

THE ROPES

At ABC, orientation is a quick review of "benefits, company policies, company history, etc. It lasts only a few hours with a human resources representative." After that, work begins; you train as you work. One desk assistant explains, "I was trained by my peers on the job. Outside of the heavy packet of information we were expected to study, there was no formal training process." ABC News representatives explain why: "There is no way to prepare an individual for the chaos of covering a breaking news story, so we immediately throw them into an environment [that] helps them to build a level of confidence that will carry them through the chaos."

DAY IN THE LIFE

Desk assistants' duties depend on their assignments. "If they are assigned to a show like *World News Now* or *World News Tonight,* they are responsible for supporting the show so that it runs smoothly. This means organizing scripts, routing calls appropriately, and collecting editorial information. If a desk assistant works on the assignment desk, the responsibilities include helping to coordinate news coverage, obtaining and retaining very specific editorial information about several important stories, and knowing how stories are staffed." One assignment desk assistant writes, "I had to learn where everyone was at all times and had to be up to speed on all news, especially breaking news, and who from our team was covering what stories. I worked with an assignment editor. Some nights it was so busy, I couldn't get up to go to the bathroom. The phone would be ringing off the hook, and you just have to manage. The night of the blackout [in New York] was crazy but incredibly fun 'cuz I love this stuff!" All of the desk assistants we spoke with agreed that they needed to take on jobs beyond their own to get ahead; one assistant explains, "I took a lot of initiative, and I pitched story ideas that aired, and I got to go on shoots (this is rare). You need to be aggressive or else you could get stuck. Most importantly people have to like you and have confidence in you. Network! If you don't network, you won't move. Talk to anyone who will talk to you, [and] make sure you have mentors."

PEERS

Desk assistants get to see a lot of one another at work. "We do not hang out that much after work, since we're here on average sixty hours a week together." One desk assistant writes that because they spend so much time together, "there is a lot of camaraderie among the desk assistants. During the day, we'll discuss the various ABC shows as well as what's happening in our personal lives. I also think we offer a support network for one another since we all have our days of struggling as desk assistants and the stress of worrying about moving up the ABC ladder." Desk assistants like one another, in part, because they are so much alike. One desk assistant interviewed notes that "ABC News—maybe news in general—attracts smart, interesting people with drive and talent. It generally takes a certain type of personality to withstand the [pressure-filled] environment, so while people have diverse interests, they generally share a sense of adventure, humor, and curiosity. The desk assistants I worked with all went to good schools and were your typical overachievers."

MOVING ON

According to company representatives, "The majority of the people who leave the desk assistant position are promoted to the next level job at ABC News. Some people who leave the company leave to go back to school or for other jobs in the industry." You should be aware that promotions don't always happen quickly. In fact, "promotions among desk assistants typically occur at a glacial pace. There is not a lot of movement among production staff; they don't leave, and they aren't promoted regularly, so people can be desk assistants for some time, maybe a year to two years. The unhappy people were those who had a sense of hopelessness that they would never move on to have greater responsibilities and do more interesting work."

ATTRITION

"Less than 5 percent" of the desk assistants quit within a year of taking the job; "everyone stays at least a year with the hope [of being] promoted to the next-level job." Employees who leave, as well as many who stay, "complain about working too many hours and not really doing tasks that represent their true capabilities." Ultimately, though, "people know being a desk assistant in New York is a golden opportunity [that] can lead to so much."

BEST AND WORST

Pick your favorite broadcaster as your own personal "best-ever" desk assistant from ABC's news staff; one first jobber explains, "Everyone has been a desk assistant at one point. All executive producers and vice presidents of news are former desk assistants."

ACADEMY FOR EDUCATIONAL DEVELOPMENT
Various Positions

THE BIG PICTURE

Nearly a half-century old, the Academy for Educational Development (AED) is "an independent, nonprofit organization committed to solving critical social problems and building the capacity of individuals, communities, and institutions to become more self-sufficient. AED works in all major areas of human development [and focuses] on improving education, health [care], and economic opportunities for the least advantaged in the United States and developing countries throughout the world." It's a great place for first jobbers who seek to become a part of "a really reputable organization in international development." You won't accumulate material wealth working here, but you'll probably sleep well at night knowing that your efforts make a positive difference in the lives of others.

STATS

LOCATION(S) WHERE ENTRY-LEVEL EMPLOYEES WORK

AED's headquarters are in Washington, DC; there is also an office in New York, New York, as well as regional offices, some of which are overseas.

AVERAGE NUMBER OF APPLICATIONS EACH YEAR

AED receives 3,000 applications each year.

AVERAGE NUMBER HIRED PER YEAR

AED hires sixty-six entry-level employees per year.

ENTRY-LEVEL POSITION(S) AVAILABLE

Entry-level employees are hired as research assistants, finance assistants, program assistants, receptionists, and administrative assistants.

AVERAGE HOURS WORKED PER WEEK

Entry-level employees work forty hours per week.

AVERAGE STARTING SALARY

Entry-level employees earn $26,000 per year.

BENEFITS OFFERED

AED offers three domestic health care plans and one international health care plan, dental and vision insurance, and medical flexible spending accounts. AED also offers a 403(b) retirement plan, twenty days of annual leave, educational and professional development assistance, transportation and parking expenses (in Washington, DC), and software training.

Contact Information

Academy for Educational Development
1825 Connecticut Avenue, NW
Washington, DC 20009-5721
Fax: 202-884-8413
E-mail: employ@aed.org
www.aed.org

Getting Hired

AED is a big organization, with "a highly diverse staff of more than 1,400," and it seeks new hires in such areas as international exchange, education, democracy building, free-market enterprise, workforce and community development, social marketing, health care, environmental protection, population control, disabilities, and evaluation. Most jobs available to recent college grads are entry-level, with many falling within the realm of administrative support jobs. Open positions are listed at the organization's website and sorted by salary grade; AED encourages those interested to "apply for specific positions as they become available" by "sending a resume to the address or fax number at the bottom of each position description." Applications are reviewed carefully, and strong applicants are contacted for initial interviews (others are not, however, due to time and personnel constraints). One successful applicant reports, "My interviewers asked about work experience, problem-solving skills, regional experience (as it's an internationally-focused position), and work style. The tone was pretty standard [for an] interview. It was not overly jovial, but it was not a grilling either." Another job seeker who passed muster writes, "I think that the key to my interview being successful [was] that I was personable and honest, in a tactful way."

Money and Perks

Start dates with AED can be negotiable. Salaries are harder to negotiate; one first jobber explains, "Given the nature of the pay structure, which is contract-based, there's not that much room to negotiate an increase in starting pay." Raises come annually; the organization explains, "Performance reviews are conducted twice a year. One of these reviews is a performance appraisal [at which time the company] reviews the employee's salary." Most of the newbies here agree that the best perk is the education benefits program, which "gives full-time employees $2,400 per year to spend on professional development. It's absolutely fantastic. You can take courses, buy books or newspaper and journal subscriptions, and travel to conferences. It's a great benefit."

The Ropes

Orientation at AED is a "half-day seminar" covering introductions of the various departments, an overview of the organization and its work, an outline of employee interest groups, and a review of billing procedures and benefits. Subsequent training is generally handled on the job, most often by a coworker or supervisor.

Day in the Life

Many first jobbers at AED handle administrative duties, many of which may be referred to as grunt work. One writes, "A typical day involves taking care of my boss's calendar, screening her phone calls, working on various projects she assign[s] me, making travel arrangements, ordering supplies for the center, and assisting other staff in their projects. I [may] work on a PowerPoint presentation or graphs for a proposal, various things like that." Another reports, "When first hired, I was responsible for managing e-mail and fax communication between the home office and international field offices, making payments to vendors and service providers, and assisting program specialists with procurement and program implementation issues." Over time, however, "new hires receive more responsibilities, and their work becomes focused on more interesting projects suited to their talents." All the same, there are some who "often feel that the menial tasks eat up any time that could be used to create more interesting work and come up with creative ideas."

Peers

AED is "definitely a vibrant place to work," as it is home to "a lot of young professionals who are very passionate and very social outside of work." Young hires are typically "very smart and very diverse. They come from all over the United States and from all over the globe." They tend to hang together when the work day is done. One reports, "There are many opportunities to interact with those in your grade level." Another elaborates, "There are a number of interest groups operating here, including school-mentoring programs, sports teams, and language classes. Folks also get together with people they work with directly. There are several people around my age in my unit, and we get together for happy hour once in a while. So, yes there is a measure of camaraderie here. And you're free to create more of a social scene and start interest groups here if you feel so inclined."

Moving On

Those who leave AED take jobs in private industry or seek employment at other nonprofit organizations with a government entity. Some leave because of "the increasing bureaucracy at the lower grades and the perception that the pay "is really not sufficient for the amount of work that most of [the entry-level workers] do." While it's true that AED's pay "is fairly consistent with the DC nonprofit market," some gripe that "it's really not enough to live comfortably in DC."

ACCENTURE
Consulting Analyst

THE BIG PICTURE

Consulting analysts are the cavalry of the business world. They save the day by solving problems that businesses can't solve on their own. Accenture is well-known for its consulting work in IT services and technology; with $11.8 billion in annual revenues, there are few areas in the business world in which Accenture *isn't* a major player.

STATS

LOCATION(S) WHERE ENTRY-LEVEL EMPLOYEES WORK

Accenture has locations across the United States.

ENTRY-LEVEL POSITION(S) AVAILABLE

Accenture hires entry-level employees mostly for consulting analyst positions; candidates are chosen according to the company's skill and capability needs, as demanded by individual markets.

AVERAGE HOURS WORKED PER WEEK

Employees generally work more than forty hours per week, but this varies based on factors such as level and position.

BENEFITS OFFERED

"Accenture offers total rewards packages that consist of professional growth opportunities, competitive compensation, and a broad and flexible range of benefits that include medical, dental, disability, and life insurance; paid holidays; and paid time off. In addition, Accenture provides a range of services to employees that can include financial planning, apartment listings, consumer resources, and many others."

CONTACT INFORMATION

For more details, visit Accenture on the Web at http://campusconnection.accenture.com.

GETTING HIRED

Candidate screening at Accenture is a four-step process. First, the company begins with a review of resumes and qualifications. Selected individuals may then be scheduled to begin the interviewing process, which consists of three steps. The first round—a twenty- to thirty-minute interview—offers a chance for those who wish to work at Accenture to present their resume in person. "This initial conversation allows us to get to know [one another], understand objectives, and evaluate qualifications. The second round— a forty-five-minute interview—gives the interviewee a chance to share experiences [in] greater detail. This interview will hone in on candidates' educational and personal experiences as they would relate to their potential performance at Accenture. Recruiters may ask for specific examples of situations encountered and how they have been handled. The final step in the process is an office visit. During the office visit, analysts, consultants, and executives further assess qualifications. There will also be presentations to explain further some of the nuts and bolts of working at Accenture." Company officials tell us that "individuals who excel during the interview process are those who are well prepared and demonstrate that they have done research on the company and the position. Many times these candidates have attended an event or talked to company representatives to gain a better understanding of the company and position."

MONEY AND PERKS

Accenture offers "competitive compensation"; representatives did not provide further details, but rest assured the pay is pretty good by first job standards. Perks include "many personal and professional development opportunities," a new laptop for business use, personal use of airline miles accrued during business travel, discounts from a variety of vendors, and "a transit transportation program that allows Accenture employees to pay for transportation using pre-tax dollars."

THE ROPES

Accenture's orientation program occurs in stages. The first, which lasts several weeks, is called the new employee orientation and the core analyst local course. Once they complete the course, analysts head to core analyst school at the center in St. Charles, Illinois. One analyst describes the experience: "My first few weeks comprised [of] local training with my start group and central training with others from around the world. The local training gave me the opportunity to create instantly a network with my start group and others I met in the office. It also provided an introduction to skills that were very valuable at central training in St. Charles. It was hard work but also fun. The training simulated a real project. It really provided background on what the Accenture culture is like—work hard as a team and play hard as a team." Continuing training is a fact of life for all Accenture employees, regardless of their seniority; "as part of continuous training throughout a career at Accenture, training can be completed either in person or virtually."

DAY IN THE LIFE

Consulting analysts meet with the businesses they advise, explore the parameters of the problem they are hired to address, and begin solving that problem. One analyst writes, "a typical day at my current project includes meeting with my team leader to ensure all tasks are being addressed, completing those tasks, and raising any issues found along the way. Currently, we are still in the concept phase. The workload will pick up significantly within the next couple of months as we head into the design and implementation phases." The firm adds that "responsibilities can vary across client engagements. On any given day, an analyst may [need to] leverage skills that include building industry skills; developing technology-based solutions; analyzing, designing, and implementing business process improvements; defining user requirements; and specializing in business process design, business validation concepts, testing and quality assurance, system building concepts, programming, and development [skills]." You won't be on your own here, as "many times [older alumni] also make a special effort to ensure that they are progressing. Accenture offers both informal and formal mentoring programs and encourages participation on all levels."

PEERS

New consulting analysts at Accenture are "constantly impressed by the people here. Coworkers are intelligent, amiable, helpful, and very committed to the quality of their work. People are always willing to help [one another] out or answer questions. There is a feeling of camaraderie that always develops when working on a team project, and those friendships extend beyond the workplace." One newbie reports, "The people are fantastically motivated and accept nothing but the highest level of work ethic and achievement. That said, most of the employees are very laid-back and down-to-earth, [which creates] a relaxed but productive work environment." Employees also praise the diversity of their coworkers; one employee reports, "When I attended new analyst training in St. Charles, I was astonished by the diversity of backgrounds, cultures, and nationalities represented by Accenture employees. The company is truly a global one."

MOVING ON

Consulting analysts make tons of contacts in the business world; thus, it is not surprising that some employees leave the firm to join one of Accenture's clients. Others leave to return to school. Representatives note that "Accenture has a well-established alumni program to [stay up-to-date] with the exciting opportunities that many of our alumni pursue."

ATTRITION

"Globally, our attrition rate (company wide) is below the industry average."

ÁEGIS ASSISTED LIVING
Various Positions

THE BIG PICTURE
Named America's third-fastest growing private company by *Inc.* magazine in 2003, Áegis Assisted Living is a business that will likely be creating many new jobs for years to come. If you're interested in working for Áegis, that's especially good news; employee satisfaction levels there result in a turnover rate that's among the lowest in the assisted-living industry.

STATS

LOCATION(S) WHERE ENTRY-LEVEL EMPLOYEES WORK
Corporate headquarters are located in Redmond, Washington; regional offices are located throughout Washington, Nevada, and California.

CONTACT INFORMATION
Visit the website at www.Áegisal.com/Positions.html.

GETTING HIRED
Áegis advertises job openings on its website and on www.monster.com. Most applicants undergo multiple interviews before the company decides to hire them. One support staffer explains, "The office manager, director of recruiting and retention, chief marketing officer, and accounting manager all interviewed me. My interview process began with a call from the office manager. She asked me a few basic questions over the phone and then invited me to a group interview. The group interview consisted of approximately sixteen candidates and was conducted by the office manager, the director of recruiting and retention, and the chief marketing officer. My third interview was conducted by the office manager, director of recruiting and retention, and the accounting manager. This was a panel interview. My fourth interview was one-on-one with the president of Áegis." While not *everyone* we spoke with interviewed with the president, all of our correspondents were vetted by many levels of company hierarchs prior to receiving a job offer.

MONEY AND PERKS
Most entry-level job offers at Áegis aren't negotiable, employees tell us, but some found the company flexible on the start date. Our correspondents speak highly of Áegis' Enhanced Benefit Program; they also tell us that "the company offers a lot of soft benefits such as luncheons, group activities, etc." Those who work at corporate headquarters report that the hometown of Redmond is a major plus.

THE ROPES

Orientation at Áegis, one worker reports, "begins on your first day of work. I met with everybody in the office separately and sat with [each of] them for a little while to learn about their roles in the company. This gave me a better feeling for the culture of Áegis and also the business itself. My orientation lasted for the first few days on the job." After that, "you sit down and dive right in." Most employees receive some specialized training early on to teach them how to deal with Áegis' clients; a chef writes, "I was new to Alzheimer's/dementia care and to Áegis itself, but the company took the time to train me on the aspects of care . . . so I felt comfortable and informed of what to expect. I also received training in CPR and first aid."

DAY IN THE LIFE

Áegis hires first jobbers in almost all areas, from client care (in positions such as activities director, care manager, concierge, cook, and wellness nurse) to behind-the-scenes business management (in capacities such as bookkeeping, marketing, and office administration). As such, there is no typical day; most would agree that "as the company is growing, so is the challenge of keeping up with it." Nearly all the employees we spoke with feel they have ample contact with higher-ups in the company. One typical employee writes, "I have plenty of access to upper management. I feel as though I can approach any of them if I need some information. We have an all-staff meeting once a month; [this] allows everybody to find out what is going on in the other departments."

PEERS

There is "a fairly high degree of camaraderie" among coworkers at Áegis; only a few people we spoke with distinguished between their relationships with fellow first jobbers and the company workforce at large. Everyone agrees, "the camaraderie is very strong, and it doesn't matter how long someone has been with the company. It feels [as if] we've all been here forever." Most employees enjoy getting together after-hours; one says, "Everybody is outgoing. I have met a couple of coworkers outside [of] the office for social occasions."

MOVING ON

Áegis has a very low employee turnover rate, a testament to the satisfaction level of its employees. One exuberant Áegis booster writes, "I don't hear anything but praise about the company. It's a really great place to be. It's challenging, busy, friendly, caring, and funny, and sometimes [it is] better to be at work than at home!"

AIR PRODUCTS
Career Development Program (CDP)

THE BIG PICTURE

Established in 1959, Air Products' Career Development Program is one of the longest-running entry-level programs profiled in this book. The deep roots of the program mean that there are always plenty of CDP graduates around to mentor the incoming class, and that's a real advantage for first jobbers here. Air Products supplies gases (oxygen, hydrogen, helium, etc.) and chemicals to a wide range of clients in the health care, technology, industrial, and energy markets.

STATS

Location(s) Where Entry-level Employees Work

"Corporate headquarters is in the Lehigh Valley in Southeastern Pennsylvania. About 40 percent of our college new hires start at our headquarters." Others start at one of the company's many locations throughout the mid-Atlantic, southeast, and west coast regions of the United States.

Average Number of Applications Each Year

Air Products receives 350–400 applications each year.

Average Number Hired Per Year

Air Products hires thirty-four entry-level employees per year.

Entry-level Position(s) Available

There are numerous positions available, predominantly in engineering.

Average Hours Worked Per Week

Entry-level employees work forty hours per week.

Percentage of Entry-level Hires Still with the Company After Three, Five, and Ten Years

Ninety-six percent of entry-level hires remain with Air Products after three years; 87 percent are still with the company after five years; and 67 percent stay on for ten years and beyond.

Average Starting Salary

Starting salaries are "competitive within the industry."

Benefits Offered

Air Products provides a medical/prescription plan, mental health coverage, dental plan, and an optional vision plan. "New hires must satisfy a waiting period of thirty days before coverage begins for most benefits." Additional benefits include life insurance, disability, long-term care, adoption assistance, ConSern Education loans, education assistance, matching gifts, a retirement savings plan, and flexible spending accounts.

Visit www.airproducts.com/Careers/NorthAmerica.

GETTING HIRED

All Air Products job seekers must submit applications via the company's website; while Air Products "does recruit on campus, all students we meet are directed to the website." Ideal candidates "demonstrate strong technical competencies, good teamwork skills, strong interpersonal skills, good leadership skills, and a willingness to be flexible in assignment content and geographic location." Those who don't make the cut, writes one successful hire, "are those who are just too one-dimensional. Air Products seeks well-rounded engineers with more than just strong technical skills. Strong interpersonal skills are also a must." The interview process is rigorous; one product coordinator reports, "Thirteen of us [prospective employees] traveled to Allentown for the same interview. The night before our interview, several Air Products employees met the interviewees at our hotel to take us out to dinner and get to know each other a bit better. We were told at dinner what to expect the next day in terms of our schedule. We were also told only two interviewees were going to be hired. The interview itself consisted of two technical interviews in the morning, a technical exam, an open-floor discussion among the interviewees about the exam question (which was monitored by the interviewers, who outnumbered the interviewees), two impromptu presentations about the exam-question discussion to two different interviewers, two nontechnical interviews, and finally an human resources debrief info session about Air Products. Although we were given meals and breaks between each section of the interview process, the stress of the *very* thorough interview may have weighed more on some interviewees than others." A number of the first jobbers we spoke with began their careers through college co-ops, then became full timers after graduation.

MONEY AND PERKS

All Air Products employees "are eligible for variable compensation. It is based on individual performance." Most first jobbers felt that their starting salaries were not negotiable, but most were also happy with their initial offer. Top perks include flexible work arrangements (called FWAs; one worker writes, "The company strives to be the best company to work for, and, therefore, offers this perk. As long as you complete your work and put in your forty hours, you are able to arrange your schedule as four days a week, ten hour days, or '9-80s,' which entail putting in eighty hours in nine days, with the tenth day off, etc."). First jobbers also love the work-related travel ("visiting customers is usually a good time"), relocation benefits, and "the onsite dry cleaner."

THE ROPES

Entry-level hires at Air Products participate in the Career Development Program (participants are referred to as "CDPs, for Career Development Participants"), during which "each CDP rotates through three different assignments, with each assignment averaging approximately twelve months in length. The CDPs have input as to which assignments they prefer, so it is somewhat self-directed. This is a strength of the program; the CDPs begin their careers by taking three different developmental assignments in areas of interest to them."

Formal orientation is short and sweet, just a half-day introduction to the physical plant and reviews of benefits and company policies. One first jobber writes, "A new employee handbook was sent to my door a few weeks before I began work. A human resource representative contacted me to discuss the process and go over the forms and paperwork. When I began work, my supervisor and I went through the handbook. [We] discussed my benefits, such as retirement packages, and [my supervisor] directed me to the resources to manage my options. Later, training was conducted at corporate headquarters for new employee orientation." There's plenty of subsequent training "conducted by supervisors on the job," as well as "various safety classes (since we work at a chemical plant)."

DAY IN THE LIFE

The rotational nature of the CDP means Air Products' first jobbers "perform many of the different engineering functions [including, but not limited to] process engineering, project engineering, product engineering, safety, environmental [projects], design, maintenance, production, etc." A product coordinator recounts his experiences as a CDP: "What was great . . . was the autonomy and experience it afforded me as an engineer. At my first assignment, I was put in charge of two high-pressure emulsion-production processes. Every day when I first got to work, I would check on the overnight production runs to ensure reactor efficiencies were at par. I would investigate and place controls on those [reoccurring] inefficiencies in the process, by either placing control changes, procedure changes, or process changes. I would also interact with the plant operators to get feedback on any process issues they may be facing in the plant to help streamline their jobs a bit better. After my first assignment, I moved into a similar one-year role as a process engineer at a plant location near Baton Rouge, Louisiana. After that second assignment was completed, I worked my way into the business area, where I have become a permanent employee and rolled out of the CDP program. The advantage of the CDP program, and what attracted me to AP, was the fact that new hire graduates are given a chance to figure out where in the company they best fit and what jobs are best for them."

PEERS

"There is a lot of camaraderie with fellow employees" at Air Products because of "corporate-sponsored intramural sports leagues, clubs, etc." CDPs "get together for happy hours, [form] committees, and [partake in] community service days. Again, it's up to the individual to determine [his or her own] level of participation, but the opportunities are there. There is a common e-mail chain for all CDPs (and some recent CDPs) that circulates frequently, which tells where the next big social gathering will be on weekends and after work." Participants appreciate that "due to the size of the CDP program, there is instant camaraderie amongst all CDPs." And sometimes there's more than camaraderie; one first jobber reports, "I married another one of the CDPs!"

Moving On

Young hires who leave Air Products usually do so to "return to school for an advanced degree (typically in engineering or business)" or because "their spouse works in a different geographic location." Some "decide to change careers and do something different [from] engineering."

Best and Worst

"Our CDP program has turned out some of the best in the company. Our current CEO, as well as his two predecessors, all joined Air Products as CDPs. This program has been in place since 1959. We truly use this to develop the leaders of the company. Many of our managers, senior managers, and executives at Air Products joined the company through this program."

AMERICAN BIOPHYSICS CORPORATION

Various Positions

THE BIG PICTURE

If you hate mosquitoes—and besides frogs and bats, who doesn't?—and love the idea of a growing business, American Biophysics may be the right place for you. The producer of the Mosquito Magnet, a machine capable of capturing up to 1,500 of the pesky biters in one night, was the number one growth company on the 2003 *Inc. 500* list. It was also named one of *Forbes* Magazine's "Top 25 Hot Private Properties in 2004." This company plans to continue growing within this realm. According to its website, American Biophysics is "single-mindedly focused and dedicated to the business of biting insect control."

STATS

LOCATION(S) WHERE ENTRY-LEVEL EMPLOYEES WORK

Corporate headquarters are located in North Kingstown, Rhode Island.

AVERAGE NUMBER HIRED PER YEAR OVER THE LAST TEN YEARS

There are 108 employees, twenty-five of whom are entry-level employees. The company predicts a relatively substantial increase in the number of new hires.

ENTRY-LEVEL POSITION(S) AVAILABLE

There are anywhere from fifteen to twenty entry-level positions available.

AVERAGE HOURS WORKED PER WEEK

Depending on the position, employees may work more than forty hours per week.

PERCENTAGE OF ENTRY-LEVEL HIRES STILL WITH THE COMPANY AFTER THREE, FIVE, AND TEN YEARS

After two years, 90 percent of all entry-level hires remain with the company; after three years, 80 percent of all entry-level hires remain.

AVERAGE STARTING SALARY

The average starting salary ranges from $25,000–$30,000.

BENEFITS OFFERED

The company offers Blue Cross/Blue Shield (20 percent employee contribution) and Delta Dental (20 percent employee contribution). Additional benefits include a 401(k) and 529 college savings plan.

Contact Information

Human Resources Manager

140 Frenchtown Road

North Kingstown, RI 02852

Tel: 401-884-3500, ext. 139

Fax: 401-884-6688

www.mosquitomagnet.com

Getting Hired

American Biophysics representatives tell us that they seek candidates who are "adaptable to ever-changing environments, have an entrepreneurial spirit, are willing to make decisions, have a drive to succeed, and have excellent communication skills." Currently the company does not advertise job openings on its website, but it does recruit at area campuses. One of the company's recruiters says, "Applicants who stand out are [those] who have researched the company already, who seem confident and natural, [who don't give] canned answers to questions, and who have insightful, creative answers to our questions. We ask them how they handle pressure, ask them to describe a high-stress situation they feel they have handled well, and why, and then describe one they feel they didn't handle as well and what they would have done differently and what they have learned. We also talk to them a lot to see how well they listen, which is very [crucial]." One successful hire says, "The interview process was very casual. Both people who interviewed me explained the history and the goals of the company. The human resources manager called me a few weeks later and told me I had the job."

Money and Perks

Because the company is quickly growing, new opportunities become regularly available for current employees. The company bases pay increases on "annual increases and changing roles." The benefits package is "evolving," and the company is working to expand and add extras as it grows more profitable. According to some employees, the greatest perk is the excitement of working at a fast-growing company; it's "the best company in the world at what we do, and we're sitting on the verge of helping to create something truly groundbreaking," gushes one new entry-level hire.

The Ropes

As with most everything else at American Biophysics, orientation and training is a work in progress. According to company representatives, "We have some established training for our specialized products that involve hands-on experiences with our product. Training in regard to specific jobs is still being developed." Most of the employees we spoke with tell us that at first they "did not receive much training at all." One person says, "I was definitely thrown into the mix and left on my own to find my niche. How I dealt with that is what enabled me to advance in the company." Others add that they "receive constant training on company policies, procedures, and products, but none specifically on the job functions" and that, because the company is so small, "all employees have some knowledge of all operations."

DAY IN THE LIFE

American Biophysics is still in the process of defining the jobs its new hires will fill. If the company continues to grow at its current rate, the experiences of new hires will be much like that of those already working at the company. A current employee explains, "My responsibilities varied from day to day. The company was moving so fast with so few employees that everyone had to pitch in." Because American Biophysics workers usually have several coals in the fire at any given time, "There is always a level of multitasking that needs to occur so you can get each of your projects completed on time and [within] budget." One of the great things about working at such a small company, entry-level employees agree, is the relatively easy access they have to everyone from the shipping room to the board room. One worker reports, "There is no isolation at American Biophysics. All departments have close contact [with one another]. The high-level executives know everyone's first name. They regularly interact with all employees on both a business and personal level."

PEERS

There's "a mix of young and old workers" at American Biophysics, which "helps maintain a balance of youth and experience" and maintains a level of comfort in an otherwise hectic work environment. "We're all good friends, even when things get intense in the office," writes one employee. "Everyone respects [one another] even when there's a conflict. At the end of the day, all issues are forgotten." Workers "spend a lot of time together inside and outside of work. We all go out a few times a month after work."

MOVING ON

American Biophysics was founded in 1991, but its business has only moved into high gear since it introduced its first mosquito trap in 1998. As such, it doesn't have much of a history of employees who "move on," and only a few people could offer insights into where departed employees have gone. In fact, the vibe we get from them is that most people are happy to work here and bullish about their prospects of advancement within the company. Their few complaints concern poor communication. One first jobber says, "When a company is growing as fast as we are, some things slip through the cracks without all the appropriate people knowing about them. When the customer knows and you don't, it can be embarrassing. That's the main issue that comes up."

AmeriCorps
Various Positions

The Big Picture

AmeriCorps representatives note, "This year [AmeriCorps will] engage 75,000 people in service to their communities and country. Every AmeriCorps member gains the personal satisfaction of making a difference by helping others. You can teach or mentor youth, build affordable housing, teach computer skills, clean parks and streams, run after-school programs, and help communities respond to disasters. You can also put your college skills to work strengthening the capacity of charitable organizations by recruiting volunteers, expanding programs, providing training and technical assistance, and updating technology, thereby helping grantees to become more self-sustaining."

Stats

Location(s) Where Entry-level Employees Work

AmeriCorps has offices in all fifty states; Washington, DC; Puerto Rico; and other U.S. territories

Average Number of Applications Each Year

People apply directly to the nonprofit organizations that AmeriCorps members serve, and there isn't a centralized database of all applications; as a result, the exact number is unknown.

Average Number Hired Per Year over the Last Ten Years

AmeriCorps currently hires 75,000 people a year.

Average Hours Worked Per Week

Full-time members work forty hours per week. A full-time member works 1,700 hours over ten to twelve months. Some part-time members work 900 hours over the course of ten to twelve months.

Percentage of Entry-level Hires Still with the Company After Three, Five, and Ten Years

"AmeriCorps members typically serve for a year. Some of them, however, continue for another year or accept positions as employees with the nonprofit organizations [at which] they've served."

Average Starting Salary

Members receive "a living allowance of about $8,000 a year, plus a $4,725 education award that can be used to pay back student loans or put toward future tuition. Each member receives the [education] award after completing a year of service."

Benefits Offered

Health care coverage is included in the living allowance. Additional benefits include forbearance on interest for student loans during the term of service.

CONTACT INFORMATION

To learn more or apply online, visit www.americorps.org or call 800-942-2677 or 800-833-3722.

GETTING HIRED

There is no surefire route to attaining an AmeriCorps position because "the hiring criteria are determined by the nonprofit organizations [that] select AmeriCorps members. The only general criteria [are] that you must be at least seventeen years old and a U.S. citizen, national, or legal permanent resident alien of the United States. For some programs, such as the AmeriCorps*National Civilian Community Corps (AmeriCorps*NCCC), members must be between eighteen and twenty-four years old, but for most [programs] there are no upper age limits." Openings available through AmeriCorps are listed on the website. Successful applicants recommend that interested candidates post their resumes online. One applicant writes, "I posted [my] resume and cover letter on the AmeriCorps Web page. This was the better way to go since there was a much quicker response time than sending any application via mail."

MONEY AND PERKS

AmeriCorps representatives describe the living allowance that makes up its pay as "modest," so you know you won't be getting rich from this job. You will gain valuable experience, however, and you may also be eligible for other helpful perks such as student loan deferments, a grant toward paying off student loans (paid at the end of your term of service), health insurance, child care assistance, and money to relocate. For most, though, the greatest perk is the experience itself. As one AmeriCorps veteran tells us, "I really met some great people. I am still in contact with fellow members six years after we served together. I have gained valuable skills that transfer into everyday life and my current positions. Finally, I have gained confidence in my abilities and myself."

THE ROPES

As with the hiring process, orientation for AmeriCorps jobs varies depending on the organization with which members are placed. A two-term AmeriCorps veteran reports, "Orientation was an intensive experience for the two AmeriCorps programs I participated in. The concept was to challenge the corps to learn about diversity, conflict, and other challenges they would be facing in the coming year. For one of my assignments, we actually went on a three-day retreat as part of the orientation process—which allowed for quick and deep bonding to occur." For many organizations, corps members receive training through various federal, state, and local agencies; the training sessions can focus on everything from intensely practical skills (i.e., how to fight a fire or how to build a house) to maddeningly bureaucratic chores (i.e., how to complete government forms).

DAY IN THE LIFE

Because AmeriCorps workers undertake so many different projects for so many different organizations, there is no typical day. According to organization representatives, "Some typical assignments for AmeriCorps members are running after-school programs, tutoring, developing and maintaining nature trails, addressing issues of homelessness, and responding to natural disasters." The work can certainly be gratifying, as the experiences of one graduate who worked at a domestic violence center illustrate: "I was responsible for answering the crisis hotline. I went to court with victims who needed help in obtaining restraining orders against their abusive partners. I did shelter intakes and talked with people who needed someone to talk to. I provided information and support to victims and survivors of domestic violence. I also did outreach events in the community to help spread awareness of the issues. Over time, I was given more and more things to do. I came up with projects that I wanted to do. I was really able to branch out and find my own niche. The experience I received was invaluable and has helped me in every position I have had since."

Peers

Peer relationships at AmeriCorps depend on the assignments members have. One member says, "We are spread out around the state, so there is no peer network." Conversely, an alum of AmeriCorps*NCCC reports, "The corps bond was very tight. I was a team leader, and this group was also very close-knit. This was my social circle, since I had moved to a new city to participate in the programs. To this day, I still maintain contact with many people with whom I served. Despite the fact that we are spread out all over the country, we commit to getting together at least once a year for a reunion." Another first jobber sums up the situation this way: "[During] the months you spend on projects, you are limited to interaction with your team, or if you are working at a site with other people, then [you interact with] coworkers. Some projects are team-based, and during other [projects], you work individually. Most after-work hours are spent privately or with your team if you choose to fraternize."

Moving on

AmeriCorps is a one-year program, and most people leave after their term is finished. Quite a few people, however, sign up for a second and even a third tour of duty. An organization representative notes, "One of the benefits of AmeriCorps is that it provides members with the opportunity to explore different career paths. Many members discover a love and talent for the service they have provided as members, including teaching and nonprofit management."

Attrition

About one in five people who start an AmeriCorps assignment don't make it through the year of service. Some members find themselves working on projects they deem trivial; other members find they can't handle the demanding workload and/or the low pay.

APPIAN CORPORATION
Associate Consultant, Software Engineer, Quality Engineer, and Marketing Associate

THE BIG PICTURE

A business-process management company founded in 1999, Appian Corporation breaks the mold in many ways. One employee explains, "What we do is somewhat unique, and it requires a fair amount of faith in the vision of the company's leaders to understand where we want to be in one, three, or ten years." Because Appian is both young and small, the company "likes to stay aggressive to compete with some of the competitive giants out there (the Microsofts, the Lockheed Martins, the Booze Allens, etc.)." As a result of its innovative philosophy, Appian is not, as one employee points out, "your typical consulting or software company."

STATS

LOCATION(S) WHERE ENTRY-LEVEL EMPLOYEES WORK

All positions are located in Vienna, Virginia.

Average Number of Applications Each Year

Appian receives about 10,000 applications each year.

Average Number Hired Per Year

Fifty entry-level employees are hired each year.

Entry-level Position(s) Available

Entry-level employees may be hired as associate consultants, software engineers, quality engineers, and marketing associates.

Average Hours Worked Per Week

Entry-level hires work about forty-five to fifty hours per week.

Average Starting Salary

Starting salaries vary based on applicants' majors and degrees, with additional compensation available in bonuses and revenue appreciation rights.

Benefits Offered

Appian offers medical, dental, and vision coverage; and all employees are eligible from first day of employment. Employees may also participate in Appian's 401(k) program with matching employer contribution. The company has revenue appreciation rights, as well.

CONTACT INFORMATION

Visit Appian Corporation on the Web at www.appian.com.

GETTING HIRED

Appian "recruits at five to ten schools per recruiting season in the United States and internationally. Recruiting on-campus includes attending university career fairs, [giving] company presentations, and [conducting] on-campus interviews. Schools that we regularly attend are: The University of Virginia, Duke, Dartmouth, the University of Pennsylvania, MIT, Harvard, Princeton, Yale, Cornell, Georgetown, the University of Texas, Tec de Monterrey, and IIT—Bombay. Students from other universities are encouraged to apply and may do so online." One first jobber who was recruited at Duke writes, "The first round of interviews was with two Appian employees who were alumni of my university. The interviews were mainly behavioral, with a few technical questions based on my academic focus, which was computer science. The second round—and admittedly the round that sold this company to me—was with two of the four founders of the company: the CEO and the CTO, respectively. Both of these interviews were challenging: the CEO's interview was centered around my experiences in college. For example, I described a particular project in one of my classes, and he changed a few of the parameters of the assignment and asked me to explain how these changes would [affect] the result. The CTO, [however], presented me with a technical case study, drew his conclusions, and asked me to challenge them. It was a fast-paced interview, and I realized very quickly in both interviews that these two founders, like myself, enjoyed being challenged, [and] challenging others to think in different ways and generally liked finding problems and solving them. The final round of interviews took place at the company's headquarters. [This] included an office tour, meeting most of the employees, two more interviews with senior employees, and a very nice night out on the town."

MONEY AND PERKS

Start date is negotiable at Appian, as is one's specific work assignment; location and salary generally are not, at least not for first jobbers. Employees "receive performance bonuses during their annual reviews," which are "based on the employee's individual performance throughout the year, as well as [the] company's performance."

The best perk here, everyone agrees, is the annual corporate retreat, "which has traditionally been a seven-day cruise." One employee reports, "We use this opportunity to take stock of the state of our company and the market, to transfer knowledge gained on specific projects to the rest of the company, and to just have a good time. It's always an incredibly well-organized event that offers everyone the opportunity to get friendly with new faces and catch up with old ones we haven't seen since Appian Academy [the company's orientation program]."

THE ROPES

Appian has an "extensive orientation process," a five-week long "Academy Program" during which new hires "hear from representatives from the different departments throughout the company about policies, procedures, and the role of each department. Employees also start to learn about our product and begin to work on projects that will ultimately result in a presentation for their peers and supervisors." One first jobber describes it as "a crash course on all things Appian featuring various units on specific technologies that Appian uses, Appian's products and history, how to consult (consulting etiquette), an understanding of the market in which Appian does business, and much more. During the academy, new employees have lectures, papers, projects, presentations, and yes, even tests! The purpose of the academy is to give all new employees a chance to bring whatever skills they have garnered in their college experiences and round them out with the skills that every Appian employee needs to succeed."

DAY IN THE LIFE

First jobbers come aboard at Appian in a variety of functional areas. Once new hires complete their academy training, they take on consulting and technical assignments. No two jobs are the same—though nearly all the positions demand hard work, creativity, and the ability to work with others. A first jobber brought on as a software consultant writes, "My job consisted of gathering client requirements, developing prototype solutions, demonstrating them to the customer, and implementing (coding) and deploying them. A typical day early in my career at Appian would see me meeting with my manager to do a technical review of earlier work, spending a number of hours working on my current software task, then preparing for and meeting with the client to flesh out requirements for future enhancements to the system that Appian developed and delivered to the customer. Early on, these meetings were nearly always attended by my manager, and afterward, we would discuss our impressions of the client's needs to ensure that I took away from these meetings what I needed. As time went on, I would conduct these interactions with more and more autonomy, until my manager moved on to another project and I stayed on [this project], managing the team myself."

PEERS

Appian is a magnet for young, smart, ambitious hires. One writes, "I think the common thread among Appianites (as we like to call ourselves) is the desire to engage and be engaged intellectually. This translates directly into the ways that we like to have fun (organized brainteaser contests are never hard to find on the cruise) and the fact that we are all driven to see this company succeed." Workers enjoy "a terrific camaraderie thanks to the common experience of the Appian Academy." One reports, "Not three months goes by that I don't try to organize dinner or a bar night with my academy mates to catch up on how work, Appian, and the rest of life is treating them."

MOVING ON

First jobbers leave Appian "to pursue another position or to return to school," according to the company. Very few leave before they've completed at least one year here; the average tenure is two to three years, though that figure should increase as the company ages (it was founded in 1999).

ASSOCIATED PRESS
Various Positions

THE BIG PICTURE

The Associated Press (AP) is the framework for the world news industry; the organization maintains 242 bureaus around the globe and provides copy, photographs, graphics, audio, and video to more than 1,700 newspapers and 5,000 television and radio outlets. If you want your stories to be seen, there's no better place to work: AP news services reach a billion people every day.

STATS

LOCATION(S) WHERE ENTRY-LEVEL EMPLOYEES WORK

"Generally speaking, every major city has a bureau. We hire at all locations, if there are appropriate openings."

AVERAGE NUMBER OF APPLICATIONS EACH YEAR

The AP receives "hundreds" of applications per year.

AVERAGE NUMBER HIRED PER YEAR OVER THE LAST TEN YEARS

The number of people who the AP hires "depends on turnover and various economic forces."

ENTRY-LEVEL POSITION(S) AVAILABLE

Entry-level employees work as editorial assistants, temporary news people, and interns.

AVERAGE HOURS WORKED PER WEEK

Entry-level employees work full-time hours.

AVERAGE STARTING SALARY

"[Starting salaries] depend on location. Salaries are covered by a collective bargaining agreement."

BENEFITS OFFERED

The AP offers "health, dental, mental health/substance abuse, [and] life insurance."

CONTACT INFORMATION

E-mail the AP at apjobs@ap.org.

GETTING HIRED

The AP makes its hiring decisions locally; "the bureau managers generally review the applications," organization representatives tell us, and the three qualities they look for are "experience, experience, experience." The AP visits "a number of colleges, especially those with strong journalism/communications departments." The most important part of the application process, first jobbers tell us, is the AP test. One new hire explains that "among other things, it has exercises in spelling, grammar, AP style, and current events. There are hypothetical situations posed that require you to write a news story based on tidbits of information provided. The AP also expects its news staff to write for broadcast media, so there are exercises related to that as well." Passing "puts your name in the AP system as someone who [is] interested in working for the AP and has passed their test. After that, it's a matter of a position opening up. If they call you up for an interview, it's already a done deal; they've already formed an evaluation of you because they've seen your test." Many employees begin with temporary assignments; people who make a good impression have the inside track when a permanent position becomes available.

Money and Perks

Salary at the AP is entirely determined by its union contract. Available jobs usually require first jobbers to work in specific locations on specific shifts; only in rare cases are start time or location negotiable. First jobbers point out that the "AP does, however, have posts in every state and most countries, so sometimes people will take the test in one bureau, then wait for a position to open up somewhere else." Young employees love "being exposed to breaking news all over the world on the wire (it's an extremely exhilarating feeling)" and "the feeling of learning nonstop." One person says, "You have to [have] a very humble attitude. Sometimes a topic will be thrown [at] you that you know nothing about." Employees also say, "It's neat to see your copy in newspapers around the state and sometimes around the country, even if it isn't credited."

The Ropes

Each local AP bureau runs slightly different. At some bureaus, first jobbers are thrown into the job with little preparation or training; others receive an orientation and training that lasts several weeks. A first jobber at one end of the spectrum tells us, "I was sent out on a story on the very first day. I didn't even know how to use their internal computer system. You learn as you go. They're so short staffed; when they need you, they need you." At the other end was the writer whose orientation "involved a couple of weeks of work on each part of the job—writing and reporting, dictating stories from the scene, writing broadcast copy, and working a supervisory shift that requires heavy editing." A former first jobber states, "Training [at most bureaus] is in the form of shadowing more experienced staff. For instance, I worked several broadcast shifts with the broadcast editor before I was left to man that desk on my own."

Day in the Life

Working at the AP means you'll always be in the middle of the action. One first jobber explains, "One of my first jobs was driving to the scene of an explosion in downtown St. Cloud, Minnesota. I collected information from people at the scene, law enforcement officials, and rescue workers, and then phoned in a story to the day supervisor. I also gathered information from energy companies about gas leaks. I phoned in a story to the broadcast desk, then updated both the newspaper and broadcast stories throughout the day." The sheer volume of work required is often overwhelming; many of the writers tell us they are expected to "write two or three stories on happenings of the day. There is also the expectation that you will write more extensive weekend stories a couple of times a month." Promotions usually entail more responsibility, higher-profile stories, the responsibility of coming up with original stories (rather than simply covering stories assigned by an editor), and more work. It's a news junkie's paradise.

PEERS

AP peer networks vary from bureau to bureau. In the larger bureaus, "there is ample camaraderie." "I often socialize with my colleagues," explains one first jobber in just such a bureau, adding, "I constantly interact with my peers at work, and I probably spend two or three nights out with at least one other AP person." At some bureaus, social life is limited by the demands of work; "there isn't much on the social plane here, since we're all at work twenty-four hours, and if you're not on, someone else usually is," writes one newbie. At smaller bureaus, there may not be any other young hires; "there weren't any other entry-level people when I started," reports one staffer.

MOVING ON

AP first jobbers are generally future lifers in the news industry. People who leave often take jobs with newspapers or in broadcast news; however, many people stay with the organization and work their way up the ranks.

ATTRITION

Most AP writers know what they're getting into, so the attrition rate is low. The "pressure from editors," the "heavy workload," and the "tedium of some routine jobs, such as editing" are things that may drive others to leave this organization; but AP employees generally take these issues in stride and accept them as the cost of working at a world-class news outlet.

BALTIMORE CITY TEACHING RESIDENCY
Teacher

THE BIG PICTURE

The Baltimore City Teaching Residency (BCTR) is "an initiative of the Baltimore City Public School System (BCPSS) that recruits, selects, and trains outstanding college graduates to become teachers in the schools that need them the most." Program hires, called residents, "become part of a cohort charged [with raising] student achievement." BCTR looks for "individuals interested in teaching in all subject areas, especially middle and high school math, science, and special education. Following an intensive and rigorous Training Institute, residents will enter the classroom [as teachers] while taking classes to obtain their teaching certification;" they also "have the option to earn their master's degree at The Johns Hopkins University or at the College of Notre Dame."

STATS

LOCATION(S) WHERE ENTRY-LEVEL EMPLOYEES WORK

All positions are located in Baltimore, Maryland.

AVERAGE NUMBER OF APPLICATIONS EACH YEAR

The Baltimore City Teaching Residency program receives 1,500 applications per year.

AVERAGE NUMBER HIRED PER YEAR

The program hires about 200 teachers each year.

ENTRY-LEVEL POSITION(S) AVAILABLE

Employees are hired as teachers/residents.

AVERAGE HOURS WORKED PER WEEK

Teachers work about forty-six hours per week.

PERCENTAGE OF ENTRY-LEVEL HIRES STILL WITH THE COMPANY AFTER THREE, FIVE, AND TEN YEARS

Seventy percent of entry-level hires are still with the program after three years.

AVERAGE STARTING SALARY

The base salary is $38,112 for those with a bachelor's degree and $40,973 for those holding a master's degree.

BENEFITS OFFERED

The Baltimore City Teaching Residency offers employees a choice of health insurance plans as well as dental, prescription, and vision coverage. Additional benefits include a 403(b) plan, a pension plan, and a "generous tuition reimbursement policy to defray the costs of certification and master's degree coursework." In addition, "during the summer pre-service training session, residents are provided with a stipend to help defer living costs. This year's stipend has not yet been determined and is dependent on the budgetary constraints of the Baltimore City Public School System. Last year, the stipend was $2,500 (pre-tax)."

CONTACT INFORMATION

The Baltimore City Teaching Residency
Baltimore City Schools
200 East North Avenue, Room 110
Baltimore, MD 21202
Tel: 410-396-7383
Fax: 410-545-0897
E-mail: info@baltimorecityteachingresidency.org
www.bcteachingresidency.org

GETTING HIRED

BCTR recruits on eastern college campuses but "will consider applications from all institutions." The organization does not conduct on-campus interviews; all potential residents must apply online by completing an application and attaching a resume, a personal statement, and academic transcripts. Applicants are "notified two weeks from the application deadline of their status. If granted an interview, candidates will have the ability to select their interview date and time via an online scheduler." One successful hire reports that "the interviewers asked questions about [my] successes and challenges in past jobs, why I thought that I would be successful in this position, what I thought the challenges of the position would be, etc. I also had to teach a demonstration lesson." Following the interview, candidates are "notified of their status within two weeks. At this time, selected candidates are supplied with an enrollment package that contains additional information on the program and states the program enrollment deadline. To finalize the process, candidates must pass state teacher tests before entering the classroom as teachers." Successful applicants "span a wide range of ages and backgrounds and bring to the program a diverse set of talents and skills. Strong candidates are those who are committed to having a positive effect on student achievement, who display excellence in their previous endeavors, and who are dedicated to reaching and influencing students—especially those in under-resourced areas—on a daily basis." Placements in schools are determined "through a variety of processes including, but not limited to, interviews and placement fairs and coordination of interviews between individual schools and residents. All candidates should be prepared to teach wherever they are needed most."

MONEY AND PERKS

Salaries, raises, and benefits for Baltimore City teachers "are governed by the collective bargaining agreement in place between the district and the teachers union. The teacher salary scale is a step-based system in which employees increase a salary step each year they teach. Additionally, residents are compensated based on their highest-earned degree: bachelor's degree, master's degree, master's plus thirty credits, and PhD." Teachers here tell us that the best part of their job is "working with students every day. It's very stimulating."

THE ROPES

All residents begin their work "with a paid Training Institute that is designed specifically for members of the BCTR. Residents will be exposed to seminars and workshops on standards, [the] foundations of teaching, and classroom management. During this training, residents will also participate in discussions and activities focused on the challenges and benefits of teaching in a diverse educational setting. The BCTR Training Institute consolidates a great deal of training time into only a few weeks;" as a result, "training is extremely demanding." During the training, "residents typically begin their days at 8:00 A.M. [teaching] in a summer school classroom, paired with an experienced teacher. For part of the morning, they may observe or teach; and they may work with small groups of students for the remainder of the session. In the afternoons, residents meet with an advisory group, led by excellent veteran teachers, for two- to three-hour sessions. These advisory groups are designed to build on residents' teaching experiences in the mornings and provide them with the key knowledge and skills necessary to begin teaching at the end of training. After this portion of the day ends, residents may have reading to do before the next day, preparation for work with their students, or graduate coursework to attend [to]." Residents accepted into the winter program begin training in January; those accepted into the summer program begin training in late June or early July.

DAY IN THE LIFE

Residents handle all the chores of a classroom teacher; in particular, they count among their duties the responsibility "to ensure that all students are achieving at the desired levels for their grade and skill levels and to complete any additional school requirements set by the principal or district (e.g., attending all staff meetings and participating on committees)." The school day lasts six-and-a-half hours; residents "on average work an additional two to three hours per day planning lessons, grading papers, or participating in after-school activities."

PEERS

"There is a high degree of camaraderie with first-year and new teachers at my school," writes one resident, observing that "most of the teachers I've encountered are smart and committed." Social life is hampered by the busy schedule residents keep, but they try to get together occasionally outside the confines of school.

MOVING ON

BCTR started up in 2002, so the program is relatively new. Consequently, relatively few of its hires have "moved on." Those who do typically move to other areas within education (in other districts, for example); a few leave education altogether.

ATTRITION

According to BCTR, "Individuals who leave the school system do so for a wide variety of personal and professional reasons." One teacher writes, those who are unhappy "usually criticize the administration. They tend to be negative types who don't really offer any solutions to problems." Over the past few years, between 12 and 15 percent of residents have left the program before completing two years.

BEST AND WORST

"There is not [a single] mold of a successful resident teacher," BCTR tells us. Great teachers have "diverse backgrounds, experiences, and skills [that] drive their success as classroom teachers." All of them share "a deep commitment to students and student achievement," the "ability to trouble-shoot, problem-solve, and develop innovative solutions rapidly," a "strong sense of responsibility for student outcomes," a "desire to become part of the school and neighborhood community," and a "commitment to working with parents and guardians." Less successful teachers include "individuals interested in 'easy work,'" such as those attracted by the "8:00 A.M. to 2:00 P.M. day with summers off."

BANK ONE

Development Programs and Other Entry-level Programs

THE BIG PICTURE

Bank One covers much of the financial universe, and it provides not only traditional savings and checking services, but also credit cards, insurance, financial planning, mutual funds, and annuities. The bank offers a variety of programs designed to integrate recent college graduates into each of its divisions.

STATS

LOCATION(S) WHERE ENTRY-LEVEL EMPLOYEES WORK

Bank One has locations in various cities in Arizona, Colorado, Delaware, Illinois, Indiana, Kentucky, Louisiana, Michigan, Ohio, Oklahoma, and Texas.

ENTRY-LEVEL POSITION(S) AVAILABLE

There are numerous entry-level positions available, including those that are part of the Bank One Scholar Program: Card Services' Business Associate Program and First Leader Program; Capital Markets Analyst Program; Finance, Accounting, and Audit Development Program; Chicago Sales Management Development Program; National Retail Management Development Program; Relationship Banker Development Program; National Enterprise Operations Management Development Program; and the Technology Development Program. Other opportunities may exist at any given time.

AVERAGE HOURS WORKED PER WEEK

Hours vary by position.

AVERAGE STARTING SALARY

Salaries also vary by position; they range from $25,000–$50,000 for people with bachelor's degrees and from $51,000–$85,000 for people with master's degrees, depending on the program.

BENEFITS OFFERED

Bank One and its employees share the cost of medical and dental insurance, 401(k) plans, training and education benefits, and adoption assistance. Bank One pays the full cost of disability and business travel accident insurance and has a wellness program. It also pays the full cost of life insurance and pension accounts. It provides sick leave, vacation time, holidays, and service awards.

CONTACT INFORMATION

Visit Bank One on the Web at www.bankone.com/careernav.

GETTING HIRED

Bank One "actively recruits on campus at many schools in the Midwest and South (a copy of our recruiting schedule can be found on our website)" and also accepts online applications. An entry-level employee in the National Enterprise Operations Management Development Program describes the process: "I got the interview after turning in one of my standard resumes. I believe that my past work experience and GPA are what got me the interview. I was interviewed first by a Bank One finance manager on campus. After passing that first round, I was invited to the operations center for a tour and two more interviews, one with an operations manager and the other with a senior vice president and division manager. All of the interviews used a standard Bank One format consisting of behavioral questions like, 'Describe a time when . . . .'" Interviews for full-time jobs "typically occur in the fall of each year; internship interviews are conducted in the spring. Offers are typically extended in November and December for full-time positions and in March and April for internships."

MONEY AND PERKS

Entry-level salaries vary at Bank One by program: "Each program determines if and how bonuses will be distributed as well as how salaries will increase. Some individuals receive increases once they graduate from their specific programs; others receive merit increases at their annual performance reviews." Starting salaries are rarely negotiable, although they can be for candidates with well-developed skills (i.e., in technology areas). Respondents to our survey praise the long-term financial benefits of working for Bank One: "There are great 401(k) and pension plans. Also, we get fees waived or better rates on other financial products." One entry-level employee adds that "the best fringe benefit[s] for the short-term [are] the discounts. Bank One is partnered with several companies, from restaurants and cell phone companies to clothing stores and gyms." Other fringe benefits include "exposure to senior management of the company (their guidance was invaluable and very motivating)" and "four weeks of vacation!"

THE ROPES

Everyone in Bank One's development programs starts off with "a week-long orientation, which includes an in-depth overview of Bank One as well as exposure to the heads of our lines of business. Each line of business continues from there with some form of orientation [and] training for their new hires during the individual's first 120 days of employment." One undergraduate hire reports, "The orientation process was the very best part of the program. They bring you in first to the corporate orientation, where you have an overview of the company and meet people from all different departments. The second day was the in-store orientation, where we were introduced to the program manager and were given our training schedules for the next 120 days. It made me feel very secure and eased my nerves about coming into a bank, knowing basically nothing about banking!" Training continues throughout the development programs and often includes substantial amounts of classroom learning.

DAY IN THE LIFE

A typical day depends on the program in which a given entry-level employee participates. Bank One scholars work six-month rotations in various positions by day, then attend an MBA program in the evening.

Card Services Business Associates Program is a "fast-track management program" that places trainees in one of the bank's many credit card-related areas. Capital markets analysts rotate through positions in the bank's Capital Markets departments, supplementing their training with formal classroom instruction. Development programs also entail rotations that expose participants to all the different specializations within their selected area. A participant in the Technology Development Program describes his work experience this way: "My job has been to take graphs of metrics [that] are reported manually each week and help automate them and make them viewable in a Web environment. To accomplish this task, I have spent a large [amount of] time learning the Java language and other technologies [that] I do not have much experience with. A typical day consists of learning new technologies, applying them to my metrics-reporting projects, and a daily meeting with the team on the project to go over our progress."

PEERS

"There is a huge camaraderie within the members of our program," writes one program member. "I think the main reason is because for all of us, this is our first real introduction to the corporate world, so we have lots we would like to discuss, but more as friends than as coworkers." Another adds, "We spent a lot of time together in Chicago [during training], and that was a real bonding experience for all of us. A few times, we have gotten together after work, and most days I eat lunch with at least one or two people from the program."

MOVING ON

Most entry-level employees remain with Bank One. "I plan to stay for as long as I can continue to grow and feel satisfied with my job," one person puts it. Typically, they advance through the ranks of the area for which they received training. "I left after graduating from the six-month program when I was placed in a supervisory position," writes one such entry-level hire. Others move elsewhere within the bank; "I have moved through the program to [become] an assistant manager, a branch manager, and now I'm moving to a different program—the In-Lines—as a branch manager," explains one employee.

ATTRITION

According to Bank One representatives, fewer than 5 percent of first jobbers leave within twelve months. "Given that the majority of the new hires are recent college graduates with limited work experience, those that choose to leave the bank do so to pursue career opportunities outside of banking," writes a company representative. First jobbers add that some people leave because they "feel they were placed in a department that didn't utilize their skills, [feel] undervalued, or [feel] there was poor communication about [things] happening within the program."

BEST AND WORST

Bank One representatives tell us that "individuals who are successful at Bank One tend to possess our core values [and] competencies: a customer focus; interpersonal effectiveness and teamwork; a drive for quality and results; ethics, integrity, and character; and courage."

BASES
Research Analyst

THE BIG PICTURE

"Researching new, innovative products" is the business of BASES; entry-level employees quickly find themselves immersed in the world of product development and marketing. The job, which "combines math, statistics, and analytical thinking," is a great fit for people "who love puzzles" and being on the cutting edge.

STATS

LOCATION(S) WHERE ENTRY-LEVEL EMPLOYEES WORK

BASES has offices in Westport, Connecticut; Chicago, Illinois; Covington, Kentucky (Cincinnati metropolitan area); Parsippany, New Jersey (New York metropolitan area); and a number of international offices.

AVERAGE NUMBER OF APPLICATIONS EACH YEAR

BASES receives thousands of applications each year.

AVERAGE NUMBER HIRED PER YEAR OVER THE LAST TEN YEARS

"In the last six years, we have averaged about twenty to thirty entry-level hires per year."

ENTRY-LEVEL POSITION(S) AVAILABLE

"The majority of our entry-level recruiting efforts are focused on the research analyst position. We do, however, fill other entry-level positions that occasionally become available."

AVERAGE HOURS WORKED PER WEEK

Employees typically work forty to fifty hours per week, but the hours may vary given client needs.

PERCENTAGE OF ENTRY-LEVEL HIRES STILL WITH THE COMPANY AFTER THREE, FIVE, AND TEN YEARS

"BASES has very little turnover. The vast majority of our college hires stay with the company for years. Specific retention statistics are not available."

AVERAGE STARTING SALARY

"Competitive—salary varies depending on location."

BENEFITS OFFERED

The company offers "medical and dental insurance, life and disability insurance, vacation and personal days, a 401(k) savings plan, pension plan, tuition reimbursement, flexible spending accounts, and an incentive compensation program."

CONTACT INFORMATION

Find out about career opportunities at www.bases.com.

GETTING HIRED

BASES recruits on select college campuses; students at campuses that BASES does not visit may apply online for jobs. Company representatives "review your resume and, if [they] feel that your experiences and qualifications may be a good fit [for] the position, contact you to schedule an interview. In addition to multiple interviews, you will also be asked to submit transcripts, as well as complete a seventy-five-minute analytical skills assessment." One entry-level employee says, "BASES values people who have diverse backgrounds and interests. During my interview process, I was not only asked about my academic and work experience, but also about my extracurricular activities." Another employee reports, "My first interview was with an analyst who had been at the company for [only] one year and had been hired right out of college. This surprised me, and at first, I thought that the company was not serious about hiring [me] since they sent a fairly new employee to interview me. However, I learned that this is often done, and it is representative of BASES culture (young, casual, everyone's ideas and thoughts are respected, etc.). Most of the questions I was asked required me to [discuss] a specific event or example from my life (behavioral-based questions). I was later invited to the office for several second-round interviews. The second round of interviews included more hypothetical questions specifically related to marketing research and consumer behavior." Company representatives tell us that "interviewers are interested in learning more about the candidate's background and experiences, career interests, analytical skills, communication skills, attention to detail, organizational skills, and work ethic, among other things."

MONEY AND PERKS

"BASES rewards employees based on their contributions and overall performance. All employees receive their first performance appraisal after six months of employment. Annual performance appraisals are accompanied by a salary increase." First jobbers tell us that "the job offer [is] not negotiable in terms of salary, office location, and duties," but that start time is sometimes flexible. First jobbers discuss perks, which include "the laid-back but highly driven atmosphere. Everyone is friendly but takes [the] work seriously. We deliver a superior product to our clients but enjoy ourselves while we're doing it!" Employees also enjoy "having insider information [about] new product launches. It is a pretty rewarding feeling to have clients look to you for multimillion dollar launch/no launch decisions. It is also gratifying to see a new product on the shelf and know that your insight went into its launch. (Plus, we get a lot of free new products.)"

THE ROPES

Orientation at BASES "is quite quick" and includes some "meet-and-greet" around the office and a day with a human resources representative "learning company policy and filling out paperwork." Training, however, is extensive and "lasts roughly six weeks. Training sessions have been led by almost everyone in the office, from relatively recent hires to senior-level managers. The first two weeks consist of full-day sessions, and the last three weeks consist of half-day training classes. The training sessions consist of presentations, case studies, and various exercises. At that point, we begin working with our managers on small projects, which is a great way to immediately apply the learning from the training. I really enjoyed this training model because it allowed us to get to know a large number of coworkers very quickly." In addition, "several formal job-specific training courses [are] conducted throughout the first few months of the new hire's employment, [and] other company specific and miscellaneous training opportunities are offered through the year."

DAY IN THE LIFE

BASES research analysts hit the ground jogging and soon after reach full stride. One analyst says, "When I was first hired, my responsibilities mainly entailed data gathering and summarizing. However, as soon as training was over, I was given more extensive responsibilities. While my manager reviewed all of my work (from reports to e-mails), it was [ultimately] my work that was being sent to our clients. This was a great feeling: to have an entry-level job that really allowed you to think for yourself and contribute to the success of the company." Another analyst agrees and adds, "The responsibility curve at BASES is incredibly steep. I was put on my own project right away, which entails analyzing in-market and consumer data, checking marketing plan inputs, entering data into a complex model, drafting e-mails to clients, and writing toplines and lengthy (100-page) reports and presentations." First jobbers appreciate that "there is no typical day." One first jobber reports, "I am always working on something new. I am typically on one to four projects at a time. There is no set schedule to follow. I have a lot of independence as to how I spend my time."

PEERS

"I feel like there is a definite BASES personality," writes one research analyst. "Nearly everyone I have met here is young, intelligent, and fun. No one tries to get ahead by stepping on other people's toes. Even though everyone is obviously trying to get ahead, no one is willing to do so at the expense of others. There is a definite team feeling at BASES." Another analyst adds, "I am constantly interacting with peers at the office. BASES encourages employees to bounce ideas off of one another. I would say I interact with my peers half (or more) of the hours I am at work." The camaraderie continues even after the computers are shut down for the day: "Socializing outside of the company with coworkers is big," explains one entry-level employee. "There is an organized off-site happy hour at least once a week and frequent weekend parties. There are also several company sports teams."

MOVING ON

Many new hires come to BASES expecting to stay for the long haul, and few are disappointed. Most first jobbers like the work and stick around as long as opportunities for growth and advancement exist. "The majority [of people who leave the firm after a few years do so to] return to school and obtain a master's degree. Others leave the company to start a family or pursue outside interests."

ATTRITION

Dropouts from the BASES entry-level job program are rare. Some who do leave "have voiced concerns about lack of managerial training—that people are promoted to management levels but not properly taught how to manage their direct reports. This leads to frustration among the newer hires." Others "complain about the workload or high expectations [from their managers]. However, the people with these types of criticisms are far less common than people who hold a positive view of their job[s] here at BASES."

BEARINGPOINT

Various Positions

THE BIG PICTURE

BearingPoint is a major consulting firm that provides "application services, technology solutions, and managed services to Global 2000 companies and government organizations." Clients include nearly half the *Fortune 1000*, all fourteen Cabinet-level departments of the U.S. Federal Government, the top thirteen global pharmaceutical companies, and many, many other heavy hitters.

STATS

LOCATION(S) WHERE ENTRY-LEVEL EMPLOYEES WORK

The BearingPoint headquarters are located in McLean, Virginia, but company officials note that BearingPoint has entry-level positions "in a number of its offices worldwide."

AVERAGE NUMBER OF APPLICATIONS EACH YEAR

BearingPoint receives about 40,000 applications each year.

AVERAGE NUMBER HIRED PER YEAR

BearingPoint hires approximately 500 entry-level employees each year; this number may vary given changes in corporate performance.

ENTRY-LEVEL POSITION(S) AVAILABLE

Entry-level employees are hired as management analysts, or in other entry-level positions.

AVERAGE HOURS WORKED PER WEEK

Entry-level employees work about forty hours per week.

AVERAGE STARTING SALARY

Starting salaries are competitive with the industry standard.

BENEFITS OFFERED

"Our employees are offered an exceptional benefits package here at BearingPoint," reports a company official. Included in this package is "an employee-contributed health care plan, dental plan, prescription drug plan, disability insurance, health care for [the] employee's family, and health care for domestic partners." Other benefits include a 401(k) plan, stock options, maternity and paternity leave, subsidized child care, and health club discounts.

CONTACT INFORMATION

Visit www.bearingpoint.com, and click on the "Careers" tab.

GETTING HIRED

BearingPoint "advertises at selected colleges and universities," at which they also "conduct on-campus interviews," which are "followed by office visits." Many successful hires report that "my school has a strong working relationship with BearingPoint." Additionally, BearingPoint "collects resumes through career fairs, referrals, and networking." The firm seeks candidates who "exhibit our company's core values, possess strong leadership skills and integrity, are team players, have an interest for the consulting industry, are quick learners, can be flexible, exhibit an entrepreneurial spirit, and have a strong sense of customer commitment." "Good communications skills" are also a major asset.

One entry-level employee reports, "About a year and a half ago [the Public Services practice at] BearingPoint started a campus initiative in which they would hire people, but not to a specific project, and put them on the 'bench.' As you approached your start date, you would work with your resource manager to get set up on a project that had an open position that you were interested in. Through this campus initiative, they would have campus days at the McLean office with interview sessions. My interview session was in the afternoon, and [I] was brought in with about ten to fifteen other students. We interviewed with managers from the same industry sector, but as I said, you weren't interviewing necessarily for a position within their group, just a position within the company."

MONEY AND PERKS

"Start date is fairly flexible" at BearingPoint. Salary, however, "is competitive but pretty much nonnegotiable and don't expect a signing bonus. The exception to this is those [who] come in with an MBA [or a] graduate degree or at the consultant level or above. Sometimes a relocation stipend is offered." Salary increases are based on performance reviews and productivity. First jobbers are eligible for bonuses, which "are given based on individual and company performance." Top perks include a personal laptop and "car benefits; we can buy cars [from certain dealerships and suppliers] at a company discount."

Employees may also take advantage of "performance-based bonuses, stock options, and a 401(k) plan," as well as "matching of employee contributions, maternity and paternity leave, employee referral program, health club discounts, subsidized child care, health and health-education programs, employee assistance program, telecommuting, flex time, and compressed work weeks, funding for attending professional conferences/trade shows, paid association memberships, a minimum of forty hours per year of on-site and off-site training, formal mentoring program, leaves of absence for education or specialized training, and an online-training system that offers over 10,000 courses (technical, operations, and strategic)."

THE ROPES

"BearingPoint offers a new hire orientation called BearingPoint Beginnings, which is held each week in Northern Virginia," explains the firm, pointing out that "by bringing new hires together face-to-face and by giving them a high-touch, hands-on program, we help them assimilate more quickly into our company and culture. Through case studies, role-plays, and activities, participants learn about our vision and values, our business strategy and global operating model, and our financial management principles and tools. They also learn about our staffing and performance management processes, all of which are important to getting a great start with our company." One first jobber adds, "After about three months of working at BearingPoint, all consulting employees attended a three-day workshop where we learned about our company's financial system, marketing campaigns, and internal tools. In addition, we attend networking workshops." Beyond this, "there is little [other] formal training; it's all on the job, and you learn from other, more experienced management analysts and from your mistakes, as may be the case with most jobs—and life."

In addition, each new hire is assigned a peer advisor/performance manager. The peer advisor serves as a "guide, confidant, information resource, network resource, counselor, and advocate." New hires are also "assigned a specific managing director," who serves as a "team leader."

DAY IN THE LIFE

We spoke with a number of management analysts at BearingPoint; all took the position immediately out of college. Here's how one describes a typical day: "At first, my main responsibility was to learn as much as I could about all facets of the BearingPoint systems that I would be working with. Learning and understanding this required a great deal of hands-on work and developing tracking tools to trace my pathways through the various tools and databases within the company and my group. A typical day would look like this: 9:00 A.M. to 10:00 A.M.—review e-mails from my boss; catch up on administrative tasks associated with on-boarding; take an online training course; 10:00 A.M. to 12:00 P.M.—receive training on systems in my boss's office; 12:00 P.M. to 1:00 P.M.—lunch; 1:00 P.M. to 5:00 P.M.—work through the systems I was trained on and reconcile what I learned with the spreadsheets I received; 5:00 P.M. to 6:00 P.M.—review documents that my boss sent me; compile a list of questions to ask my boss the following day; and begin to develop my own spreadsheets."

After gaining some experience and expertise, employees report taking on additional responsibilities and managing their projects with greater levels of independence.

PEERS

First jobbers at Bearing Point are "constantly impressed by the resumes" of their peers, all of whom seem to have "attended impressive schools, engaged in many extracurricular activities, and worked in very interesting jobs for noteworthy companies before coming to BearingPoint. They are also energetic, driven, hard workers." Friendships are easily made here, though the after-hours scene is subdued. One newbie reports, "We have happy hours every once in a while, and they're always a good time. I wish we had more of them, and I think a fair amount of others do, too. I know those [who] work on projects in the intelligence community have frequent happy hours and are a fairly tight community, even with people they don't work on projects with."

MOVING ON

Top reasons for leaving BearingPoint, in descending order of frequency, are personal reasons, career advancement, a return to school, a move to an industry position (nonclient). For some, the consulting business just isn't a good fit; one management analyst notes, "Some people simply do not like the client-consultant relationship. Clients can be cranky and have unreasonable expectations, or they can be amazing friends for life. Some people do not like the ups and downs of that world. The good news is that I have seen my peers who feel this way easily and seamlessly placed in internal jobs in the company in fields like finance, accounting, and operations."

BOEING

Various Positions

THE BIG PICTURE

Boeing, maker of commercial airplanes, military aircraft, satellites, spacecraft, and missiles, is the largest U.S. exporter, and it conducts a pretty tidy business within the nation's borders, as well. There are a myriad of opportunities to work on groundbreaking projects and advance through the ranks for a go-getter with a flair for aeronautics or the aeronautic business. And they can be had in many far-flung locations, across the country and around the globe.

STATS

LOCATION(S) WHERE ENTRY-LEVEL EMPLOYEES WORK

"Most [of the] company locations have opportunities for entry-level work. Boeing operates in more than seventy countries and thirty-eight states within the United States, with major operations in the Puget Sound area of Washington State; Southern California; Wichita, Kansas; and St. Louis, Missouri."

AVERAGE NUMBER OF APPLICATIONS EACH YEAR

Boeing receives "thousands" of applications every year.

AVERAGE NUMBER HIRED PER YEAR OVER THE LAST TEN YEARS

Boeing has more than 150,000 employees total. There are no figures for the number of new hires per year.

ENTRY-LEVEL POSITION(S) AVAILABLE

Entry-level hires work in engineering, information technology (IT), and business.

AVERAGE HOURS WORKED PER WEEK

"Forty hours is the typical work week for Boeing employees, with part-time work options also available. Boeing offers virtual work options, allowing employees to telecommute from their homes or use 'hoteling' or transit work spaces at company work sites."

AVERAGE STARTING SALARY

Engineering salaries start at $50,000; IT salaries start at $46,000; and business salaries start at $41,000.

BENEFITS OFFERED

"Boeing offers a competitive program of health and welfare plans to help take care of employees and their families. Employees in most locations can choose from among several types of medical plans. Prescription drug, vision, dental, mental health, and substance abuse insurances are also covered. For more information, please visit www.boeing.com/employment/benefits/index.html." Additionally, "Boeing offers competitive total compensation. Employees represented by labor unions negotiate their pay and benefits—including incentives—through collective bargaining. Nonunion employees enjoy salary reviews, retirement and 401(k) plans, profit sharing, vacation time and holidays off, [and] other financial/recognition programs."

Contact Information

Visit Boeing on the Web at www.boeing.com and www.boeing.com/employment/flash.html.

Getting Hired

Although Boeing "does target schools and maintains an on-campus visit schedule based on curriculum and locations of schools," the company values all schools. "By having an online application process, every student is able to apply for open positions." The company seeks new hires who demonstrate the ability to work with a team and who posess "integrity, technical proficiency, and the ability to communicate effectively." The hiring process can drag on from start to finish. One electrical engineer writes, "A few weeks after submitting my application, Boeing gave me a phone interview. The interview was behavior-based ('Tell me about a time when . . .'). I'm sure that my having had a couple of these already and having brainstormed and practiced answering some of those questions helped." Boeing now holds "one-day events that allow job seekers to [have] pre-scheduled interviews with hiring managers. On-the-spot job offers and follow-on job offers are typical." The schedule for these events is posted on the company's website.

Money and Perks

The negotiability of Boeing positions varies widely from function to function; obviously, the more specialized your skills, the better your negotiating chances. Most first jobbers find that "location, activity, and salary are specified [in] the offer." One first jobber explains, "In my case, the first two [offers] were specific and seemed nonnegotiable. I did ask to negotiate the salary. They listened to my arguments, but didn't change it." A new hire in one of Boeing's rotational training programs reports that "the program is flexible in terms of the job you're hired into. You get to choose [what] department you start in and have a large degree of discretion in where you go over the two-year rotational period (mandatory rotations occur every four months)." Newbies love Boeing's flex-time arrangement, which "with proper approval (that is usually given), allows you to take a whole Friday off, and make up the hours during the rest of the two-week pay period. Or, you can work an extra hour one day and leave an hour early the next." They also appreciate "the Learning Together Program, known as one of the most generous corporate tuition reimbursement programs. It offers 100 percent paid tuition at accredited schools."

The Ropes

Boeing offers "a standard half-day schedule for orientation used by all company locations" that is "designed to congratulate and celebrate the success of the employee's newly obtained position at Boeing. In addition, it is an opportunity for Boeing to impart some very important values, responsibilities, and standards of conduct." In addition, "certain regions may add an afternoon session that is specific to their own region." Participants in the rotational training program have a longer formal orientation; a person in the Business Career Foundation Program writes, "We had a week-long orientation seminar that gave us an overview of the company and of the positions we would be rotating through." Other new hires complete the four-hour orientation, then jump right into their new jobs. Subsequent training is a mix of "on-the-job training as well as formal training," including some online instruction. How much of each an employee gets depends on his or her job. The more technical the position, the more likely it is to require specialized training classes.

DAY IN THE LIFE

Entry-level employees work in just about every department in every location in which Boeing does business; as company representatives explain, "The responsibilities for newly hired employees vary; there is not one standard set of responsibilities." Much of the work at Boeing is project oriented, so new hires often jump in *in media res;* one engineer writes, "When I was first hired, there was a project that most of my coworkers were working hard to finish up. So, at first, I spent a lot of time doing the online training and learning the computer tools from coworkers. My first assignment was to draw up the wiring to install a new device, following the example of one that had already been done. Most of that time was spent using a 2-D drawing package on the computer, as well as using other tools to look up information I needed (guided, again, by my coworkers)." Mentoring plays a large part in the life of a new Boeing employee, as does "a program that is a network for new college hires. It allows college hires to network with others that are in the same circumstances." Those new hires participating in a rotational program tell us "the benefit of a rotational program is that each position only lasts for four months, which gives you a chance to figure out where you fit."

PEERS

Because Boeing is such a big company, there are plenty of first jobbers. The company is even large enough to hire a number of students from the same school; one Texas A&M graduate writes, "Contact and camaraderie among the new hires from the same school [are] extremely good. There is a big after-hours social scene organized by different people from Texas A&M." Regardless of your alma mater, though, "there is definitely contact and camaraderie with other young workers. Not all of them are first jobbers, but several are still around [the same] age." Everyone we spoke with agrees that they "have a great group of supportive, intelligent, and driven peers. Friends are easy to make here." Another newbie writes, "It is a challenge and a privilege to work with so many brilliant minds."

MOVING ON

Most first jobbers stay at Boeing; one reports, "I've been told it's relatively easy to move around in the company." People who do leave, according to company representatives, go to work for "competitors in the aerospace industry and/or companies requiring technical professionals such as Lockheed, Raytheon, Northrop Grumman, BAE Systems, Honeywell, Microsoft, Rockwell, Sandia National Labs, Los Alamos National Labs, and Ball Aerospace."

ATTRITION

Boeing representatives report that some employees who leave the company do so because "the work was not what they expected." One electrical engineer concurs: "One or two of my peers have commented that this job doesn't seem to use our training." Company representatives also tell us that "money, level, and promotion ability" sometimes drive first jobbers to seek work elsewhere.

BOOZ ALLEN HAMILTON
Junior-Level Consultants and Researchers

THE BIG PICTURE

Booz Allen Hamilton is a very big and very well-known "strategy and technology consulting firm" that offers aspiring consultants opportunities in numerous cutting-edge fields. One entry-level employee explains the appeal of this demanding, but rewarding, program: "[The company has] a very good reputation in the government business sector."

STATS

LOCATION(S) WHERE ENTRY-LEVEL EMPLOYEES WORK

"With more than 16,000 employees serving clients on six continents, we are truly a global organization. The majority of our undergraduate new hires join the firm in our Washington, DC metro area corporate headquarters in McLean, Virginia (also known as our McLean Campus). We also have undergraduate opportunities in our Atlanta, San Diego, Colorado Springs, and Omaha offices."

AVERAGE NUMBER OF APPLICATIONS EACH YEAR

For the undergraduate program, "we receive between 8,000 and 10,000 [applications] each year."

AVERAGE NUMBER HIRED PER YEAR OVER THE LAST TEN YEARS

The company has hired an average of 150 undergraduates each year for the last ten years.

ENTRY-LEVEL POSITION(S) AVAILABLE

"We offer two entry-level positions: junior-level consultants and researchers, with concentrations in functional areas such as IT, systems, business, economics, public policy, and engineering within our national security, civil, and defense business segments."

AVERAGE HOURS WORKED PER WEEK

Employees work between forty-five and fifty hours per week. The firm "is committed to helping our staff keep their lives in balance. Our team members enjoy flexible schedules."

PERCENTAGE OF ENTRY-LEVEL HIRES STILL WITH THE COMPANY AFTER THREE, FIVE, AND TEN YEARS

After three years, 72 percent of all entry-level employees remain with the company; and after five years, 70 percent of all entry-level employees remain with the company.

AVERAGE STARTING SALARY

"We offer very competitive starting salaries ranging from $35,000–$60,000, depending [on] specific job functions and skills."

BENEFITS OFFERED

"We offer generous medical and dental benefits from top providers with plans that fit individuals [needs]." Furthermore, the company offers profit sharing and 401(k) plans, income protection, reimbursement accounts, tuition assistance ($5,000 per year per employee), an award-winning training program (that offers technical and business strategy certification courses), work/life programs, family centers, family-friendly policies, and a generous paid leave policy.

CONTACT INFORMATION

Interested students should visit www.boozallen.com. Access "Careers," then "College Opportunities" to create a profile and submit a resume.

GETTING HIRED

Booz Allen Hamilton does much of its undergraduate recruiting at select college campuses. You can also submit applications online, so you don't need to attend one of the company's "core schools" to land an interview. First interviews are held on campus, with subsequent interviews conducted at a Booz Allen office. Interviews typically consist of "behavioral questions; some examples are, 'Tell me about a time when you had a deadline for an assignment, had many other things that interfered with meeting that deadline, and how you handled it?' Another question is 'Tell me about a time when you had to work on a team and rely on other people to deliver a final project and how you handled conflict within the group.'" An entry-level hire describes the entire interviewing experience: "I submitted my standard resume and was interviewed by a recruiter and a senior consultant. They were both very friendly and fairly laid back. I was asked to come back for a second interview at their McLean, Virginia, headquarters. I went to a nice dinner with about thirty other candidates, stayed in a hotel overnight, and then went through a pretty tiring day of interviewing. They set us up to interview with teams they thought we would be compatible with based on our resumes and previous interviews, and they also had a mini-career fair with the other teams if we wanted an interview with them. I received my offer a couple of months later."

MONEY AND PERKS

Undergraduate hires disagree as to whether their starting salaries were negotiable. One "negotiated a higher salary and signing bonus," while others say that "there was no negotiation." All agree that location "and assignments were not negotiable," but that new hires are "able to move onto different tasks that better suit [their] interests" once they've been with Booz Allen for a while. By all accounts, the best perk is flex time: "We can work from home or work more on one day to make up the hours from another day," explains one consultant. The firm also offers "tuition assistance, an award-winning training program, employee discounts and special buying services, mentoring, benefits for domestic partners, tax-deferred reimbursement accounts for medical and dependant care, family centers, paid parental leave for new parents (mothers *and* fathers), and a plethora of [minority and interest] groups and forums."

THE ROPES

Orientation is relatively brief at Booz Allen. Firm representatives tell us that initial training consists of "a half-day training class that helps staff become familiar with the culture and what to expect in the beginning of their career at Booz Allen. Within the first thirty days, new hires attend a two-day training class. Within the next few months, employees attend another two-day training class focused on consulting skills." Here's how one beginning consultant describes the process: "The orientation included filling out benefits paperwork and learning more about Booz Allen and getting our badge printed. We had a four-hour orientation. My peer team member came to meet me at noon, and we had lunch. She got me situated at my desk. I met my boss after lunch to find out what specific project I was going to be working on."

DAY IN THE LIFE

Booz Allen Hamilton representatives tell us that "most new hires will work within a team environment, have frequent interaction with clients, and be challenged to make change happen. Functionally, they are often assigned roles requiring keen data-gathering and analysis skills." Because the firm consults for such a wide range of businesses and government offices, there is "a vast variety of opportunities for new hires with different functional skills, [and] each role requires different responsibilities." Here's how one entry-level employee describes her integration into the firm: "I supported a couple different projects here and there for my first couple weeks until I was [assigned to] a project full-time. My typical day on my first project was meeting with military subject matter experts to gather requirements for an integrated HR system for the Department of Defense." Another entry-level employee says, "[My first task] was to debug this application that we are investing in as a new service offering. I would come in and do Google searches, ask other team members for their expertise, and keep trying new solutions to debug the entire application that was created by another company. Now I am solely developing Web portals by myself; I lead the code review team, and I am the team's graphic designer." The longer you're at the company, the greater your responsibilities. All the consultants we spoke with praise the mentoring skills of their supervisors and approve of their frequent contact with upper-level management.

PEERS

Consulting is all about teamwork, so it should come as no surprise that "[Booz Allen Hamilton] managers encourage us to go out after-hours." One newbie reports, "We go to happy hours on Thursdays, and on Fridays or Saturdays, we go out to clubs. Sometimes we [take] weekend trips like white-water rafting or [go to] barbeques at coworkers' houses." Another young consultant adds, "We are a very close group of friends and colleagues."

MOVING ON

The entry-level employees we interviewed have little intention of leaving Booz Allen Hamilton; they all hope to remain with the company as long as possible. Firm representatives explain one possible reason: "Our people don't have to leave the firm to try something new. Booz Allen offers an internal transfer process through our Career Mobility Program. Staff can transfer between teams to pursue new opportunities and learn new skills." When entry-level staff members do move on, they usually do so to return to school or to "pursue a technical concentration versus consulting."

ATTRITION

Firm representatives say, "Naturally, people pursue new passions and new opportunities—and we encourage our staff to explore the world around them. Booz Allen has an active 'Come Back Kids' program that works with people who want to come back to the firm, and some [may] even say that many of our best clients were once Booz Allen employees who have taken the expertise they gained serving many clients to one institution."

BORDERS GROUP
College Graduate Training Program

THE BIG PICTURE

The Borders Group, owner of both the Borders and Waldenbooks chains, has had "great success" with its College Graduate Training Program, which aims "to hire and develop college graduates to build a strong foundation of future leaders within [the] Borders Group." The program includes mentoring, cross-functional team projects, on-site training at stores and warehouse facilities, and seminars.

STATS

LOCATION(S) WHERE ENTRY-LEVEL EMPLOYEES WORK

The headquarters is located in Ann Arbor, Michigan.

AVERAGE NUMBER OF APPLICATIONS EACH YEAR

Borders Group receives more than 750 applications each year.

AVERAGE NUMBER HIRED PER YEAR

Borders Group hires six entry-level employees per year.

ENTRY-LEVEL POSITION(S) AVAILABLE

Entry-level employees enter the College Graduate Training Program, with placements in corporate finance, marketing, IT, and human resources.

AVERAGE HOURS WORKED PER WEEK

Entry-level employees work forty to forty-five hours per week.

PERCENTAGE OF ENTRY-LEVEL HIRES STILL WITH THE COMPANY AFTER THREE, FIVE, AND TEN YEARS

More than 80 percent of entry-level hires remain with the company after three years; and 80 percent stay on for five or more years.

BENEFITS OFFERED

Borders Group offers medical and dental insurance (the premiums for which are shared by the company and the employee). Additional benefits include basic life insurance, business travel insurance, short-term disability, a 401(k) program, store discounts and other corporate discounts, adoption assistance, and alternative work schedules.

CONTACT INFORMATION

Candidates should apply by September 1. They may do this by e-mailing their resumes to collegeresumes@bordersgroupinc.com. The company cautions: "We receive a large number of questions and resume submissions for the above-described university relations programs. Due to the high volume, we are unable to specifically respond to every inquiry. However, we do thoroughly review every resume and will directly contact individuals who meet our specific background requirements and qualifications."

Getting Hired

Borders Group recruits on campus and online. The company reviews the "academic performance, leadership traits, previous internships, analytical skills, results orientation, and flexibility" of all of its candidates. Preference is given to college graduates with relevant degrees (e.g., a bachelor's degree in computer science for IT applicants), a GPA of at least 3.0, and a record of campus involvement. Resumes are reviewed by human resources, and "the most qualified students are selected for our initial round of interviews [that are] conducted by a Borders Group human resources team member. Students selected for second-round interviews are brought on-site for additional human resources and functional team interviews. Roundtable discussions occur after that point to [review the qualifications of] all final candidates; all candidates are notified of their status shortly thereafter."

One successful applicant writes, "The interviews were very comfortable. The thing that stuck out most in my mind was that all three of the people I interviewed with mentioned career advancement to me. Considering I was just trying to get my first job, I was very excited that everyone would be so interested in what my second job could be. I also noticed that the entire company seemed very casual. I received a lot of smiles and nods from people in the halls who noticed that I stuck out in my full business suit."

Money and Perks

As is the case with many first jobs, base salary levels are predetermined by functional area at Borders Group. Annual raises "are based on performance evaluation," as are bonuses. The company explains: "The Performance Bonus Pool is a fund that is used to reward the highest-performing employees at the corporate office. These top performers are employees who continually go above and beyond expectations while delivering outstanding results. The Performance Bonus Pool is a tool to reward exceptional employees. It also reinforces our 'pay for performance' compensation philosophy."

Perks include "amazing employee discounts," "flexible work schedules that allow for four ten-hour days per week or nine nine-hour days with alternate Fridays off," and "at least one concert per quarter open to all employees at the home office."

The Ropes

The College Graduate Training Program commences with a one-day orientation, followed by a structured six-month plan that includes mentoring, diversity training, seminars, team projects, and on-site training at stores and warehouses. One trainee in finance reports, "The program gives you the opportunity to work on cross-functional projects, to visit and work in the stores and warehouse, and to learn about areas of the company [from] executives. In the finance area, it also allows you to go on a rotational program through three areas of finance, staying in each area for six months." Another trainee notes, "Each week, leaders and executives from the company talked with the College Grad group about their areas of the business, their key strategies and initiatives, and how they got to where they are."

DAY IN THE LIFE

The College Training Program is rotational; details of rotations vary according to the new hire's specific job function. A human resources trainee tells us that "I spent the first three months supporting our Borders stores in recruitment. I then moved to the training department and learned to develop and facilitate training programs. I was also responsible for some project management in this role. After four months in training, I moved into corporate human resources, where I learned how to interview and select top talent, manage employee relations concerns, become a strategic partner to my client groups, and communicate with all levels of employees within the organization." An IT hire writes, "During a typical day, I'd receive requests to schedule [and] automate a process. I had to contact the requestor to collect requirements and determine if the requirements fit with the company standards for automation. I would take that information and summarize it into a document that my manager would approve before the request was fulfilled. After approval, I would create documentation of the new process." A trainee in promotions reports that "a typical day is pushing at least three different projects forward each day. On most days, I respond to questions and concerns from the field, work with vendors to solicit the best products, work with vendors to execute the details of our tests, and find ways to add incremental revenue to the bottom line by building awareness tactics or with promotions."

PEERS

Meeting peers "is what the College Graduate Training Program is great for," writes one participant. "You automatically have a peer group spread throughout the company whom you can ask questions of and whom you continue to work with. In my different positions, I have had many business relationships with [my original] group. You also have someone to call on to relate subjects that you may not know much about. If I know I need to talk to the person in marketing that's responsible for X, I call one of the people in marketing [from] the program, and they tell me who to talk to." After work, "there is a significant amount of camaraderie" among new hires, "though as the years go on, you tend to split up into groups that continue to have more things in common (married/single, finance/merchandising, etc)." The connections continue after the program ends; one grad reports, "We have actually created a group called 'Momentum' that people can join after the College Graduate Training Program is completed. This organization allows [us] to continue to get the exposure and access to the things that will help us in our careers." The group facilitates "access to working on special projects for the New Business Development area, roundtable discussions with executives and managers, volunteer opportunities with our Employee Foundation, etc."

MOVING ON

Borders Group informs us that "Our College [Graduate Training Program] has only been in effect for four full years (just starting out the fifth year as we speak). Of the forty participants in the program, 20 percent have left the company. All have had very positive things to say about Borders and their experience with us." Those who leave typically do so "to change industries or career focus (from retail to financial services, for example, or from marketing to education)." Some seek a change of venue, with many looking to move to a bigger city than Ann Arbor. Others go back to school; one such first jobber writes, "I [may] leave the company if I elect to pursue my MBA. However, I would like to secure my next position here at Borders before I would consider leaving. Borders has offered me challenging projects that many companies would not allow an entry-level employee to handle. I appreciate their merit-based advancement and enjoy the variety and challenging pace of a project management role here."

ATTRITION

Borders Group loses less than 3 percent of its college graduate hires within twelve months of initial employment.

BOSTON BEER COMPANY
Sales Representative

THE BIG PICTURE

Remember when you stopped dreaming of being a firefighter or an astronaut and instead started dreaming of a life surrounded by beer? Dream no more, stalwart brew-phile! Boston Beer Company offers you the chance to promote, sell, and, yes, drink beer, *and get paid for it.*

STATS

LOCATION(S) WHERE ENTRY-LEVEL EMPLOYEES WORK

Boston Beer has sales positions at locations in major metropolitan areas throughout the United States.

AVERAGE NUMBER OF APPLICATIONS EACH YEAR

The company receives thousands of applications each year.

AVERAGE NUMBER HIRED PER YEAR OVER THE LAST TEN YEARS

The company has hired approximately forty entry-level employees per year for the last ten years.

ENTRY-LEVEL POSITION(S) AVAILABLE

There are entry-level sales representative positions available at the company.

AVERAGE HOURS WORKED PER WEEK

Employees work over forty hours per week.

PERCENTAGE OF ENTRY-LEVEL HIRES STILL WITH THE COMPANY AFTER THREE, FIVE, AND TEN YEARS

After three years, 75 percent of all entry-level employees are still with the company.

AVERAGE STARTING SALARY

The base salary is in the mid-$30,000 range, with a 10 percent bonus potential.

BENEFITS OFFERED

The company offers medical and dental insurance, long- and short-term disability, life insurance, and a flexible spending account. Furthermore, the company offers a 401(k) plan (the company matches), gym membership discounts, paid vacation, discounted movie tickets, tuition reimbursement, and a car allowance (for sales personnel only).

CONTACT INFORMATION

Visit the website at www.samadams.com/company.

GETTING HIRED

Boston Beer Company recruits on campuses and through its website, which offers valuable information for potential candidates. One current employee writes, "I thought it was important to find out what skills [the company] was looking for in a college recruit candidate and then pull out and magnify those skills on my resume. For example, I knew they were looking for someone with high levels of customer service, especially in the restaurant/bar area. Obviously, I focused on my bartending experience both on my resume and in interviews." The interview process itself can be extensive. One entry-level employee reports, "I interviewed with four different employees, and each one of them asked numerous questions about my college career and work history. Questions like: 'Provide me with a time when you had to manage your time between work and school in order to more efficiently and effectively accomplish both? What questions do you have about the company?' The interviews were all about one hour long. The entire process took about three months, from the career fair to the actual start date." Part of the interview process includes spending a day in the field with an account manager. One employee writes, "The great thing about [the company] is that a step in the interview process is actually riding with an experienced sales rep, so you know exactly what the job is like."

MONEY AND PERKS

Account managers say, "The area where we [were first assigned] and what we actually did were pretty much nonnegotiable. You knew the requirements for both these things throughout the interview process." Starting salary is negotiable, but only within relatively narrow parameters. Everyone agrees that the best fringe benefit of all is the product itself and their access to it. "If anybody tells you it's not the free beer, they're lying!" declares one respondent. "The great relationships you build with accounts" is also cited as a big plus.

THE ROPES

Aspiring account managers agree that "the training program at Boston Beer Company is awesome!" Here's how one new hire describes the process: "Our orientation class was held at the main office [in Boston]. It lasted an entire week, with five days of extensive information about brewing, beer, brief sales training, and how it all works together." One entry-level employee notes, "I was definitely on information overload." The highlight of orientation, according to one new hire, is "getting to sit down one evening with Jim Koch [the founder of Boston Beer] and having him sample and taste-profile the products with us." After the weeklong orientation, trainees return home and "receive three full months of training from [their] managers. We began reviewing information from orientation and then gradually worked our way into accounts, watching our managers deliver sales presentations, doing it all together, and from then on presenting on our own."

DAY IN THE LIFE

Account managers are responsible for managing and developing business within a specified region. Here's how one person describes his job: "I was in charge of developing business in seventy-core accounts, most of which already carried our product. Half of the accounts were grocery or liquor stores, and the other half were bars and restaurants. My job was to drive availability and visibility by gaining new or additional distribution and selling the customer on how displays, extra visibility, product position, and features could help their business. A typical day for me starts in a grocery store at 8:00 A.M. I may try to get into five stores to sell displays and get better visibility. My afternoon might be spent in the bars trying to get accounts that [carry] our beer in the bottle to put it on draft or [to bring] in some additional Samuel Adams products. I set up staff beer educations, features, and promotions. Three evenings a week, I have a promotion set up to help support an account that had brought in a new product of mine."

PEERS

Account managers work in the field, so they don't have much daily personal contact with their peers as employees in many of the other jobs featured in this book. Even so, "the camaraderie was there throughout training, and five of the six college recruits I trained with became close and have remained in contact over the phone and/or e-mail." One employee adds, "Most of my contact with my fellow trainees has been via cell phone; phone conversations asking advice or sharing ideas were the norm for me. The camaraderie was still there despite the distance. I still keep in close contact with my original college recruit class." One entry-level employee writes, "To this day, the other college recruits that I started with are some of my best friends. They are all going to be at my wedding, and one is actually in my wedding party."

MOVING ON

Boston Beer doesn't track where employees who leave its account manager program end up, and all the account managers we spoke with hope to remain with the company for the forseeable future. This is not a two-and-out program; most who take the job do so with hopes of building a career, and apparently, many do. An employee who's been with the company for several years writes, "My job has changed several times in four years, as I have been promoted three times and relocated four times in four years (from Colorado to Chicago to Indiana to Chicago and back [to] Colorado again). With each new position, I was challenged with another area, gaining new responsibilities, including managing point of sales materials, distributors and their inventories, and now managing people (three account managers)."

ATTRITION

Some employees resent having to relocate as part of the job, even though the company makes this aspect of the work clear from the beginning. One current employee writes, "It made a couple of the college recruits a little apprehensive to have to move to another market, but that is the main requirement of the program: You *had* to be willing to take a promotion and relocate to another market where we needed reps. Other than that, everyone loved everything else about the program: the company, the peers we worked with, our bosses, the level of training we were receiving, [and] how fun the industry is."

BEST AND WORST

One of the company's best recruits rose through the ranks, beginning as a sales representative and then becoming an account manager, then a senior account manager in New York City, and finally ascending to the position of district manager in Boston ("one of our most visible and high-impact markets"). The worst first jobber never really got started; "he decided that he did not want to relocate and resigned in the midst of moving."

BP

Various Positions

THE BIG PICTURE

"BP was formed by the union of British Petroleum, Amoco, ARCO, Castrol, and Vastar." It hires many entry-level workers every year; its blue-chip entry-level opportunities are in the early development programs found in every segment of the company. BP's Exploration and Production segment, for example, offers a three-year rotational program called Challenge. According to people in the company, "all university hires are immersed in a formal development program that includes extensive training opportunities, a variety of work experiences, and an induction event with university hires from all over the globe."

STATS

LOCATION(S) WHERE ENTRY-LEVEL EMPLOYEES WORK

"BP has offices or operations in all fifty states. States with the greatest number of employees are Alaska, California, Illinois, Ohio, and Texas."

AVERAGE NUMBER OF APPLICATIONS EACH YEAR

BP receives 10,000 applications every year.

ENTRY-LEVEL POSITION(S) AVAILABLE

There are 150–175 multiple hires per entry-level position at BP.

AVERAGE HOURS WORKED PER WEEK

New hires work forty hours per week.

BENEFITS OFFERED

BP offers "several medical plan options, depending on job and location." Additional benefits *may* include a "dental plan, vision plan, basic [and] supplemental life insurance, short- and long-term disability plans, a 401(k) plan, [and] retirement accumulation plan."

CONTACT INFORMATION

Visit the company's website at www.bp.com/careers/us.

GETTING HIRED

BP representatives report, "There are a number of ways for students to apply for entry-level jobs. Each discipline decides [what] schools its teams will visit, but since we can't send teams to every school, we have an online process that is available to all students. Our recruiters are also active with the student chapters of numerous professional organizations and associations." An engineer who ultimately landed his dream job in Alaska describes the vetting process this way: "I don't recall much about the interview other than that it went well and seemed more like a conversation than a grilling. The interviewer invited me to dinner with the rest of the BP folks and interview candidates that evening. I went (knowing full well that it was an additional step of evaluation) and was invited shortly thereafter to come to Anchorage on a site visit with other candidates from around the country. During the visit, BP put us up in great hotels—really wined and dined us. They showed us around town and nearby areas and introduced us to lots of staff, from the newest hires to powerful managers. Interactions were mostly social and informal. There were a few actual interview sessions during the site visit. Some of the questions were clearly designed to catch you a little bit off guard— but [there was] nothing truly underhanded. The interviews were predominantly conversational in nature, each conversation focusing specifically on some portion of my preparation for the job." A number of employees we spoke with had previously interned or worked co-op jobs with BP while they were in college.

MONEY AND PERKS

Entry-level workers at BP tell us that their job offers were "somewhat negotiable." One explains, "Essentially, I gave them my preferences [of] where and what and communicated my priorities. BP then took those priorities and preferences and placed me in the organization. In my case, my top priority was honored." Another adds, "Starting salary was excellent, so I didn't bother to negotiate." Most people agree that the best fringe benefit is the "Flex Fridays" work schedule. Here's how it works: "We work nine hour days instead of eight, and then we get to take every other Friday off. Two three-day weekends a month goes a long way toward home/work life balance."

THE ROPES

Orientation and training at BP is a combination of formal courses, on-the-job training, and mentoring. For one employee, "On day one I had a number of briefings starting with job location safety, team/business orientation, benefits, and meeting my team. By six months, I had a mentor, a junior staff 'buddy,' and attended an induction event at another BP location. All together, I received about one month's worth of training in my first year, away from the office, at courses. The courses were either recommended for my job function by my manager or were health/safety/environment related. After my first several years, I ventured out into other courses that were outside of my core job function or behavioral/leadership related." There's a lot of information for newbies to process; as one explains, "The nature of the petroleum industry is that college is where you learn the very basic material, and then your work life builds on the fundamental understanding that you have. I didn't come in on day one and understand everything. It probably took me six months to feel like I had a good idea [of] what I was doing—looking back, I understand that I still had a lot more to learn (and probably still do). [I have] no regrets about what I did or didn't know."

DAY IN THE LIFE

BP hires entry-level workers in many different areas for many different jobs; all require newcomers to be prepared to learn a lot quickly. One explains, "My responsibility was to look after about fifty oil wells, the same as [that of] other more experienced engineers. I did my job by asking a lot of questions and getting a lot of help. I was learning to use new software packages, find information on the company networks, analyze available data, and use the analysis to move toward a solution (a solution is usually a project of some type to improve production)." Some newcomers to BP spend their first three years in the Challenge Program, a rotational program that places them in three different assignments; one participant we spoke with spent a year as a reservoir engineer, later moved into a position as a production engineer, then finally worked as a petroleum engineer and production coordinator. Most people tell us that they rarely interact with upper-level people in the company, but no one saw this as a major issue; as one puts it, "I don't need face time with bigwigs right now. I need to be technically proficient, and if I want to progress, it will be my skills in concert with my networking that will get me there. Networking is very important in BP, but skills are more important. An emphasis is placed on contact with folks from other teams and departments. We do a lot together."

PEERS

"The social scene is pretty good" for BP newcomers, though the particulars vary depending on one's placement as well as "your status: single/married, kids or not, where you live relative to work, and interests." One typical newbie reports, "The majority of my friends now are from the company, and I interact more with my peers outside of work than I do at work. At work, the focus is with my team (though we will meet up for lunch a time or two each week). Outside of work, something is going on virtually every weekend and occasionally on weeknights." Our correspondent in Alaska tells us that "I'm on two hockey teams made up solely of young BP folks, and there [are] always parties, hikes, runs, climbing, and all sorts of activities going on. Most of my friends in Alaska also work at BP, so I spend the majority of my time outside of work with them."

MOVING ON

BP did not provide us with data on former entry-level employees, and those we spoke with have no plans to leave the company.

ATTRITION

"The frequency of downsizing exercises," as one employee puts it, is a major reason some newcomers don't stick with BP. Some people leave because they find their jobs too demanding, while other people leave because they feel that opportunities for advancement and interesting assignments are too difficult to come by.

BRIGHTPOINT

Various Positions

THE BIG PICTURE
Brightpoint "offers the most comprehensive selection of brands and products in the wireless industry," including a variety of telephones, PDAs, modems, and software. The company also sells logistics and subscriber services, channel development services, and advanced wireless services to corporate clients. Brightpoint's customers include such heavy hitters as Virgin Mobile USA, Cingular Wireless, and Motorola. First jobbers join the Brightpoint team in sales, customer service, operations, product testing, and accounting. Because Brightpoint is in the burgeoning wireless industry, "our business continues to grow." One first jobber reports "We have room for growth [at work], and I also have the ability to obtain a master's degree with 100 percent reimbursement. As a result, I believe my pay and responsibility within the company can only grow."

STATS

LOCATION(S) WHERE ENTRY-LEVEL EMPLOYEES WORK
Entry-level employees work in Plainfield, Indiana and Reno, Nevada.

AVERAGE NUMBER OF APPLICATIONS EACH YEAR
Brightpoint receives 1,200 applications for entry-level positions per year.

AVERAGE NUMBER HIRED PER YEAR
Brightpoint hires about 150 entry-level employees per year.

ENTRY-LEVEL POSITION(S) AVAILABLE
A variety of positions are open to entry-level employees at Brightpoint.

AVERAGE HOURS WORKED PER WEEK
Entry-level hires work forty-five hours per week.

AVERAGE STARTING SALARY
Average starting salaries range; production assemblers, for example, earn $17,000; financial analysts earn $38,000–$40,000; and operation supervisors earn $40,000.

BENEFITS OFFERED
Employees receive a choice of medical plans and supplemental medical insurance as well as dental and vision coverage; Brightpoint also offers flexible spending accounts.

Additional benefits include short- and long-term disability; life, accidental death, and dismemberment insurance; an employee stock-purchase program; a 401(k) plan; tuition reimbursement; paid time off; holiday pay; an on-site cafeteria and on-site fitness center; and discounts on telephone accessories.

CONTACT INFORMATION

Interested parties should visit www.brightpoint.com, click on the "About Us" link and then on the "Career" link.

GETTING HIRED

All initial job applications to Brightpoint are made online. The Human Resources Department reviews all applications and then conducts a phone-screen interview with potential new hires. Those who sufficiently impress human resources have their files forwarded to hiring managers for review, who may contact them to schedule the first of a minimum of two face-to-face interviews. Reference checks, a background check, and a drug screen conclude the hiring process. The company "looks at technical skills; but in addition, we look at the soft skills necessary to position an employee for short-term and long-term success." Several of the first jobbers we spoke with here began their tenure with the company as temp workers or interns; once they had demonstrated their abilities, they were brought on as full-time employees.

MONEY AND PERKS

Salary, location, and job responsibilities are typically not negotiable for most Brightpoint first jobbers; start date is, however, "somewhat negotiable." Some entry-level hires, depending on their positions, "can be eligible for bonuses [that amount to] up to ten percent of their pay. These bonuses are based on company performance, department performance, and individual performance." New hires in sales earn a commission on top of their salaries. Prime fringe benefits here include "great discounts on electronics and accessories," "lots of travel to trade shows and company events," a "laid-back atmosphere" in the workplace, and the satisfaction of sharing in the "company's involvement with the community." Best of all, perhaps, is the fact that the company offers "many opportunities for growth."

THE ROPES

Orientation at Brightpoint includes a detailed discussion, led by a company executive, of Brightpoint history and the responsibilities of the core divisions. "A great deal of time is spent going over the company policies and benefits," writes a company official. According to one newbie, the process "lasts about a day and a half;" it also includes lunch, a tour of the building, and an introduction to the fitness center. Subsequent training occurs on the job. An operations supervisor explains, "My training included instruction in how to process using the company's system and the standard operating procedures pertaining to the area in which I worked. I was trained by associates, team leads, and supervisors." A marketing coordinator adds, "I'm constantly learning how our internal processes work. I go through training with my immediate manager. I also have the opportunity to utilize Brightpoint University for any additional training needs [I may have]. An example of this would be Adobe Photoshop classes or time management skills training." One first jobber agrees, "The company is very good at [providing] on-the-job training. There is [always] the opportunity to learn from one of the many offered classes."

DAY IN THE LIFE

Brightpoint hires first jobbers across a wide range of positions. Operations supervisors work in the distribution center, managing teams to ensure that orders are filled promptly. Project coordinators "manage and coordinate various sales and customer service projects and activities with the account managers." Staff accountants handle standard entry-level accounting duties by generating operational and financial reports. Financial analysts "develop, interpret, and implement complex financial and accounting concepts or techniques for financial planning and control" and "assist in determining operational cost evaluation of business performance." Product/test engineers "write, update, and maintain all customer files at Brightpoint while providing support (hardware, software, and troubleshooting) to all customers both internally and externally." The company also hires customer service representatives and production line workers at the entry level.

PEERS

"Everyone is very friendly" at Brightpoint, and as a result, the work environment is "very comfortable." One first jobber writes, "Everyone here is very positive and upbeat. The company president is just as easy to get along with as those in entry-level positions." Workers "frequently go to lunch together," "participate in community service events," and enjoy an occasional night out as well.

CATAPULT TECHNOLOGY
Various Positions

THE BIG PICTURE

Catapult Technology is an established consulting firm that provides comprehensive, quality technology solutions, human resources, and management consulting to the federal government and private sector. The company "offers a positive work-life environment, professional development opportunities, competitive salaries and benefits, and recognition and rewards for outstanding performance."

STATS

LOCATION(S) WHERE ENTRY-LEVEL EMPLOYEES WORK

Entry-level employees work in Washington, DC; Northern Virginia; suburban Maryland; Denver, Colorado; Las Vegas, Nevada; Oklahoma City, Oklahoma; and Miami, Florida.

AVERAGE NUMBER OF APPLICATIONS EACH YEAR

Catapult receives 1,000-plus applications per year.

AVERAGE NUMBER HIRED PER YEAR

Between ten and twenty-five entry-level employees are hired each year.

ENTRY-LEVEL POSITION(S) AVAILABLE

Numerous positions are open to entry-level hires.

AVERAGE HOURS WORKED PER WEEK

Entry-level employees work forty hours per week.

PERCENTAGE OF ENTRY-LEVEL HIRES STILL WITH THE COMPANY AFTER THREE, FIVE, AND TEN YEARS

Eighty percent of entry-level hires remain with Catapult Technology after three years.

AVERAGE STARTING SALARY

The median salary range for new hires is $29,000–$34,500.

BENEFITS OFFERED

Catapult Technology offers employees medical, hospitalization, and prescription plan coverage, as well as dental and vision coverage. The company also allows flexible spending accounts. Catapult Technology provides life and accidental death and dismemberment insurance; short- and long-term disability; supplemental life and disability; eighteen days of paid leave (vacation, personal, and sick days) annually; ten paid holidays annually; a 401(k) plan; direct deposit; confidential employee assistance program; employee referral bonuses; and an annual bonus plan.

CONTACT INFORMATION
Visit Catapult Technology on the Web at www.catapulttechnology.com/careers.

GETTING HIRED

Hiring at Catapult is driven by the status of its contracts; as a result, hiring occurs on a rolling basis. The company does not recruit on college campuses. Applicants should submit their resumes online via Catapult's website. Resumes "can be submitted for specific open positions or [as] stand-alone [submissions]. All resumes are cross-referenced for the experience and background necessary for each open position; if the minimum qualifications match, an human resources specialist will review the resume further and determine if the candidate should [be reviewed] by the hiring manager. If the hiring manager is interested, the candidate may be interviewed and offered the position." Catapult seeks "candidates who demonstrate an aptitude for quality, timely work, teamwork, and attention to detail. Qualities consistently avoided in prospective employees include lack of demonstrated ability to complete tasks in a timely manner and inability to work as a team player." One successful hire advises, "One thing to always remember is to remain professional in your appearance and actions. Also, no matter how you got hooked up with the interview, whether through a family member or friend or through [the online] application, have someone double- and triple-check your cover letter and resume for typos." Many of the first jobbers we spoke with began their tenure with Catapult as temporary hires and transitioned into full-time hires after demonstrating their worth during their first assignments.

MONEY AND PERKS

Because Catapult is a government contractor, "work assignments for entry-level employees are not always available." That said, "Catapult does successfully place entry-level employees regularly and rewards employees for work well done." Employees at the firm love the rewards programs; one explains, "Employees are rewarded in various ways, such as on-the-spot awards and the big-time awards [at the annual awards banquet]." Company officials note that "all employees are eligible for on-the-spot rewards for doing something notable that their supervisor wants to acknowledge." A newbie notes, "I have received an on-the-spot reward. It was within the first few months of working here, and it was for great customer service." First jobbers here also love the "travel subsidies we receive as well as many other benefits, such as discounts on rental cars, movie tickets, various discounted memberships, etc. We are often treated to lunch as a show of gratitude for hard work."

THE ROPES

Catapult offers an orientation that provides "an overview of benefits and Catapult's corporate make-up." Training for specific jobs is usually provided by the contracting employer, with support from Catapult. One first jobber explains, "Catapult employs a lot of subject matter experts, and I was fortunate to work with some who didn't mind answering the myriad questions I had every day."

Day in the Life

Entry-level hires at Catapult "typically engage in a broad variety of duties that require a depth of understanding and appreciation for learning as well as the aptitude to learn." Depending on the position, a new hire may spend his or her day fulfilling any number of tasks. A newbie in human resources, for example, reports that "a typical day would be to come in at 8:30 A.M. and stay until 5:00 P.M. filing documents. We have customers visit with questions regarding their files, [and] we send [them] to the human resources specialists." A quality assurance specialist tells us that he "sorts the data entry from the previous day and isolates at least 10 percent of the total number. Ten percent is our minimum contractual percentage needing quality assurance, but I often [quality assure] a higher percentage. This can possibly take me up to about lunchtime. The rest of my time is spent fulfilling other parts of the data entry process and assisting others in any way I can."

Peers

One of the drawbacks of working on-site for a contract is that first jobbers sometimes feel "isolated" from other company worksites. One's peers here are a mix of workers at the contracting company and other Catapult contract workers. Given the circumstances, the after-hours scene here is predictably subdued. "There are social events that take place, but [the prevalence of those] depends on the team you are placed with," explains one employee. In general, however, "newcomers are greeted very kindly and welcomed with open arms."

Moving On

Catapult is a relatively new company, so there is little data on the career paths to which work at Catapult leads. Some who leave here find work at other firms or within the federal government.

Attrition

First-jobbers typically remain with the company for three to four years, though that figure may be artificially low because of the relative youth of the company. Some find positions in the federal government; others continue their formal educations. According to the company, more than 90 percent of first jobbers stay on for at least one year here.

Best and Worst

Catapult tells us that "The most successful entry-level employees demonstrate aptitude and interest in achieving professional goals, including long-term and short-term goals and opportunities for training and education. The least successful entry-level candidates are those who seek employment for reasons that are not in the best interests of themselves or the company."

CATERPILLAR

Various Positions

THE BIG PICTURE

Come work for the company that makes the big machines. According to the company's website, Caterpillar is "the leading manufacturer of construction and mining equipment, diesel and natural gas engines, and industrial gas turbines." Caterpillar is one of America's most successful industrial companies; employees enjoy a salary that they call "competitive" and a benefits package that they rate as "top-notch."

STATS

LOCATION(S) WHERE ENTRY-LEVEL EMPLOYEES WORK

"Caterpillar is a global company, with nearly 250 company facilities worldwide. While many of the entry-level new hires would begin their career at the company's Peoria, Illinois headquarters, Caterpillar has independent dealers and customers on every continent."

AVERAGE NUMBER OF APPLICATIONS EACH YEAR

"Caterpillar receives about 50,000 applications each year for all positions across the company. About one-third of those applications are from recent college graduates."

AVERAGE NUMBER HIRED PER YEAR OVER THE LAST TEN YEARS

"Over the last ten years, Caterpillar has hired about 1,000 people per year on the management payroll, which is where the majority of entry-level hiring takes place."

ENTRY-LEVEL POSITION(S) AVAILABLE

"Caterpillar hires entry-level employees in a variety of disciplines. The primary areas include engineering, information technology, manufacturing, marketing and communications, business, accounting, and finance."

AVERAGE HOURS WORKED PER WEEK

"The majority of positions within Caterpillar are full-time [and require] forty hours per week minimum. Many jobs offer varying degrees of travel as a part of the position responsibility. Management employees are expected to manage their time and workload appropriately, often requiring time at work beyond the forty-hour minimum."

PERCENTAGE OF ENTRY-LEVEL HIRES STILL WITH THE COMPANY AFTER THREE, FIVE, AND TEN YEARS

"Among employee management, which is where the majority of entry-level position hiring takes place, 92 percent of new hires are still with the company after three years. After five years, 79 percent of new hires are still with the company. After ten years, 73 percent of new hires are still with the company."

AVERAGE STARTING SALARY

"At Caterpillar, you'll earn what you're worth—we're firm believers in higher rewards for higher performers. In addition, our more-than-competitive salary package includes a base salary along with incentive compensation."

BENEFITS OFFERED

"Caterpillar offers one of the most generous benefits packages in the corporate world, including 100 percent matching on 401(k) contributions; portable pension equity plan; paid vacation and personal time; tuition reimbursement; comprehensive medical, dental, and vision coverage; a preventative care program; and life and disability insurance."

CONTACT INFORMATION

For more information about opportunities and how to apply, visit www.catcareers.com. General company information is available on www.cat.com.

GETTING HIRED

Caterpillar recruits on campuses and also accepts applications through its website. Company representatives tell us that "the development of a diverse, global workforce within an environment that encourages innovation and rewards individual and team performance is critical to its future success. Caterpillar values diversity, not only in the race or gender of its employees, but also in their background, skills, and experience." First jobbers from Caterpillar's more than twenty different business units similarly describe the hiring process. Here's how one newbie in human resources recalls it: "The director of compensation and benefits, the director of succession management, the corporate [human relations] manager, and the director of human relations interviewed me. Each interview was one hour in length and was a structured behavior-based interview. The questions revolved around how I have responded in the past to given situations (i.e., 'Tell me about a time you had to convince a boss or coworker of your idea'). During my interview, the program coordinator gave me an overview of the program. She also took me to lunch. At the end of the day, I was given a drug test. The program coordinator contacted me approximately a week later with a job offer."

MONEY AND PERKS

"Salary increases are based on business conditions and strongly tied to job performance" at Caterpillar. "The highest performers are rewarded with the highest salary increases," company representatives report. First jobbers rave about the benefits package; one new hire tells us that "the entire package is excellent. If I were forced to pick one as the best, I would say the 401(k) plan. Caterpillar matches employee contributions to the 401(k) plan dollar-for-dollar up to the first 6 percent of gross salary. These contributions are immediately vested." Other new hires say the best perk is "working in a team environment. This allowed [us] to meet a large group of [our] people in a short time. Also, there were after-work sporting and social events that allowed everyone to get acquainted with [one another] outside of the work environment."

THE ROPES

Orientation and training regimens at Caterpillar "vary by business unit or functional area." Many of the employees we spoke with describe a one-week orientation period; however, some (such as those in marketing) recount orientation periods that lasted over three months, and others describe being briefly introduced to their bosses before getting to work. For most positions, orientation and training are both thorough and rigorous, designed to ensure that new hires are familiar with both Caterpillar's corporate culture and the tasks for which they were hired; these processes typically involve classes and seminars, team-building exercises, plant tours, and equipment-specific training. New hires in manufacturing participate in a special three-year rotational development program, as do some beginners in human resources.

DAY IN THE LIFE

Caterpillar is a huge company that hires entry-level employees for numerous jobs in most of its divisions. There is no typical day for all of these employees; they do, however, participate in a common corporate culture. Part of that culture involves close contact with upper management. As one new hire tells us, "One of the best things about this program is the amount of exposure you get to leadership. I've met with several vice presidents and upper-level managers." Another agrees: "It is sometimes scary [to think about] the extent to which I have interacted with high-level employees within the company. So far in my career, I have interacted with [many] vice presidents, and a group president and have given presentations to division managers. When averaged on a weekly basis, the time would be very minimal (not even an hour), but the time spent is very valuable." Another aspect is the emphasis on taking initiative. Supervisors, one entry-level worker reports, "are not afraid to let me take on as many challenges or responsibilities as I want (as long as I demonstrate that I'm capable of handling them). They do a great job of providing coaching and support as I take on tougher, more demanding responsibilities."

PEERS

Caterpillar's emphasis on teamwork helps build strong relationships, both among entry-level workers and between entry-level workers and their bosses. One employee reports, "There is definitely camaraderie with our new hires. Part of my responsibility in my current position is to organize events for our new hires. These events have ranged from facility tours to bowling outings." After-hours socializing varies from division to division and from city to city. A manufacturing trainee says, "There is a large after-hours social scene at Caterpillar. I usually interact with my peers about ten to twenty hours a week at work, and after work I usually spend about eight hours a week interacting [with them]." A new hire in accounting tells a different story and says, "I do not live in the same city as most of my peers, so my social interaction with them outside of work is limited, but it [does exist]."

MOVING ON

Caterpillar doesn't lose many employees; over 90 percent of new hires remain with the company for at least three years. Company representatives brag that "the average length of service for full-time Caterpillar employees in Illinois is 18.7 years—nearly *four times* the manufacturing industry average of just five years. Since 1972, more than 17,000 current and retired employees have reached their thirty-year service anniversary." The few people who fly the co-op usually do so "for personal reasons because they determine that the job isn't a good fit for them or because they identify another opportunity that they feel better meets their goals."

BEST AND WORST

"Four of the five group presidents started with Caterpillar soon after college. Their first jobs were in accounting, engineering, finance, and marketing. Today, their years of service with Caterpillar range from twenty-nine to thirty-six years, and each of these senior executives has administrative responsibilities for a group of business units."

Centra

Various Positions

The Big Picture

Centra provides software and support for real-time business-to-business collaboration via the Internet and corporate networks. The company conducts everything from one-on-one virtual classroom sessions to meetings with more than 500 executives from across the globe. Only a decade old, Centra could develop into a major growth company. If it does, today's first jobbers could be tomorrow's fat cats because—as they say on Wall Street—a rising tide lifts all boats.

Stats

Location(s) Where Entry-level Employees Work

Most Centra employees work in Lexington, Massachusetts; some positions are available in other locations.

Entry-level Position(s) Available

Various entry-level positions are available.

Benefits Offered

Centra offers its employees medical and dental insurance. Additional benefits include life and disability insurance, flexible spending accounts, a 401(k) plan, stock options, an employee stock purchase plan, a tuition reimbursement program, paid time off, holidays, vacation days, and sick days.

Contact Information

Visit the website at www.centra.com/corporate/jobs.

Getting Hired

Centra posts available positions on its website. One employee we spoke with found his job online; several others say they found their jobs through placement agencies. Some people were attracted by "the company, the people, and opportunities available at a small, fast-growing company." The hiring process is fairly standard; one employee explains, "I interviewed in two rounds; the first interview was with the hiring manager and human resources. The second interview was with the chief financial officer, to whom the department I would be working for reported. I was then called to confirm references and then called [with the] verbal offer by the hiring manager, which I accepted." Interviewers "ask very basic questions about computer skills. The interviews were very friendly. I think the interviewers were just trying to get a read on my long-term interests, my working style, and my work experience." Successful hires suggest you "express a willingness to learn and an interest in the industry."

MONEY AND PERKS

Centra first jobbers tell us that their "start date was somewhat negotiable," but "salary, what [we] did, and where [we] did it were not." Employees appreciate the company's extensive benefits package. They also praise the "informal work environment," which makes it easy to make friends. One newbie especially liked how he "was able to interact with all of the different departments and talk with people in various positions to determine areas of interest for [himself]. This was invaluable to [him]."

THE ROPES

Most of the employees we spoke with started at jobs that didn't require much training. Since those we spoke with moved on to better positions relatively quickly, they didn't really mind. One writes, "I think the receptionist position [I held] was a perfect entry-level job. I learned a lot from this position, interacted with everyone in the company, and learned how the company worked." Another employee, who also began at a reception desk, agrees: "I viewed the position as a means to get to other positions in the company. My duties were very much day-to-day administration and not too difficult to learn or perform." Another new hire adds, "[That orientation and training is generally informal] because it's a young, small company. On my first day, I walked around and met everyone. By my second day, I was contacting customers and prospects." She also tells us that she had "no formal training, but [she] learned a lot from [her] coworkers."

DAY IN THE LIFE

The core of Centra's business is facilitating e-Learning (college courses, training sessions, etc., conducted via the Internet) and virtual business meetings. Many first jobbers play a crucial role in these Web events as event managers; they "host" the event by coordinating logistics, training clients to use Centra software, and serving as moderators. Other new hires provide the type of support found in all businesses: clerical, human resources, sales, [and] customer service. While some consider this "mostly grunt work, it *is* important. Every company needs someone to manage those day-to-day tasks. Centra is very busy since it is growing. There are many interviews taking place and new hires coming on board, lots of equipment that has to be ordered on a daily basis, and many other tasks to complete."

PEERS

As do many young companies, Centra has a large population of fresh-faced go-getters, many of them first jobbers, among its employees. These workers enjoy "a lot of contact with other first jobbers at the company."

MOVING ON

Centra does a good job of promoting from within, and many first jobbers find themselves quickly moving on to better jobs in the company. Two of our correspondents began as receptionists; today, one works in human resources, and the other has become a marketing specialist.

CHILDREN'S RIGHTS
Paralegal

THE BIG PICTURE

Some of the nation's child welfare programs are, tragically, underfunded and/or poorly managed. When such programs fail to execute their missions, children ultimately suffer. Formerly a project of the American Civil Liberties Union, Children's Rights became an independent organization in 1995. This small legal advocacy group combats the neglect and abuse of foster children with class action suits designed to force reform of failed child welfare systems. College graduates here serve a two-year tenure as paralegals; one explains: "Since Children's Rights is so small, paralegals are integral members of the litigation teams. We sit in on almost all important meetings. Paralegals work closely with the executive director and the other attorneys on a daily basis." The job is a great way to prep for a career in the law or social services and an even better way to serve a powerless constituency.

STATS

LOCATION(S) WHERE ENTRY-LEVEL EMPLOYEES WORK

All positions are located in New York, New York.

AVERAGE NUMBER OF APPLICATIONS EACH YEAR

Children's Rights receives 200 applications each year.

AVERAGE NUMBER HIRED PER YEAR

Children's Rights hires two or three paralegals each year.

ENTRY-LEVEL POSITION(S) AVAILABLE

Entry-levels hires are brought in as paralegals.

AVERAGE HOURS WORKED PER WEEK

Paralegals work forty to forty-five hours per week.

PERCENTAGE OF ENTRY-LEVEL HIRES STILL WITH THE COMPANY AFTER THREE, FIVE, AND TEN YEARS

Most paralegals stay for two years, then move on to graduate school.

AVERAGE STARTING SALARY

The starting salary for paralegals is $29,500.

BENEFITS OFFERED

Children's Rights offers full medical and dental benefits that vest the first of the month after thirty days of employment. Additional benefits include flexible spending accounts (which vest the first of month following three months employment), life insurance and long term disability insurance (which vest the first of month following three months employment), and a 401(k) plan.

CONTACT INFORMATION

Children's Rights
Human Resources
404 Park Avenue South, 11th Floor
New York, NY 10016
E-mail: info@childrensrights.org.

GETTING HIRED

Children's Rights is "too small an organization to interview on campus." Instead, the organization posts job openings at such sites as www.Idealist.org. The applications come pouring in, [at a ratio of] about 200 for the two or three positions that open annually. The organization looks for evidence of "attention to detail, good editing skills, critical analysis capabilities, a solid work ethic, and the ability to juggle many tasks." Initial screening of applicants is done by current paralegals, whose choices are "then approved in a final interview by the paralegal supervisor, who is a senior lawyer in the office." One successful hire reports, "My first-round interview was with the four paralegals who were working at Children's Rights at the time. I had to do the interview over the phone, as I was far away from New York. The tone was quite friendly, though I was definitely asked questions that related to [what] I think about child welfare and the role of the law in advocating for children. We also talked a lot about my previous work experience, and I was given an opportunity to ask all the questions I had, as well. The second-round interview was in the New York office with a staff attorney who was also the paralegal supervisor; that interview was more formal. After I was offered the job, the then-paralegals gave me their contact information, including their cell phones, so that I could call them with any questions I had about the job. They were very helpful and generous with their time, and in the end, they definitely had me convinced that I should take the job."

MONEY AND PERKS

"Job location, tasks, and pay were all nonnegotiable," writes one Children's Rights paralegal, adding that "I was able to work out a mutually convenient start date." The starting salary makes living in expensive New York City difficult, but not impossible. Raises are awarded annually "and are generally in accordance with across-the-board raises throughout the organization," so the second year of the job is easier than the first. Overtime pay "is generally available." Paralegals brag about the "good vacation time" (they receive fifteen vacation days, four personal days, two floating holidays, and ten sick days per year) and the "good daily work schedule" but agree that the best perk of all is that "the work here positively [influences] the clients we serve."

THE ROPES

Training of newcomers is handled by "the current paralegals, who train you on basic paralegal duties and case-specific duties. The attorneys on my cases also provided some training. Most of the training is on-the-job throughout the first few months of work." One paralegal writes, "I was paired up with an outgoing paralegal who oriented me to office logistics and trained me on the specifics of the cases I would be working on. I worked with her for about two weeks, though for part of that time I began performing tasks on my own with her supervision, and I was given time to read background materials to help me understand the nature of the work we do. I had lunches with the attorneys and paralegal on each of the case teams I was to be working on, during which I was taught the history of the cases and given the opportunity to get to know the people working on the cases. It was a generally informative and fun time."

DAY IN THE LIFE

Paralegals at Children's Rights are assigned to work on specific ongoing cases, so "it's very difficult to explain a typical day here because the work varies tremendously depending on what cases you're assigned to and how active the litigation is on those cases. However, as best as I can describe it, a typical day begins with press monitoring; I check the websites of newspapers relevant to the cases I work on to find articles related to child welfare, child abuse, fatalities in foster care, etc. The rest of the day could include editing correspondence for attorneys and finalizing it to be sent out, reviewing discovery documents to find key information, reading over a monitoring report and culling out key areas of concern, answering intake phone calls from concerned foster parents or biological parents who have problems with their state's child welfare system, researching data related to the systems we're investigating, keeping track of contacts made with stakeholders in the jurisdictions where we're working, organizing and managing documents, sitting in on conference calls with local co-counsel or local advocates, or doing basically anything else for the attorneys you are there to support." Another first jobber adds, "Because Children's Rights is primarily involved in litigation, work follows the litigation cycle. Some weeks are slow, whereas other weeks are incredibly hectic. I never feel that I cannot handle the workload, though."

PEERS

Children's Rights employs no more than five paralegals at any given time, so first jobbers here form a small contingent. Paralegals agree that their peers are "fantastic. We have all become close friends" who enjoy "a great deal of camaraderie. Happy hours occur on a weekly basis." The camaraderie extends beyond the bottom rung of the office hierarchy; one paralegal explains, "We hang out frequently outside of the office, and we all really enjoy [one another's] company. That includes the supervising attorneys. The office environment is generally laid back, even though we often work under lots of pressure."

MOVING ON

Paralegals at Children's Rights make a two-year commitment to the job. They "generally leave after two years and go on to graduate school as planned," with "many going to law school, but some pursuing degrees in social services (MSW or MPA)."

BEST AND WORST

Children's Rights has "had the good fortune to work with many exceptional paralegals who have moved on to graduate-level education at prestigious institutions, either in the law or in social services." The organization has had "very limited experience with unsuccessful hires. This has occurred when it was mutually determined that a new hire's skill set and interests did not dovetail well with those of the organization."

CITIZEN SCHOOLS
Teaching Associates and Teaching Fellows

THE BIG PICTURE

Citizen Schools offers after-school programs that "deliver a creative and effective learning model that addresses community needs while building student skills through hands-on experiential learning activities," primarily in poor, urban settings. It's the kind of company that advertises its employment opportunities on websites like Idealist.org. In short, this is a job that you seek out if you're interested in challenging, rewarding work that has the potential to affect others' lives directly.

STATS

LOCATION(S) WHERE ENTRY-LEVEL EMPLOYEES WORK

Citizen Schools has programs in Tuscon, Arizona; Redwood City, California; San Jose, California; Boston, Massachusetts; Framingham, Massachusetts; Lowell, Massachusetts; Malden, Massachusetts; New Bedford, Massachusetts; Springfield, Massachusetts; Worcester, Massachusetts; New Brunswick, New Jersey; Baytown, Texas; and Houston, Texas.

AVERAGE NUMBER OF APPLICATIONS EACH YEAR

The company receives 300–400 applications per year.

AVERAGE NUMBER HIRED PER YEAR OVER THE LAST TEN YEARS

"The Teaching Fellowship has grown from one teaching fellow in 1997 to fifty-seven teaching fellows in thirteen cities in 2004. The number of teaching associates has grown to eighty-eight nationwide."

ENTRY-LEVEL POSITION(S) AVAILABLE

"We hire approximately thirty to forty new teaching associates in the fall and an additional ten to twenty in the spring. Every June we hire twenty-five to thirty AmeriCorps Teaching Fellows. The fellowship is a two-year position that includes earning a master's degree through Lesley University."

AVERAGE HOURS WORKED PER WEEK

Hours vary according to the position. Teaching associates work from twenty to thirty hours per week; program staff, (including teaching fellows), work from forty to fifty hours per week (in addition to master's course work); headquarters staff work from twenty-four to fifty hours per week.

PERCENTAGE OF ENTRY-LEVEL HIRES STILL WITH THE COMPANY AFTER THREE, FIVE, AND TEN YEARS

After three years, about 80 percent of all entry-level hires remain with Citizen Schools.

Average Starting Salary

"Compensation varies by position and is commensurate with experience. Teaching assistants begin at $11.30 per hour; this wage increases with each year of employment. AmeriCorps Teaching Fellows earn a salary of $20,000 per year plus $4,725 in education awards."

Benefits Offered

"All full-time employees have the opportunity to enroll in [a] health care plan (currently HMO Blue, a provider of Blue Cross/Blue Shield). Citizen Schools pays 80 percent of the monthly premium, and the employee pays 20 percent. This amount is deducted from his or her paycheck on a pre-tax basis. Health insurance, like all benefits, is pro-rated for part-time FTE staff. Teaching associates are eligible to enroll in health insurance on entering their fifth semester with Citizen Schools; Teaching fellows receive free health care. Citizen Schools offers both individual and family plans, which includes health insurance benefits for domestic partners." Furthermore, while working with Citizen Schools, "staff can concurrently receive a master's in education with a specialization in out-of-school time from Lesley University (assistance provided by Citizen Schools)." They have the "opportunity to enroll in a 403(b) retirement plan (currently with TIAA-CREF). Citizen Schools matches up to $500 annually after one full year of employment." Time off includes "fifteen vacation days, nine sick days, three personal days, and eleven paid holidays per year. After four years of continuous employment, employees are eligible for a twenty-day vacation splash." There is also an "opportunity to enroll in Section 125 flexible spending account (for nonreimbursed medical expenses) and dependent care account program. Long-term disability insurance [comes] at no cost to the employee." When junior comes along, staff members are eligible for "six weeks paid parental leave for primary caregivers [and] two weeks paid parental leave for secondary caregivers."

Contact Information

Teaching Fellows Program
Museum Wharf
308 Congress Street
Boston, MA 02210
Tel: 617-695-2300
Fax: 617-695-2367
www.citizenschools.org

Getting Hired

Citizen Schools scours its applicant pool for candidates who demonstrate "experience in education/ working with kids; commitment to nonprofit/social service work in urban communities; flexibility and patience; excellent communication skills (written and verbal); enthusiasm; and entrepreneurial spirit. Bilingualism/multilingualism is a plus." All applicants fill out the online application available on the organization's website and submit a cover letter and resume with the application. One successful candidate writes, "I e-mailed my cover letter and resume and followed [up] with a call to the human resources specialist. The director of development called me back to arrange an interview. I then met with her, along with the manager of individual giving. The interview was casual, and they inquired about my goals, interests, and intent for the position. They stressed the importance of enthusiasm, flexibility, and dedication. The energy around the office was high, and I was impressed by the fact that employees seemed to be enjoying their jobs." Sample interview questions include "What about Citizen Schools most excites you? After reading and filling out the job application, what is your understanding of the impact we are trying to achieve? Tell me about your past work experience and how it relates to this position? What are your three greatest strengths and weaknesses for this job?"

MONEY AND PERKS

Teaching associates earn $11.50 per hour during their first semester of work; the starting salary for Teaching fellows is $20,000. According to organization representatives, "salary reviews occur on an annual basis. Annual increases typically are in the 2–5 percent range." The best perk, employees tell us, is "working with kids!" The organization points out that "the education award pays for the Teaching Fellows' master's."

THE ROPES

"When an employee arrives on his or her first day, he or she already has a voice-mail account, an e-mail account, a network login, and a mailbox. All new employees meet with the human resources manager for an in-depth review of benefits and policies (typically one hour). New employees also receive technology training on computer systems, e-mail, voice-mail, etc. New employees are also given an office tour by the office manager. This orientation usually takes about half a day." One new hire adds, "I got a thorough overview of the job and what my responsibilities were [before I started work], so I felt like I knew what I was getting into. Everyone was very accommodating to me [considering] the fact that I was both new to the organization and new to the workforce. I learned by asking questions, watching others, and using my best judgment. All of these things have helped me do my job well and improve many projects and processes with my own ideas."

DAY IN THE LIFE

"There is no real typical day at the job" at Citizen Schools. As an organization representative explains, "Citizen Schools turns children into community heroes; children apprentice with lawyers, Web designers, [and] architects and culminate their learning apprenticeships by arguing trials before federal judges, designing websites for their school, organizing public events, publishing newspapers, and much more." Citizen Schools' Teaching Fellows "work primarily as front-line educators and community builders, leading hands-on activities for small and large groups [of] children, designing and teaching curriculum, leading peers in the planning and implementation of educational activities; recruiting students and volunteers; communicating with and engaging parents; and fostering partnerships with school faculty and community organizations." They also recruit volunteer Citizen Teachers from the local community. Teaching associates also handle a wide range of duties, including leading curriculum, designing and leading learning games, organizing sports activities, and directing hands-on learning experiences. They also confer with students' parents to keep them apprised of their progress.

PEERS

"Citizen Schools attracts a wide variety of people. Most of them are very intelligent, friendly, and come with a unique array of past experiences," offers one employee with the organization. They're the type of folks who believe "that all communities are blessed with thousands of born teachers (old and young, professional and laborer, athlete and artist); [these are] people who would like to enrich their own lives and contribute to their community by sharing their skills with children." Many are young; one employee writes, "There is large camaraderie largely due to the young age of the teaching fellows. My peers are the coolest cats in town."

MOVING ON

Among those employees who use Citizen Schools as a springboard to land another job, "approximately 70 percent are involved in community-based education initiatives as program directors and teachers. Some are involved in graduate studies. Several graduates have become campus directors or start-up captains at our affiliate sites. Because of their excellent teaching, leading, and community-organizing skills, and Citizen Schools' strong reputation, teaching fellows are highly sought-after employees."

ATTRITION

Current employees warn that teaching for Citizen Schools is hard work. "I wish I had known about the amount of hours that would be needed after work," one employee tells us. The organization adds that "Teaching associates often leave to find more full-time employment or because of scheduling conflicts. Other staff may leave due to new opportunities and/or better salary."

BEST AND WORST

According to organization representatives, the best new hire ever "began with Citizen Schools as a teaching associate, became a teaching fellow, and is currently a successful campus director." The worst new hire was "a recent college graduate who moved to Boston to become a teaching fellow and was overwhelmed by living in such a big city and not prepared to work with children nine to fourteen years old. She resigned after only six weeks. This shaped how we recruited for teaching fellows. All potential candidates now spend a day at a Citizen Schools campus as part of their interview process."

CITY YEAR
Corps Member

THE BIG PICTURE

City Year is one of the larger service programs that is part of the Federal AmeriCorps initiative. Through a year of community service, leadership development, and civic engagement, participants mentor and educate children in public schools; they also lead major physical service projects.

STATS

LOCATION(S) WHERE ENTRY-LEVEL EMPLOYEES WORK

"In the 2005–2006 corps year, City Year will have service opportunities at fifteen sites: Boston, Massachusetts; Chicago, Illinois; Cleveland, Ohio; Columbia, South Carolina; Columbus, Ohio; Detroit, Michigan; Little Rock, Arkansas; Stratham, New Hampshire; New York, New York; Philadelphia, Pennsylvania; Providence, Rhode Island; San Antonio, Texas; San Jose/Silicon Valley, California; Seattle/King County, Washington; and Washington, DC."

AVERAGE NUMBER OF APPLICATIONS EACH YEAR

"For the 2005–2006 corps year, City Year received 21,400 inquiries and more than 3,000 completed applications for slightly more than 1,000 corps member positions."

AVERAGE NUMBER HIRED PER YEAR OVER THE LAST TEN YEARS

"Corps member enrollment in the 2004–2005 corps year was more than 1,000."

ENTRY-LEVEL POSITION(S) AVAILABLE

"Corps members work full-time in service to their community and country as tutors and mentors to children in the classroom and after-school programs and as leaders of physical service projects, such as painting schools, planting community gardens, building play spaces, and revitalizing urban spaces."

AVERAGE HOURS WORKED PER WEEK

"Corps members serve full-time every week for ten months to complete at least 1,700 hours of service."

PERCENTAGE OF ENTRY-LEVEL HIRES STILL WITH THE COMPANY AFTER THREE, FIVE, AND TEN YEARS

"The City Year model is a one-year term of service, with approximately one-third of City Year corps members returning to serve a second year in a leadership capacity."

AVERAGE STARTING SALARY

"Corps members receive a very modest living stipend, based on their region's cost of living and other factors."

BENEFITS OFFERED

"City Year provides corps members with standard health care benefits." Additional benefits include "a $4,725 education award that can be applied toward existing student loans or future higher education tuition. Meeting the 1,700-hour service requirement secures this full-education award."

CONTACT INFORMATION

To learn more, visit www.cityyear.org.

To apply online, visit www.cityyear.org/joincorps/gateway.

GETTING HIRED

City Year scans each application for evidence of "the four Cs: character, cooperation, commitment, and competence." Volunteers must be between the ages of seventeen and twenty-four; according to the organization, individuals in the age range are "young enough to want to change the world—[and] old enough to do it." A complete application includes personal information, two letters of reference, and three personal essays. A screening interview follows, with most applicants receiving a second, in-depth interview later in the process. One successful applicant tells us that the process "was a real mix between an application for school and an application for a job. There was a standard form with questions and essays. I also had to send in letters of recommendation. [Subsequently] I got a letter from City Year offering me an interview, and I set one up while I was home for winter break. I interviewed with the recruitment director. She provided me with a lot of information about the job that I couldn't get from the website. She told me about the particular challenges that the type of work presented and asked how I would deal with them. The process was formal but not intimidating."

MONEY AND PERKS

Individuals do not take positions with City Year for the money. You may be able to negotiate the location in which you work, but all other aspects of the job offer are "a take-it-or-leave-it proposition." Several of the volunteers we spoke with said that City Year offers "great networking opportunities. With all of the community service we do and with all the service partners that we work with and attract to the organization, [we] get to make a lot of connections if [we] put [ourselves] out there." Others feel that the best perk was "being able to put your idealism to work." Organization representatives note that "alumni have a well-earned reputation as hard-working, dedicated, and idealistic leaders who bring passion, competence, and a can-do attitude to subsequent endeavors," so City Year service should be a help on future job applications.

THE ROPES

City Year orientation, one newbie tells us, "lasts for five weeks and is provided by a host of people. Some training is given by local City Year staff, but at least half is not. We have members of the community and representatives from numerous agencies come in and speak to us. We also go out to several places for workshops and lectures. Each team also has its own particular training with the community service organization it works with on a regular basis. For example, the Case Foundation Young Heroes Team (my team) had several training sessions with an organization [called] For Love of Children (FLOC)." Ongoing training continues throughout a volunteer's ten-month tenure; one first jobber explains, "We receive all kinds of training from all kinds of people, and it goes on throughout the year. Every other Friday all the teams are together for training in self-defense, different social issues, the government process, health, and wellness. We [corps members] could suggest themes for any of these days as well."

Day in the Life

One corps member notes, "There really is no such thing as a typical day, or even a typical week, which is one of the great things about the job." While some volunteers spend the bulk of their time teaching in the classroom or producing educational dramas for school children, many others shift from role to role, serving whatever project the local City Year office has undertaken that day, week, or month. Those projects could include anything from delivering meals to shut-ins, to serving as course guides on a homeless walk, to providing day care, to organizing press conferences and other media events. As one volunteer puts it, "The job changes every day, and the teams achieve more and more independence throughout the year both for individual service and initiatives (our service projects) and within our schools. The work itself doesn't really change, but the level of independence and individual initiative does increase throughout the year."

Peers

Most City Year volunteers enjoy a strong peer network. One offers, "The camaraderie is excellent—[there is] a ton of outside-of-work social gathering, hanging out, etc. Some of my best friends are corps members I serve with." Of course, the amount of peer interaction varies according to the individuals involved and the locations; in some areas, "because teams have different focuses, there are times when we can go without seeing a team for a week or more. Regardless, there is some camaraderie across teams since we spend so much time in training together." Many people tell us that corps members "have such different backgrounds," which they see as a major plus. As one member puts it, "One of the cool things about working with so many different people is that there is always somebody to go to with a unique perspective on things or with information that you don't have. My peers, for the most part, are nothing like me, and it is really the first time that I have been in a situation like that."

Moving On

City Year is a ten-month program, and many members move on after one term of service, "having earned their education award." Some use their education awards to "bear the costs of higher education, making college and graduate school the top destination after City Year." One volunteer says, "Some people do come back for a second year, and that's something I'm seriously considering." Returnees constitute about one-third of the volunteer force; those who return usually find themselves "in a leadership capacity."

ATTRITION

Members who leave early generally complain about "the staff and the hours of the work. Those people looked at the experience more as a conventional job than as a learning experience that would lead to other things." Some people leave when they discover they cannot survive on the living stipend.

BEST AND WORST

According to organization representatives, "some of City Year's most successful corps members now advocate for social justice, lead foundations, work in schools, and create new opportunities for service. Other very successful corps members are those who incorporate an ethic of service and commitment to community in their work as doctors, lawyers, and businesspeople. City Year alumni are also in government positions and on City Year staff."

COLLEGE SUMMIT
Various Positions

THE BIG PICTURE

"Low-income students who get A's enroll in college at the same rate as high-income students who get D's," notes the College Summit website. This nonprofit seeks to redress this inequity; to that end, it pursues its mission "to transform the college admissions process and increase the college enrollment rate of low-income students" by helping "low-income, academically midtier students" navigate the college admissions and financial aid processes to "ensure that the community harnesses the talent of all college-capable students." First jobbers serve a wide variety of support roles at College Summit.

STATS

LOCATION(S) WHERE ENTRY-LEVEL EMPLOYEES WORK

College Summit's headquarters are in Washington, DC; the organization also has regional offices in Chicago, Illinois; Los Angeles, California; Denver, Colorado; St. Louis, Missouri; and Charleston, West Virginia.

AVERAGE NUMBER OF APPLICATIONS EACH YEAR

College Summit receives about 1,000 applications per year.

AVERAGE NUMBER HIRED PER YEAR

Nine entry-level employees are hired by College Summit each year.

ENTRY-LEVEL POSITION(S) AVAILABLE

The entry-level positions available vary. "The general focus is on providing broad support to the department or manager, as well as contributing significantly to specific projects or initiatives."

AVERAGE HOURS WORKED PER WEEK

Entry-level employees work about fifty hours per week.

PERCENTAGE OF ENTRY-LEVEL HIRES STILL WITH THE COMPANY AFTER THREE, FIVE, AND TEN YEARS

After three years, 10 percent remain with the company; and after five years, 4 percent remain.

AVERAGE STARTING SALARY

The starting salary for entry-levels hires is $28,000.

BENEFITS OFFERED

Employees receive a fully-covered PPO health insurance plan, which encompasses medical, dental, vision, and prescription expenses. Additional benefits include a 401(k) program; $1,000 per year in professional development funding; flexible spending accounts; and a generous vacation policy (ten personal days, five sick days, seven company holidays, and the full week between December 25 and January 1).

CONTACT INFORMATION

Visit College Summit online at www.collegesummit.org. To apply for a job, click on the "Join Us" link or send an e-mail to jobs@collegesummit.org.

GETTING HIRED

Job openings at College Summit "are posted internally and on external recruitment websites, as well as [on] our own [website]." College Summit encourages applicants "to submit their materials via e-mail." The organization notes that because "our recruitment function is currently understaffed, our primary outreach is through websites such as www.Idealist.org, Teach for America's alumni network, and Net Impact. We do not yet target specific colleges, and [we] welcome applicants from any college." Model candidates evince enthusiasm for the organization's mission, have an entrepreneurial inclination, and demonstrate excellent communication and interpersonal skills. Applicants who meet these criteria "are invited to participate in a phone interview with the human resources department, [after which the pool] narrows down to final candidates to interview in person with the hiring manager and often other team members. In some cases, final candidates are asked to interview with other staff [members], as well; additionally, reference checks are performed as necessary, though less often with entry-level candidates."

One successful hire reports, "During the interview process, I spent an afternoon visiting College Summit in Washington. I was interviewed by many of the younger staffers and the founder and CEO of the organization. The interviews with the younger people were genuine and kind in nature. I was just struck by the humility of everyone, the like-mindedness of everyone (out of college, ambitious, [and] passionate about education). My interview with the CEO was very professional, rather short, but pointed nonetheless, centering on the principles that guide me. I was then offered the job a few weeks later."

MONEY AND PERKS

As at most nonprofits, there's little room for salary negotiation at College Summit, especially for entry-level hires. Raises "are performance-based and are typically given following the annual performance review process. When an employee has demonstrated superior results, he or she would be eligible for a raise or promotion outside the standard process." The organization also offers "additional professional development opportunities around time management and prioritizing tasks." Among the most appreciated perks are the "excellent health insurance," "a full week of vacation between Christmas and the New Year," and "the entrepreneurial environment of a fast-growing and successful nonprofit organization."

THE ROPES

Orientation at College Summit "lasts about two days and is designed to welcome new employees to their teams and the organization and to give them the background information they need. A typical day would include a welcome breakfast with the office; a series of one-hour meetings to get new hires acclimated to their computers, office systems, and benefits; lunch with their supervisors; and then another series of meetings giving them background on College Summit's values, history, and program. All employees also receive a thorough introduction to the organization's growth plan." One first jobber writes, "The orientation process was great. There was a wonderful binder made for me, and I had a set of meetings organized for me during my first few weeks on the job. It was really nice, and I was impressed that people had been thinking of me in advance of my arrival."

DAY IN THE LIFE

College Summit hires first jobbers for a wide range of positions. A development coordinator writes, "When I first started, some of my main responsibilities included grant management, fundraising data management, creating budgets and attachments for proposals, coordinating the annual appeal, supporting college sales and workshop set-up, supporting the deputy director, and drafting letters and other correspondences." A new sites coordinator explains that her first tasks involved "a lot of grant writing and research. I'd work on a draft of a proposal to a potential donor and do some preliminary research on other potential donors."

PEERS

"My peers are some of the smartest, most idealistic, fun, talented, inspiring people I have ever met," writes a typical first jobber at College Summit, adding that "We are all like-minded and hang out together." Another agrees: "It's beyond friendship. It's like family." This is especially true for those who work in DC, where "we have hung out outside of work many, many times."

MOVING ON

Most first jobbers at College Summit remain with the organization for a period of one to two years, after which they typically find another job or move on to graduate school. Some leave because of the heavy workload; one young hire explains, "College Summit is a very output- and results-driven place. In other words, it's not about how much time you put in, when you leave, and when you show up; it's about [the degree to which] you are on top of your stuff. This [ethos] offers many perks, flexibility, and the feeling that you are an executive—but also can make work more consuming than one [may] plan."

ATTRITION

Less than 5 percent of College Summit first jobbers leave within twelve months of starting on at the organization. Relatively few remain for more than three years, though several have moved up into management-level positions. For most, however, this is a significant way station on the path to other career goals.

BEST AND WORST

Excellent first jobbers at College Summit are those "who have remained committed to the organization, who have pursued opportunities to grow within the organization, and [who] have advocated for themselves. Additionally, these are people who have stuck it out through jobs that may not have matched their interests until better opportunities opened up (or until they helped create those opportunities)."

Poor matches for the organization are those who expect to work directly with students; an organization representative explains, "Most of our positions involve working behind the scenes to move the organization forward in our effort to generate social change in low-income communities."

comScore

Analyst

The Big Picture

First jobbers tell us that comScore "is very unique and specializes in market research and consumer behavior." The company measures the Web activity, attitudes, and lifestyles of more than two million participating consumers who give comScore permission to "measure what matters across the entire spectrum of consumer surfing and buying behaviors." comScore uses this anonymous information to help hundreds of leading companies develop more effective marketing strategies. Good starting salaries and exposure "to a more innovative, technology-based aspect of research" are among the top allures of a comScore gig.

Stats

Location(s) Where Entry-level Employees Work

Entry-level employees who join as part of the firm's training program "begin work at comScore's headquarters in Reston, Virginia, but can ultimately work in any of the firm's offices, which are located in New York, New York; Chicago, Illinois; Seattle, Washington; San Francisco, California; Toronto, Canada; and the United Kingdom."

Average Number of Applications Each Year

comScore receives about 150 applications each year.

Average Number Hired Per Year

Seven employees were hired each in 2004 and 2005; comScore is looking to hire twenty-four entry-level employees in 2006.

Entry-level Position(s) Available

Entry-level employees start as customer data analysts, client service analysts, and specialized technology analysts.

Average Hours Worked Per Week

Entry-level employees work forty-five to fifty hours per week.

Average Starting Salary

The average starting salary varies based on individual qualifications, but is competitive with the industry standard.

Benefits Offered

Full medical (PPO) and dental coverage is available on the first day of the month following an employee's start date, and comScore pays 80 percent of the premium. The company also has an employee assistance program with a twenty-four-hour hotline for health inquiries and other personal needs.

Additional benefits include a 401(k) program with company contribution. "Generous vacation and holiday time off and allowance for [sick] leave" are also provided. The company finances basic life, supplemental life, and AD&D insurance, as well as short-term and long-term disability insurance. Supplemental optional benefits include vision care and legal services.

CONTACT INFORMATION

Visit comScore on the Web at www.comscore.com, or send your resume and cover letter to jobs@comscore.com.

GETTING HIRED

comScore seeks "energetic, enthusiastic, self-motivated, highly engaged individuals who are comfortable in an intellectually challenging, fast-paced environment where change is the norm." The company recruits on college campuses and accepts applications online. Applicants who make the first cut "visit comScore's Reston office for day-long interviews with comScore employees from various levels of the organization." One applicant reports, "The interview was a two-day process. The night before the actual interviews, there was a three-hour reception at a restaurant. It was nice to informally meet some people in the company before being thrown into a day of interviews. The next morning started with breakfast at the office, followed by a short test. They also had us fill out a personality profile, which I assume is currently being used to best manage each new hire personally. I went through four forty-five-minute interviews. I was impressed by the fact that everyone in the company seemed to be involved in the interview process." Another applicant adds, "The tone of the interviews was very informal, relaxed, and conversational. They just wanted to find out who you were, what you liked, etc." The company typically notifies successful applicants within a few weeks of the interview. One successful applicant notes, "My education made me a perfect fit for comScore, [since I have] both people skills and an analytical mind."

MONEY AND PERKS

Most first jobbers we spoke with were satisfied with their starting salaries at comScore. The company points out that "employees are eligible for annual salary increases, which are based on performance," but that entry-level hires are not eligible for bonuses. First jobbers tell us that the potential to receive incentive stock option grants when the company has its IPO is a huge perk. They also appreciate the "free snacks and sodas provided in the kitchen," as well as the fact that "everyone has his or her own laptop with wireless internet access." The company also offers summer hours "to add more flexibility for work-life balance.

THE ROPES

Some new hires at comScore experience a brief orientation (a "formal two-day boot camp," one first jobber called it), followed by supervised immersion in work supplemented by the occasional "training class in such areas as effective listening, negotiation skills, etc." Others participate in a more formal training program that "employs a three-month orientation process, beginning with an introduction to the company and its structure, followed by team-specific data analysis instruction. Candidates participate in an intensive series of meetings interspersed with work on live projects and simulations. Business- and management-skill workshops in conflict resolution, performance management, negotiating, and listening are [also] provided." One first jobber notes, "We've have had at least twenty-five different people train us, each filling us in on a different piece of what comScore does. This gives the new hires enough understanding of the company to think about what areas they would like to work in."

DAY IN THE LIFE

Entry-level employees at comScore may work in one of a few positions. Client service analysts "provide analysis of data, client support, and support to the sales and client service teams in delivering customized analysis of consumer behavior." Custom data analysts "conduct data analysis, support internal clients, generate reports, and act as the conduit between the data warehouse and the sales and client service teams." Finally, technology specialists keep the whole system up and running. A client service analyst reports that "it is very difficult to describe a typical day because I still haven't had one. Every day [brings] something different. Basically, I am given pieces of projects to work on. This is meant to give me exposure to our clients and familiarize me with Excel, PowerPoint, our data collection, etc. It can be overwhelming at times." One custom data analyst reports, "Relatively quickly I started working directly with internal clients, from obtaining business requirements and translating them to delivering the project. I was pretty much on my own by the third month of my employment at comScore, but if I wanted, there were plenty of people to go [to] for help. It was up to me how much help I wanted to get." For technology specialists, "A typical day starts by fixing any errors that occurred over the previous night (the programs that a data stream engineer writes run each day, and they [have the potential to have] errors). After all errors are fixed, I work on coding more programs or researching the necessary information in order to code a new program. I also [assure the quality of] the data produced by the programs in order to ensure the program is working properly."

PEERS

First jobbers at comScore are "very happy about the work environment," which "surrounds them with young people who are, for the most part, really fun." One notes, "There is camaraderie [among] the new hires. We sit together in the same area throughout training and work on some assignments together." Another agrees, "I rave to my friends that I am so lucky because I get to work with so many cool people in such a relaxed, yet intellectual, environment." Workers note that "Monthly happy hours are held at the corporate headquarters, [and] everyone is encouraged to come and socialize with employees of all job levels. There is little distinction between 'newbies' and those employees who have been at the company for a while; everyone is part of the comScore family."

Moving On

Because comScore's formal entry-level program is only two years old, there isn't much data on former trainees who move on. The company held onto half its first-year program participants; at the time of our survey, all the second-year participants were still with comScore.

Attrition

According to the company, people who leave the entry-level program do so "to pursue other opportunities," "to work [directly] for clients," or "to attend graduate school." For some, the company is "not a good culture fit." One employee notes that some leave because they are unhappy with "the pay-to-work ratio." Such sentiment, however, "did not cause employees to work less or provide less than superior work."

Coro Fellows Program in Public Affairs
Fellow

The Big Picture

The Coro Fellows Program in Public Affairs is a full-time, graduate-level leadership development and civic engagement program. During the nine-month period of the program, fellows "develop an understanding of leadership and decision-making by working on challenging issues with the powerful individuals and institutions that influence our communities." Participants spend up to sixty hours per week in "a unique series of consultancy roles with various organizations representing government, business, nonprofit, labor, and political campaigns." The program also involves Focus Weeks in which fellows examine such topics as the media, health and the environment, education and information technology, economic development, and public finance. Through face-to-face meetings with decision makers in a variety of fields and guided discussions with one another, fellows work to refine their inquiry skills and gain a substantial understanding of the various issues affecting a city. One fellow writes, "I was impressed by the amount of hands-on experience I would be getting during the year. There was an academic component to it that attracted me, too, but it was rooted in experience. That's what sold me."

Stats

Location(s) Where Entry-level Employees Work

Fellows work in New York, New York; Los Angeles, California; Pittsburgh, Pennsylvania; San Francisco, California; and St. Louis, Missouri.

Average Number Hired Per Year

Coro selects about sixty-eight fellows each year.

Entry-level Position(s) Available

Members of this program are referred to as fellows.

Average Starting Salary

Coro's Fellows Program in Public Affairs "features both practical and academic value." Tuition is $3,500, but fees are "often waived, deferred, or reduced, and monthly stipends may be awarded based on demonstrated need."

Benefits Offered

Financial assistance and benefits vary from one center location to another. In addition, Coro is partners with select graduate programs at colleges and universities in the cities in which their centers exist; in such cases, Fellows may earn academic credit in some cases and be given preferred or automatic admission status for graduate school applications.

Outreach & Communications
Coro New York Leadership Center
42 Broadway, 18th Floor
New York, NY 10004
Tel: 212-248-2935, ext.242
www.coro.org

GETTING HIRED

Coro "seeks bright, self-motivated individuals committed to ethical, effective leadership and to strengthening democracy through civic involvement." These individuals typically demonstrate "evidence of leadership experience or leadership potential as well as a concern for the well-being of the community." Candidates may apply while completing undergraduate academic work or after graduation by submitting a formal application, academic transcripts, three required essays, and three letters of recommendation. One successful candidate writes, "The application has three difficult essays that force you to understand where you were, are, and will be. There are three references that are specific, too." Applications are used to screen final candidates, who are invited to a day-long Selection Day, which applicants call "the hardest part of the process."

MONEY AND PERKS

Coro fellows don't get paid; on the contrary, the program is supported by tuition, though it may be waived, reduced, or deferred in some cases. Financial assistance is available to help those with demonstrated need to cover their living expenses for the duration of the program. Fellows tell us that one of the best perks of the experience is "the level of interaction with high-level executives and officials [in the public service sector]. The national Coro network is highly esteemed." They also appreciate "the friendships made with other Coro fellows."

THE ROPES

Orientation procedures vary at different Coro centers. At some, orientation is "a week-long community immersion process spent with the rest of your fellows program cohorts. It included a pre-program interview, the purpose of which was to clarify my goals in the program and to clarify expectations, those that I had of Coro staff, my colleagues in the program, of myself, and those that Coro had of me." This orientation also includes classes on effective meeting facilitation, public speaking, effective communication, graphic recording, giving and receiving feedback. At other centers, orientation at Coro "is a bit jarring" because "you hit the ground running with a full-time project on your first day. You meet everyone, including the director, you introduce yourselves, and then you move as a group." It's "training by fire" that "really forces teams to build on other team members' strengths."

Day in the Life

"Dealing with the unknown is part of the pedagogy," writes a former fellow. Fellows need to be prepared to think on their feet. "There is nothing typical about any day in the Coro Fellows Program" because "over the course of nine months, a fellow works in very different organizations doing meaningful work that results in a final deliverable, all while being able to access high-level decision makers within the organization." One fellow explains: "Each month we are assigned to an organization. They give us a project with a deliverable, and we work on it from nine to five, and sometimes on weekends." The experience took a Pittsburgh fellow to all the following places: the city's Department of Planning, the office of an electoral judge, a Hispanic-language education center, a nonprofit, the state education association, a community project, and a for-profit biotech company. A former fellow reports, "As a Coro fellow, I had very important interactions with high-level people in all of the sectors that I worked within. Coro fellows conduct interviews with former governors, Supreme Court justices, heads of multinational corporations, and elected officials. In these interviews and interactions, we were able to ask thoughtful questions of these leaders."

Peers

Coro attracts unique candidates who are ambitious and eager to be involved in public affairs. They are exceptionally bright and extremely energetic; one writes, "My peers brought unique perspectives to the table and were able to teach me their talents." "I have life-long friends from my experiences." Fellows find both the time and inclination to share downtime with one another after work is done.

Moving on

Coro does not have a formal job placement service for fellows program graduates; once you complete the nine-month program, you're officially on your own. Informal resources (including "networking opportunities and potential mentors") abound, however, and prove highly valuable for many. Some fellows have even found work as a result of one of their field assignments. Others who choose to pursue graduate study may receive credits toward a degree for having completed Coro's Fellows Program.

DC TEACHING FELLOWS
Teacher

THE BIG PICTURE

Established in 2001, the DC Teaching Fellows (DCTF) program "recruits elementary to secondary teachers within the DC Public Schools. DCTF looks for candidates [in] a range of subject areas, including math, science, special education, English, and elementary education. Fellows will receive their Washington, DC teaching licensure while they teach in a high-need school within the district."

STATS

Location(s) Where Entry-level Employees Work

The teaching positions are in high-need Washington, DC public schools.

Average Number of Applications Each Year

The DCTF program receives 1,400 applications each year.

Average Number Hired Per Year

The program hires 100 teachers per year.

Entry-level Position(s) Available

Program hires become teachers.

Average Hours Worked Per Week

The DC Teaching Fellows program has a standard thirty-five-hour work week, "plus before- and after-school planning, organizing, and tutoring."

Percentage of Entry-level Hires Still with the Company After Three, Five, and Ten Years

More than 67 percent of entry-level hires remain with the DC Teaching Fellows program after three years; and about two-thirds stay beyond five years.

Average Starting Salary

"The starting salary for these teaching positions is the same as that for all other first-year teachers in the DC Public Schools system; a first-year teacher can expect to make $38,434 annually. Teachers with a master's degree related to their teaching assignment receive $40,966 in annual pay."

Benefits Offered

The DC Teaching Fellows program offers a choice of health insurance plans that include dental, prescription, and vision coverage. Additional benefits include a pension plan and 403(b) investment plan. Fellows are also "automatically enrolled in a rigorous six-week summer training institute," for which they "are paid a stipend for living expenses. Included in the training is a minimum four-week teaching practicum at a DCPS summer school. In their first year, fellows begin a course of study (one to two courses) for their district teaching licensure. There is a significant negotiated discount for fellows to attend one of two local universities. The district also gives the fellows a full-tuition reimbursement for two years of graduate coursework within their fields of study."

CONTACT INFORMATION

DC Teaching Fellows
825 North Capitol Street, NE
Human Resources, 6th Floor
Washington, DC 20002
Tel: 202-442-5022
Fax: 202-442-5027
E-mail: info@DCTeachingFellows.org
www.DCTeachingFellows.org

GETTING HIRED

DC Teaching Fellows does "limited campus recruiting in the tri-state area," but the program "does not actively recruit on college campuses." DC Teaching Fellows is, however, "very much interested in college graduates who want to enter the field of teaching." All candidates must "complete and submit an online application, [submit] a resume and personal statement, and provide the program office with copies of college transcripts. Applicants who submit a complete application will be notified of their application status within two weeks. If granted an interview, candidates will have the ability to select their interview date and time via an online scheduler." During the interview, applicants must teach a brief lesson and answer questions that are "mainly centered on how we would react to hypothetical situations in the classroom." Afterward, candidates are "notified of their status within a designated time frame. At that time, selected candidates will be given an enrollment package."

MONEY AND PERKS

All compensation issues—salary, pay, and benefits—"are governed by the collective bargaining agreement in place between the district and the teachers union. Teachers receive [increased] compensation for each interval of fifteen education credits received with the proper university documentation." Top perks include the tuition reimbursement program, which is "unique to teacher candidates recruited by DC Teaching Fellows. Fellows are reimbursed for two years of university coursework toward state licensure. In many cases, these two years of reimbursements will cover the entire cost of becoming a licensed teacher."

THE ROPES

Because DCTF "is a fast-track program into teaching," all fellows "participate in a six-week training institute that starts in late June." This training "consists of two parts: classroom observation and teaching in the mornings and sessions [that focus] on designing instruction [plans], teaching strategies, managing student behavior, and understanding the diversity and culture in your school." This training regimen "is very intense but rewarding. Fellows typically begin their days at 8:00 A.M. in a summer school classroom [and are] paired with another fellow under the guidance of an experienced DCPS teacher. After the day ends—typically at 5:00 P.M.—fellows attend university classes held at the summer institute site."

DAY IN THE LIFE

Daily life for a DC Teaching Fellow consists of fulfilling "the responsibilities of a classroom teacher." This involves teaching, planning lessons, grading student work, and sometimes attending staff meetings. The job is difficult and demanding, but fortunately support is available in a variety of forms. A program representative explains, "Throughout the summer training institute, we encourage the fellows to develop relationships with others in the program and to seek [one another] out for support, best practices, and insights over the course of the school year. Furthermore, the DC Teaching Fellows program staff employs a full-time professional development manager" who addresses "specific topics or the needs of fellows throughout the year [and makes] regular classroom visits. Additionally, fellows can contact the program office at any time for help with teaching or logistical issues."

PEERS

Fellows in the DCTF program tell us that their peers are "smart and cool." There isn't much socializing after the bell rings; most teachers have too many other responsibilities (family, certification training, grading, lesson plans) to enjoy a booming extracurricular social life.

MOVING ON

DCTF reports that "fellows [who leave the program] largely stay within the field of teaching and education. They may become department and school leaders, seek out additional roles and responsibilities within their schools and the district, and may even apply to be school principals." The program has only been in existence since 2001, so information in this area is limited.

ATTRITION

DCTF loses about 10 percent of its first-job hires each year, most often because of "personal reasons" and "the challenges of their school placements."

BEST AND WORST

The most successful first-year fellow was a woman who "rationally and realistically faced every challenge she encountered as a secondary math teacher. After leaving a lucrative career in technology, she transferred her dedication and commitment to the students in her math classes. She was a diligent and creative lesson planner; she went above and beyond to foster positive relationships with her students; and she made significant efforts to involve parents in their children's education. [Her] most admirable traits were a mix of achievement and personal responsibility [that] she internalized and transferred to her students. She was and still is committed and dedicated to her students' achievement and personal growth."

Among the least successful was a teacher who "did not demonstrate flexibility or a realistic vision of teaching in a difficult school. Focusing on her students' achievement became secondary to classroom behavior, administrative problems, and parental struggles. In a nutshell, this teacher did not embody any [positivism] toward her students or her school."

DELOITTE TOUCHE TOMAHTSU
Various Positions

THE BIG PICTURE

Enter the expanding universe of professional services and advice at Deloitte Touche Tomahtsu, a firm that serves more than half the world's largest companies. Deloitte's services include everything from assurance to enterprise risk services to management solutions to tax services. Does this sound intriguing? Then maybe you're perfect for one of the nearly 2,000 entry-level jobs that open at Deloitte each year.

STATS

LOCATION(S) WHERE ENTRY-LEVEL EMPLOYEES WORK

"Deloitte hires entry-level candidates in nearly all of our eighty U.S. offices."

AVERAGE NUMBER OF APPLICATIONS EACH YEAR

"We review more than 10,000 resumes [and] applications each year."

AVERAGE NUMBER HIRED PER YEAR OVER THE LAST TEN YEARS

Deloitte hires 1,900 people per year.

ENTRY-LEVEL POSITION(S) AVAILABLE

"We hire a range of entry-level candidates [who have majored in] accounting, finance, information systems, computer science, business, marketing, economics, and others areas."

AVERAGE STARTING SALARY

Employees earn from $45,000–$50,000, depending on the market.

BENEFITS OFFERED

Deloitte offers a comprehensive medical benefits plan for employees, their families, and domestic partners and includes a prescription drug plan, dental plan, and discount vision care. Additional benefits include a 401(k) plan, a flexible spending plan, a pre-tax transportation program, various forms of flexible work arrangements, parental leave, adoption assistance, adoption reimbursement, a child care resource and referral program, an elder care consultation and referral service, a mortgage assistance program, and paid time off programs.

CONTACT INFORMATION

"Students can either visit us on the Web (www.deloitte.com) and apply online or apply through their campus career centers."

GETTING HIRED

Deloitte seeks candidates "who can provide evidence of excellent client-service skills; marketing, sales, and communication skills; management effectiveness (time management, project management, and people management); and leadership skills (team playing and driving results)." If that describes you, apply through your campus career center or online. "All resumes and applications are reviewed and selected for interview," firm representatives tell us. They use "a structured, behaviorally-based interview to hear real experiences that provide evidence of the skills/attributes that [they're] interviewing for." One successful hire in tax services describes the application process this way: "On my resume, I focused on experiences and knowledge that were specifically related to the job I was applying for. I was very truthful and genuine in my cover letter. I had a total of five interviews, and they were with partners and senior managers during first and second rounds. The tone of the interview depended on who I was interviewing with. They were all very friendly and asked questions to get to know who I was and why I wanted to be at the firm."

MONEY AND PERKS

Newcomers to Deloitte tell us that "the start date is definitely negotiable, and the office where you work is also, to some extent, but that typically requires another interview in that office." As for salary, everyone we spoke with agrees with the first jobber who states, "I do not think that if I asked for more, I would have gotten it." Company representatives note that "salary increases are based on performance, business growth, and marketplace." Full-time workers "generally start in August, September, and January." Most of our respondents say the best perks are "the great people who you work with" and "being able to work [with] so many clients from so many different industries."

THE ROPES

A first jobber in tax services tells us that orientation at Deloitte "lasts, on the whole, about two weeks. We had one-day new-hire orientation that covered benefits, a general overview of the firm, different support functions, etc. Then we went to a national training for four days. Although it was technically training, the new hires and I were all so new it was like an orientation into the firm as well as tax training. When we got back into the office, we had a week-long new-hire training that focused on more technical tax training as well as software training." Once orientation and initial training is done, newbies "are assigned 'buddies,' 'counselors,' and 'mentors.' These individuals are generally selected and developed for their roles—often based on their team-working skills and their involvement in recruiting generally. We consider the involvement of our client-service professionals as personal and professional development."

DAY IN THE LIFE

After orientation and initial training, "New hires commence working on teams dealing directly with clients" at Deloitte, and "they fulfill these responsibilities through a fairly structured team-support approach." One entry-level worker explains, "A typical day involves coming in and checking our e-mails, then we start on our work. Sometimes we work on more than one project, so we have to balance our workload. The day involves our preparing the work papers and then getting them reviewed by our seniors. During this whole process there is also a lot of communication between the staff and the senior staff." Adds another, "My responsibilities [from day one] were to have a good attitude, learn from every engagement I was assigned to, and ask questions. A lot of this job is on-site, learn-as-you-go training." There's rarely down time; one newbie tells us, "I am almost never bored. When I am at work, I am always thinking and keeping myself busy, and the time flies by. Sometimes the amount of work can be a little overwhelming, but that makes the time go by faster."

PEERS

There are many first jobbers; therefore, new hires describe an atmosphere that is "like a college class. We have a great camaraderie. We usually go out together for a while at least every Friday, and more often than not, we get together for something on the weekends." One worker says, "[Other new hires are] smart, nice, and hardworking. We also share a lot of similarities because I feel that every company has its own culture of people, and all of us were hired by Deloitte." Those in accounting tell us that they enjoy their peers' support and help in preparing for the CPA exam.

MOVING ON

Many entry-level employees come to Deloitte in the hopes of building a career. Those who use it as a way station often go on to business school, capitalizing on their experiences to build a more compelling business school application. Others "wind up working with clients they met through their work engagements; so in a sense, they continue to work with Deloitte."

ATTRITION

According to Deloitte representatives, "there's no overarching reason that stands out" for why some entry-level hires don't stick around long, "but generally when a person leaves that early in the process, it's because of a disparity between the job responsibilities and the person's goals or expectations." Some new hires, we're told, simply can't take the long hours required of them. "It isn't for everyone," concedes one audit associate.

DEMOCRATIC NATIONAL COMMITTEE
Various Positions

THE BIG PICTURE

The Democratic National Committee (DNC) coordinates the political party's presidential nominating convention; supports Democratic candidates for public office at the national, state, and local levels; and publicizes and promotes the positions of the Democratic party as a whole. Working here is a great way to break into politics and provides an equally stellar opportunity to move to Washington, DC, a fun town and a good place to start a career.

STATS

LOCATION(S) WHERE ENTRY-LEVEL EMPLOYEES WORK

First jobbers work in Washington, DC.

AVERAGE NUMBER OF APPLICATIONS EACH YEAR

The DNC receives 100 applications per year.

ENTRY-LEVEL POSITION(S) AVAILABLE

Entry-level hires work as administrative assistants to directors and offer administrative support.

AVERAGE HOURS WORKED PER WEEK

New hires work fifty hours per week.

PERCENTAGE OF ENTRY-LEVEL HIRES STILL WITH THE COMPANY AFTER THREE, FIVE, AND TEN YEARS

After three years, 5 percent of new hires remain with the DNC.

AVERAGE STARTING SALARY

New hires earn $30,000 per year.

BENEFITS OFFERED

The DNC offers its employees major medical, dental, and vision insurance. Additional benefits include life insurance, short-term disability, supplemental medical insurance, a 401(k) plan, and flexible spending accounts.

CONTACT INFORMATION

Democratic National Committee
430 S. Capitol Street, SE
Washington, DC 20003
Tel: 202-863-8000
E-mail: Jewelle Hazel, Director of Human Resources, hazelj@dnc.org
www.dnc.org

Getting Hired

The DNC lists job openings on its website; internships, first jobbers tell us, provide an excellent gateway to subsequent employment. (According to DNC representatives, "Most of our entry-level hiring is done by word-of-mouth. We also hire prior DNC interns and people who have prior campaign experience.") Because interns are already known by human resources and other staffers, they usually avoid a prolonged vetting process (including resumes, letters of recommendation, etc.). All other applicants, however, must take the conventional route. Here's how one applicant describes it: "I sent my resume via e-mail, actually for another position at the DNC. However, my resume was noted and sent to the director of the Women's Vote Center, where I was eventually hired. When I heard that my resume was drawn from a pool of other resumes, it appeared that the DNC internally communicated; this impressed me. Since I was in Texas at the time, I interviewed via teleconference with the director. The questions were both [general] and specific, ranging from, 'Why do you want to work with the DNC Women's Vote Center?' to specific questions about my previous work experience." "Individuals who are [good at multitasking] and who are quick and creative thinkers are DNC material."

Money and Perks

The primary objective of most first jobbers is to acquire experience and gain a foothold in democratic politics; accordingly, few people worry much about their starting salaries. "I didn't try to negotiate. I was perfectly happy with the start date and salary," writes one first jobber in the research department. One employee says, "The health benefits [we] receive [are] unbelievable. I am covered so completely that I have nothing to worry about." Other excellent perks include "working at the pulse of the DNC, so you get to interact with the entire staff. It's also a great way to make connections."

The Ropes

When candidates accept an offer, "a human resources package is mailed to them at least one week before the start date. This package includes their confirmation letter, benefits, and personnel information. On the first day a welcome package is awaiting the new employee, which includes information technology information, basic DNC information and policies, information on public transportation, and places to eat. Department directors conduct specific department orientation on the first day. Each department's orientation is different and based on how the department works. A human resources orientation is scheduled for several days after." While most DNC employees receive some formal training during their tenure, it is primarily "a learn-as-you go process. As I was working and questions arose, I asked them and had them answered by my colleagues."

Day in the Life

The first jobbers we spoke with at the DNC work on a wide range of assignments; for example, some assist senior strategists and organizers, others supervise and coordinate events for interns, and others perform basic clerical and administrative tasks. What all of them share in common is that they're very busy;

one explains, "There is always something to do in our office. I always have a lot of work and long-term projects. While anyone can get bored during office work, I know that I have things I can be doing. If I find myself either overwhelmed or bored, a quick Internet read, such as a newspaper clips, can help with that. It's about pacing your day and allowing yourself to merge into the day and your work." They also get to mix and mingle with party bigwigs. As one newbie tells us, "Even as an intern, I was given the opportunity by my boss and other high-level people to sit in on meetings. I have the opportunity to work directly with them on a regular basis, depending on what we are working on and what kind of meeting is being held."

PEERS

DNC staffers tell us that their peers "are extremely friendly. We often hang out at happy hours and events, and we have other outside contact. Sometimes it is just our department, and other times it's the entire staff." One first jobber notes, "One thing unites all of us, even if our personalities differ: [for example,] all of us [were] determined to win back the White House in 2004. From there, great, and even unexpected, relationships can form." The ubiquity of "mostly young, diverse individuals" on the staff means first jobbers have "people with whom one can talk with if [they feel] overwhelmed."

MOVING ON

"Since we are a campaign headquarters and a fundraising operation, employment with the DNC is very cyclical," officials tell us. "Most people move on after a particular campaign cycle to work for either candidates who have won a particular campaign or to work for other democratic organizations or nonprofit organizations to expand their campaign portfolio." Some leave to go back to school. The average tenure of a DNC first jobber is two years.

ATTRITION

Turnover rates are high at the DNC; approximately 50 percent of employees leave within a year of starting. Most people find work with an elected official or another political organization.

DOMINO'S PIZZA
People Pipeline Program

THE BIG PICTURE
The "People Pipeline," Domino's leadership training program, is "a cross-functional rotational program through three core assignments (store operations, distribution, and franchise services)" that is "designed to foster ongoing learning and development and prepare participants for future leadership positions within the company."

STATS

LOCATION(S) WHERE ENTRY-LEVEL EMPLOYEES WORK
HR officials note that "we have opportunities nationwide, but most are concentrated in Ann Arbor, MI."

AVERAGE NUMBER OF APPLICATIONS EACH YEAR
Domino's receives 400–500 applications each year; of those, fifteen applicants are invited to complete the extensive application process.

AVERAGE NUMBER HIRED PER YEAR
At present, Domino's hires three entry-level employees each year; however, the company hopes to expand the program in coming years.

ENTRY-LEVEL POSITION(S) AVAILABLE
Entry-level hires participate in the People Pipeline Program for leadership development.

AVERAGE HOURS WORKED PER WEEK
Entry-level employees work 40–50 hours per week.

AVERAGE STARTING SALARY
Employees receive starting salaries of $30,000 to $45,000, plus bonuses.

BENEFITS OFFERED
"On the first of the month following three months of service, team members are eligible for...medical, dental, and vision" coverage, for which "a small biweekly premium [is] paid by [the] team members [themselves]."

Additional benefits include generous short-term disability coverage; healthcare flex spending accounts; dependent-care flex spending accounts; stock option awards; 401(k) plan; adoption assistance; paid time off; and bereavement leave.

CONTACT INFORMATION
"Interested parties should visit our website at www.dominos.com to check for employment opportunities."

GETTING HIRED

People Pipeline is an elite leadership training program, and the selection process is commensurately rigorous. The application starts when the applicant submits a resume. Human Resources contacts likely candidates for an initial interview, and those "who demonstrate they have the competence needed to do the job based on their answers to the interview questions... are asked to submit a formal application and complete an essay. Next, candidates interview with an advisory team . . . of senior team members from across the organization. At this point, all candidates' references and backgrounds are checked prior to completing the application process, which involves an interview with a group of executive vice presidents and concludes with the offer of employment." Explains one applicant who survived the ordeal, " The interview and application process was unlike any other company's. The interviews consisted of one-on-one interviews with the Leadership Team of Domino's Pizza (the executive vice presidents) and then a formal PowerPoint Presentation to the Leadership Team. Once you are successful in those steps, you move on to an interview with the CEO. It was a challenging process, but it reaffirmed the fact that Domino's would be willing to invest a lot of time and effort into my development process." The entire process, from initial contact to job offer, can take up to four months.

MONEY AND PERKS

Because People Pipeline fast-tracks participants up the corporate ladder, starting salary is not a matter of primary concern for most in the program. Even so, most find their pay more than adequate. Observes one Pipeliner, "Monetarily, the little extras like paid travel to each city we move to, paid housing in each city we are in (paid utilities, rent, etc.) are perks of this position. With no expenses going out, I basically put my entire paycheck in the bank every time!" Others tout the Team Achievement Dividend, which "rewards every team member for reaching our annual EBITDA target. As you know, EBITDA is an excellent measure of the profitability of a company and its controllable expenses. This bonus program has a 10-to-1 leverage element for exceeding the company's EBITDA target. This means that if we hit 101 percent of our annual EBITDA target, we get 110 percent of our annual bonus. We've never missed our target since the plan's inception, and have exceeded the goal every year but one." The job offers other perks, including "Domino's Days (extra days around each holiday which extend a three-day weekend to four days), and the holiday party, at which we receive huge picnic baskets filled with holiday-themed plate and silverware sets, baking goods, coupons, toys, and so much stuff."

THE ROPES

All new hires at Domino's corporate headquarters start their tenure with the STAR Welcome program, "a day-long orientation in which we review various aspects of the company culture, review our benefit programs, go on a building tour and to meet key people from various departments, and learn how to make pizza in the test kitchen." The rest of the first week is spent at Pizza Prep School, "a four-day, 42-hour intense training program during which Domino's office members don uniforms, split into four-person teams, and immerse themselves into every detail of store culture. Team members learn about store operations and procedures during morning classroom sessions and work in the pizza theater in the afternoon to learn order taking, pizza making, oven tending, pizza routing, and store closing procedures. The training culminates with a written exam and a timed pizza-making test. Team members then have the opportunity to put their knowledge into action as they work a Friday night dinner rush in a store." Training continues throughout the People Pipeline program; notes one Pipeliner, "At the beginning of each assignment, there has been specific training and orientation provided by team leaders. There are also online training courses that we are responsible for taking."

Day in the Life

Domino's reports that "Leadership Development Associates are integrated into new positions in a series of rotational assignments.... Typical position assignments are approximately six months in duration. The associate will complete four to five various position assignments while in the Leadership Development Program. . . . In addition to completing assignments, the associate is also provided with leadership and organizational training defined in a customized plan known as a learning map. Mentors are assigned to aid in the development of the associate. . . . Each Leadership Development associate graduates from the program once he or she has successfully completed all assignments and courses identified in the learning map, over [the course of] approximately 24 to 36 months." Writes one Pipeliner, "With each rotation I complete, I am given more responsibility, larger-impact projects, and more visibility in the organization. The contact with management is great. We present case studies to the Leadership Team, and they present synopses of their duties and departments to us. We also have outings with the Leadership Team, [among which was] a recent golf tournament at the CEO's country club."

Peers

The People Pipeline is a very small program (it had seven participants total as of this writing), and its rotational nature means that participants are not always in the same location. Occasionally there are opportunities for them to get to know one another; reports one, "A few of us have the chance to room together during some rotations, and we became really close. It was helpful moving to a new city with other people you know and being able to share our experiences with each other." Notes another, "Twice a year the seven of us in the program get together for a week-long training/team-building session." Pipeliners can make friends with other Domino's first jobbers, of course, "but this requires initiative on your part. There isn't a huge after-hours social scene; I would say that I probably go out for drinks or dinner with people from work approximately once a month."

Moving on

Graduate school and other career opportunities are the main reasons young workers leave the Domino's fold of their own accord.

ATTRITION

The company reports: "Domino's has worked tirelessly to provide a development program for recent graduates that [offers] both the training and support needed to be successful. We are proud that not a single person who has entered the Leadership Development program has left without successfully completing it." The program had been in operation for 18 months when we spoke with Domino's representatives.

BEST AND WORST

According to HR officials, the best entry-level hire fit this description: "Among all the exceptional people who work here, M. H. has been incredibly successful. Starting as an intern in 1988, M. H. established himself as a winner. Upon graduating from college, he came back to work full time as a Corporate Controller and worked his way up to VP of Financial Analysis.... When asked why he has been so successful at Domino's, M. H. answers modestly that he enjoys the work and the people."

DYNETECH
Event Planner and On-Site Coordinator

THE BIG PICTURE

Think of Dynetech as an "instant company"-maker. Say you have a great new product that you've been toting all over the country to sell at trade shows. Your overhead is high; your ability to reach potential customers is limited; and as a result, the growth of your business is constrained. That's where Dynetech comes in. The firm partners with its clients to provide consulting services, media and marketing strategies, software support, a direct-to-market sales campaign, and a number of other, similar services. Dynetech, in short, becomes the fully-staffed support company that clients need to spur "dynamic growth" in their businesses. First jobbers here assist clients by helping to plan training and sales events and then managing those events to make sure they run smoothly and successfully.

STATS

LOCATION(S) WHERE DYNETECH HIRES ENTRY-LEVEL WORK

Entry-level employees work in Orlando, FL.

AVERAGE NUMBER OF APPLICATIONS EACH YEAR

Dynetech receives 80 applications each year.

AVERAGE NUMBER HIRED PER YEAR

Dynetech hires six entry-level employees each year.

ENTRY-LEVEL POSITION(S) AVAILABLE

Entry-level employees work as event planners and on-site coordinators.

AVERAGE HOURS WORKED PER WEEK

Entry-level employees work 40 hours per week.

AVERAGE STARTING SALARY

Salary depends on the position for which the recent grad is applying, his or her major at school, as well as participation in extracurricular activities, internships, part-time jobs, GPA, and other such factors.

BENEFITS OFFERED

Dynetech offers employer-paid medical and dental insurance. Other benefits include life insurance, a prescription plan, short- and long-term disability, and a company-matched 401(k) plan, which is fully vested after five years.

CONTACT INFORMATION

Organizational Development

255 South Orange Avenue, Suite 600

Orlando, FL, 32812

E-mail: hr@dynetech.com.

Fax: 407-206-6565

GETTING HIRED

Dynetech seeks hires who demonstrate "'Shine Values,' which are: Accountability, Flexibility, Entrepreneurialism, Integrity, Excellence, and Open Communication." The firm recruits at numerous local school-based job fairs, especially in the central Florida region. The firm also posts job openings on its website. According to company officials, "The first step of the application process is for the Organizational Development Department to review resumes. After reviewing the resumes, the Organizational Development Department will select which applicants warrant an in-person interview and, if needed, pre-employment testing. The first interview is with Organizational Development, the second…with the hiring supervisor/manager, the third…with the Director, and the fourth…with the Vice President." Interview questions "are tailored to the applicant." The firm advises that "applicants should research the company ahead of time on the internet" and "come prepared…with a portfolio with examples of their work (even if it's related school projects), letters of recommendation, etc. This demonstrates that the applicant is prepared and takes initiative. Also, during the interview, applicants should take their time, listen to the question, think about the question, and provide an articulate response with examples. Often, applicants are so nervous and want to tell you everything about themselves that they either just blurt out any response, or go off on a wild tangent without even answering the question. Silence during interviews is okay. It means that the applicant is actually thinking."

MONEY AND PERKS

For many first-jobbers at Dynetech, starting salary is not negotiable. Employees note that "start date can be flexible, though." First jobbers we spoke with, however, reported satisfaction with the initial offer and did not try to negotiate a better deal. Raises "are given during annual reviews, which are completely performance-driven. Dynetech also offers promotional opportunities to Associates. It's possible that an Associate would receive a promotion during the year, at which point his/her salary would be readjusted to reflect the responsibilities of the new position."

Most beloved perks include the "great insurance program," "all the training opportunities," and a generous vacation plan. Writes one first jobber, "We get two weeks vacation [after one year of employment; newbies get one week], four paid personal days, and our birthday off. We also benefit from nine additional paid vacation days." Also, on-site coordinators collect their own frequent flier miles, "a great benefit considering how extensively they travel."

Dynetech also offers a myriad of training programs designed to facilitate personal and professional development among associates. Training programs include Management Training, Business Communication, and Associate Mentorship Certification.

Other perks of working at Dynetech include free parking ("a great perk when working in a major downtown area"), organized athletic teams, planned recreation with family participation, and workout facilities.

The Ropes

Employment at Dynetech starts with a week-long orientation; reports one first jobber, "The orientation includes getting assigned a mentor and a lunch date with your mentor as well as your boss." It also includes an introduction to Dynetech's "visions, goals, and values" as well as its "processes, procedures, products, and service lines." Toward the end of the week, new hires receive "departmental training with their manager and colleagues. Departmental training is unique to each department and is tailored to each position. Finally on Friday afternoon, new hires participate in the orientation wrap-up with the Training and Development department." Subsequent training is ongoing—"from the minute you report to work the first day until the present day. We learned about everything and everyone," writes one event planner.

Day in the Life

Recent college graduates often enter Dynetech as event planners or as on-site coordinators. The former are "in charge of planning each day of an event. . . . event planners are assigned by DMA (Designated Market Area) and are responsible for researching the event city's demographics. . . . Once the research of the city is completed, contact is made to the best and most appropriate locations in which to hold the events that correspond with the demographic research the event planner has put together. Mostly hotel space is contracted, but depending on the event, other locations, such as convention centers or large meeting spaces, could be used." According to one employee, "Event planners embody the following characteristics: they are extremely organized and detail-oriented, they have the ability to work in a constantly changing environment, and they are flexible when changes and/or challenges occur. They also have the ability to be extremely effective team players." Observes an event planner, "I normally have two or three campaigns that I am working on at a time." Once the event is planned, the on-site coordinator takes over. He or she attends the event and is "responsible for its successful execution"; this entails handling everything from corporate credit card authorizations to troubleshooting for clients and customers.

Peers

"There are a lot of younger people" at Dynetech," and so it's relatively easy for new hires to find friends and join a social scene. Writes one first jobber, "I've come to really appreciate the camaraderie and friendship I have here at Dynetech. This place is like my extended family." Explains another newbie, "Every Friday, there is a happy hour crew heading out to the local bars, clubs, and restaurants. This is a company where we eat lunch together almost every day. We have parties and get-togethers on the weekends; we have a running program; we do charity drives together. . . . We're a pretty tight-knit group here with a lot of big ideas."

MOVING ON

On-site coordinators are most likely to leave Dynetech, we're told, because "they don't want to travel anymore and they are not interested in a position in the office." Event planners typically move on "when they want to plan larger-scale events and conferences" beyond what Dynetech offers.

ATTRITION

Our contact in Dynetech Organizational Development reports that the "turnover rate is very low. It is rare that a recent graduate comes on board and leaves during the first year. Out of all the recent grads we've hired, I can only recall one person who left Dynetech during their first year." Our contact also notes that "Dynetech has hired most of its associates (both experienced and entry-level) since 2001, so the average tenure company-wide is approximately three to four years (but this is only because we've grown from fifty Associates to more than 500 associates during this time)."

There are several associates who have enjoyed careers of twenty-plus years at Dynetech. They started with Dynetech in the early phases of its existence and have since been promoted to senior-level managers, directors, and vice presidents. HR officials note that there are many career advancement opportunities at Dynetech for those "who wish to apply themselves."

EDWARD JONES

Various Positions

THE BIG PICTURE

Repeatedly named in *Fortune* magazine's "100 Best Companies to Work For," Edward Jones is one of those rare companies that continued to grow rapidly during the recession. Edward Jones was also ranked number one in *SmartMoney*'s annual full-service broker survey. It isn't just the growth-related job security that employees love, though; the *Fortune* ranking reflects worker satisfaction on a whole range of quality-of-life issues, including benefits, workplace culture, and advancement opportunities. Many new hires start in a rotational program—ideal for those who know they want a career in the world of finance but aren't sure what area best suits them.

STATS

LOCATION(S) WHERE ENTRY-LEVEL EMPLOYEES WORK

"Edward Jones is headquartered in St. Louis, Missouri; home offices [are] in Tempe, Arizona; Toronto headquarters [are] in Mississagua, Ontario; and United Kingdom headquarters [are] in Canary Wharf, UK; and [there are more than] 9,000 one-broker branch offices across the country, as well as [in] Canada and the United Kingdom."

ENTRY-LEVEL POSITION(S) AVAILABLE

New hires may work as investment representatives or hold positions in accounting, compliance and licensing, human resources, information systems, marketing, operations, products and sales, research, and training at a headquarters location.

AVERAGE HOURS WORKED PER WEEK

Employees work forty or more hours per week.

BENEFITS OFFERED

Benefits vary according to the position.

CONTACT INFORMATION

Visit the website at www.edwardjonesopportunity.com/usa_home.html.

GETTING HIRED

Many first jobbers get their start at Edward Jones through the rotational development program, "a year-long rotational program through four different product and marketing areas of the firm. During the course of the year, [employees] were also required to become Series 7 licensed (Series 7 is an exam that qualifies an idividual to trade in corporate securities). The program has recently changed to include areas beyond product and marketing." Many new hires find their way into the rotational program through internships they held while they were still in college; "the internships helped me get the initial interview," explains one trainee. The interview process, a first jobber reports, "is pretty unique. They have a three-interview minimum. The first one is just a sit-down, face-to-face interview; nothing complex. Then they do a phone interview/personality profile. What I liked was they knew what they were looking for, and I was able to answer the questions [honestly]. They were asking about my childhood, how I looked at things, that sort of thing. After that, if they think you're a good match, they extend an offer for a final interview."

MONEY AND PERKS

As far as working in the company's rotational program goes, one new hire says, "The salary is pretty much set. They were willing to negotiate the start date; they were really willing to work with me on that. [Rotations] were set when I got hired. However, I was told by my department leaders I would do better somewhere else and was able to move. A lot of people don't end up where they originally thought they would. The program is flexible in that way." Outside the rotational program, according to company representatives, hard-working, first-year investment representatives "can net an average income of $55,000." Since that takes long hours and above average work, "the firm has developed a unique 'first year' compensation package: regular paychecks during training, salary support during the first twelve-selling months, and bonuses." First jobbers love "the fact that there's a lot of flexibility. If you need to go to an appointment, you just tell your leader. If [you] need to get something done, it's not like they're going to make you take away from vacation time or sick days." They also "like that it's a very big local company. Somewhere down the line, if [you] want to expand [your] horizons, [the company has] campuses in St. Louis, Tempe, Toronto, and London."

THE ROPES

"Edward Jones does a terrific job with orientation," writes one first jobber who adds, "We had a week-long orientation in which they told us about the culture of the firm. We learned about the history of the firm, where they come from, what they do. Orientation sucks at most places, but everybody in the room was like 'This is great. There's a great corporate culture here.'" For noninvestment representative positions, following orientation, "You go to the main campus where you start your job. You're told ahead of time who and where, so you know where to go. I sat down with my department leader, and she told me what was in store for me. Being part of the rotational program, I was encouraged to visit other departments." Ongoing training is a major component of the rotational program. Another first jobber explains, "I still get [trained] to this day, long after I started. During each of the three-month rotations, my first year I worked very closely with one or two associates in the department I was in and was trained by them. I also attended training sessions both internally and externally, ranging from diversity training to Web-content workshops. There are also a plethora of learning courses to sign up for on the learning site of our Intranet. They offer both independent study and class courses on the applications and software, presentation skills, leadership courses, etc."

DAY IN THE LIFE

According to one trainee, most first jobbers' daily tasks "really depend on the department. You come in at the assigned time, maybe seven or eight. If I had a meeting, I'd go to that. If not, I'd work on old projects, try to get information on upcoming projects, and have meetings with other associates in the department to get ideas [from] them." Another trainee agrees, "My responsibilities changed, of course, with each rotation. Although looking back on it, I had some pretty important responsibilities for an entry-level training position. My responsibilities included working on ideas for a redesign of the public website entry page, designing fliers and posters, creating Web pages, designing and implementing contests for the branches, setting up a Trade Show Booth program for our branches, designing the trade show booths, and many more projects. I don't really have an example of a typical day because each and every day is different." One new hire warns that "when you start a new rotation, it sometimes takes awhile to get going, and you can get a little bored, but from then on, you stay busy. I always have something exciting going on. I have felt overwhelmed a few times, but everything always works out great in the end."

PEERS

First jobbers at Edward Jones "see one another a lot, especially with rotational associates, which is the number-one entry-level position." The company provides plenty of opportunities to socialize; one associate explains, "What's good about being a big company is they have tickets to every sporting event, every concert, any outing you want. We do an annual Founders' Day; we have baseball and softball tournaments. Our division took us to the Cardinals game. It's definitely a fun atmosphere." Another associate adds, "During our rotations, [all of us] had to work in groups on a competitive-strategies project together and present it to management. That was work, but a good experience to work with others." Associates usually remain close with their work group for the first year: "After a year, you're placed in your own department, and you've moved on to your other 'real' job, and you're kind of wanting to work as hard as you can to be beneficial to your department."

MOVING ON

Edward Jones is a great place to start a career, but it's not for everyone. One trainee writes, "It's just not a good fit for some. Maybe the rotations aren't what [some] thought they'd be. Maybe they thought they'd be earning more than they get here." People we spoke with agree that "there are more positives than negatives," but also explain that "sometimes people just don't like their actual job duties. It may not be what they really wanted to do or may not be related to what they studied in school, but it's the job they were offered." Some are turned off by the fact that "it's very challenging. If you're a slacker, it's not going to work for you. Also, it's a very conservative atmosphere. [People] wear suits every day. It's very structured." Some people who leave return to school for an MBA; others seek opportunities elsewhere in the world of banking and finance.

ELECTRONIC ARTS (EA)
Various Positions

THE BIG PICTURE

For many, it's a dream come true: a job that pays you to develop and test games for PCs, PlayStation, Xbox, and Nintendo. Electronic Arts (EA) is a major producer of sports games, role-playing games, war games, driving and flight simulators, and all other manner of blissful diversions. It's kind of like the way you spent your free time in college, except that EA pays you for it.

STATS

LOCATION(S) WHERE ENTRY-LEVEL EMPOYEES WORK

EA has locations in Redwood City, California; Los Angeles, California; Orlando, Florida; Chicago, Illinois; Vancouver, Canada; Burnaby, Canada; Montreal, Canada.

AVERAGE NUMBER OF APPLICATIONS EACH YEAR

Approximately 82,000 applications are submitted to EA every year.

AVERAGE NUMBER HIRED PER YEAR OVER THE LAST TEN YEARS

EA has hired approximately 2,100 people per year over the last ten years.

ENTRY-LEVEL POSITIONS AVAILABLE

New hires work as software engineers, technical artists, computer graphic artists, production assistants, marketing assistants, and financial analysts.

AVERAGE STARTING SALARY

"EA offers a competitive total compensation package." This includes base pay, a performance bonus, stock options, and the benefits outlined below.

BENEFITS OFFERED

"EA offers a choice of two medical programs through United Healthcare. One is a PPO, and the other is an EPO." For California employees, an "HMO is also available through Kaiser Permanente." Additional benefits include a 401(k) plan with matching program, an employee stock purchase plan, $100 toward a game console, and ten "EA points" per year for use toward games.

CONTACT INFORMATION

An HR official writes, "Please visit our website at http://jobs.ea.com to register on our EA Recruiter system."

Getting Hired

EA posts available positions on their website, at which "an applicant can complete a profile and electronically attach a resume. The EA Recruiter system will automatically notify each applicant of an opening that matches his or her skill sets and interests via e-mail." The company visits "several campuses during the fall and spring seasons" (to find out which ones, visit the website). Many first jobbers we spoke with begin their tenure with the company as interns; internship opportunities are also posted on www.jobs.ea.com. One former intern reports, "I was not interviewed for my full-time position, but when applying, I attached screenshots of my personal projects, and I believe this helped set me apart from the rest of the applicants."

Money and Perks

Entry-level workers at EA warn that little is negotiable in the job offer: "The position is quite popular given the number of gamers out there, so [the company] can be picky," explains one first jobber. Most newbies report that the "start date was flexible and accommodative," but that other aspects of the job were not. Key perks include "working in a field that is very much 'now' and the center of attention. [Getting] this kind of experience right out of school seemed almost impossible." Employees also enjoy "game rooms on-site to play the latest games, $100 toward the purchase of a gaming console, world-class facilities (state-of-the-art gym, cafeteria, indoor basketball court, sand volleyball courts, etc.), and free games!"

Other perks include an education reimbursement program (for which "regular full-time employees can receive up to $5,000 per year for education directly related to their position or career path") and invitations to special events ("such as private screenings of *Harry Potter*, *James Bond*, and *The Lord of the Rings* movies prior to general public viewing").

The Ropes

Orientation at EA takes a half day and includes "completing the required paperwork [as well as getting] information on benefits, corporate culture, ergonomic equipment available, travel, and events." Subsequent training depends on the position. Newbies inform us that "Electronic Arts offers a variety of courses in all areas of game production. These are open to all employees." A designer we spoke with, for example, explains that he had "attended a couple of seminars/conferences. They were all related to design. One was a seminar on interface, and another was on Flash." A 3-D production artist reports, "I'd learned 3-D fundamentals from school, but most of what I do at work I learned during my Electronic Arts internship. Training was a steep and hectic process, but I'm really glad I came through." HR notes that "by offering training, the company not only ensures that employees are keeping abreast of the latest technologies and principles, but that they are also participating in education that will lead to their own personal development."

DAY IN THE LIFE

There's much more to creating and selling games than you may imagine, and there are a myriad of tasks for first jobbers to perform at EA. One software engineer tells us that her typical day consists of "working with the game designers to figure out how they want the enemies to act, then working out how to implement that, and finally working with the artists to get any new animations that this behavior may require." An artist on the production team often spends the day "modeling props and environments for the game. I receive my task(s) in the morning, complete the task(s) by the afternoon, and receive critiques from [an] art director, then refine the model based on the feedback. Sometimes certain tasks may take up to three to four days." Other positions at EA may require an employee to "resolve player disputes, take report information about hacked accounts, report bugs, fix bugs that affect the general player base that are easily resolvable, action customers that use harassing language, fix doors; if they did not have us, the game world would be anarchy." No matter what the task, new hires are "expected to strive for the goals that their supervisor has set for them and learn as much about the project and skill sets needed for the task they are working on."

PEERS

"Most people here are really smart and cool," say EA entry-level employees. "We also play a lot of video games!" One worker characterizes his colleagues as "a diverse group of people from all around the world.... I've gotten to work with people from all ages, walks of life, and several different cultures." EA "provides many opportunities for social and personal interaction. This is not only for first jobbers, but [also for] anyone in the company. You can become great friends with producers and executives; no one is out of reach professionally or personally."

MOVING ON

Because "EA is very successful and constantly growing in every way," few first jobbers are anxious to move on." They like the security EA provides, as well as the excellent on-the-job training that they receive. People who leave, for the most part, move on to other gaming companies or return to school for an advanced degree.

EMC
Various Positions

THE BIG PICTURE

EMC is a leader in information lifecycle management and helps its customers "maximize the business value of their information" with "industry-leading information storage systems, software, networks, and services." It's a "vibrant, fast-paced" industry that places a premium on "creative ideas, innovative thinking, and unparalleled commitment" in its work force. The company offers a variety of entry-level opportunities, including several rotational training programs.

STATS

LOCATION(S) WHERE ENTRY-LEVEL EMPLOYEES WORK

Major facilities are located in Massachusetts; California; North Carolina; Toronto, Canada; and Cork, Ireland; 100+ sales offices and distributions partners; and fifty countries across the globe.

AVERAGE NUMBER OF APPLICATIONS EACH YEAR

EMC receives "5,000 applications per year for entry-level positions. The majority of the positions are college-level."

ENTRY-LEVEL POSITION(S) AVAILABLE

Entry-level hires typically work as software and hardware engineers, or enter into one of the following programs:

MLDP—Marketing Leadership Development Program

PERC—Program for Engineering Rotation in Clariion

FTP—Finance Training Program

HRLDP—HR Leadership Development Program

AVERAGE HOURS WORKED PER WEEK

Entry-level employees work forty hours per week.

MEDICAL BENEFITS OFFERED

EMC offers medical, dental, and vision coverage; basic group term life insurance; supplemental life insurance; dependent life insurance–CIGNA; portable term life insurance–Boston Mutual; short-term disability; long-term disability; health care flexible spending accounts; dependent care flexible spending accounts.

Additional benefits include HealthLink, an online personal health manager; an employee stock purchase plan (three-month vesting period); a 401(k) savings plan; a 529 college investing plan; a group legal plan; a long-term care plan; personal voluntary plans from AFLAC; ClubOne (on-site fitness facilities) or Global Fit (discounted fitness facilities throughout United States).

CONTACT INFORMATION

Visit www.EMC.com or e-mail work@emc.com.

GETTING HIRED

EMC interviews on college campuses; first jobbers may also apply directly via the company's website. The company reports that "entry-level employees typically start at the end of the academic year." Interviews focus on behavioral questions that "allow the interviewer to get a sense of how someone will perform in a job and in various circumstances." One participant in the Marketing Leadership Development Program reports, "The tone of the interview was professional and direct. They asked me to describe academic and professional situations entailing decision-making processes, team projects, and work group collaboration. They inquired about how I would act in a given situation among these topics and scenarios." Most applicants endure several rounds of interviews before receiving a final offer. One who was interviewed three times writes, "The most impressive thing is how fast they moved. They had a quick debriefing and all three rounds were in quick succession. They made me a job offer on the same day of the third round. They demonstrated a 'sense of urgency,' which is big in the culture here." EMC points out that it "also hires a high percentage of co-op/interns as full-time employees."

MONEY AND PERKS

Some of the first jobbers we spoke with told us that their start dates were somewhat flexible, but that otherwise, their job offers were "not negotiable." For many here, the key issue is not salary but the opportunity to learn and advance. "The most attractive factor was that it was a structured program with classes and a curriculum. There were rotation opportunities, and it seemed like a very steep learning-curve experience," explains one first jobber. Another agrees, "The program's attributes fulfilled my notion of the ideal entry-level job." Some first jobbers travel frequently for EMC; their fringe benefits include "a monthly car allowance" and "lots of frequent flyer miles and hotel points." First jobbers also love the stock options.

THE ROPES

All incoming employees at EMC receive an orientation that "covers a broad overview of the company, its organizations, recent financial results, and medical and 401(k) benefits. We were given an overview of the hierarchical structure of the company, a tour of the intranet and important links that we need to know about, and an introduction to the product line of the company. What was very clear at the end of this session was the sense of being a part of the company's vision and a feeling that we will be considered as important contributors to its success." Subsequently, first jobbers in rotational and training programs take classes that can last anywhere from a couple of weeks to a couple of months. An implementation specialist reports, "The training program was an intensive nine-week program in which we covered most of the EMC offerings in lecture, which was often followed by a lab section, during which we had the opportunity to get hands-on experience."

DAY IN THE LIFE

EMC hires first jobbers to serve in a wide range of functions, and their daily responsibilities vary considerably. Many training programs here "entail a mentoring/shadowing phase during which we are assigned only to projects where there are other EMC employees on-site. This has provided a great opportunity to get important questions answered while gaining familiarity with the available software, tools, etc." Frequent rotations mean that trainees rarely remain in one role long enough to become bored.

PEERS

EMC first jobbers see a lot of themselves in their peers, whom they describe as "intelligent, conscientious individuals" who "range from the highly experienced to people having diverse backgrounds but who have been in this industry for a while now to fresh graduates. Everyone has something to share and contribute. The work culture is elite, competitive, and yet fun." Many describe an enjoyable *esprit de corps* that forms during training classes but add that once in the field, they typically have regular contact with only one or two other first jobbers, and so "there's not much of an after-hours scene."

MOVING ON

EMC does a good job of holding onto first-time employees. Those who leave do so for various reasons. One worker explains, "I have heard some people complain that the office they are based out of doesn't have enough projects for them to be on, and so they have been stuck with more routine work. I have also, however, heard some people say they are working on so many projects that they are being overloaded, so I guess it really depends on what location you are being hired for. In general, though, I haven't heard of anyone with major complaints about EMC as a company." Many who leave return to school to earn an advanced degree.

ENTERPRISE RENT-A-CAR
Management Trainee Program

THE BIG PICTURE

Entry-level employees in Enterprise's Management Trainee Program love the "company's extremely performance-based philosophy for business" under which "everyone at the company starts [at] the same place and succeeds through [his or her] own work and determination." The chance for advancement and a solid, well-nurtured sense of community combine to make Enterprise a great place to begin your working life and build a career.

STATS

LOCATION(S) WHERE ENTRY-LEVEL EMPLOYEES WORK

"Enterprise Rent-A-Car hires entry-level employees company wide in five countries."

AVERAGE NUMBER OF APPLICATIONS EACH YEAR

The company receives 220,000 applications per year.

AVERAGE NUMBER HIRED PER YEAR OVER THE LAST TEN YEARS

Enterprise hires from 5,000 to 6,000 people per year.

ENTRY-LEVEL POSITION(S) AVAILABLE

Entry-level hires between 6,000 and 7,000 new college graduates per year.

AVERAGE HOURS WORKED PER WEEK

New hires work from forty-five to fifty hours per week.

AVERAGE STARTING SALARY

"Though starting salaries vary by location, all are highly competitive and range from the high $20,000s to the high $30,000s."

BENEFITS OFFERED

"Enterprise offers a complete benefits package. Employees have a choice of medical benefits through either an EPO or a PPO. Full-time employees can also participate in a health care reimbursement [or flexible spending] account, which sets aside up to $3,000 in pre-tax dollars to pay for noncovered medical expenses such as deductibles and copayments. Additional medical benefits include a dental, prescription drug, and vision plan." Additional benefits include "a pre-tax [flexible spending] account for dependent care in which employees can set aside up to $5,000 pre-tax to pay for child care; a matching 401(k) plan; profit sharing; ChoiceTime (paid time off for illness or personal use); discounts on renting, purchasing, or leasing a car; monetary rewards for new employee referrals (up to $2,500); education assistance; adoption assistance;

clothing allowance (in some locations); LifeMatters Resource program (a professional service that assists employees in finding resources for any number of needs—from serious matters such as child care or parental care to other issues like finding a realtor, pet care, and a health club).

CONTACT INFORMATION

Go to www.enterprise.com/careers.

GETTING HIRED

Enterprise tells us that "we hire management trainees that have already been out in the workforce; our company [also] regularly visits campuses across the nation looking for management trainee candidates. If an applicant proactively decides to apply for a position, an application is available online at www.enterprise.com/careers. The company welcomes candidates from all backgrounds, schools, and experiences." It seeks candidates who display "a strong work ethic, team player mentality, self-motivation, leadership potential, confidence, a customer service-centered attitude, flexibility, persistence, and social deftness." One trainee explains, "I posted my resume [at my school's career website], then logged onto the Enterprise website. I had to take a test online, and then I waited for a phone call. I had three interviews. The tone was professional. I felt very comfortable, and they asked many questions about my ambitions." Another agrees, "The tone of the first interview was serious, yet laid back. The interviewer was very nice and personable; he encouraged me to relax and talk to him as if I [were] an old friend. He asked me situational questions as well as questions about my experience in sales. I then spoke with a regional recruiter; I asked her for more specifics about the position. She was very excited and energetic and passed that along to me. I then interviewed at the branch where I'd be working. That interview was very short; I was offered the job the next day."

MONEY AND PERKS

All management trainees at Enterprise are "initially taught how to manage an Enterprise location. Normally, employees who successfully complete this training program can expect to become assistant managers after one year. Their next step is to become a branch manager. They typically attain that level two to two-and-a-half years after joining Enterprise." Trainee salaries vary slightly depending on location (i.e., trainees earn more in expensive locations such as San Francisco than in areas where the cost of living is lower) and whether they have completed internships at Enterprise. Subsequent pay raises occur "as employees become management assistants, assistant managers, or branch managers; their management compensation is determined by the success of the business. Assistant managers and managers receive a base salary plus a percentage of profits from their operation, and they have the potential to earn a lot more by driving the growth and increasing the profitability of their operation." Employees agree that "the best perk is the opportunity to be promoted based on performance;" they also appreciate how "Enterprise does a great job of taking care of [employees] through office outings, a summer party, and a holiday party. In addition, the 401(k) plan, profit sharing, and generous vacation times are also nice fringe benefits."

THE ROPES

Orientation at Enterprise is a one-week program. One entry-level employee explains, "The experience was extremely positive and informative. There were nine other management trainees and the overall feeling from all of us was that orientation introduced us to the start of our careers." Enterprise officials tell us that "because of the decentralized nature of the company, orientation programs vary slightly by region of the country. While the orientation is designed by and catered to specific regions, each program teaches the basics of the business and introduces employees to the philosophy of the company." Following orientation, trainees are sent to a branch location, where they "develop skills in sales, marketing, customer service, accounting, and finance. Managers meet with trainees weekly to go over their progress and any questions they may have. Throughout the seven to twelve month training program, the trainee will receive opportunities for increased responsibility, bonuses, and pay increases." One first jobber notes, "Enterprise understands the importance of continuous employee development. Every employee undergoes some type of formal training at least once a month. These training sessions are designed to inform the employees of other departments of the company and how they relate to the functions of the rental branch."

DAY IN THE LIFE

The management trainee program at Enterprise is designed to teach trainees every aspect of running a business. This means that trainees must master a wide range of duties. Here's how one trainee describes a typical day: "In the morning before opening, we have to make sure all the cars for the day's reservations are ready. After opening, it's a balancing act of helping customers who come in, picking up customers who need rides, marketing, cleaning cars as they're returned, and making sure the cars get their regular maintenance. I spend just as much time on the road as I do in the branch—this helps break up my day, so I am not burned out. Every day the same concepts of business are applied, but to different situations. The ability to multitask is essential to this job." Because of the company's unique business model, "Employees at Enterprise have an opportunity essentially to run their own business—in essence, to have a franchise without paying a fee. To prepare employees for that opportunity, we offer an extensive training program, which many employees make reference to as the 'virtual MBA.' Every employee serving customers at the front counter is quietly learning the ins and outs of the business world, including profit-and-loss statements, controlling expenses, and implementing a comprehensive business plan."

PEERS

One new employee says, "There is no separation among 'first jobbers' and other employees at the company. Each branch becomes a team that depends on each member. The company provides chances for employees to interact outside of work, which takes the pressures off of the daytime grind by providing a more social atmosphere. I spend a good amount of my free time with those I work with, whether it be just hang out or participate in an organized flag football team." Another new employee adds, "Besides knowing the people who work at branches near yours, the training sessions are one way to network and get to know other management trainees. There is a big 'after-hours' social scene. Many managers will reward performance by offering a happy hour after work. It is very easy to make friends mainly because the majority of employees here are very outgoing."

MOVING ON

Company officials report, "Realizing the potential for growth that exists within the company, many first jobbers stay on to become the company's leaders. Regardless of background, employees at Enterprise progress purely on their own merit." The employees we spoke with confirmed the company's assertions; all of them told us they plan to stay here, work hard, and rise through the ranks.

BEST AND WORST

"Pam Nicholson began her career at Enterprise Rent-A-Car in 1981 as a management trainee. Fresh out of college with a bachelor of arts degree, she started in St. Louis behind the rental counter learning the importance of customer service, an Enterprise trademark. Within nine months, Pam was promoted to assistant branch manager, and within a year, accepted a position in the company's fast-growing Southern California group. Over the next twelve years, she was promoted through the ranks to one of the top operating positions in Southern California: regional vice president. While there, she assisted in growing the region's fleet from 1,000 to more than 27,000 vehicles. Her efforts were rewarded with a position back in her hometown of St. Louis as a corporate vice president at Enterprise's world headquarters. Proving that professional growth with Enterprise is constant, Pam was soon promoted to general manager of the New York Group, a top job in that region. Overseeing rental car, fleet services, and car sales operations for the company's second largest operating group, Pam led the group to double its profitability. In acknowledging her top performance in New York and throughout her career, Pam was promoted back to St. Louis as a senior vice president of their North American operations and soon after to executive vice president of their North American operations. Today, as C.O.O., she oversees the activities of more than 61,000 employees; 667,000 rental cars; 150,000 fleet services vehicles; and 6,500 branch offices in five countries. She is a corporate officer and one of the company's top operating employees."

GEICO
Various positions

THE BIG PICTURE

GEICO's formal college recruiting program is relatively new (it started up in August 2003), but it has already delivered a lot of fresh faces to this sixty-eight-year old insurance giant. The company offers entry-level positions in nearly all its functional areas.

STATS

LOCATION(S) WHERE ENTRY-LEVEL EMPLOYEES WORK

Offices are located in Washington, DC (corporate headquarters); Buffalo, New York; Woodbury, New York; Fredericksburg, Virginia; Virginia Beach, Virginia; Macon, Georgia; Lakeland, Florida; Dallas, Texas; Tucson, Arizona; and San Diego, California

AVERAGE NUMBER OF APPLICATIONS EACH YEAR

Geico receives about 22,000 applications each year.

AVERAGE NUMBER HIRED PER YEAR OVER THE LAST TEN YEARS

Geico hires about 200–300 entry-level employees each year.

ENTRY-LEVEL POSITION(S) AVAILABLE

Positions are available as "actuarial associates, product management analysts, underwriting analysts, claims representatives, sales associates, customer service representatives, auto damage adjusters, and management-training programs in operations management and information technology. We have also hired recent graduates into our IT-project management office, marketing and HR departments, and our competitive analysis group."

AVERAGE HOURS WORKED PER WEEK

Entry-level hires work forty to forty-five hours per week.

AVERAGE STARTING SALARY

Starting salaries vary by position and typically range from $30,000–mid-$40,000s.

BENEFITS OFFERED

Medical, dental, flexible spending accounts are available. Additional benefits include life insurance, paid vacation and holidays, disability, long-term care, scholarships, tuition reimbursement, dependent care, business-casual dress, profit sharing, sports teams, on-site fitness facilities and cafeterias, commuter assistance, and a 401(k) plan.

GEICO College Recruiting

5260 Western Avenue, 1CE-HR

Chevy Chase, MD 20815

Fax: 301-986-3092, Attn: College Recruiting

E-mail: jobs@geico.com

www.geico.com/oncampus

Getting Hired

GEICO "strongly encourages students to do their research on the company prior to the interview," reporting that the best job interviews are distinguished by "the amount a student has researched and knows about the company. When their knowledge comes across as true interest in GEICO, this helps students shine." The company also seeks "strong communication and customer service skills, analytical and computer skills, well-rounded experiences, leadership potential, and work/internship experience." The interview process can be drawn out for applicants to the Emerging Leaders Management Development Program; one writes, "The process was long (one and a half months) but worth the time. There were four phases of interviews that ended in a meeting with very high ranking company officers." For other positions, the process is less formal—typically, a screening call from HR, followed by a behavioral-based interview with the hire's prospective supervisors. One hire writes, "I was asked about specific situations and how I reacted (i.e., 'Name a time in which you showed leadership skills/teamwork abilities/etc.'). I was given a tour of the facility and an overview of the different departments. I used the S.T.A.R. (situation, task, action, result) approach to answer. The interview concluded with a final employment offer."

Money and Perks

Starting salaries are rarely negotiable at GEICO. First jobbers have better luck negotiating their start date, but tell us that most other aspects of the job are off the table. GEICO reports that salary increases and promotions are based on performance, adding that the company "promoted nearly 1,700 of our entry-level employees in 2003. Promotion from within is serious business at GEICO." Employees tout the profit-sharing program; they also enjoy "the discount on car insurance, discounts with partner companies such as Microsoft and Dell, and the shorter workday than normal (we work for 7.75 hours and get .75 hours for lunch." Also, for some "the schedule is pretty flexible."

THE ROPES

Formal orientation at GEICO begins with "a two- or three-day boot camp explaining benefits and GEICO in general, followed by a six-month certification period." The company notes that "different positions have to attend classes and/or complete rotations [that range] from days long to months long." Emerging Leader participants "rotate through all the areas: licensing, sales, service, and underwriting. All of the trainings are created and administered by different trainers (depending on their areas of expertise) in the training department." Those with more traditional positions "receive training on specific tasks on a need-to-know basis, informally (by asking questions). Usually this training is from a supervisor or other members of the department."

DAY IN THE LIFE

GEICO hires first-jobbers to serve a variety of functions, ranging from "selling insurance policies, to investigating claims, to special projects for upper management." Among the first-jobbers we contacted were a programmer analyst, a cost-benefit analysis coordinator, a college-recruiting assistant, a business analyst, and two Emerging Leaders. Those in rotations "start with a one- to three-month training class, then work the phones. Eventually we get to shadow and interact with management."

PEERS

First jobbers tell us that their peers "are all very intelligent, driven, team-based, professional, and hard-working individuals. Everyone brings their own uniqueness to the company." Some are "big on the bar scene, others are homebodies, but they are mostly great people in general." One new hire reports that she and her peers "frequently get together outside of work in several cliques. The HR department supports this with newsletters, a pizza party, and recruiting opportunities. Some groups of associates have social outings in the evenings, but it is rarely in large groups."

MOVING ON

The average overall tenure for all GEICO employees is thirteen years; the company does not currently have data for first jobbers. Those who leave do so to return to school or to pursue other career options. Those who plan to stay praise the "great exposure to business and leadership" and the "relaxed atmosphere and flexible schedules."

GENERAL ELECTRIC
Corporate Leadership Development Programs

THE BIG PICTURE

General Electric (GE) offers Corporate Leadership Development programs in many divisions. Typically they are "two-year rotational training programs [that] consist of formal classroom, digital, and on-the-job training" that prepare participants to continue their careers at GE when they end.

STATS

LOCATION(S) WHERE ENTRY-LEVEL EMPLOYEES WORK

GE has locations in more than 100 countries.

AVERAGE NUMBER OF APPLICATIONS EACH YEAR

The company receives about 50,000 applications per year in the United States alone.

AVERAGE NUMBER HIRED PER YEAR OVER THE LAST TEN YEARS

About 1,000 people are hired in the United States per year.

ENTRY-LEVEL POSITION(S) AVAILABLE

Entry-level positions are available in sales and marketing, engineering, finance, human resources, information management, and operations.

AVERAGE HOURS WORKED PER WEEK

The number of hours worked per week varies by position.

PERCENTAGE OF ENTRY-LEVEL HIRES STILL WITH THE COMPANY AFTER THREE, FIVE, AND TEN YEARS

After three years, about 80 percent of all entry-level employees remain with the company; after five years, 60 percent of all entry-level employees remain with the company; and after ten years, 50 percent of all entry-level employees remain with the company.

AVERAGE STARTING SALARY

The average starting salary ranges from $50,000–$90,000 per year.

BENEFITS OFFERED

The company offers competitive, full medical coverage, and a generous tuition reimbursement program.

CONTACT INFORMATION

Submit resumes online at www.gecareers.com, or contact your career center to see if GE will be interviewing at your school.

GETTING HIRED

Applying for one of GE's Corporate Leadership Development Programs requires two interviews. The first, conducted on campus or over the telephone, is with a company representative and involves "many questions about working in teams, situations in which failure occurred, and how it was dealt with." Next, "candidates selected for on-site (second) interviews will be interviewing for a position with a specific GE business. Students are given the opportunity to choose up to three GE businesses they are interested in joining. We try our best to align student geographic and business preferences with internal business hiring needs; however, there is no guarantee that you will be offered a position at your preferred location," writes one company official. A former program participant who now organizes recruiting says, "I'd encourage candidates to be energetic and engaging. Ask a lot of questions! The goal of the process is to determine whether there is a fit between the candidate and the organization. Sometimes it is clear that a candidate has the technical and nontechnical skills to excel, but [it is] unclear whether the candidate is engaged with the environment and really wants the job. Asking questions about the work, organization, and program is the best way for both parties to accurately predict whether there is a fit." Another entry-level employee adds, "Entry-level positions at GE usually require work that isn't a direct outflow of previous work, so specific technical skills are less important than a strong and consistent demonstration of the capability to learn, adapt, and excel."

MONEY AND PERKS

Participants in all GE development programs tell us that "the job offer is negotiable in terms of when you start, but nonnegotiable in terms of salary and placement." Many hasten to add that "the offer [GE makes] is highly competitive, so there's no need to negotiate the compensation." Pay increases come semiannually and are based on performance. One entry-level employee says, "Those raises are based [on] your on-the-job evaluations and your class grades, and they add up quickly during the two-year program." Perks include "discounts on products, ranging from GE appliances to gym memberships to Dell computers to automobiles." Program participants also love the educational package; as one student explains, "GE paid for my master's degree, [gave me] two full-time quarters off [of] work [while still earning my] full salary, and paid for [all my books]. It was a great opportunity; I got a master's degree at a top twenty-five engineering graduate school in about two-and-a-half years."

THE ROPES

General Electric's Corporate Leadership Development Programs start with a brief orientation, usually half a day or one day long. One entry-level hire writes, "My orientation process was a three-hour long seminar-style event that entailed a presentation about the big picture of GE and how the research center [to which I was assigned] serves the business, overviews of how programs are funded, and how time accounting should be performed, procedures related to security and safety, and other rather unexciting, but necessary, topics." Orientation is only the beginning of a long and thorough training process, however. In fact, since first jobbers rotate through jobs throughout the two-year program, the training period never really ends. One engineer offers, "I received so much training it's hard to recall it all, so I'll give the highlights: two trips to [a] GE corporate training facility at Crotonville [in Ossining, New York] for business leadership courses and jet engine teardown training [where] we disassembled and reassembled aircraft engines. In addition, Six Sigma green belt classes and training also were provided." Six Sigma is a management philosophy that holds sacrosanct the goal of constantly improving operational efficiency. Many employees also pursue master's degrees while working for GE; the company offers substantial support in this area [see "Money and Perks"].

DAY IN THE LIFE

GE is number five on the *Fortune 500* list, and so it generates a great deal of revenue. Accordingly, the variety of tasks performed by entry-level employees is incredibly broad. According to company officials, "The average program member works about fifty hours per week. Additional time commitments may be required depending on job assignments. Course work, on average, will add another five to eight hours to your week." One program participant writes, "Responsibilities vary depending on the area of the first job assignment, but typically program members are directed [or] given work by a manager and given a mentor or engineer who provides help [and] advice in the area. As a program member progresses onto different assignments and gains more on-the-job engineering competency, the program member is typically given the same amount of work and responsibility as any other engineer in the area of work." Everyone in the program rotates positions within his or her business every six months; company officials tell us that "rotations outside your function or your GE business do exist, but [they] are an exception, rather than a rule, for all program participants. Assignments of these types are dependent on the GE business need and participant preferences and are also often based on merit."

PEERS

"One attractive thing about a big program like this is that there is a continual stream of young, bright, and motivated folks coming in," notes one first jobber. The scope of the after-hours scene varies widely by division and location, program participants tell us, but all agree that there's "a tremendous amount of camaraderie" among people starting out at GE. One program participant explains, "You're in classes with twenty to thirty people [who are] your age every week, so it's kind of like being in college again. All of us made friends pretty quickly [and] went out after work [or] on weekends; and now, three years later [we] are still going out to happy hours and dinners together. We've all been to [one another's] weddings and have established a very close group of friends through this program."

Moving On

GE regards its Corporate Leadership Development programs as stepping stones to careers with the company. Its website states, "GE's Leadership Programs prepare graduates for positions with significant levels of responsibility and challenging off-program assignments. Some graduates join the GE audit staff. Others enter positions in one of the GE businesses. Cross-functional assignments are also a possibility. If someone successfully completes one of our leadership programs, other advanced educational degrees or certifications are not required to succeed at GE. Training and experiences gained while in a program may accelerate an individual's career growth in much the same way an advanced degree [may] at another corporation. Inevitably, some program graduates feel the need to seek further education. In these instances, GE's support, whether it is in the form of tuition reimbursement, leave of absence, executive MBA, etc., is considered on a case by case basis and differs according to the GE business."

Attrition

People who leave GE site the lack of "work/life balance" as their reason, and report that this is something that GE as a whole struggles with. Most jobs require pretty long hours, especially during programs where you have to work until late at night on homework every week. There's not much time for friends or spouses outside of work. Also, "the traveling aspect of the program turns a lot of people off, even after they take the job knowing they [may] move every six months. Above all else, [employees] say the lack of [geographic] stability is the number one criticism."

GO DADDY
Sales and Support Representative

THE BIG PICTURE

Did you ever wonder how Internet domain names are assigned and secured? Wonder no longer; the process is handled by companies like Go Daddy, which happens to be "the world's largest domain name registrar, both in terms of daily new registrations and domains under management." In fact, Go Daddy manages "more than ten million domains" and offers "a complete product line, including comprehensive hosting solutions, website creation tools, secure SSL certificates, personalized e-mail with spam and antiphishing filtering, e-commerce tools, and more." First jobbers here handle sales and support at this mega manager.

STATS

LOCATION(S) WHERE ENTRY-LEVEL EMPLOYEES WORK

Jobs are located in Scottsdale and Gilbert, Arizona

AVERAGE NUMBER OF APPLICATIONS EACH YEAR

Go Daddy receives 1,500 resumes each year.

AVERAGE NUMBER HIRED PER YEAR

Go Daddy hires more than 400 entry-level employees each year.

ENTRY-LEVEL POSITION(S) AVAILABLE

Entry-level hires work as sales and support representatives.

AVERAGE HOURS WORKED PER WEEK

New hires work forty to fifty hours per week.

PERCENTAGE OF ENTRY-LEVEL HIRES STILL WITH THE COMPANY AFTER THREE, FIVE, AND TEN YEARS

Thirty percent of employees are still with the company after three years.

AVERAGE STARTING SALARY

In 2004, the average starting salary was $28,000.

BENEFITS OFFERED

Go Daddy offers medical, dental, and prescription plans that vest after ninety days; all employee benefits are paid by Go Daddy. The company also offers short- and long-term disability, life insurance, vacation (three weeks in the first year of employment), and sick leave as well as paid holidays and paid personal days. Employees may take advantage of Go Daddy's education assistance program after six months of employment.

CONTACT INFORMATION

Visit www.GoDaddy.com, and click on the "Jobs" link.

GETTING HIRED

Company officials note that successful applicants at Go Daddy demonstrate "career ambition, customer focus, adaptability, problem-solving skills, functional/technical job skills, communication skills (e.g., an ability to influence/persuade), and a results orientation." The company interviews at Arizona State and a few other local colleges and encourages students at all other schools to "apply by completing an application online." Applications are screened by human resources; those that show promise prompt a phone prescreen. Those clearing that hurdle are invited for a face-to-face interview. During the interview, company reps "ask behavioral-based questions of all applicants. We are looking for specific answers that reflect how the candidate would handle specific situations. We are looking to learn about past work history, as well as how well they listen, answer, and provide examples. Candidates who do not provide specific examples are not selected to continue in the process." Sound stressful? Worry not; according to current employees, the interview process isn't as taxing as it seems. One successful applicant writes, "The application process was very informal. I was interviewed by the domain services manager. The tone of the interview was informative and relaxed. She asked me about what I was looking for in a company, my background, and my knowledge of computers and the Internet. I was offered the job the next day and accepted it."

MONEY AND PERKS

Entry-level hires at Go Daddy are eligible both for bonuses "based on meeting established criteria in the areas of sales, quality, and customer satisfaction surveys" and for "contests based on sales performance. We have given away cars [and] trips and have even paid employees' mortgages or rent for a full year. Most recently, we ran a 'debt relief' contest, paying off various debts held by several employees." The company also "subsidizes lunch for our employees three times a week. For example, Subway comes on-site, and our employees only pay $1.00 for a sandwich. The company pays the rest." Sounds good, right? But wait, there's more! Go Daddy also has "a wide range of partnerships with local businesses that offer our employees discounts" on such key products and services as gym memberships and childcare.

THE ROPES

Formal orientation at Go Daddy "has three objectives. First is teaching the learners the technical and product knowledge, a core component that contributes to their success. Second, we focus on defining the expectations of Go Daddy in keeping customer satisfaction high. Finally, we show our learners [that] they are the voice of Go Daddy and [emphasize how much] that is a special role inside of our organization." The training lasts two weeks, beginning with "company values, the basics of domain management, and product knowledge based on relevancy. By the end of week one, our team members understand Web hosting concepts, how to drive website traffic, and how to keep information secure. To ensure the best customer experience, our team members are required to pass a final exam before continuing into week two." During the second week, "We teach the team members soft skills: proper call control, phone etiquette, and how to help customers make the most of their domain names. We define team goals, employee expectations, and career opportunities. All team members are taking live calls midweek under the close observation of our training specialists."

DAY IN THE LIFE

Sales and support specialists at Go Daddy handle telephone and e-mail support duties. One explains, "When I first started, I was responsible for answering e-mail questions from customers about their domain names. I fulfilled my job duties by responding to the customers after investigating their issues. In a typical day, I would respond to about sixty to eighty customer questions. These questions [included] how to change ownership of their domains, how to purchase domains, how to transfer domains to Godaddy.com from other registrars, and [what] the differences [were] between the many different TLD extensions. I would research each incident and find the solution to the problem from resources on the Web and internal resources." According to the company, employees in these positions "need to have troubleshooting skills and be fairly [technically savvy.] And they must have knowledge of the inner workings of the Internet."

PEERS

"There is huge camaraderie among the new employees in our company," writes one first jobber, pointing out that "we have a great mentoring program in place to assist new employees and to make them feel welcome immediately." Many "find lasting friendships here." The after-hours scene, however, is surprisingly muted for a company with so many young hires. The first jobbers we spoke with did not spend much time with their coworkers outside the office. "There are pockets of after-hours social buddies," though.

MOVING ON

First jobbers most often leave Go Daddy to return to school. Some take offers from "other noncompetitive call centers in the valley." Turnover is moderately high; one first jobber explains "A lot of times, you will find the wrong people in the wrong positions." This "is both ineffective for the company and for the person. Our biggest challenge is to find the right people for the right jobs. The main complaint comes from people who don't believe they can sell; they claim they didn't know it was a sales job and thereby walk in the door without the drive to succeed."

ATTRITION

About 15 percent of new hires remain at Go Daddy for less than a year. The average tenure of a first jobber here is fourteen months, though this number is artificially low because Go Daddy is "such a young company."

BEST AND WORST

Go Daddy has had "numerous entry-level employees who have started out in entry-level positions [and] have been promoted [within] the company. The promotions [are often to] supervisor, manager, and director titles. These promotions are in all phases of our company, from development to IT to management." Those who fail here are those who are "unable to show the appropriate level of commitment to our customers."

GOLDMAN SACHS
Various Positions

THE BIG PICTURE

Goldman Sachs is "a leading global investment banking, securities, and investment management firm." Most entry-level hires are analysts who help the company "provide a wide range of services to a substantial and diversified client base that includes corporations, institutional investors, governments, nonprofit organizations, and individuals." Goldman Sachs conducts business "in increasingly complex markets," and so employees must "continually find new ways to provide access to capital, manage risk, and provide investment opportunities" to help clients realize their goals.

STATS

LOCATION(S) WHERE ENTRY-LEVEL EMPLOYEES WORK

"We hire a vast majority of first-year analysts in our New York and London offices. While analysts could be placed in any of our offices throughout the United States, Europe, and Asia, other top hiring cities are Paris, Frankfurt, Chicago, Hong Kong, and Tokyo."

AVERAGE NUMBER OF APPLICATIONS EACH YEAR

Approximately 53,000 applications are submitted to the company every year.

AVERAGE NUMBER HIRED PER YEAR OVER THE LAST TEN YEARS

Anywhere from 800–1,000 people are hired per year.

ENTRY-LEVEL POSITION(S) AVAILABLE

Available entry-level positions vary by year.

AVERAGE HOURS WORKED PER WEEK

The hours vary widely, depending on the position. Generally, a Goldman Sachs employee can expect substantial workdays, with the rewards commensurate with their commitment.

PERCENTAGE OF ENTRY-LEVEL HIRES STILL WITH THE COMPANY AFTER THREE, FIVE, AND TEN YEARS:

"Most of our new hires begin in our Analyst Program. We regard the Analyst Program as a two- to three-year experience. After completing the Analyst Program, analysts pursue various exciting opportunities." Some stay, while many return to business or law school or move on to pursue other career opportunities; obtaining an analyst position at Goldman Sachs opens doors in the financial services community and beyond.

AVERAGE STARTING SALARY

New hires earn salaries that are competitive with those at other investment banks.

BENEFITS OFFERED

"We offer a competitive benefits package. We also offer [an] on-site fitness center or subsidized memberships at local clubs; on-site health units for physician-ordered testing, vision testing, prescription services, facilities for nursing mothers, and Lamaze classes; on-site physician services; wellness/health fairs and seminars; free on-site screenings such as flu vaccinations; cholesterol, skin cancer, [and] prostate cancer [tests]; and mammograph[ies]." In addition, "a partial list of the services we provide for employee convenience, professional development, and charitable efforts [includes] online employee discounts to retail stores; complimentary admission to local museums and discounts at gift shops; no-fee ATM machines on site; discount banking and mortgage programs; and financial exam classes (with manager approval) provided on- and off-site, for those who need certification. [Furthermore,] second- and third-year analysts have access to a How to Apply to Business School seminar and on-site receptions with admissions officers from top business schools; GMAT Princeton Review classes; numerous classes available on various topics (with manager approval); and one paid day off a year to volunteer in the community."

CONTACT INFORMATION

Visit www.gs.com/careers, or visit your campus career services office.

GETTING HIRED

Goldman Sachs "actively markets and has a physical presence on campus at a select number of universities across the United States, Europe, and Asia, but [the company] hires from a great number of universities. Students from all colleges and universities are encouraged to apply." The firm reviews all applications, which can be submitted online (see "Contact Information" above), then invites the most likely candidates to interview. The first-round interview "consists of a Goldman Sachs 'firm wide' interview, rather than a divisional one. The interview focuses primarily on past candidate experiences and accomplishments and is designed to help [the firm] get to know the candidate and for the candidate to ask questions." The second-round interview "focuses on candidate suitability for a particular division and may be more technical in nature" than the first. One entry-level employee writes of the experience: "The interviews were, in general, challenging but fair. I did not receive any trick questions, but the nature of the questions did force me to be thoughtful and think on my feet. Overall, it was an extremely positive experience." Another notes, "Prior to the interview, I scoured the Goldman Sachs website for information on what the interviewers may ask of me as well as tips for a successful interview. I found the website to be extremely helpful in my preparation."

MONEY AND PERKS

Salaries, according to Goldman Sachs officials, "generally move according to 'class.' Typical packages consist of a base salary, [a] discretionary bonus, private health care, [a] pension, and other benefits." The employees we interviewed say the firm's initial offers were not negotiable but also note that "the pay scale and other employment terms were competitive with the other industry players." Perks include the extensive benefits package outlined above, as well as "the extremely high quality of coworkers, both in terms of intellect and motivation/dedication."

THE ROPES

Orientation programs at Goldman Sachs "vary by division" and "are designed to provide the skills, background, and tools candidates need to do their job within their chosen division, business unit, or product group." They can last "anywhere from two to twelve weeks." An investment-banking analyst reports that her program "was taught by both university-level professors as well as internal presenters and revolved around long days of economics, financial math, and business products and services, as well as soft skills training. There were a number of social and networking events, as well." Training is also facilitated by "formal mentoring programs that are administered by human resources professionals working within our divisions" and a "big buddy program" in which newbies have contact with "an experienced associate who answers questions, helps [them] figure out how to complete [their] work, shows them where to find the information they need, and, more generally, looks out for their well-being."

DAY IN THE LIFE

Although their duties differ depending on the division in which they work, all starting analysts "learn a great deal about [Goldman Sachs'] businesses, develop important relationships, and build the skills necessary to carry them through to the next level of their careers." Starting jobs are designed to "help analysts learn critical business skills while gaining fundamental skills in their respective divisions." Here's how one employee describes his experience: "On first joining the group, my responsibilities were typical of those of an entry-level analyst and included general administrative tasks, such as setting up calls and preparing notes/slides for meetings, coordinating meetings, spreading numbers and running models for various counterparties or banking clients, and making sure that I was being diligent and retaining the significant volume of information that was being presented to me." Another investment-banking employee writes, "As a first-year, I was assigned to three industry teams and one product team. On any given day, I could have been working on projects on any or all of the four teams. This aspect of the work kept things interesting, fast paced, and challenging, and really made working a pleasure. Over time, I have taken on more responsibility; people expect more of me in terms of value-added opinions and critical analysis, and people seek me out as a source of information. My work has gotten more challenging, and I have been able to begin weaning [myself] off the administrative tasks I was performing as a first-year analyst."

PEERS

Friendships among newbies are forged during Goldman Sachs' intensive training programs, according to the analysts we surveyed. One writes, "Just like at the start of college, the groups getting together after work and on weekends tend to be very large at the beginning and for the most part eventually dwindle down to your closest friends." Because "everything is done collaboratively here," close working relationships are key. Fortunately, "coworkers are definitely friends, and there is a young, fun atmosphere at work. Not a single hour goes by without interaction with my peers."

MOVING ON

Goldman Sachs officials say, "Some of our departing analysts are often accepted into top graduate business and law schools or receive offers from private equity shops, hedge funds, or other outstanding companies throughout the world. Our program has an excellent reputation among academic and business leaders worldwide." Many employees who complete the analyst program stay on; officials note that "the analyst program is also an integral component of our associate-recruiting strategy. After completing the analyst program, some top-performing analysts are promoted to the associate level. We also keep in touch with our departing analysts and frequently rehire them at a later time in their careers." As one analyst tells us, "At this point, and given my extremely positive experience thus far, I cannot imagine why I would really ever want to leave Goldman Sachs for good. I *would* eventually like to go back to business school. However, following that, I would ideally like to return to Goldman Sachs."

ATTRITION

Employees sometimes gripe that they frequently stay late into the evening. People who quit usually cite the unusually long hours and the "seemingly endless workflow" at Goldman Sachs; as one analyst told us, "Even the jobs with 'good' hours are still much more intensive than your standard forty-hour workweek. This is a firm where people work hard, play hard, and then go back and work harder."

BEST AND WORST

Successful employees at Goldman Sachs "create and sustain positive working relationships with others," "show initiative," "earn and deserve increased responsibility," and "maintain high ethical standards." Failures are those who just can't cut it in Goldman Sachs' high-pressure, high-stakes atmosphere.

GOOGLE
Various Positions

THE BIG PICTURE

Not many new companies grow so big that their name becomes a verb, but Google's has. And if you don't believe us, google it and see for yourself. Besides presenting a really cool product, Google is also a place at which go-getters can rise through the ranks relatively quickly. No wonder the company receives thousands of job applications every day.

STATS

LOCATION(S) WHERE ENTRY-LEVEL EMPLOYEES WORK

Google has locations "in Mountain View, New York, Santa Monica, and most of our twenty-plus sales offices."

AVERAGE NUMBER OF APPLICATIONS EACH YEAR

Google receives "thousands per day."

ENTRY-LEVEL POSITION(S) AVAILABLE

Positions are available as AdWords representatives, legal assistants, and administrative associates.

AVERAGE HOURS WORKED PER WEEK

Entry-level hires work forty hours per week.

AVERAGE STARTING SALARY (BY POSITION)

AdWords representatives earn $30,000–$40,000 per year. Legal assistants earn $40,000–$50,000 per year. Administrative assistants earn $40,000–$50,000 per year.

BENEFITS OFFERED

"Employees receive several HMO and PPO medical plans, plus vision and dental. They receive coverage beginning on the date of hire. We pride ourselves on providing extremely generous employee benefits," writes a company official. These include three weeks of vacation for the first three years of employment, increasing in subsequent years; eleven paid holidays per year; free healthy lunch and dinner buffets, Monday through Friday; on-site doctor, dental, dry cleaning, oil change, and more services; on-site gym; subsidized yoga and Pilates classes; subsidized on-site massages; and maternity coverage and parental leave.

CONTACT INFORMATION

Interested parties should send an e-mail to jobs@google.com.

Getting Hired

Many first jobbers start at Google as contract workers: They are brought on as temps without benefits. A typical hire explains: "Initially, I was a temporary employee for a stipulated twelve-week period. During the twelve-week time, I would be evaluated as well as have an opportunity to evaluate the position, and a mutual decision about conversion to full-time employment would be made sometime after week eight. Once I became a full-time employee, the salary and contract I committed to were based on multiple factors. These factors included my educational background, relevant work experience, performance within the first twelve weeks, as well as my potential growth within Google." Google tells us it seeks "smart, flexible" hires with "interesting experience, unique accomplishments, a passion to learn, and creativity. We are not inclined toward inflexibility, overly process[-based] orientation." In interviews, the company "tries to learn what makes [candidates] passionate, how they think, and how they approach problems. The best interview is when a candidate, no matter at what level, has researched the position and our products. He/she has a passion for the job and the responsibilities, and the clear ability to succeed in the role and develop beyond it." The company "actively seeks employee referrals, so having a friend in the company helps."

Money and Perks

"The job is not negotiable other than in terms of start time," most first jobbers at Google report, and that's fine: They agree with the respondent who told us that "I was happy with what they offered me, so I signed my offer letter without trying to negotiate. I cared much more about finding a place I wanted to work than about salary—otherwise, I would have joined an I-banking firm or something." Google notes that "entry-level employees are eligible for the same bonuses as other full-time Googlers, which are based on individual, team, and company performance" and that "for some employees, there may be promotion opportunities at six-month intervals. The goal is to keep our employees challenged and engaged with new opportunities." Perks are numerous and beloved; they include "a great, free shuttle service that runs from two locations in San Francisco down to Google's offices in Mountain View, which will save you years of life in commuting stress, as well as lots of money in gas, insurance, and maintenance!" Also, "all of our meals are provided to us free of cost. I save a significant amount of money on food and definitely factor this fringe benefit into my overall compensation package."

The Ropes

For many new hires at Google, "the contractor program is like an extended orientation. It lasts eight weeks, giving you the opportunity to learn the function of your job and the skills you need to succeed." Formal orientation occurs after employees land permanent positions; it takes place on Monday, lasts half a day, and includes "brief introductions of all new employees, a review of Google's history and culture, and an overview of policies and benefits. Orientation concludes with a tour of the building and lunch with the new hires' mentors." AdWord representatives and coordinators "get a 'buddy bag' on their first day with a toy and some Google goodies, and they meet a buddy from their new team. The buddy is their guide for the first week at Google and beyond this time, as needed." Google's internal website "contains myriad information" that helps newbies learn their various responsibilities.

Day in the Life

AdWords representatives spend their days checking ad content, quality, and relevance, as well as screening ad submissions based on fixed guidelines. They also work on the advertisers' keyword lists, provide customer service and support, and train new hires. Administrative assistants "perform a host of administrative duties, including scheduling, interacting with visitors, attending meetings, and keeping a steady flow of office communication. One consistency in most days is to communicate on behalf of my manager and team to individuals from different departments within our office. The job has the potential to be entirely different from one day to the next, which is nice." Legal assistants "do legal research, correspond with outside parties, write reports, etc." They "also continue to do some administrative work, which is fine—after eight years (high school and college) of nothing but reading and writing, I don't mind doing some filing. And since I'm going off to law school in the relatively near future, I welcome the opportunity to take a little mental break now and then."

Peers

Google first-jobbers tell us that they are "continually impressed workers. They are an incredible and diverse group of individuals with a wealth of talent and enthusiasm for what they do." Most are bright, young, ambitious, and friendly, and the company capitalizes on that, "placing a strong value on socializing and maintaining a sense of fun within the company's corporate culture. This breeds a great sense of contentment amongst employees. Work becomes less of mundane duty, but rather a membership into a special large extended family that coworkers feel privileged to be part of." Workers enjoy "happy hours, TGIF, and offsite gatherings regularly. There is much contact and camaraderie. This is a very social place to work."

Moving On

Google's turnover rate is extremely low. Those few who leave generally do so to pursue advanced degrees, to pursue new job opportunities, or to relocate out of the area. Most stick around because they "feel like there is a lot of room to grow here at Google." One first jobber reports, "I have already had two promotions in terms of job responsibility, and two raises within a year, and I think that that is achievable for anyone who is willing to work hard and show their initiative."

GREEN CORPS
Field Organizer

THE BIG PICTURE

"Hey, you titmice, let's have a little more chirping, okay? Frogs, don't all bunch up in one spot—spread out! And who in blue blazes cut the grass so short?" No, that's *not* what Green Corps field organizers do, but wouldn't it be cool if it was? What they do is just about as cool: They coordinate with local activists to affect Green environmental goals. Working with this organization is a great introduction to the world of ecoactivism.

STATS

LOCATION(S) WHERE ENTRY-LEVEL EMPLOYEES WORK

"Nationwide—placements are temporary (usually two to three months), and entry-level employees move to a couple of locations throughout the year."

AVERAGE NUMBER OF APPLICATIONS EACH YEAR

Green Corps receives 800 applications each year.

AVERAGE NUMBER HIRED PER YEAR OVER THE LAST TEN YEARS

The organization hires twenty-four people per year.

ENTRY-LEVEL POSITION(S) AVAILABLE

New hires work as field organizers.

AVERAGE HOURS WORKED PER WEEK

Hours are "highly variable based on campaign schedule[s]." When big events approach, field organizers work "approximately sixty to seventy hours [but] less during other times."

PERCENTAGE OF ENTRY-LEVEL HIRES STILL WITH THE COMPANY AFTER THREE, FIVE, AND TEN YEARS

"The program is a year-long training program, so all employees leave for other organizations after one year."

AVERAGE STARTING SALARY

New hires earn $23,750 during their year-long program.

BENEFITS OFFERED

Field organizers get health insurance. Additional benefits include a loan repayment program, paid vacation, holidays, sick days, and job placement assistance.

CONTACT INFORMATION
Jesse Littlewood

Recruitment Director

E-mail: jobs@greencorps.org

Tel: 617-426-8506, ext. 1

GETTING HIRED

Green Corps interviews "on as many college campuses as possible and conducts first-round phone interviews for all other qualified applicants." A successful applicant describes the process this way: "Green Corps has a three step application/interview process. First, there's a short, written application, at which point you provide your resume. It was helpful that my resume showed that I had been active on campus. Second, I interviewed on campus with the assistant director of the program. What made my first interview work was that I made a personal connection with the person interviewing me. I told stories that got her attention, made her laugh, and showed her that I was smart and motivated. On that basis I was invited to the interview weekend. Third, Green Corps takes the best candidates from the round of first interviews and invites them to group interview weekends. There are about five around the country during the hiring season, and they have about forty to fifty candidates per weekend. Over the two days, Green Corps runs you through a couple of skills sessions and another individual interview and evaluates overall chemistry and social skills. Even those who don't get hired generally agree that it's inspiring to meet so many smart, committed people like them."

MONEY AND PERKS

For Green Corps field organizers, "the salary and length of employment are fixed. Because Green Corps is a fellowship program, it runs thirteen months, and all of the thirty or so fellows [who] are hired each year work from the beginning of August until the end of the following August, when Green Corps staff helps them find more permanent positions in the environmental or social-change fields." The best perks include "a loan repayment program (for student loans), full staff-subsidized vacation in Aspen, Colorado, in December, spending time organizing in communities around the country, and a great outplacement service. Because Green Corps has such a great reputation in the environmental field, other organizations end up competing with one another for the chance to hire Green Corps organizers."

THE ROPES

All field organizers start at the beginning of August with a four-week orientation in Boston. The training is run "by Green Corps staff, alumni, and veteran leaders from across the environmental field. That's where you learn how to write a press release, run a meeting, recruit and develop volunteers, organize an event, build a coalition, etc." One corps member adds, "Green Corps is very much based around building a team among the organizers and on learning by doing, so we jumped right into classroom training the day after we arrived. There were different social events every night where all of the fellows could hang out—the people in each

Green Corps class remain close friends, and a lot of times people become close friends with other Green Corps alumni who weren't in their class." Organizers then set off on two-month campaigns in the field, after which they "meet for a week to debrief the previous campaign, get some additional training, and prepare for the next project."

DAY IN THE LIFE

Perhaps the most appealing—and intimidating—aspect of Green Corps' program is the amount of responsibility first jobbers take on. One newbie explains: "Basically Green Corps organizers are the directors of their campaigns in the cities where they work—so they don't have a boss overseeing them on the site, and they recruit and train everyone they work with. On my first campaign, I was responsible for signing on dozens of organizations to a coalition letter, holding media events, meeting with reporters, and recruiting and training citizen volunteers. On a typical day, I'd come into the office at 8:30 A.M. or 9:00 A.M. and make a detailed plan for my day. I'd spend the next two hours calling potential coalition groups and talking to them about the campaign. At noon, I'd take a break for lunch and meet with one of my student interns about her plan for the week and what she was going to accomplish for the campaign. In the afternoon, I would nail down the logistics of a press conference in the coming week, including the site and permit, and prep the speakers for the event. I would talk to existing coalition partners about turning out members to the press event. In the evening, I would spend a couple of hours [on the] phone [with] banking volunteers to [get them to] turn out for the press event."

PEERS

Because "most Green Corps organizers are in their campaign cities without any other Green Corps organizers there," the organization lacks the regular after-hours social scene present at many entry-level jobs. Even so, the peer network is a potent one. One organizer explains: "One of the biggest perks about the job is that you are in a class with an incredible group of Green Corps organizers. You bond with them during the classroom training in Boston. Then you keep in touch via phone and e-mail during the campaigns. When you get back together between each campaign for the follow-up trainings, it's like a mini-reunion. And then after the year is over, these people become your friends, colleagues, and support system. It's incredible to have such a tight network of such talented, motivated, creative people who are out there making a difference day in and day out."

MOVING ON

According to Green Corps, about 85 percent of its program graduates continue in "the social change and environmental field." Others travel, study abroad, or head to graduate school. Some of the graduates we spoke with now work for the Sierra Club, the Campaign to Ban Landmines, and Physicians for Human Rights.

ATTRITION

Green Corps isn't for everyone. Those who don't make it through the program usually cite "being overwhelmed, having too much responsibility, [and] working hard when their friends [who] care less about their jobs leave at five" and get paid much more. As one Corps graduate puts it, "The same things that are great about the job also make it tough."

BEST AND WORST

"For more than a decade, the oil and gas industry has lobbied to exploit the pristine Arctic National Wildlife Refuge. Now the industry is pushing to include drilling as part of the federal budget. Green Corps organizer Josh Buswell-Charkow needed to rally pro-Arctic groups and leaders in Minnesota to convince Senator Norm Coleman to protect the Arctic. Using skills learned from our classroom training, Josh recruited volunteers, and in just ten days, generated more than 8,000 phone calls and 300 letters to Senator Coleman's office. Hours before Senator Coleman made his final decision, Josh organized a press conference outside his St. Paul office. The press conference was covered in more than thirty newspapers and media outlets across the state and country. In the end, Senator Coleman voted no on drilling in the Arctic—helping to deliver a very narrow fifty-two to forty-eight victory. With the House set to vote on the budget this fall, the fight to protect the Arctic is far from over. And the Alaska Coalition has one again asked Green Corps to serve as their field team. In the 2005–2006 year, eleven Green Corps organizers are working across the country to raise media attention to protect the Arctic. The Green Corps organizers helped mobilize more than 5,000 Arctic supporters to travel to Washington, DC for Arctic Refuge Action Day."

HABITAT FOR HUMANITY INTERNATIONAL
Entry-level Jobs, Internships, and Externships

THE BIG PICTURE

Habitat for Humanity International describes itself as "a nonprofit, ecumenical Christian housing ministry" that "seeks to eliminate poverty housing and homelessness from the world and to make decent shelter a matter of conscience and action." The organization "invites people of all backgrounds, races, and religions to build houses together in partnership with families in need." Over the years, Habitat has succeeded in building more than 200,000 homes across the globe. The pay isn't great, and the work is hard, but few organizations offer the potential to experience satisfaction from having accomplished important work.

STATS

LOCATION(S) WHERE ENTRY-LEVEL EMPLOYEES WORK

The headquarters are located in Americus, Georgia; the organization has field offices across the United States.

AVERAGE NUMBER OF APPLICATIONS EACH YEAR

About 2,400 applicants seek out positions at Habitat for Humanity International each year.

AVERAGE NUMBER HIRED PER YEAR

Habitat for Humanity International hires about 100 people each year.

ENTRY-LEVEL POSITION(S) AVAILABLE

"Habitat for Humanity International has both internship and externship opportunities, which are particularly helpful to both current students and recent college graduates acquiring on-the-job skills and experience."

AVERAGE HOURS WORKED PER WEEK

Entry-level hires work about forty hours per week.

PERCENTAGE OF ENTRY-LEVEL HIRES STILL WITH THE COMPANY AFTER THREE, FIVE, AND TEN YEARS

Forty percent of entry-level hires remain with Habitat after three years.

AVERAGE STARTING SALARY

Entry-level hires earn $25,000 a year.

BENEFITS OFFERED

Habitat offers health insurance. Additional benefits include a 403(b) plan, ten paid holidays, disability insurance, an employee assistance program, flexible spending plans for both health care and dependent care, life insurance, and paid vacation/sick leave.

Contact Information

"For a list of positions or to apply, please visit www.habitat.org."

Getting Hired

Habitat for Humanity International does not recruit on college campuses; rather, it posts openings on its website and encourages prospective employees to apply online. Hiring is determined annually in accordance with the organization's budget and areas of need. The organization seeks those who have "a true commitment to the mission of Habitat for Humanity—people with the heart and faith to eliminate poverty housing worldwide." One successful hire notes, "I was convinced to apply because Habitat's Christian values appealed to me, and I saw the potential for meaningful work." Screening involves "asking candidates what their goals are, what they know about Habitat for Humanity, and how they learned of the open position." According to one first jobber here, "My resume and application were reviewed by the Human Resources Department. [I was then called] for an interview a few weeks after I sent my information. The interview was fairly casual; it worked in my favor that I had the qualifications they were looking for in education and experience and was willing to come as a volunteer (i.e., live on a small stipend) and live in the housing they provided. As best I can remember, the interviewer asked the expected questions about why I wanted to work for Habitat and my experiences working on my college newspaper. Also, she was able to answer my questions about the office environment and arranged for another employee in the department to call me later to answer my questions about living in volunteer housing." According to the organization, top interview performances show that "the candidate has done homework on Habitat for Humanity and is thoroughly versed in the organization's work, structure, and philosophy." The worst interview ever? "A candidate who thought that Habitat was an organization geared toward helping animals."

Money and Perks

You won't get rich monetarily working for Habitat for Humanity International—but you are likely to find the experience soul enriching. There's not a lot of wiggle room to negotiate about your position, either; first jobbers we spoke with described their offers as pretty much take-it-or-leave-it affairs. A few even came on as volunteers; their positions morphed into "real" jobs over time; or they worked as volunteers until a paying job opened up. There can be "some flexibility in terms of when you start," but "position description determines the salary, department, and job duties." Merit-based increases "are considered after one full year of employment, during the annual performance review. Salary or wage increases are based [on] performance." Workers agree that "the best fringe benefit of working for Habitat is the satisfaction that the organization's work changes people's lives for the better, in a permanent and sustainable way." One first jobber writes: "I'm not working to further someone else's bottom line; rather, our work makes an impact on communities all over the world."

The Ropes

Habitat for Humanity International hires on a rolling schedule and holds orientation sessions every Monday for new hires. Orientation is a one-day affair that "involves general information, benefits counseling, online training, and technology training." One first jobber writes, "During orientation, we learned about the phone system, e-mail software, benefits (time off, insurance, etc.), the history of the organization, and functions of different departments." Subsequent training is handled by one's supervisor.

DAY IN THE LIFE

Entry-level hires at Habitat for Humanity International serve in all types of roles. They perform typical entry-level tasks and are carefully supervised. One newbie in editorial writes, "My responsibilities were to check facts, edit articles for length, write short articles on assigned topics, and generally be helpful to my boss, the editor. I used the Internet to fulfill a lot of research and fact-checking assignments and [made] many phone calls to complete articles." A first jobber in information systems notes, "My main responsibilities were data entry and backup. I would receive a batch of donation pieces, and I would enter the names, address info, donation amounts, or any other partner information that was made available for our partners into the database. I would [then] save the changes and pass [it] to the next person, who would manually total all the donation amounts and compare [it] to my total, for reconciliation purposes." First jobbers tell us that "there is room to grow for people in certain, but not all, positions" and that "pay probably won't grow very much because we are a nonprofit ministry." That said, "the potential to develop your skills to a higher level are very good."

PEERS

Habitat for Humanity International is home to "a healthy-sized group of people in their mid- to late twenties who have come to Habitat early in their careers; and they are a fascinating, diverse group of people! Habitat's work tends to attract people with similar values but very different skills and life experiences, so getting to know them has been wonderful." Around the home office in Americus, "There is a social scene, but as one would expect in a small, Southern town, it's very casual and low-key. Front-porch sitting is still a major pastime in Americus!" First jobbers enjoy the "many opportunities to meet and greet newcomers. There are potlucks and other events that welcome newcomers to our organization." Employees also appreciate the "very open environment" within the organization.

MOVING ON

Those who leave Habitat for Humanity International, we're told, do so most often because of "family/spouse relocation" or "a new job in a different location." One first jobber writes, "The most common criticism I hear is from people who feel a bit overwhelmed by the rate of change in the organization. The last year, especially, has seen a lot of staff turnover and policy changes, and it can be difficult not to fear that your position will be the next casualty." Another agrees: "Lately [there] has been stress created by turnovers and the [possibility] that we may relocate."

HEADSETS.COM

Various Positions

THE BIG PICTURE

Headsets.com is an online retailer of telephone headsets; the company also operates www.headphones.com (which sells headphones) and www.conferencers.com (which sells—you guessed it!—conferencing telephones). This Bay Area company hires first jobbers in all areas of the business, though the majority start in customer service and product support.

STATS

LOCATION(S) WHERE ENTRY-LEVEL EMPLOYEES WORK

The company has offices in San Francisco and Walnut Creek, California.

AVERAGE NUMBER OF APPLICATIONS EACH YEAR

Headsets.com receives 2,600 applications per year.

AVERAGE NUMBER HIRED PER YEAR

Fifteen entry-level employees are hired each year.

ENTRY-LEVEL POSITION(S) AVAILABLE

Entry-level positions at Headsets.com are available in customer service, shipping and receiving, marketing, and web design.

AVERAGE HOURS WORKED PER WEEK

Entry-level employees work forty-four hours per week.

AVERAGE STARTING SALARY

The average starting salary for an entry-level hire at Headsets.com is $34,000.

BENEFITS OFFERED

An HR official reports, "Medical and dental insurance are available after an employee has been with the company for ninety days." Beyond the basics, Headsets.com also offers some additional benefits: "Once an employee has earned over $5,000, [he or she is] eligible for a company matched simple IRA. After a year of employment, most employees are eligible for stock options, which continually vest over a three year period."

CONTACT INFORMATION

Visit the company online at www.headsets.com/headsets/company/employment.html, or e-mail HR at employment@headsets.com.

Getting Hired

Many of our survey respondents found their positions at Headsets.com advertised on www.craiglist.org, "which is a listing of local jobs, apartments, personals, etc." Positions are also posted at the Headsets.com website. The hiring process is atypical; one first jobber observes, "I was interested in the position mainly because the company requested that instead of sending a resume, you write a letter to the hiring department about yourself and why you would like the job. I'm what you would refer to as 'antiresume,' so [that process] sounded ideal to me." The initial interview is done by telephone. One successful hire describes the experience: "An HR [rep] called and informed me that he was calling everyone who'd sent in an e-mail [for] preliminary phone interviews. Did I have a few minutes? I said, 'Sure,' and he [began] to ask a series of mostly silly questions ('What state is Wisconsin in?') just to test my phone manner. After several minutes of this, he informed me that I had passed this stage of the interview process, and that he'd like me to come in for some face-to-face interviews and testing," a procedure that includes "various personality tests." Finally, there is "an all-day, eight-hour interview that consists of sitting with a few customer service representatives while they take calls." Our contact in HR explains, "Throughout the interview process, we're trying to understand a potential employee's suitability for long-term work and his/her sustainability in the development and growth of the company."

Money and Perks

"The job was definitely negotiable as far as when I started, but I had no say over where I worked, what I did, and how much I was to get paid," writes a typical Headsets.com first jobber. Bonuses can be earned "by offering ideas to help the company and by participating in a weekly sales revenue guessing game." Also, "after a certain amount of time, employees [in the Customer Service Department] become eligible to participate in the GPB—the Group Productivity Bonus—which shares the rewards of the company's productivity on a bi-weekly basis." The GPB bonus may range from an additional $2.00–$5.00 per hour; it typically falls in the $2.00 to $3.50 range. Perks include "free cellular headsets every quarter and a $500 reimbursement for every sick day not taken per quarter (assuming we're profitable in the given year); [this] leads to a potential $2,000 bonus at year's end." Also, "for every record sales day, employees get a gift card to a store (Circuit City, Trader Joe's, etc.) or a set amount of money to spend on shoes, clothing, electronics, etc."

The Ropes

Orientation at Headsets.com "lasts two weeks. During this time, a new employee listens in to live calls, is given product and company training, and is given a daily checklist of things to do and learn." One first jobber writes, "Training/orientation consisted mostly of sitting in with other customer service representatives while they took calls. We had daily check-ins via telephone with our CEO, Mike Faith. We also watched several business videos regarding phone etiquette and customer service, and we were asked to read two short books of similar inspirational business-related wisdom." The final day of training "includes a follow-up with the CEO [about] everything we've learned."

Day in the Life

Many first jobbers enter the Headsets.com workplace performing customer service and product support roles. Most tell us that "you are given full CSR responsibilities from the get-go: answering phones, processing orders, doing basic product support, data entry, etc. A typical day is basically eight-and-a-half hours of that, with occasional breaks to check e-mail over at the 'personal use station' (we're not allowed to do any nonwork-related browsing or e-mail-checking at our work computers, so we have to take a break to do so)."

The job doesn't change over time; it does, however, provide opportunities for advancement. One former product support employee reports, "Within two months of joining the company, I was made the Product Support Lead, and now I'm also the Co-Customer Service Lead responsible for coleading the entire call center."

Peers

The Bay Area is a magnet for young, talented, creative people, many of whom take in jobs such as customer service while aspiring to succeed as artists and musicians. Headsets.com certainly has its share of these employees. One notes, "The people are the best part of the job. All of my peers are a lot like myself and are a lot of fun to hang out with. We're all actually pretty good friends and get together outside of work for drinks almost every Friday." The same worker observes that "My manager is twenty-four, and the whole company is like that. Young people really get a bad rap, so I enjoy that the people running our company are so young; it shows our CEO is thinking outside of the box."

Moving On

People leave Headsets.com when they "develop interests outside of customer service," when they "need a change of workplace," or when they "decide to continue their education." The turnover rate here is relatively high; about one-third of new hires stay with the company for less than a year, and the average tenure for entry-level employees is two years. As one explains, "The job can be pretty repetitive, and answering the phones for eight hours straight can start to take its toll. People mostly complain about wishing they had more downtime between calls or that they had additional responsibilities [beyond] answering the phones. We hire people [who], for the most part, are overly qualified for the position they're in. This means they can get bored doing the same thing every day."

Best and Worst

The company tells us that "at any given time, we have between five [and] ten superstar employees who shine through their ability to go above and beyond company expectations while providing world-class customer love." The worst first jobber ever "would be one who didn't make it through training."

HEWLWTT-PACKARD COMPANY
Various Positions

THE BIG PICTURE

Hewlett-Packard Company (HP) is a manufacturer of computers; but the company also provides much more, such as "technology solutions for consumers, businesses, and institutions across the globe; IT infrastructure; global services; and imaging and printing for consumers, enterprises, and small and medium businesses." In its literature, HP emphasizes the importance of a comfortable, positive work environment.

STATS

LOCATION(S) WHERE ENTRY-LEVEL EMPLOYEES WORK

Entry-level employees work in Cupertino, California; Palo Alto, California; Roseville, California; San Diego, California; Mountain View, California; Colorado Springs, Colorado; Fort Collins, Colorado; Atlanta, Georgia; Boise, Idaho; Marlborough, Massachusetts; Corvallis, Oregon; Austin, Texas; Houston, Texas; Richardson, Texas; Vancouver, Washington; Indianapolis, Indiana; and Omaha, Nebraska.

AVERAGE NUMBER OF APPLICATIONS EACH YEAR

"HP receives more than 250,000 external applications each year for all levels of positions in the Americas."

AVERAGE NUMBER HIRED PER YEAR OVER THE LAST TEN YEARS

"On average, the number of entry-level employees hired in the United States each year over the past ten years is 600."

ENTRY-LEVEL POSITION(S) AVAILABLE

Entry-level hires work as computer engineers, computer scientists, electrical engineers, management information systems analysts, sales representatives, supply chain management analysts, chemical engineers, chemists, materials scientists, and physicists, among other positions.

AVERAGE HOURS WORKED PER WEEK

New hires work forty hours per week.

AVERAGE STARTING SALARY

"Each year HP researches the market and adjusts its university compensation guidelines accordingly. Research shows that the company offers competitive salaries appropriate for entry-level university hires. The details of this information are confidential."

BENEFITS OFFERED

The company offers medical, dental, and vision coverage. Additional benefits include short- and long-term disability, flexible spending accounts, life and accident insurance, employee assistance program, retirement medical savings account, a 401(k) plan (which vests after five years), a share ownership plan, vacation and paid holidays, an employee purchase program, and an annual company performance bonus program.

CONTACT INFORMATION

Interested parties may apply online at www.hp.com/GO/jobs and are encouraged to contact their university's career services office to see if Hewlett-Packard recruits on campus.

GETTING HIRED

HP "focuses its proactive campus recruiting efforts and long-term relationships on HP partner schools;" but students at other schools are encouraged to apply via the company website. Company officials tell us that they most highly value a prospective employee's ability to work in a team, to take initiative when required, and to write and communicate effectively. Many jobs require technical expertise; one employee notes that during the interview process, "they asked a lot of C++ questions, so if someone didn't nail those, I suppose [he or she] probably wouldn't get the job." The interview process proceeds in several stages; one employee recalls, "Originally I did a phone interview with the recruiter, then a phone interview with the hiring manager. I was then flown in for a round of interviews with several people currently working in the group. The phone interviews were about gauging interest and job/education background. The on-site interviews [focused on] job and education experience, along with [my] technical abilities." HR officials note that "the best interview performances are typically done by those candidates who have spent a significant amount of time researching the company prior to their interviews. It is essential that candidates distinguish themselves from their peers by learning as much as possible. They [may] then leverage that information by showing the interviewer how their background can benefit the company." Successful interviewees also "listen well to the interviewer, engage in an active two-way conversation, and give examples of results they've achieved." Many newbies also report that working as an intern during college presents a great way to get your foot in the door.

MONEY AND PERKS

According to the company, "HP has an annual review date and increase process, at which time consideration is given to increasing an employee's salary based on market comparisons, performance, and time in position." HP also has a "bonus program that is available to all employees;" bonuses are "based on meeting company performance goals."

New hires report that their starting date can be "totally flexible" and that there's occasionally some latitude in their choice of location; the company representatives similarly report that "there is a lot of flexibility offered to employees [regarding] work-life options, [as] arranged between manager and employee." Employees' favorite perks include "discounts associated with a large company [as well as] local discounts (percent off, reduced price tickets, etc.), free books, and tons of online technical material, [and] the work-life balance: Your personal life is valued very, very highly here."

THE ROPES

New HP hires begin their tenures with the You + HP program, in which they "learn about the company strategy, culture, metrics, and organizational structure. They are also given individual [orientations] by their managers and mentors (if assigned);" these guides teach newbies "about working at HP and [serve as] someone to go to for questions." The amount and kind of training workers receive varies from one department to another. A software/firmware developer tells us that he "spent a month working with the group that tests the firmware that [his] group develops" before doing any work on his own. A marketing manager, however, reports having received "no training. It took me a long time to figure things out." Mentor relationships are not uncommon and often serve as a new hire's informal training; one first jobber writes, "I learned about some of the software processes by reading documentation or books. The majority of what I learned was guided by a team leader [who] was designated as my mentor."

INTERNATIONAL RESCUE COMMITTEE
Various Positions

THE BIG PICTURE

"Refugee relief, respect, renewal" is the slogan of the International Rescue Committee (IRC), an international organization that provides housing, food, water, medical assistance, and other essentials to people uprooted by war, violence, disease, or natural disasters. The organization also offers long-term relief in the form of education programs, job training, and employment services.

STATS

LOCATION(S) WHERE ENTRY-LEVEL EMPLOYEES WORK

"[There is] potential for entry-level positions in any IRC office—domestic (including headquarters in New York or any regional resettlement office) or international."

AVERAGE NUMBER OF APPLICATIONS EACH YEAR

The IRC receives "roughly 2,600 applications per year (domestic and international) for entry-level positions."

AVERAGE NUMBER HIRED PER YEAR OVER THE LAST TEN YEARS

The IRC fills "roughly 100 (domestic and international) entry-level positions per year."

ENTRY-LEVEL POSITION(S) AVAILABLE

Domestic new hires work as "volunteers, administrators, and specialists." International new hires work as "volunteers, interns, and officers."

AVERAGE HOURS WORKED PER WEEK

New hires work a little over thirty-seven hours per week.

PERCENTAGE OF ENTRY-LEVEL HIRES STILL WITH COMPANY AFTER THREE YEARS

"After three years, domestic, 28 percent; international, 5 percent (these are, by nature, short-term positions)."

AVERAGE STARTING SALARY

"International volunteers/interns [earn an] average $500 [per] month. International officers [earn from] $20,000–$24,000 per year. Domestic [officers earn from] $27,000–$30,000 per year."

BENEFITS OFFERED

"International [hires receive] major medical, life insurance, emergency evacuation, travel insurance, and workers' compensation. Domestic [hires receive] major medical, dental, life insurance, emergency evacuation, travel insurance, workers' compensation." Additional benefits for "international employees, including volunteers and interns, [are] round-trip transportation, housing, travel within country, coverage of visa expenses, immunizations, medical exams, and a 403(b) and pension plan. [Additional benefits for] domestic employees [include] options for a 403(b) plan, a transit-saver program, and a cafeteria plan."

CONTACT INFORMATION

Visit the website at www.ircjobs.org.

GETTING HIRED

"Volunteering is a great way to start with IRC—both in the United States and overseas," employees tell us. One employee writes, "[Volunteer work] gave me the opportunity to show my interest in the organization and my commitment to working with refugees. When a position opened, I already knew a lot about the organization and the programs in Atlanta and had already demonstrated some of my strengths." Internships are also an excellent gateway to full-time work. Those without volunteer or internship experiences may still apply through the organization's website. The organization seeks in its prospective hires "international experience, strong writing skills, excellent interpersonal and communication skills, [an] ability to work productively and independently in a team environment, flexibility, and a sense of humor." So how do you wow IRC's recruiters? "I definitely think that my enthusiasm for the work, matched by my studies at college and extracurricular activities, as well as the fact that I had found IRC on my own demonstrated to the recruiter that I was very serious about working for this organization and that it fit into my long-term career plans," reports one successful hire.

MONEY AND PERKS

Your IRC salary is "not really negotiable," but "at the same time, it is the ideal job" for many people who take it. Low wages often come part-and-parcel with a satisfying career, especially in the world of nonprofits. Organization officials report that it "has an annual [salary] increase system in place for domestic and international employees. Additional increases are based on performance." First jobbers identify numerous perks; they tell us that "it's hard to beat getting paid to run around the African bush in a Land Rover and attend regional meetings in Zanzibar. But better than any of that is the chance to meet firsthand and talk to the people IRC assists and works with. These are people who have suffered through some of the worst oppression and privation one can possibly imagine and yet are, in many cases, some of the most optimistic and inspiring people you will ever meet." They also appreciate that "there is flexibility within the organization" and that "it's not terribly formal. You have to wear your suit when you go to meetings at the United Nations, but you can wear jeans otherwise."

THE ROPES

Orientations at IRC are "held on a quarterly basis and bring together new staff from headquarters, [from] regional resettlement offices across the United States, and from field offices around the world for three days in New York." The orientation "typically covers payroll and benefits, IRC policies and procedures, a general introduction to other IRC programs, security and safety procedures when working for IRC overseas, how to manage stress while working overseas, and other topics." International staff members "receive an orientation in-country on arrival." One staffer who worked in Guinea and Ethiopia reports, "When I arrived in Guinea, my supervisor immediately took me out into the field for a week to visit all of the refugee camps and meet the staff in three different field sites. My boss met me at the airport, helped me change money, and showed me my accommodations. In Ethiopia, my immediate supervisor actually met me at the airport at 2:00 A.M. when I arrived. I had a two-day orientation [at] headquarters and then flew to the field to visit two refugee camps and to meet my staff." Training is often on-the-job and handled by mentors. One first jobber writes, "Although there was a steep learning curve, I didn't find this to be a problem and never felt like I did not know enough. You have to quickly absorb a lot of information about subjects as diverse as public health surveys, international social work, U.S. government grants and contracts, and U.N. peacekeeping operations."

DAY IN THE LIFE

The IRC calls on its first jobbers to perform a wide assortment of jobs, both at home and abroad. The tasks are enormously complex and often difficult, complicated by the variety of governments with which the IRC must work. That the IRC only operates in trouble spots makes the job more challenging still; so too does the organization's modest budget. One program specialist explains, "Budgets at nonprofits are tight, and there's a lot of administrative work that needs to get done, so program specialists wind up bearing the burden of photocopying, making travel arrangements, scheduling meetings, and other not so intellectually rigorous tasks. At the same time, the nature of international assistance is that it is constantly overwhelming, but usually in a positive, up-to-your-eyeballs-and-loving-every-minute-of-it sort of way." First jobbers may find themselves a little overwhelmed at first, but eventually they hit their stride. One writes, "Someone new to the world of international humanitarian assistance simply does not possess the knowledge and experience to weigh in on substantial issues. With time (and in particular, by getting the chance to travel to the field and see firsthand how IRC assists refugees and partners with communities to help them recover from conflict), [we] develop into experts on their programs and their part of the world and are able to make substantive contributions to the organization." And of course, there's another payoff: As one first jobber puts it, "The work is rewarding, and the people I work with are highly motivated, intelligent, compassionate, and cosmopolitan."

PEERS

IRC first jobbers in the United States tell us that "there's a lot of camaraderie and a solid after-hours social scene. Informal happy hours happen approximately once a month or so." Overseas workers state, "All of us expatriates live together. Thus we work *and* live together, and we socialize all the time. As we are all living away from friends and family, we tend to largely socialize with [one another] outside of work. We often eat together, etc. In overseas work, I think expatriate staff spend a great deal of time together (which is also why personality and an ability to cope with overseas life is very important). Even if we are different, we are going through a similar experience and facing similar challenges." Another perk of the peer network is "making friends with colleagues around the world. After working at IRC, odds are you'll have friends [in every continent on] whose couches you can crash."

MOVING ON

The IRC tells us that "domestically, most staff leave to pursue higher education and professional growth. For our international employees, much of our work takes place in high-security areas, such as Afghanistan or the Congo. Therefore employees may leave to work in a more stable environment or to take a break from the rigors of overseas work." The average tenure of an overseas employee is two years; domestic employees tend to last longer.

ATTRITION

"Some people have real difficulty adjusting to the fast pace of the NGO (nongovernmental organization), the heavy workload, and the stress of living overseas," workers at the IRC tell us. "There are also a lot of frustrations in terms of logistics, working through the bureaucracy of overseas governments, dealing with donor limits and demands, and the challenge of working with and managing staff of different nationalities and cultures." These challenges, plus the challenge of living on a low wage, drive some first jobbers to other pursuits. One employee writes, "I have no plans to leave at this point, though it is always tempting to go to the for-profit world and make more money. That said, I am very aware of the intangibles that I would be giving up here, and so I stick around."

J.E.T. PROGRAMME

Coordinator for International Relations and Assistant Language Teacher

THE BIG PICTURE

J.E.T.s—that's what participants in the Japanese Exchange and Teaching Programme are called—spend a year (or more) in Japan, primarily teaching English, though the program also offers some other community service jobs. The J.E.T. Programme offers a great way to visit Japan and immerse yourself in Japanese culture while doing worthwhile work.

STATS

LOCATION(S) WHERE ENTRY-LEVEL EMPLOYEES WORK

The J.E.T. Programme has many locations across Japan.

AVERAGE NUMBER HIRED PER YEAR OVER THE LAST TEN YEARS

Approximately 2,500 people are hired per year.

ENTRY-LEVEL POSITION(S) AVAILABLE

New hires work as assistant language teachers, coordinators for international relations, and sports exchange advisors.

AVERAGE HOURS WORKED PER WEEK

New hires work thirty-five hours every week.

PERCENTAGE OF ENTRY-LEVEL HIRES STILL WITH COMPANY AFTER THREE, FIVE, AND TEN YEARS

Not applicable. "The programme is for one year with the possibility of extending twice."

AVERAGE STARTING SALARY

New hires earn 3.6 million per year (calm down; that's yen, not dollars!). Exchange rates fluctuate daily; you may use an online currency converter to see how much this amounts to in U.S. dollars.

BENEFITS OFFERED

New hires receive Japanese national insurance and accident and medical insurance.

CONTACT INFORMATION

Visit the website at www.jetprogramme.org.

GETTING HIRED

The application process is "run by Japanese embassies and consulates in forty countries and differs slightly accordingly." Applications may be downloaded at Japan's Ministry of Foreign Affairs home page;

the application is standard and asks for education and employment background information, a statement of purpose essay, academic transcripts, and letters of reference. After reviewing applications, the Japanese government contacts likely candidates to schedule interviews. One new hire writes, "I was interviewed by three people: a former J.E.T. employee, a university professor, and a Japanese consulate representative. It was a formal interview; all questions had been prepared by the interviewers and written down beforehand. Each interviewer asked three to four, mostly situational, questions. Some examples are: 'Since you are a vegetarian, what would you do if the principal at your school invited you over for dinner and offered you meat?' [and] 'Boys can be curious about female bodies. What would you say if one of your students asked for your bust-waist-hip measurements?'" Another adds, "I was intimidated when being interviewed by three people, but it wasn't bad. The interviewers were friendly. The application process is long, and you don't find out where you are placed until after you accept the position, which could be a drawback for some."

MONEY AND PERKS

J.E.T.s think you should know that "the terms of [their] contract are government policy and in no way flexible," so don't bother trying to wrangle a few extra yen during the interview. J.E.T.s mostly think they get a fair deal. One writes, "I was supplied an apartment; was helped getting set up with a bank account and phone, etc.; and was paid well." They also appreciate the fact that "J.E.T. is affiliated with both the Japanese and United States governments, so you know it isn't a back-door, monkey bars company." For the teachers, the best fringe benefit—besides the free trip to and from Japan—is the work schedule, which includes many vacation days.

THE ROPES

New J.E.T.s start out with "a couple of orientation sessions at the Japanese embassy in DC," then continue in Tokyo once they arrive. One J.E.T. writes, "The [Tokyo] orientation was a grueling three days in an overpriced hotel. It was a series of meetings and seminars relating to the J.E.T. Programme and teaching ideas." Another new J.E.T. adds, "They told us things like 'Don't stick your chopsticks in your rice' and 'Never put sugar in green tea.' Yes, their orientation programs need some help. I know that most J.E.T.s (including me) were disappointed that we didn't get more practical information or teacher training." Afterward, "most training was on-the-job, learning the boundaries of what was and wasn't expected of me."

DAY IN THE LIFE

The vast majority of J.E.T.s serve as assistant language teachers. Here's how one describes her typical day in Japan: "Arrive at 8:20 A.M. Sit through a five-minute morning meeting in Japanese. Drink green tea. Begin reading my teaching materials or the textbooks to make a lesson plan. (I typically had two to three classes, fifty minutes each, a day.) Read a book or the newspaper. Eat lunch in the teachers' room. Go to the convenience store to buy chocolate. Continue making a lesson plan for the week. Talk to students in the hall. Drink more green tea. Leave by 4:00 P.M." Another J.E.T. agrees that the workload is often surprisingly light: "Typically, I taught anywhere from one to three fifty-minute classes per day (out of an eight-hour work day). The rest of the time I [planned lessons], e-mailed, read, wrote, studied Japanese, spaced out, and observed. Teaching consisted of reading a one-page passage out of the textbook that my kids would repeat and then write in their notebooks. About every two weeks, I would plan a game or speaking activity." Despite occasional bouts with boredom, most J.E.T.s describe their experience as a valuable one. As one notes, "I worked with some incredible teachers and some mediocre ones. The best ones helped me with my Japanese-language studies and answered questions I had about Japanese culture. I learned both what I wanted to aim for in my teaching career and what I wanted to avoid in terms of style of teaching."

PEERS

Peer relationships in J.E.T. depend largely on the assignment. As one newbie tells us, "I was the only J.E.T. in my town, so it was pretty much up to me to meet other J.E.T.s and make plans with them. There were other towns that had, like, thirteen J.E.T.s, and some of these people hung out exclusively with other J.E.T.s at western-type bars, clubs, and restaurants. I tried to [balance hanging out] with other J.E.T.s and [with] Japanese people." Another J.E.T. offers, "I made friends, but the other J.E.T.s were all across the board. I definitely met some great people; I even met my boyfriend through the J.E.T. Without fellow J.E.T.s, life in Japan can get lonely;" as one teacher explains, "I felt isolated. There was the language barrier, as well as the fact that an outsider, especially a foreigner, is not really welcome into the larger group or expected to do real work or take on real responsibilities."

MOVING ON

The J.E.T. Programme is a one-year deal, though J.E.T.s have the option to renew their contracts twice and extend their stays to three years. Most of them return home to attend graduate school or seek teaching jobs in the United States. One recalls, "I left after one year. I had a great time and would recommend the [programme] to anyone, but it was time for me to go. I felt that I had a good experience and staying any longer would have dragged it out to the point that it [would become] unpleasant."

ATTRITION

Homesickness and loneliness are the chief causes of attrition, but there's a huge disincentive to leaving the programme early: Participants are then responsible for their airfare home, plus other related expenses (rent and fees on a participant's apartment in Japan, for one) that quickly add up to a small fortune. If they fail to complete the contract for any but the most dire reasons (i.e., a death in the immediate family), they must pay all of these costs.

Johns Hopkins University Applied Physics Lab
Various Positions

The Big Picture

The Johns Hopkins University Applied Physics Laboratory does a ton of work for NASA and the U.S. Navy. It also performs research for other government agencies. There is no formal entry-level program, but there are plenty of jobs available for those with highly developed technology and/or science skills.

Stats

Location(s) Where Entry-level Employees Work

Entry-level employees work in Laurel, Maryland.

Entry-level Position(s) Available

There are opportunities in many of APL's 130 labs and technical facilities.

Average Hours Worked Per Week

Entry-level hires work forty hours per week.

Benefits Offered

"APL's flexible benefits plan offers different health care options to meet the needs of staff members and their families. Covered services from designated providers generally require small co-payments; covered services received outside the designated provider network (opt-out benefits) are covered after a deductible amount is satisfied. Two dental insurance plans cover preventive, diagnostic, and restorative services for employees and their eligible dependents." Additional benefits include paid leave, a flexible spending program, a pension plan, continuing education funding, and scholarships.

Contact Information

Visit the website at www.jhuapl.edu/employment.

Getting Hired

One entry-level employee at APL tells us that the application process "is rather simple. I gave my resume to the recruiter at the college career fair, and I received an e-mail a month later inviting me to interview. APL sends your resume to all [of the] departments, and you interview with all [of the] departments that have an interest in you. For the interviews, the tone was very casual, and I interviewed with four members of my current group. After all of my interviews were conducted, I received a job offer that afternoon." Many first jobbers describe the hiring process as surprisingly pleasant. One first jobber offers, "I had a great experience communicating with APL prior to attending the interview. All accommodations were taken care of, and everything was explained to me prior to flying out to interview." New employees recommend that you "ask intelligent questions that show you've taken the time to look around [the] website. Also, indicate a department [in which] you are interested in working." Those who serve successful internships have an inside track on being hired.

MONEY AND PERKS

Salary, start date, and the nature of the job are "somewhat negotiable," new hires tell us. One writes, "My group had some tasks in mind for me when they hired me, but they remain somewhat flexible as to which projects I get to work on (based on my preference). If I decide one day that I don't like what I'm doing at all, I'm of the impression that I can apply for a position in another group at APL, so there's also opportunity for lateral movement here." Workers praise the retirement plan; one employee says, "APL matches my donation to my retirement account two-for-one up to a fixed percentage of my salary. Other than that, an APL employee is entitled to discounts throughout Maryland. So another example of a fringe benefit of working here is that I get 12.5 percent off of my cell phone bill every month."

THE ROPES

"There are a few layers to the orientation process" at APL. "On the first day of work, there is an orientation process which lasts about half a day and provides information on the various employee benefit programs, goes over adherence to national security guidelines here at APL, and outlines some basic company policies. After that half-day session, you start working. There is an additional week-long orientation that is held twice a year." That training, called Professional Staff Orientation Program (PSOP), "lasts for one full week, and each day you learn about two departments at APL, take tours of those departments' facilities, and meet people [who] you would have otherwise not been able to meet." Regarding an employees' tenure, a new hire says, "When there is a need for some explanation of something specific to my job here, it's usually done by my supervisor or one of my more experienced coworkers. The only formal training I've had since coming here was a week-long class I took at Penn State University, which provided a good background for the field I'm working in."

DAY IN THE LIFE

APL has many divisions working on so many different projects. There is no typical day within a single division, much less within the entire enterprise, according to workers. All work is project-based; sometimes workers are assigned to several projects at a time. Here's how one employee describes his first assignment at APL: "When I was first hired, my responsibilities were to spend half my time researching a new technology that my group was considering implementing and half my time becoming familiar with a project that was started by a former group member. Originally, I was supposed to continue work on the project where the former employee left off. Within that framework, a typical day for me included reading textbooks and journal papers for half the day and looking through and experimenting with existing Matlab code for the other half. The goal in looking through the Matlab code was first to assess the performance of the existing project, then to make a recommendation of whether or not we should move forward with the project, and if so, then to suggest a methodology for moving forward with it. Within a few weeks, I stopped working on both projects and began working on a few different existing projects, but I was adding to and enhancing them as opposed to just analyzing them. Now I spend most of my day writing code using Matlab."

PEERS

Other than orientation, "there aren't many structured social activities for new employees," first jobbers tell us. "However, there is an active network of younger employees at APL called the Recent Graduate Network that gets together both at and outside of work. I've definitely made some friends and good acquaintances this way. The actual number of hours per week that we interact varies, but often times, we'll do lunch during the week, and we'll go out to happy hours or clubs about once a week." Another worker adds, "APL has great camaraderie! There's always a group doing something after-hours or somewhere to go with other employees. There are all kinds of sports and clubs [over two dozen, according to APL representatives]."

MOVING ON

The APL is a great place to build a career, and the folks we spoke with have no intention of leaving. Complaints are few and far between; "APL has a tendency to promote brilliant scientists to management [positions]," writes one employee wryly. "However, not all scientists have management skills." Another writes, "Most APL employees are pretty happy with their jobs, and I definitely fall into that category. People here like the relaxed atmosphere. You don't have dress up to come to work, and APL is very flexible in letting you schedule your forty hours per week. Some people work nine hours per day and take every other Friday off. APL also has a great employee benefits package." People who do leave most often move onto positions with other movers and shakers in the world of applied physics; other people return to academia.

ATTRITION

APL representatives say that "volunteer turnover [terminations excluding retirements, disability, and for-cause releases] is very low, particularly among the technical professional staff ([fewer] than 2 percent)."

KATZ MEDIA GROUP
Sales Assistant

THE BIG PICTURE

Katz Media, which includes the Katz Radio Group, the Katz Television Group, and Clear Channel Radio Sales, sells commercial time for more than 2,600 radio stations and 400 television stations across the country. If you love the media, advertising, and schmoozing, Katz Media could be the gateway to your dream career.

STATS

LOCATION(S) WHERE ENTRY-LEVEL EMPLOYEES WORK

Katz Media has twenty-one regional offices at which entry-level employees work.

AVERAGE NUMBER OF APPLICATIONS EACH YEAR

Katz receives 10,000-plus applications every year.

AVERAGE NUMBER HIRED PER YEAR OVER THE LAST TEN YEARS

The company hires 300 people per year.

ENTRY-LEVEL POSITION(S) AVAILABLE

New hires work as sales assistants.

AVERAGE HOURS WORKED PER WEEK

New hires work forty hours per week.

AVERAGE STARTING SALARY

The starting salary for entry-level hires is $23,000+ per year.

BENEFITS OFFERED

The company offers medical, dental, and life insurance, as well as short-term and long-term disability. Additional benefits include an employee stock purchase plan, a 401(k) plan, tuition reimbursement, commuter check, and employee assistance program.

CONTACT INFORMATION

Anne Strafaci
Vice President of Recruitment
125 West 55th Street
New York, NY 10019
Fax: 212-424-6110
E-mail: anne.strafaci@katz-media.com

Getting Hired

Katz's on-campus recruiting consists of "interviewing on campus with a few area colleges that are close to our offices" and "attending many career fairs that usually consist of several colleges." A resume referral program is available for interested students from out-of-area colleges; the firm will "accept applications from anyone with a strong interest in media, strong background in client relations, and the personality to match." Here's how one successful hire describes the interview process: "I was interviewed initially by human resources. My interviews went very well, and the next step was to see where my specific skills could be put to use. A week later I was called in to interview with two different divisions. [For] each division I was interviewed by three different individuals who gave me a feel for what each department did and how I would fit into the scheme of things."

Money and Perks

During their first year at Katz, sales assistants "could receive one to two pay increases, depending on performance and the department's budget. After that, there are yearly performance reviews" to determine raises. The firm engages in other "employee morale efforts," such as "an Instant Rewards Program (employees recognized with gift certificates for a job well done), on-site yoga classes (in New York), and on-site personal development seminars like financial planning, parenting, nutrition, etc." First jobbers appreciate that "there are many opportunities for upward mobility within the company."

The Ropes

Orientation at Katz is a half-day affair, and it is "very informative." One employee recalls, "It basically gives you an overview of the company and the services that it provides to its clients. The orientation also goes over basic paperwork necessary for any new job. Additionally, the orientation allowed us to find out about the most important clients: the employees. Learning about the different perks and services available to employees was definitely the highlight of orientation." New hires subsequently "receive training in how to use the various computer systems specific to [their] industry. The computer information systems department holds weekly workshops to help new hires adjust to working with the new programs. [Employees] also [get] additional training from [their] supervisors and fellow sales assistants." Firm officials note that "there are a number of veteran employees who informally act as mentors to new employees." One sales assistant explains, "We are constantly having assistant sales-training classes taught by the account executives; and my own rep, who I assist, is very helpful in showing me anything he can to help me in the job."

Day in the Life

Sales assistants "are the backbone of Katz Media Group's sales teams because they assist account executives with the high-volume work of television, radio, or Internet sales," a representative from the firm tells us. As their title suggests, these entry-level employees "assist all the sales reps on a team. [They] input orders, send revisions, process 'make-goods,' request contracts, and interact with the stations and agencies via e-mail and telephone." It's a job that requires newbies to stay on their toes; one newbie writes, "My most important job is to maintain my contracts and make sure that spots are running. If they are not running, I troubleshoot to fix the problem. My job entails a lot of troubleshooting and management of relationships!" At first, sales assistants have to run everything they do by their supervisors, but "as time goes on, you're given more responsibility and do not have to report to your sales rep for as many things." Another new hire says, "For me, a trust developed between us, as the reps saw what I was capable of and knew that my understanding of the business was growing." As they work their way up the corporate ladder, sales assistants appreciate that "high-level people are very accessible; that is what makes [their] division at Katz a good working environment. [Their] execs are very visible, and this allows for a better rapport to be established between the execs and employees."

Peers

Because "this industry is *very* social at all levels of employment, and entertaining clients is an important part of the job," Katz employees participate in a "huge after-work social scene." Their socializing, though, is more often with "reps, their assistants, and media buyers" than with other Katz first jobbers. A new hire writes, "All of us entry-level employees definitely get along very well, and there is a sense of friendship among us. We don't hesitate to help [one another] out and ask one another questions when they arise. We occasionally go out hour together (maybe once a week), which is a great opportunity to know your coworkers on a more social level. All in all, it's nice to have other young people around you; [it] makes the transition into your first job an easier experience."

Moving On

Sales assistants generally stay in their position for one year, then either move up or move out. Some leave to work at "ad agencies, radio and television stations, and other sales-related companies." A first jobber here "take[s] it day by day," telling us that "as long as I enjoy what I am doing, I will stick with it. When the day comes that this gig or company is [no longer] fun, then I will make a change."

Attrition

People who leave before their first year is up—and that's about 30 percent of all first jobbers, according to Katz—usually "complain about the pay, but who is ever satisfied with their salary?" A few people find themselves assisting account executives with whom they are incompatible; employees who cannot get themselves reassigned usually leave the firm.

KPMG
Client Service Professionals

THE BIG PICTURE

KPMG is one of the "big four" in the assurance and tax services business (the other three are Deloitte Touche Tohmatsu, Ernst & Young LLP, and PricewaterhouseCoopers). Aspiring accountants can hone their skills at KPMG while preparing for their CPA exams, for which the company offers study materials and other support services.

STATS

LOCATION(S) WHERE ENTRY-LEVEL EMPLOYEES WORK

Entry-level employees work at 122 offices across the United States.

AVERAGE NUMBER OF APPLICATIONS EACH YEAR

KPMG receives many applications; approximately 5,000 candidates reach the interview stage.

AVERAGE NUMBER HIRED PER YEAR OVER THE LAST TEN YEARS

KPMG hires approximately 1,500 people annually.

ENTRY-LEVEL POSITION(S) AVAILABLE

"Assurance associates [work] in our Business Measurement Process (Audit), Financial Advisory Services, and Risk Advisory Services practices. Tax associates [work] in our Federal Tax, State, and Local Tax; International Executive Services; International Corporate Services; and Economic Consulting Services practices."

AVERAGE HOURS WORKED PER WEEK

New hires work fifty hours per week.

AVERAGE STARTING SALARY

"Average starting salaries for our new hires vary greatly by practice, degree, and geographic region."

BENEFITS OFFERED

Company benefits include a point-of-service health care plan with choice of network or nonnetwork physicians; a number of medical plans, with no physician networks, that vary by deductible and coinsurance levels; HMOs (available in most locations); prescription drug program; dental plan; vision care; Vision One discount plan; short- and long-term disability; and life insurance. Additional benefits include twenty-five paid personal days accrued monthly for vacation, illness, or other absence; eligibility for the incentive compensation program; bonus for passing the CPA, Bar, or Enrolled Agents Exam; free MicroMash CPA Exam review software and discounts for CPA Exam review courses; flexible spending accounts of up to

$3,000 pre-tax for nonreimbursed eligible medical expenses and up to $5,000 pre-tax for eligible dependent care expenses; a 401(k) plan with KPMG match, including Merrill Lynch Benefits OnlineSM (assistance in preparation and management of retirement savings and financial investing); KPMG pension plan; paid time off for new parents; an adoption reimbursement program; child care discounts; emergency backup dependent care program; METPAY auto and home insurance discount program; and mortgage assistance programs and financial assistance.

CONTACT INFORMATION

Visit the website at www.kpmgcampus.com.

GETTING HIRED

KPMG recruits on a number of college campuses across the country. In addition, "students from all schools can submit their resumes online." At many schools, "representatives from each of the big four firms make trips prior to accepting resumes for specific positions. Firms set up social events to meet potential interview candidates and have a presence at university-hosted career fairs." These events, our respondents say, offer the perfect opportunity to meet face-to-face with recruiters and hand out resumes. On-campus interviews come next. Here's how one entry-level employee describes the experience: "The night before the interview, KPMG held a dinner, which gave candidates the opportunity to meet their interviewer, as well as other members of the firm. The tables were set up so that all the interviewees were seated with their interviewer for the next day. About seven interviewees, the interviewer, and two other KPMG employees sat at each table. The subsequent interview was relaxed and easy. A manager from the Boston office interviewed me. It was a conversation about the experiences that I had on my resume, my plans to continue my education, [and] my expectations of what the firm could offer me." Entry-level workers note that there are practice questions on the KPMG website to help you prepare for the interview. After the initial interview comes another round of interviews, similar in content, but this time at a KPMG office. The few lucky candidates who clear this hurdle receive job offers soon after.

MONEY AND PERKS

"The market generally sets salaries, and KPMG is competitive with the other firms, but there is little negotiation," entry-level employees tell us, though one of our survey respondents notes that "salary is negotiable if you have another competitive offer." Everyone agrees with the company line, namely that "salaries are commensurate with the level and competitive with the marketplace. Top performers have the opportunity to earn incentive compensation if the firm has met its revenue targets." Workers' favorite perks include five weeks of paid vacation. ("KPMG believes in a good work-life balance; the firm wants its employees to work hard when they have to but take time for themselves as well.") "Discounts with various companies, and the flexibility of the job itself" are also popular. Aspiring accountant types with a touch of wanderlust could be happy with KPMG: "One of the great aspects of KPMG is that it is an international organization, and the firm would rather keep you and make you happy than lose you. Therefore, it is relatively easy to move from one office to another, especially [at] the beginning of your career."

THE ROPES

Training at KPMG begins with a brief orientation ("new hires complete relevant paperwork and are provided a firm overview that helps them understand our business structure and core values"), followed by "local office training that provides them with information specific to their offices ([i.e.,] security badges and parking information). In addition, all professionals attend a five-to-ten day national training program soon after their start date, where they learn how to perform the client engagement responsibilities of a new associate." One employee who recently completed the process, "You begin in your office, [where you focus for three days] on KPMG's policies and procedures and becoming more familiar with the office itself. It's a combination of self-study and instructor presentations. This is also the time period during which you will meet some people from your line of business and your performance managers; you will also receive your schedules. Then you have the opportunity to train with all the individuals in your same position nationwide. This year we went to Florida for ten days. These ten days consisted of eight days of class, a day of community service, and one free day. Classes consisted primarily of lecture, and exercises reinforcing the lectures." Once back at their home offices, "all new hires are assigned a mentor. Often this is someone who graduated from the same school as the new hire. Our mentors volunteer to work with new hires and are excited to assist them in the transition process from student to full-time employee. In addition, each new hire is also assigned a performance manager who helps them set goals and measures them against their goals, providing feedback throughout the year."

DAY IN THE LIFE

Everyone we interviewed at KPMG agrees that "there is no such thing as the typical day here, [and that] keeps things interesting." One newbie reports, "My responsibilities at first ranged from administrative tasks to understanding business documentation, process-analysis documentation, and basic audit test work. In my experience, the entry-level employee will audit the lower risk, less complex areas such as cash and investments." Naturally, responsibilities increase as employees gain experience. Another employee explains, "The first two years you work as an associate, then progress to [become] a senior associate where you are responsible for managing associates on the engagement. After about five years you are promoted to manager, where you have a number of clients and are responsible for developing the audit and managing the senior associate on all engagements." Despite what you may think, folks do more than crunch numbers. As one employee puts it, "People have the impression that accountants sit in front of a computer all day. While there is definitely some time [spent] sitting in front of the computer, there is also a great deal of people contact with frequent client interviews and meetings."

PEERS

Entry-level employees at KPMG enjoy "a significant amount of contact and camaraderie." One explains that "I started with at least fifty other people my age. Going away for training was a great way to get to know [one another] and to make friends. When work is less busy, I would say that I see KPMG friends after work at least [once] every few weeks." Friendships develop easily because "KPMG does an excellent job of hiring outgoing people who are easy to talk to." The firm also works hard to promote unity among its workers. According to one worker, "There are numerous social events held by the firm and organized by first-year people. There are events almost every week."

MOVING ON

Many new hires stick around for the long haul, but KPMG concedes that some employees can be lured away. A spokesperson from the company notes, "During their tenure with the firm, KPMG professionals develop a skill set that is in demand throughout the financial services industry. Private industry (in-house accounting and financial positions in all industries) and our competitors (other big four and smaller firms)" sometimes entice KPMG entry-level employees away with higher salaries or better opportunities.

ATTRITION

Not everyone can handle the heavy workload at KPMG. Common complaints are often "about the hours," writes one newbie, explaining why some of her colleagues quit. "I understand how an individual may feel this way, but I also feel one can make the hours work easily into a work-life balance, and long hours are not required all year."

BEST AND WORST

To read about some of KPMG's successful entry-level employees, surf over to www.kpmgcampus.com/campus/know/who/about.asp, and click on the "Meet Some of Us" link.

THE LEAGUE OF AMERICAN THEATRES AND PRODUCERS

Administrative Assistant to the President

THE BIG PICTURE

Not everyone can be the administrative assistant to the president of the League of American Theatres and Producers (LATP). In fact, only one person a year enjoys this particular opportunity. That one lucky person spends a year assisting the head of the organization that promotes Broadway theater, produces the Tony Awards® and the National Broadway Theatre Awards, and supervises a myriad of business and charity enterprises associated with the theater. And, of course, if the president gets sick and can't be there on opening night, well, then, *you'll* just have to go out there and be president. (Well, not really.)

STATS

LOCATION(S) WHERE ENTRY-LEVEL EMPLOYEES WORK

The assistant works in New York, New York.

AVERAGE NUMBER OF APPLICATIONS EACH YEAR

The LATP receives 75–100 applications each year.

AVERAGE NUMBER HIRED PER YEAR OVER THE LAST TEN YEARS

The LATP hires one person per year.

ENTRY-LEVEL POSITION(S) AVAILABLE

The new hire works as the administrative assistant to the president.

AVERAGE HOURS WORKED PER WEEK

New hires work fifty hours per week.

PERCENTAGE OF ENTRY-LEVEL HIRES STILL WITH THE COMPANY AFTER THREE, FIVE, AND TEN YEARS

After three years, 50 percent of all new hires remain with the company, and after five years, 25 percent remain with the company.

AVERAGE STARTING SALARY

New hires earn $22,000 per year.

BENEFITS OFFERED

The LATP offers medical (HMO or PPO), dental, and vision insurance. Additional benefits include possible theater tickets and Tony Awards® tickets.

CONTACT INFORMATION

P. Casterlin

The League of American Theatres and Producers, Inc.

226 West 47th Street

New York, NY 10036

GETTING HIRED

With only one position to fill, LATP obviously doesn't need to recruit on campuses. One former assistant discovered the job through an ad in *Playbill;* another learned about it while working at an internship in the theater industry. The application process is quite simple. According to the LATP, you "send your resume. We interview qualified candidates." That's about all there is to it, except, of course, that you'll be competing with a horde of people for a single position. Here's how one successful candidate describes the interview process: "I sent my resume in and crafted my cover letter to express my interest in the theater and my desire to learn about the industry. I was interviewed by the president's executive assistant, with whom I would be working side by side. The first interview was very casual and comfortable. We talked about my schooling and my past experiences and internships. They, of course, asked about my interest in theater. I then came in for a second interview with the president, which was a little more intimidating. My references were checked, and I was offered the job a few days later." One former assistant notes, "During the interview, I was asked about my education and theater background and what I saw myself doing in five years. The president asked me which productions I liked and why. Coincidently, we both love one particular musical, and I think that definitely worked in my favor." The president, we're told, is "very nice."

MONEY AND PERKS

As you may expect for an exclusive, springboard opportunity like this one, very little in the job offer is negotiable. One former administrative assistant writes, "The only thing that was negotiable was when I started. Everything else was set up already, including salary." Everyone we spoke with agrees that the best fringe benefit is "getting the opportunity to see almost all the Broadway shows of the current season at no cost and, in addition, to meet the industry's top people." One writes, "Out of a five-day work week, I am seeing four plays free this week. I see an average of two plays a week."

THE ROPES

The president's assistant is trained by his or her predecessor; one who has held the job explains, "I had an overlap period with the person I replaced. We were working together for about two weeks, which I believe to be rare for the position." Usually, the overlap period is one week. "We went over the important things together, and since then I have done some adjusting on my own. I have been working directly with my boss from day one." At first, "there are a lot of names to remember and people to meet," warns another former administrative assistant. "I learned by working with the executive assistant and writing everything down. That was very important!"

DAY IN THE LIFE

"It is hard to describe a typical day because in this job each day was different," writes one former president's assistant. "Usually we met in the morning to look at the day's schedule and worked from there. There was a lot of scheduling, travel arrangements, and phone calls coming in constantly. Being in the president's office, you are often interfacing with the industry's top people, whether it be producers, executives, or actors." It's an important job, those who do it tell us, even if it isn't always glamorous. As one explains, "Keeping the president organized and happy is very important to the structure of the company, so I think I mattered. The work I was doing certainly wasn't like performing brain surgery, but I felt like my contributions were important and appreciated, even if the actual activities were somewhat mundane." On the plus side, the president's assistant interacts with the industry's movers and shakers all the time. "One of the best things about this job," writes one, "is that nearly all of the time that I am not spending sitting at my desk working is spent interacting with high-level people. On a daily basis, I am meeting the people who are shaping this industry."

PEERS

Because the training program LATP offers has a population of one, "There is not such a big social scene. Working for the 'boss' often isolates you. During the workday I would interact, but not as much after work." Those who work here share a passion for the theater, though, and that invariably creates some sense of community; as one former administrative assistant tells us, "Younger staff members definitely hang out and have lunch or see shows together, and there is certainly camaraderie within each department as well. However, there isn't a big after-hours social scene." All who have worked here would agree that "the office has a nice air to it" and that coworkers are a friendly, helpful bunch.

MOVING ON

The administrative assistant position at the LATP is a one-year-only job, and some people "usually go to other industry jobs," while other people take "arts positions or take other fields." Some find other jobs within the organization and make a career at the LATP; one of the former administrative assistants we spoke with has moved on to another department and has been with the company for more than seven years.

BEST AND WORST

The best administrative assistant is one who "learns quickly, excels at work, asks for more responsibilities, and successfully completes them, resulting in a promotion to another department" when the year is over. The worst was one who "accepted the job with unreasonable expectations and was disappointed."

LifeScan

Associate Marketing Manager, Associate Financial Analyst

THE BIG PICTURE

LifeScan, a Johnson & Johnson company, produces diabetes-monitoring equipment for home use. According to the company's website, new hires can "explore [their] entrepreneurial drive in a small-company environment that encourages personal and professional growth. At the same time, [they] discover the stability and resources of an international health care company developing life-enhancing technology."

STATS

LOCATION(S) WHERE ENTRY-LEVEL EMPLOYEES WORK

Entry-level employees work in Milpitas, California.

AVERAGE NUMBER OF APPLICATIONS EACH YEAR

Lifescan receives sixty applications per year.

AVERAGE NUMBER HIRED OVER THE LAST TEN YEARS

The company hires eleven people per year.

ENTRY-LEVEL POSITION(S) AVAILABLE

Entry-level hires work as associate marketing managers and associate financial analysts.

AVERAGE HOURS WORKED PER WEEK

New hires work forty hours per week.

AVERAGE STARTING SALARY

Undergraduates earn from $66,000–$89,000, while employees who have their MBAs earn from $77,000–$103,000.

BENEFITS OFFERED

On the health care front, the company offers medical, dental, and vision insurance. Additional benefits include life insurance, tuition reimbursement, a 401(k) plan, on-site company store (headquarters), and on-site workout facility (headquarters).

CONTACT INFORMATION

Visit the website at www.LifeScanCareers.com.

Getting Hired

LifeScan accepts applications on its website; company officials add, "We have our core schools that we recruit from, but we also accept students from other colleges and universities." The company's recruiters seek "customer market focus, interdependent partnership, mastering complexity, and creativity" in potential hires. One successful applicant describes the vetting process this way: "I was interviewed by different levels of people: the associate marketing managers, marketing managers, and directors. The interview was a mixture of behavioral and case questions. Some questions focused specifically on the competencies required for the position. After two or three weeks, I received an offer from the company. LifeScan hosted an event in January for people who received an offer. The purpose of the event was to convince us to accept the job." Applicants with prior experience in marketing and/or financial analysis have a leg up.

Money and Perks

Starting date is negotiable at LifeScan, first jobbers tell us. Job description and salary are not, though some first jobbers are able to negotiate their signing bonuses; company representatives say, "Salaries are determined based [on] the economy and internal equity." Top perks include "access to an on-site company store, where Johnson & Johnson products are sold at an employee discount, [and] a free on-site health club facility."

The Ropes

LifeScan newbies begin their jobs with their eyes wide open, they tell us. "I knew about the job before I started. The team leader for recruiting communicated a general description of the job to me. Around June, I discovered the area that I was going to be working in. I also received a call from my manager a week before I started my position. I didn't need to know more beforehand." Orientation "is very generic [and limited to] company goals and regulatory requirements. It lasts one to two days, depending on your position." Subsequent training varies according to function; some first jobbers continue with formal training "given by various marketing managers, finance, operations, etc.," while others simply learn through "on-the-job training by our manager."

Day in the Life

LifeScan first jobbers handle the nitty-gritty tasks of keeping LifeScan afloat: developing budgets, assisting with sales campaigns, and collaborating on advertising campaigns to expand the company's presence around the world. The company expects much from its employees, as "the organization is very lean." "There's no time to be bored, and sometimes it's pretty overwhelming, depending on the timing within the month," one new hire tells us. People who show promise are quickly handed "even more responsibility to cover more areas." Fortunately, "impressive lower-level managers" are there to offer guidance and support. Although the bare-bones staffing means that [all] workers [have] at least as much work as [they] can handle—this, employees admit, is often stressful—the upside of the situation is that low-level staffers have relatively good access to higher-ups. One first jobber writes, "I feel that I have exposure to senior management. I sit in on a meeting once a month with senior management—vice president of marketing, vice president of marketing and sales, directors of various areas of marketing. Also, the associate marketing managers have lunch with the vice president of marketing."

PEERS

"There is a lot of contact" among LifeScan first jobbers, especially among the assistant marketing managers, who tell us they frequently enjoy "AMM Happy Hours." "We interact every day of the week at work and probably go out together after work once or twice a month," explains one newbie. Friendships are easily forged among the workforce at LifeScan.

MOVING ON

"There is no one particular reason" that first jobbers leave LifeScan, company officials report, listing "better opportunities, more money [offered elsewhere], going back to school, and relocation" as the most common reasons. The first jobbers we spoke with report that some coworkers bristle under the heavy workload required of them; it's enough to make some people move on. Even so, most people we spoke with are highly satisfied both with their jobs and their prospects for advancement.

LOCKHEED MARTIN
Leadership Development Programs

THE BIG PICTURE

Lockheed Martin, an advanced technology company that does the lion's share of its business with the Defense Department, offers Leadership Development Programs (LDP) in communications, engineering, finance, human resources, information systems, and operations. All of these programs incorporate job rotations, technical training, and leadership development conferences to fast-track college graduates into management positions with the company.

STATS

LOCATION(S) WHERE ENTRY-LEVEL EMPLOYEES WORK

Lockheed has locations in nearly every state in the United States.

AVERAGE NUMBER OF APPLICATIONS EACH YEAR

Lockheed Martin receives 1.2 million applications for positions in the entire company; specific numbers for Leadership Development Programs are not available.

AVERAGE NUMBER HIRED PER YEAR OVER THE LAST TEN YEARS

"In the past six years, we've hired an average of 2,200 [people] per year."

ENTRY-LEVEL POSITION(S) AVAILABLE

There were approximately 2,800 available positions in 2003.

AVERAGE HOURS WORKED PER WEEK

New hires work forty hours per week.

PERCENTAGE OF ENTRY-LEVEL HIRES STILL WITH THE COMPANY AFTER THREE, FIVE, AND TEN YEARS

The percentage of employees who remain with the company after three, five, and ten years are 84 percent, 76 percent, and 66 percent, respectively.

BENEFITS OFFERED

The company offers health, dental, and vision insurance. Additional benefits include a retirement plan.

CONTACT INFORMATION

You may submit your resume at http://lmpeople.external.lmco.com/careers/secure/resume/resume_check.asp.

GETTING HIRED

Lockheed recruits on select campuses; the company accepts applications from all college students through its website. In examining candidates, Lockheed "focuses on senior projects, work experience, and skills that are job related." Interviews are "extremely friendly and somewhat casual/candid." That doesn't mean candidates don't get a good going over; most of the first jobbers we spoke with tell us they were interviewed numerous times before the company reached a decision. One writes, "Five managers, in fifteen to thirty minute increments, interviewed me. A few asked technical questions. They told me about their positions/departments and life within Lockheed, [i.e.] it is family friendly. Another thing that was discussed was the typical 'how do you work in groups?' type questions."

MONEY AND PERKS

The salaries of LDP participants are "based on certain variables, such as education level (bachelor's or master's) and previous work experience. Within that framework, salary is written in stone." First jobbers praise the company's tuition reimbursement program, telling us "it's 100 percent, and it's easy to get your reimbursement for tuition and books." They also like that employees "accrue vacation days, and if you don't have enough, you can actually debit them and make them up later." One participant says, "[I enjoy] moving every six months. It was so great to have the opportunity to live in four cool cities in two years. The company [relocated] me each time."

THE ROPES

Lockheed's Leadership Development Program runs two to three years (depending on the department), with participants rotating jobs every six months. In each rotation, "You start off slow (I took a few days to read any manuals and Lockheed documents I could find, and I asked my manager if there was anything he might recommend to shorten my learning curve), try to follow the format of what was done previously (when available), and ask lots of questions!" Some training is conducted in person by managers, but much of it occurs online; one LDP explains, "You can always take free, online training classes from a list of several hundred at different levels (and they don't have to be job-applicable!), or your department sponsors you for further training at one of our many computer labs or external computer classes." All LDP participants must attend Leadership Development Conferences, which stress teamwork, problem-solving strategies, communication skills, and familiarity with Lockheed's corporate culture, values, and goals.

DAY IN THE LIFE

An LDP participant's typical day depends on his or her program and placement, of course. One participant in finance explains, "My typical day has changed drastically with each rotation. In the Financial Analysis Department, I worked on financial models dealing with sensitivity and impact. I reported to both the director and vice president of financial planning. I updated charts and aided in financial statements management. In the tax department, I worked on federal tax packages for our three biggest sites (spending the day on the phone with our sites to make sure that everything [was] accounted for properly and using the previous year as my model). In billing and collections, I checked my computer for invoices that are declared billable, [spoke] with government payment offices to clear up any discrepanc[ies] with contract payment reconciliation issues, and deal[t] with our contract administrators to make sure that the billings [were] correctly done."

PEERS

"LDP participants tend to group together at each site, both formally and informally," program participants tell us. "At some sites we had an LDP council where we planned community service activities as well as happy hours, etc. At other sites, it was more informal gatherings. At each site my group of friends was made up of LDP participants; there is a real sense of camaraderie between us since all of us were in the same situation." There is "a big after-hour[s] social scene, with a relatively large group [who] goes out a few times a week" at most sites. These first jobbers have a lot in common with one another, we're told; one writes, "It's easy to make friends. LDP participants tend to have outgoing personalities since all of us were chosen in part because of our leadership ability."

MOVING ON

Leadership trainees at Lockheed generally enjoy the "great exposure and diverse assignments that they have" at the company, and most plan to stay at Lockheed for a long time. A few people complain about the difficulty of finding suitable rotations, and some others feel that salary and relocation packages could be more generous. Those who are unhappy at the company sometimes return to school to study business, technology, or science.

L'ORÉAL
Management Development Program

THE BIG PICTURE

L'Oréal's Management Development Program is a rotational training program with a focus on marketing. At first, hires "spend time working in the field, literally getting hands-on experience working with products in stores and working with customers." Later they are assigned to a marketing team in which "they are considered a full member of the team. They are expected to propose ideas just as any more senior person would. Responsibilities can include anything related to brand management: market research, media and promotions, budgeting and forecasting, and interacting with manufacturing and research and development."

STATS

LOCATION(S) WHERE ENTRY-LEVEL EMPLOYEES WORK

Entry-level employees work in New York (marketing), New Jersey (finance, IT, logistics, manufacturing, and research and development), and many other locations (sales).

AVERAGE NUMBER OF APPLICATIONS EACH YEAR

L'Oréal receives approximately 450,000 applications for all positions; about 1,000 applicants try for the Management Development Program.

AVERAGE NUMBER HIRED PER YEAR

L'Oréal expects to hire thirty first jobbers for its undergraduate Management Development Program in 2006.

ENTRY-LEVEL POSITION(S) AVAILABLE

L'Oréal's only structured entry-level program is the Management Development Program; other positions include opportunities in marketing, sales, finance, IT, logistics, manufacturing, and research and development.

AVERAGE HOURS WORKED PER WEEK

Entry-level hires work thirty-five-plus hours per week.

AVERAGE STARTING SALARY

Management Development Program participants earn starting salaries of $50,000.

BENEFITS OFFERED

L'Oréal offers health and dental coverage, as well as health club reimbursement. Additional benefits include a 401(k) plan, product purchase program, summer hours (Friday ends at 1:30 P.M.), and a pre-tax transportation expense program.

CONTACT INFORMATION

"Interested students should consult our website at www.lorealusa.com or contact their career services office for additional information."

Getting Hired

L'Oréal seeks "flexible, energetic individuals who are business-minded and are interested in a dynamic, innovative industry" for its Management Development Program and warns that "people who aren't comfortable in a fast-paced, highly flexible, and team-based environment will have a more difficult time at L'Oréal." While the company "focuses on certain top schools with both strong liberal arts and business programs" in recruiting, it considers all applicants and points out that "given the planned expansion of our program, we expect the list of schools where we have a visible presence (via corporate presentations, classroom presentations, sponsorship of student-run activities, etc.) to increase." Company officials also note, "Students who attend schools that L'Oréal does not visit may apply online at www.lorealusa.com/careers. Applicants submit resumes and cover letters, which are vetted to select candidates for a round of on-campus interviews. One successful hire explains, "The general tone of the interview was pretty conversational. When I left, I got the sense [that] she wanted to know me. She wanted to see if I had a passion for the industry." Those who clear this hurdle "are invited back to the New York office for a day of interviews with line management [that] includes several networking sessions and opportunities to learn more about the company (pre-evening reception, luncheon with marketers)." Another adds, "Anyone they invite to a [second-round] interview is technically qualified, so it's all about fit."

Money and Perks

First jobbers tell us that their first L'Oréal salary is generally not negotiable. Starting location is on the table for some, though others report that their entire job offer was presented as a package deal. Most here agree that the best perk is the program itself; one hire explains, "Other companies didn't have a specific brand-based training program for undergraduates. That was really attractive for me that they invested so much in new employees." Other favorite benefits include summer hours on Fridays between Memorial Day and Labor Day (the work day ends at 1:30 P.M.), healthclub reimbursement, and "cool products." One first jobber reports, "I never have to buy Christmas presents ever again!" There's also lots of "invites to events. We're very image based."

The Ropes

L'Oréal explains that "the way the program is designed, some would consider [it] in its entirety to be somewhat of an orientation and integration program. We want our new hires to become accustomed to our culture and our work, and that doesn't happen overnight. When a new hire joins, they will attend a week-long corporate orientation program [that] gives an overall picture of the company. After this, the new hire will gain hands-on experience through fieldwork and special marketing projects. We believe in learning by doing, as understanding markets, strategy, cross-functional relationships, and clients are essential to success." The rotational nature of the program means that first jobbers are often in the process of training in a new product or function. One trainee explains, "In each rotation, I was assigned to work with a manager or above, usually a director. Most times [it] was a long-term project, but [I also did] day-to-day work. I'd experience what that area does, as well as do a marketing analysis. We also take classes; the management development center offers classes on category knowledge as well as leadership, finance skills, and presentation skills. There's a whole center that manages that."

Day in the Life

Participants in the Management Development Program begin the program with "rotations in field sales." One explains, "I was living outside of Nashville, Tennessee, where I was given the responsibility to service stores. I was supposed to make sure promotionals were up, do international market research, and do day-to-day management research. I also worked on analysis of market franchises, finance, cost of consumer goods, and inventory analysis. It was always interesting, fast-paced, and always new and exciting." After rotations, trainees are assigned to marketing teams, where they take on considerable responsibility. One writes, "I've been given my own projects. Coming from not knowing anything to managing my own projects has been a great learning curve. It's been hands-on throughout, but in the beginning, it was just learning and absorbing." Another reports, "I have a good mix of short-term responsibilities and long-term responsibilities. It gives me a good scope of where business is going."

Peers

Management Development trainees are spread throughout L'Oréal, so they don't form a natural social community; they are more likely to interact with coworkers in the division to which they're assigned than with [one another]. To counter this, says L'Oréal, "the company recently has been putting together quarterly networking events to facilitate community building." One trainee writes, "Each department does a good job of creating events. I've gone to receptions and happy hours, and this is a great opportunity to network" and meet other first jobbers. Trainees also report that "it's easy to make friends here. There's a really great camaraderie. Everyone is bright and creative, and each [person] brings something new to the table. Nobody has the same background."

Moving On

Management trainees at L'Oréal see "plenty of room to grow in terms of pay and responsibility," describing the opportunity as "one of the most important things about this company." One first jobber explains, "It's the largest beauty retailer in the world. It's a network of seventeen brands now, so there's plenty of room for you to move around. Different brands have different roles. They're supportive of you finding your career path here." What's a boon for some can be frustrating for others; "everybody's experience [in this program] is different. People anticipate this super-structured program, but the first few weeks into the program, you realize the beauty of it is making it what you want. For some people, this [may] not be what they're looking for. Some people need more guidance."

Attrition

L'Oréal's Management Development Program has only been up and running for a few years. According to the company, everyone who has ever entered the program is still with the company as of January 2005.

Best and Worst

The company writes, "If you look at many of our top managers worldwide, many began their career at L'Oréal as entry-level employees. The current CEO of L'Oréal USA is a prime example of this."

LYONDELL
Engineer Development Program

THE BIG PICTURE

Lyondell is a huge chemical and polymer producer; its products provide the building blocks, literally, for automobiles, houses, clothing, food packaging, home furnishings, and many other consumer goods. Through its Engineer Development Program, Lyondell brings aboard freshly-minted chemical, electrical, mechanical, and safety engineers. The five-year program is rotational, with engineers switching jobs every eighteen to twenty-four months.

STATS

LOCATION(S) WHERE ENTRY-LEVEL EMPLOYEES WORK

Company headquarters are in Houston, Texas; the company also has operations on five continents. According to an HR official, "Entry-level engineers often work at U.S. manufacturing facilities located in Texas, Louisiana, Iowa, Illinois, Ohio, Pennsylvania, and Maryland."

AVERAGE NUMBER HIRED PER YEAR

Lyondell hires twenty-six entry-level employees each year.

ENTRY-LEVEL POSITION(S) AVAILABLE

"Lyondell seeks chemical, mechanical, electrical, and safety engineers to fill various entry-level full-time roles in maintenance-, reliability-, process-, project-, safety- and production-engineering capacities."

AVERAGE HOURS WORKED PER WEEK

New hires work forty hours per week.

PERCENTAGE OF ENTRY-LEVEL HIRES STILL WITH THE COMPANY AFTER THREE, FIVE, AND TEN YEARS

Eighty-eight percent of entry-level hires remain with the company after three years, and 75 percent stay on past the five-year mark.

AVERAGE STARTING SALARY

Lyondell offers employees worldwide a "total compensation package that includes premium pay and benefits."

BENEFITS OFFERED

Employees have at least two medical coverage options available. Lyondell also offers prescription drug benefits, a dental PPO, vision coverage, and flexible spending accounts. Additional benefits include short- and long-term disability coverage; life and accident insurance; a pension (fully covered by Lyondell); a 401(k) program; free counseling referral; 80 percent undergraduate/100 percent graduate reimbursement of tuition, fees, and textbooks; and 50 percent matching of charitable donations.

Contact Information

"Visit the College Recruiting section of www.lyondell.com, and click on 'Contact Us' to express your interest in working at Lyondell."

Getting Hired

Lyondell "actively recruits [new hires] from thirteen colleges," including Clemson, Georgia Tech, Purdue, University of Texas, Texas A & M, and Rice; the company notes that "students from other schools can express interest in working at Lyondell by visiting the college recruiting section of our website." Lyondell seeks out "results-oriented team players" who "thrive on change, communicate effectively, take prudent business risks, challenge [one another] to improve, treat [one another] with respect, and operate safely and responsibly with a focus on integrity." Interviews, according to one successful hire, "are a two-part process. For me, the first part was an on-campus interview with one of the senior engineers. I recall how impressed I was with the company sending other engineers to interview new-hire engineers. Previous companies that I had interviewed with often sent people from their HR department who had very little technical knowledge and were not able to identify with me or my interests at all. The interview was a behavioral interview that focused more on soft skills than [on] technical knowledge. The interview was very relaxed and felt like a conversation the majority of the time. I found out later that evening that I would be invited back for an on-site interview. I remember being very impressed with the quick response and high level of personal attention I was getting. About a month later, I was on a plant visit for the second round of interviews. At the plant, I interviewed with an HR representative, one of the plant superintendents, and a plant manager. In addition, I had lunch with two other engineers who worked at different plants. All of my interviews were behaviorally-based. Later that week, I had dinner with another Rice graduate who worked at the company. The following day, I received a phone call from the HR representative at the plant notifying me of my offer."

Money and Perks

"Salary is not negotiable" for starting engineers at Lyondell because the company "pays all employees of the same grade level the same salary, with a multiplier included paying those who have been at that level for a while more than those who just reached that level." "Dialog," Lyondell's term for "face-to-face, purposeful, and results-oriented discussions focused on enhancing performance and achieving business results," takes the place of traditional performance reviews. It "encourages continuous feedback among employees, supervisors, colleagues, and peers." Entry-level employees are eligible for a promotion as soon as six months after hire. Raises are also given "if the market reference for a position increases." Stellar perks include the flexible work schedule, which allows a 9-80 work week (in which employees work eighty hours in nine days and then receive the tenth day off), and 6 percent stock matching program.

THE ROPES

Work at Lyondell begins with "a two-day orientation involving corporate philosophy, policies, and benefits. At the plant, there is a written process [that outlines] types of training and topics to be addressed in the first day, week, month, year, etc. This process details training through the first five years of experience." This is followed by "a two-week course [that provides further instruction] about Lyondell's engineer development program and operational excellence, and Lyondell's process for driving continuous improvement in our operations." Subsequent training "is typically informal" and is conducted "one-on-one with peers."

DAY IN THE LIFE

Young engineers start their Lyondell careers in the Engineer Development Program, which spreads eighteen-to-twenty-four month rotational assignments over each new hire's first five years with the company. Engineers here love how quickly the program integrates them into essential and challenging functions. One production engineer writes, "We were given unit responsibilities almost immediately. Granted, you rely heavily on the specialist, the operators, and other engineers until you've learned the unit to the extent that you can make decisions about operations, etc. A typical day in the life of a new-hire production engineer is devoted primarily to learning the unit to which you've been assigned. The more you learn, the more responsibility you take on." A process engineer adds, "When I was hired, there was a multimillion dollar project going on that was going to replace the existing control system with a newer-generation one. I became an integral part of that project team when one of the principal engineers working on the project left the company. The project was completed very successfully."

PEERS

Engineers at the Lyondell's home office in Houston report a huge social network of first jobbers. One writes, "There is a lot of socializing among the new hires at the company. We often go out after work and on the weekends. Many of us live in the same area and have all come from a variety of places. There [are also many] co-ops and interns who participate in the after-hours social scene." Employees also praise the company for hiring "some of the most talented people [just] out of school. They are intelligent, hard working, and team oriented. These are very impressive people and great friends." Away from the home office, though, the ranks of young hires are somewhat thinner; one newbie explains, "Because I'm located away from [headquarters] in Houston, there is only one other young engineer I talk to regularly. But when I go to Houston for training, I meet with all the other young engineers I've met in the company (through training), and we have lunch or dinner."

MOVING ON

Lyondell is a company at which employees hope to stay for a long time; retirement is the number one reason folks stop working here, according to the company. "Continued education" and "personal reasons" are numbers two and three on the list. One first jobber reports that "less happy workers sometimes complain about the workload. We do have a lot of responsibility and a lot of work. Lyondell intentionally operates lean, [and that's] great for those of us who enjoy challenges and responsibility. This is certainly not a job for someone who is looking to slack off, though. The level of responsibility and demands in this job require strong prioritization skills and careful communication with supervisors."

ATTRITION

A negligible number of first jobbers fail to complete their first year at Lyondell, the company informs us, adding that "71 percent of entry-level employees stay with the company for at least six years."

BEST AND WORST

"Dan Smith, President and Chief Executive Officer of Lyondell, is the company's most successful entry-level employee," writes our correspondent in HR, daring you to try to top this example: "Smith began working for Atlantic Richfield Co. (ARCO) as a co-op while attending Lamar University. Following his graduation in 1968, he was hired as a full-time engineer. By 1994, Smith was president of Lyondell, and he rose to CEO two years later."

MARLABS
HR Associates, Recruiters, IT Consultants

THE BIG PICTURE

Marlabs, a full-service provider that offers "outsourced application development, managed services, and professional services" works with clients in the health care, pharmaceutical, life sciences, technology, and financial industries and also addresses a number of retail and manufacturing concerns. Founded in 1996, Marlabs now employs more than 400 people, the majority of whom hold graduate degrees. The company is growing fast and is building a reputation for being a place where go-getters can advance fairly quickly through the ranks. In 2005, Marlabs was named one of the Fifty Best Places to Work in New Jersey by NJBIZ (in partnership with the New Jersey State Chamber of Commerce).

STATS

LOCATION(S) WHERE ENTRY-LEVEL EMPLOYEES WORK

Marlabs has offices in Edison, New Jersey (sales and marketing); Cheyenne, Wyoming (regional office, development and training); Allentown, Pennsylvania (development and training headquarters); Austin, Texas (data center); Bangalore, India (global development center); and other sites.

AVERAGE NUMBER OF APPLICATIONS EACH YEAR

Marlabs receives 700 applications per year.

AVERAGE NUMBER HIRED PER YEAR

Marlabs hires about 125–150 entry-level employees each year.

ENTRY-LEVEL POSITION(S) AVAILABLE

Marlabs hires entry-level employees as human resources associates, recruiters, and IT consultants.

AVERAGE HOURS WORKED PER WEEK

New hires work forty hours per week.

PERCENTAGE OF ENTRY-LEVEL HIRES STILL WITH THE COMPANY AFTER THREE, FIVE, AND TEN YEARS

Ninety-nine percent of entry-level hires remain with the company after five years. The average tenure of a Marlabs first jobber is, according to an HR official, seven to eight years.

AVERAGE STARTING SALARY (BY POSITION)

HR associates earn $25,000 per year; recruiters earn $40,000 per year; and IT consultants earn $50,000+ per year.

BENEFITS OFFERED

Marlabs offers medical, dental, and vision coverage, all "vesting from day one." Additionally, the company helps handle employees' H-1 forms and visas. Marlabs has a 401(k) plan. Full-time salaried employees are paid for standard and floating holidays and also receive life insurance and disability coverage.

CONTACT INFORMATION

Marlabs, Inc.
2025 Lincoln Highway, Suite 110
Edison, NJ 08817
Attn: Hari Das

GETTING HIRED

Marlabs posts job openings on its website; and it cross-posts those listings at other major job websites. Applicants may apply via e-mail and are encouraged to indicate the desired position in the header of the message and then attach their resumes and cover letters. Successful candidates are those who are "trustworthy, flexible, and hard-working" and who "do their homework before they come in for their interviews. Great interviewees arrive having studied our website and [know] all about Marlabs and the position they are applying for." Poor candidates "are not at all prepared, know nothing about Marlabs, are not personable, and cannot answer our questions even though they appear on paper to have the appropriate background." One successful hire in HR reports "I had no background in HR whatsoever. I had two interviews. One was with my immediate boss, and the second was with his boss. During the interview, they were asking about my experience and why they should accept me for the job position. I had no experience, so I just told them that I really would like to work here. They liked the fact that I didn't have any experience. They wanted to be able to teach me what [to do]. Also, we talked about my schooling. I graduated high school and only have attended some college classes. We talked about starting college again and what I wanted to go for. I really wanted the job. The environment here is great; [there are many] wonderful, friendly people who are very professional, yet also very caring."

MONEY AND PERKS

Marlabs, according to its website, "offers challenging assignments, competitive salaries, and career opportunities including promotions within the organization. Marlabs provides a positive appraisal process and an open-door policy. A strong benefits package and positive work environment foster a positive attitude toward Marlabs and give employees the stability they require while performing assignments." Employees are evaluated once a year or when they earn a new assignment—"whichever comes first." Raises are merit-based. Asked to name the best fringe benefit of working here, one Marlabs employee reported that "We celebrate every employee's birthday with a cake and pizza."

THE ROPES

New hires at Marlabs "receive training in a lot of areas." One human resources first jobber writes, "I was trained in the legal aspect, finance aspect, and HR aspect. I was taught about formatting resumes, posting resumes, payroll, contracts and agreements, medical and dental insurance, general liability and workers' compensation insurance, filing for visas, employment verification letters, etc." Throughout an employee's tenure here, Marlabs provides "multiple vehicles for the continuing education and training of our consulting staff. We offer training courses conducted by various professional institutes in addition to our tuition reimbursement program." Marlabs uses Learning Tree International, DevelopMentor, Oracle, and Microsoft training systems.

DAY IN THE LIFE

Marlabs hires first jobbers in three areas. HR associates "handle all human resources activities with regard to legal, finance, contracts, bonuses, and payroll." One first jobber in this position writes, "My responsibilities were to e-mail consultants for updated information, send birthday cards/e-greetings, collect timesheets, keep records of payroll changes, prepare new hire packages, etc. A normal day would consist of sending and replying back to dozens of e-mails. I get all types of e-mails about timesheets, payroll issues, client changes, updates, etc. I answer tons of phone calls, and in between, get contracts signed and sent back to clients. That is a typical day." Recruiters do exactly what their job title indicates; they help Marlabs find top engineers and technicians in their fields. IT consultants study the IT systems of clients and make suggestions about how to improve their efficacy.

PEERS

With a majority of its workforce holding graduate degrees, it's safe to say that Marlabs employees are "extremely smart. They have so much knowledge about things I don't even know," writes one first jobber, adding, "I learn things from them every day I am with the company." Employees also praise the friendly, unpretentious work environment that Marlabs provides.

ATTRITION

Relatively few new hires—1 percent, according to our sources in Marlabs HR—leave before a year is out. Those who leave do so because they "find permanent positions in another company" or for personal reasons, such as relocation.

MERCK
Various Positions

THE BIG PICTURE

Big pharmaceuticals is big business, and Merck is one of the biggest pharmaceuticals there is. This is a place where you can parlay a degree in the sciences or engineering into a fulfilling and lucrative career. There are also plenty of opportunities to sell drugs—legal ones, that is.

STATS

LOCATION(S) WHERE ENTRY-LEVEL EMPLOYEES WORK

Engineering and science positions are available in New Jersey, Pennsylvania, California, Georgia, North Carolina, Virginia, and Washington; sales positions are available nationwide.

AVERAGE NUMBER HIRED PER YEAR OVER THE LAST TEN YEARS

Merck hires 200 entry-level employees per year.

AVERAGE HOURS WORKED PER WEEK

New hires work forty hours per week.

BENEFITS OFFERED

Health care benefits include dental, short- and long-term disability, long-term care, and on-site health services. Additional benefits include a 401(k) plan, a pension plan, mentoring program, and flexible work arrangements. On-site services include health services, fitness center, dry cleaning, credit union, and child care.

CONTACT INFORMATION

Visit the website at www.merck.com/careers.

GETTING HIRED

Merck targets schools that "meet its hiring requirements based [on its] business needs (i.e., science, engineering, information technology, etc.)," but through its website the company accepts applications from all college graduates. Many of the first jobbers we spoke with had an "in" at Merck: Some people had previously served summer internships, and others made connections through their college professors. One newbie we spoke with who didn't take either of these routes presented a strong background in her chosen field. Here's how she puts it: "Marketing of vaccines has a public health emphasis, so my joint degree in business and public health made me a perfect fit (for the available job). To prepare, I visited Merck's website and learned all about their products. I made sure to understand how I was differentiated compared to other candidates based on my public health background, and I communicated that in my resume and interviews. The interviews were very conversational. There were a few case questions [behavior based] and many questions requesting that I give examples from past experience."

Money and Perks

Starting salary at Merck is somewhat negotiable, depending on the skills and background a new hire brings to the company. Advanced academic work and previous work experience in the field should provide some leverage in these negotiations. The start date, all our survey respondents agree, is highly negotiable. The coolest fringe benefit, according to newbies, is the flex-time arrangement: "They don't care when you do it, as long as the work is getting done; I could decide not to work every Wednesday if I wanted to. It comes [down to the fact] that they completely trust everyone to perform and deliver."

The Ropes

Merck's new hires waste little time getting to work. One reports, "The orientation was very quick. I had an administrative orientation on the first day, but was then immediately introduced to my supervisor and the research group. Within one week I was running experiments." Afterward, training occurs primarily on the job. One scientist explains, "I got basic safety training from our safety officer and then received training on laboratory techniques from a colleague at my level. This colleague was referred to as 'my buddy'. The buddy-system was very effective; initially we did all [the] experiments together to ensure that my techniques met Merck standards. My supervisor also provided some basic analysis training." In some areas, formal training sessions are also part of the indoctrination process.

Day in the Life

Merck is a huge company; while primarily engaged in research, the company requires a substantial support network to handle human resources, payroll, sales, and other essential functions. For employees in the glamorous research field, every day is an adventure: "Given the proprietary nature of our job, it's difficult for me to provide an example [of what I do]. However, my responsibility includes developing a portion of a manufacturing process that would be used in producing an HIV vaccine. The work was challenging, and I did not necessarily work under another engineer—it was my primary responsibility, and I was expected to drive the development. Working at Merck Research is like trying to take a drink of water from a fire hydrant—you need to suck up as much as you can!" Employees in the less glamorous areas— we spoke with one person in payroll—also find their work challenging and fulfilling; our respondent says, "A former compensation analyst was transitioning into a new role approximately three months after I came on board. I slowly became a point of contact for people in the division concerning compensation-related matters. I was also given more projects with more complexity and became more challenged in my analytical and leadership abilities. My manager began to give me increased autonomy, meaning he would give me a project and expect me to deliver with minimal supervision."

Peers

Many Merck entry-level employees tell us that the company supports "a large social scene because so many of [the new hires] are so young. There is a large group of people [who] are less than thirty years old. There is a great sense of camaraderie, and these people have evolved into true friends. [They] routinely hang out together; [they] feel like [they are] back in school, and all of [them] are in the same lab." One first jobber writes, "Many of us were new to the area where we work; therefore we tended to socialize after work to help one another become acclimated. The great thing is that I got to meet people who like to do a variety of things and are very open-minded to my suggestions and those of others."

Moving On

Merck offers internships and co-op assignments, but it does not have a first job program *per se*. People who come on board do so expecting to start and build careers at Merck or with a related business.

Best and Worst

When asked about the best example of an entry-level hire, company representatives said, "Roy Vagelos started as an intern and became our chief executive officer."

MIAMI TEACHING FELLOWS
Teaching Fellow

THE BIG PICTURE

The Miami Teaching Fellows is "a program created specifically to bring in a cohort of high-quality new teachers, or fellows, every year." The program "helps address [the] persistent teacher shortages [that] districts face, especially in critical-need subject areas like math, science, and special education." Teaching fellows "receive their Florida state certificate as they teach," by completing coursework in addition to fulfilling their teaching duties. The job requires nine months of very hard work, but the vacations are long and the personal rewards enormous.

STATS

LOCATION(S) WHERE ENTRY-LEVEL EMPLOYEES WORK

Teaching positions are located in Miami, Florida.

AVERAGE NUMBER OF APPLICATIONS EACH YEAR

The program receives about 1,045 applications each year.

AVERAGE NUMBER HIRED PER YEAR

The program hires 50–100 fellows each year.

ENTRY-LEVEL POSITION(S) AVAILABLE

Those hired achieve the title of teaching fellow.

AVERAGE HOURS WORKED PER WEEK

Employees work about forty to fifty hours per week.

AVERAGE STARTING SALARY

The starting salary for fellows is the same as that for all beginning teachers in the Miami-Dade County Public Schools. The minimum base salary is $34,200. Bonuses are granted to those working at certain sites, those holding an education-related master's degree, and those who teach math, science, and special education.

BENEFITS OFFERED

"As employees of the Miami-Dade County Public Schools, fellows are eligible for the same comprehensive benefits as all [public school] teachers, including a pension plan; choice of health insurance plans; dental, prescription and vision coverage; and access to a 401(k) plan."

In addition, "fellows are automatically enrolled in a rigorous summer-training institute at the district. Fellows are paid a stipend to cover living expenses during this free training program. In their first year, Fellows begin a course of study for their state teaching certificate. There is no cost to fellows for this coursework."

CONTACT INFORMATION

Miami Teaching Fellows
1500 Biscayne Boulevard, Suite 129
Miami, FL 33132
Tel: 305-995-2762
E-mail: miamiteachingfellows@tntp.org
www.miamiteachingfellows.org

GETTING HIRED

Recruiters for the Miami Teaching Fellows program "want people with little or no teaching experience who are driven to succeed. We want people who have excelled as students and who want to do something that matters." Successful candidates are "committed to having a positive effect on student achievement; display excellence in their previous endeavors; and are dedicated to challenging, reaching, and influencing students—especially those in under-resourced areas—on a daily basis." Unsuccessful candidates "lack commitment, flexibility, or respect for the students and local communities in which fellows work." The application process is demanding. Applicants must submit an application, a personal statement, and academic transcripts. Those who impress recruiters are invited to interview. Here's how the interviews work, according to one current fellow: "The first part of the interview was a five-minute teaching sample. They let us know ahead of time what to expect, and they were very honest about everything. Communication before and after was *very* good. After sharing my teaching sample in front of the other nine candidates (very nerve-wracking!), we had a group discussion, a small-group discussion, and a personal interview. A woman from Teach For America interviewed me. She mostly asked situational questions and asked me to rate myself on the teaching sample. It was not a hard interview; but the whole day [had been] stressful, so by the time I got there, I was tired! It was very professional. The interviewer wrote the whole time, but made sure to look up and smile a lot, [and that] seriously helped." After these interviews, candidates are notified of their status within two weeks. To finalize the process, "candidates must pass state teacher tests before entering the classroom as teachers."

MONEY AND PERKS

Teaching Fellows' salaries are set by the Miami-Dade County Public School system and are nonnegotiable. Most other aspects of the job are similarly inflexible; as one fellow points out, "We have to be at work for the training, then teach summer school, and then be ready by August, so we can start school!" There is room to negotiate the school to which one is assigned, as "each fellow has the opportunity to interview with just about any school in the district with teaching vacancies and choose the most appropriate placement." The best perks, fellows agree, are the "winter, spring, and summer vacations!" Some say "the hours are great," though they admit that "we put in a lot of outside hours!" The free medical coverage is also considered a huge plus.

THE ROPES

The Miami Teaching Fellows program puts new hires on the fast-track to teaching with a "six-week training [program] that starts in early June." The training consists of two parts: morning classroom teaching and observation during summer school, and veteran teacher-led afternoon sessions that focus on instruction design, effective teaching strategies, student behavior management, and diversity and culture awareness. One fellow explains, "At first, we sat in training classes for eight hours and learned how to teach" by reviewing "classroom scenarios, classroom management, laws in education (federal and state), student/teacher praxis, and pedagogy and formulation of curricula." After two weeks, "We started working part-time in summer school classes." One fellow writes, "It was a pretty okay experience, [though] I wish we could have worked more in the classrooms and [spent] less time taking notes."

DAY IN THE LIFE

"Teaching is a profession that does not enable anyone to be bored during any period of time," observes one Miami Teaching fellow. "Every second of every workday is filled with opportunities to [have an] impact [on] students' lives, [both] in and out of the classroom. Teachers [must attend] meetings with their colleagues, administrators, parents, and students; plan lessons; decorate classrooms; hold detentions; [and participate in] reading, training, etc." Quite a few program participants work with the learning-disabled; one writes, "I am responsible for seventeen learning-disabled students, and I teach them reading and math. I do reading for two-and-a-half hours and math in small groups for an hour each. I am still learning how to fulfill all of my obligations and how to get things done for my students so that they can learn. It's a struggle every day!" Be prepared for there to be "times when the job feels overwhelming." One fellow cautions, "Because I was so new to everything, it took me double the time to write lesson plans, learn transitions, and deal with classroom management." Fortunately, "After a month or two in the classroom, it fell into place and was easier and quicker. Experience comes with time."

PEERS

Fellows are scattered throughout the Miami-Dade school system, so program participants don't see [one another] on a daily basis. They do participate in "happy hour meetings, cocktail parties, and barbecues and other social gatherings." These "allow fellows the opportunity to exchange ideas and interact in different settings." One fellow writes, "The camaraderie goes much further beyond happy hours. We meet to have parties at houses, go to the beach together, and go to malls and movies. We're a bunch of like-minded adults switching professions or right out of college who understand each another."

MOVING ON

The program is too new for there to be much data on where former fellows go. Program managers report that "the expectation is that the individuals who become teachers through this program will be in the classroom for years to come."

ATTRITION

"Those who leave the Miami Teaching Fellows Program to date have cited personal reasons (moving from the city) as well as challenges at their school placement," program managers tell us.

BEST AND WORST

According to program managers, successful teachers tend to enjoy spending time in the classroom and seek to assign their students meaningful, growth-inducing tasks that will foster their development.

MINDBRIDGE

Various Positions

THE BIG PICTURE

Mindbridge sells IntraSmart, an "intranet software suite" that "helps companies share information and knowledge" and leads to "improved collaboration resulting in the kind of teamwork that is necessary to dramatically increase productivity." The company works with organizations that range from nonprofits to government agencies and from hospitals to midsize and large corporations, and it is currently developing a more economical product for small businesses. And it's also hiring; Mindbridge "is currently undergoing a period of rapid growth" that has it "looking for talented and enthusiastic people." Entry-level jobs are available in sales, Web development, and graphic design.

STATS

LOCATION(S) WHERE ENTRY-LEVEL EMPLOYEES WORK

The company's headquarters are located in Norristown, Pennsylvania (near Philadelphia).

AVERAGE NUMBER OF APPLICATIONS EACH YEAR

Mindbridge receives 500–750 applications each year.

AVERAGE NUMBER HIRED PER YEAR

Mindbridge hires fifty-five entry-level employees per year.

ENTRY-LEVEL POSITION(S) AVAILABLE

Entry-level employees work as graphics designers, sales assistants, Web developers, and sales engineers.

AVERAGE HOURS WORKED PER WEEK

Entry-level hires work fifty hours per week.

PERCENTAGE OF ENTRY-LEVEL HIRES STILL WITH THE COMPANY AFTER THREE, FIVE, AND TEN YEARS

Seventy percent are still with Mindbridge after three years; 60 percent remain after five years; and half of the entry-level hires stay with the company for ten or more years.

BENEFITS OFFERED

Mindbridge offers medical and dental benefits that vest immediately. Additional benefits include life insurance and stock options, both of which are also available immediately.

CONTACT INFORMATION

Applicants should send resumes and cover letters to hr@mindbridge.com.

GETTING HIRED

HR holds in-person interviews at their Norristown, Pennsylvania office every Tuesday and Wednesday between 10:00 A.M. and 12:00 P.M. These are open interviews; slots are allocated on a first come, first serve basis. According to employees, Mindbridge "does not discriminate based on where you went to school or even if you went to school," the company tells us, noting that "we have hired PhDs, and we have hired people who have not graduated [from] high school." As a general rule, Mindbridge "looks for smart people" but "tries to avoid primadonnas." Available positions are posted at the company's website. First jobbers here often enter the company via internships or co-ops and then parlay these experiences into post-graduation jobs. One such hire explains, "I wanted to work at Mindbridge badly, but I did not have the skill set they wanted, so I took an internship and they trained me on the job. I appreciate how this company gave me a shot when other companies passed on me."

Interviews focus on practical matters. An HR rep writes, "We always ask technical people how many computers they own or have owned. We get them to talk about the make and model, what they did with the computers, and what programs they ran on them. We want people who are intellectually curious; these questions break the ice and start a dialog. People who have a lot of computers or have had them in the past generally do very well here." Want to be the best interview ever at Mindbridge? According to HR, you'll have to top the guy who "came in with a piece of code that we actually used in one of our products." Avoid the mistake made by the "worst interview performance" ever here, during which "the applicant physically struck an HR person."

MONEY AND PERKS

Full-time positions at Mindbridge offer "competitive salary and a benefits package that includes stock ownership plans, a stock option plan, medical insurance, free parking, and snacks and beverages." Full-time employees are also eligible "to share a percentage of revenue for products that they have worked on." Contract jobs offer fewer benefits, though even contract workers enjoy "free ice cream, water, and beer at all times," as well as "free lunch on Fridays" and "some sort of afternoon activity on Fridays that is free to all employees." One first jobber writes, "Summers are fun because it's not as hectic here. And we have casual Fridays, which is nice."

THE ROPES

Fresh hires at Mindbridge are "thrown to the wolves to sink or swim," according to one first jobber. Indeed, an HR official reports that newbies "are usually put on some type of project immediately." One graphics designer writes, "I learned more in my first six months on the job than I did during four years as an undergraduate." Another new hire adds, "Mindbridge is great for self-starters who want a lot of responsibly immediately."

DAY IN THE LIFE

First jobbers at Mindbridge work in a variety of positions. Graphics designers "design Web-based graphics for IntraSmart," a job that requires "a strong graphics art and Web design background and an ability to work effectively with team members." One young designer notes, "There's a lot of grunt work, but everyone does it, from management all the way down to entry-level. At the end of the day, no one is above doing what has to be done." Newbies in sales and marketing are needed for a wide range of jobs, including telemarketing and Web design. Technical hires work on developing Web applications and Middleware components; their chores require knowledge of HTML, Java, JavaScript, and SQL, as well as good communications skills and the ability to work well with others. They also require a lot of determination; one technician notes, "This place is a pressure cooker. It is Darwinism at its best and worst."

PEERS

Like many other modern tech companies, Mindbridge is the type of place that attracts "really smart people" who are "somewhat cool." There is "a lot of camaraderie among the first jobbers," as well as "a big after-hours social scene."

MOVING ON

Mindbridge is not for everyone. Some who leave here "go on to start their own businesses or go to a larger company." An HR representative reports, "We actually help place some of them at other companies, if they request that we do so."

ATTRITION

First jobbers typically last about five years at Mindbridge. About one in ten doesn't stay on past the demanding first year.

MONITOR GROUP
Various Positions

THE BIG PICTURE

The Monitor Group is a prominent and prestigious consulting firm. Undergraduate group consultants learn on the job, performing nuts-and-bolts analysis under the guidance of their mentors/supervisors. Successful hires find themselves advising businesses on increasingly important matters as their talents and knowledge develop.

STATS

LOCATION(S) WHERE ENTRY-LEVEL EMPLOYEES WORK

"In North America, we [recruit] for positions in Cambridge, Massachusetts; New York, New York; Chicago, Illinois; Los Angeles, California; and San Francisco, California. Those interested in international positions should apply through the normal process in North America, and we will coordinate with other offices on their behalf. We have global recruiting standards, so if a candidate qualifies for an offer and meets local language requirements, we will determine whether or not there are available positions in the offices in which they are interested."

AVERAGE NUMBER HIRED PER YEAR OVER THE LAST TEN YEARS

The Monitor Group hires about forty people per year.

ENTRY-LEVEL POSITION(S) AVAILABLE

Entry-level positions change annually according to growth forecasts and business needs.

AVERAGE HOURS WORKED PER WEEK

New hires work sixty-five hours per week, with a lot of variation and unpredictability. On some weeks, employees may work as few as fifty hours, while on other weeks, they will work as much as eighty-five or ninety.

PERCENTAGE OF ENTRY-LEVEL HIRES STILL WITH THE COMPANY AFTER THREE, FIVE, AND TEN YEARS

"We don't track [these] data specifically. Since there are multiple career paths depending on one's interests and development goals, many undergrads stay longer than expected because they gain the opportunity to try different types of consulting domains or focus on areas that are of greater interest. Advancement into management positions is a function of skill, not degree or tenure."

AVERAGE STARTING SALARY

The starting salary is "competitive within [the] industry" and tends to be roughly $50,000 per year.

Benefits Offered
Medical benefits are "competitive within [the] industry," and additional insurance, a 401(k) plan, and a generous paid time off program.

Contact Information
Visit the website at www.monitor.com.

Getting Hired
Monitor recruits its fledgling consultants on college campuses, primarily at Ivy League schools. Students attending other schools are welcome to submit applications online, but must be prepared to interview at a Monitor office if called. And that's a big "if." As one entry-level employee explains, "Consulting is a very competitive industry to get into, and Monitor is one of the top-tier firms in terms of appeal to college students and prestige." Another entry-level employee notes, "Getting the interview is the real major hurdle in the application process. Resume screening is notoriously tough, and there just aren't that many slots available—ten to twelve, tops. To get an interview, you must have demonstrated some meaningful work experience and/or superior academic achievement. Your resume and cover letter must tell a very compelling story." The lucky few who pass the gatekeepers' muster enjoy a "great interview process, very casual and also candid. It was more of a conversation than an interview. The interviewers immediately set the tone for Monitor as welcoming." Successful applicants go through several rounds of interviews; the first includes a case exercise, while later rounds put prospective hires through their paces in group exercises and "a client scenario role-play exercise."

Money and Perks
As is the case at most entry-level gigs, you won't get rich in your first year at Monitor. Newbies gripe a little more about the pay than do their peers in similar programs because of the long hours, but they also understand that they're receiving invaluable training that will serve them throughout the rest of their more lucrative careers. Go-getters can earn quick raises; "salary increases are based on performance and are not linked to tenure. We are flexible in our ability to award strong performers," firm officials write. Perks include "support to those interested in returning to graduate schools for MBA degrees, paid dinners, [cab] rides home, free drinks, (often) food in the office, off-site corporate retreats, [and] one to two weeks off around Christmas in addition to vacation time."

The Ropes
Orientation for Monitor new hires involves "a week-long process of all-day sessions covering subjects ranging from Excel to filing for expense reimbursements, to finding the bathroom. I was assigned to my first-case team at the end of the first week." Firm officials point out that its orientation program "is designed to familiarize new hires with overall firm history, strategy, values, and expectations. It is also intended to facilitate networking and expose new consultants to as many different facets of Monitor and people within the firm as possible." Skills training necessarily plays a small role in orientation. As one intern explains,

or had great training, but mostly I learned on the job. There really is no other way in consulting use each case and each firm is unique." Work experience is supplemented by seminar-like "modules learning" that "focus on a given discipline, i.e., corporate finance, enterprise economics, etc." Modules "are taught by subject-area experts that work at the firm. Many former Harvard Business School professors lead training seminars."

DAY IN THE LIFE

Monitor trainees spend their days performing "basic analysis, such as answering basic business questions. [One example is:] 'What organizational structure do I feel would best allow our client to achieve their strategy?' We do the analysis (including research, interviews, group brainstorming, etc.), synthesize data, make recommendations, and support them." One consultant explains, "A typical day would involve a couple of hours on the phone discussing problems with a client, a couple of hours with my case team discussing various ideas and hypothesizing solutions, several hours performing analysis on data (Excel), and some hours organizing findings and recommendations into a PowerPoint presentation." It's hardly grunt work, say the trainees; one trainee notes, "What I do matters a lot. Without me, my case teams would be unable to complete important analyses and deliver [impacting] and meaningful work to our clients." The work is "demanding, occasionally overwhelming, but never boring," and extremely educational; as one consultant puts it, "I have learned an incredible amount. For the most part Monitor bosses are a good combination of demanding and understanding." Another consultant agrees, "Some [of my bosses] are great coaches who are willing to take you under their wing and teach you and mentor you a great deal." As an added bonus, this program affords "a lot of interaction with higher-level people. The leaders on my team are very open to talking with me and make an honest effort to involve me and hear my opinions. Not only am I allowed to sit in on important meetings, [but also] I am encouraged to do so. Professional development is a priority here."

PEERS

Newbies at Monitor "are all good friends" who tell us that "the intensity of this job pulls people together. Everyone [shares] common experiences." One young consultant offers, "Some of my best friends are from the company. We hang out after work and on the weekends on a very frequent basis. I interact with friends from work anywhere from six to twenty hours a week (entire days of the weekend at times) outside of work." As work commitments increase, the social scene subsides a bit. "We went out a lot together at first, though that has waned as we've all become busier," comments another employee. Everyone seems impressed with their peers. "The people at Monitor are among the most intelligent and intellectual I've ever met," says one typical trainee.

Moving On

According to consulting firm officials, "most people tend to leave Monitor to seek other opportunities after having been with the firm for three or four years. However, a growing number are finding interesting opportunities within the firm [that allow them to] have long-term careers in areas that are of particular interest to them." More than a few consultants eventually leave Monitor to pursue their MBAs. "That's essentially the standard path," reports one consultant.

Attrition

Graduate study, opportunities outside the field of consulting, and a mismatch between the company and the employee are the most common reasons employees leave Monitor's training program early. Few people leave to pursue other consulting opportunities, firm officials report.

Best and Worst

Firm officials tell us that "the type of person who is most successful is the person who asks lots of questions, is curious about the work [he or she is] doing and how it fits into the bigger picture, is eager for constructive feedback to improve [his or her] performance, and uses [his or her] organizational and analytical abilities to produce high-quality outputs." Less successful first jobbers "tend to be the ones who do not recognize the level of commitment that consulting requires. They tend to have less valuable experiences because of a misalignment in their expectations and usually are not open to the valuable feedback they receive about how to improve their performance."

MONSTER
Customer Service Representative

THE BIG PICTURE

The world of employment agencies meets modern times at Monster, a website that lists available jobs across the country. The company hires college grads for its customer service division. "Phone experience in a call-center type of environment" and the ability to be comfortable in such a work environment are "important qualit[ies]." Entry-level employees like the fact that the company offers "strong opportunities for advancement."

STATS

LOCATION(S) WHERE ENTRY-LEVEL EMPLOYEES WORK

Entry-level empoyees work in Maynard, Massachusetts and Indianapolis, Indiana.

ENTRY-LEVEL POSITION(S) AVAILABLE

New hires work as customer service representatives.

AVERAGE HOURS WORKED PER WEEK

Employees work forty hours per week.

BENEFITS OFFERED

The company offers medical, dental, and vision insurance. Additional benefits include a 401(k) plan and life insurance.

CONTACT INFORMATION

Go to www.monster.com and search for "monsterjobs."

GETTING HIRED

To apply for a job at Monster, simply post your resume on www.monster.com. It's very simple. When the company is looking for new hires, it scours posted resumes for likely candidates. "I placed my resume on Monster and a recruiter from the company called me that day," reports one first jobber. "She explained the position to me very thoroughly, and it sounded like something I would be interested in. Plus, I knew that Monster was a great company!" Candidates go through several stages of interviews; one explains, "My first interview was with a member of the human resources department and was more informative than the second interview, which focused on my skills and explored whether I was a good match for Monster. The first visit entailed a tour of the facility[, which] immediately caught my attention due to its creative layout and relaxed atmosphere. The walls are painted all sorts of funky colors, and while people work very hard here, I could tell right away that Monster is a fun place to work. I also got a free lunch! The second interview was with the two bosses of the department [in which I would be working] and focused more on my work experience and whether I would be a good match for Monster and the Client Relations department. A few days after my second interview, I received a phone call with an offer." Sometimes the company has interviewees "shadow" current employees; "For my second interview, I job shadowed an employee of the department and then spoke with another manager. I really liked the fact that I was able to listen to a few calls during the interview process."

MONEY AND PERKS

Entry-level employees agree that the biggest perk of working for Monster is the "fun working environment." Workers enjoy, among other things, "free drinks, a den where you can relax for an hour on your break, [and] a gym on the floor where I work." Company representatives note, "Monster still has that dot-com feel, which is enticing to many people. Candidates walk into Monster and are greeted by a huge monster in the lobby and purple carpets. There is also a den that houses a ping-pong table and pool table. In the Monster kitchen, there is free soda and coffee throughout the day. The Monster motto is you work hard, but you also play hard!"

THE ROPES

Monster uses a buddy system to help new hires adapt to the Monster way of doing things: "When an offer is extended to a candidate, [he or she is] immediately assigned a buddy by their future supervisor. A buddy is responsible for showing a new hire around their first week and getting them acclimated to the company." One first jobber recalls, "On my first day I was greeted by a buddy who was assigned to show me around and help me with any questions that I might have. I got a tour of Monster and was introduced to everyone in my department. I still went to my buddy with questions for weeks after that." Newbies also undergo "a new hire training class that lasts one week and is held once a month." There is a "great deal" of subsequent training; "I sat with almost everyone in customer service and listened to them either take or make calls. These sessions were very beneficial, and all the staff members did a fine job teaching me all about Monster's products and services," says one employee regarding the training process.

DAY IN THE LIFE

For most new hires, a typical day at Monster consists of "answering inbound calls from Monster customers and making outbound calls to Monster customers." Other possible assignments include "posting jobs for employers, doing contract set-ups for sales reps/employers, and answering e-mails from customers and sales reps." What most first jobbers find appealing about the job is not necessarily these assignments, but rather the "enjoyable working environment" and the "opportunities to advance." They also love the close contact they enjoy with company higher-ups. One employee writes, "We definitely have contact with high-level people, and we sit [in] on important meetings at least once a month. They always encourage this." Those meetings "update all employees on Monster's upcoming programs, goals, etc. These meetings are very good if one wishes to learn about the company's vision for the future. I have interacted with higher level employees at Monster quite frequently. Everyone gets along very well."

PEERS

Monster's buddy system helps foster strong bonds between entry-level and more senior employees. Among the first jobbers themselves, "There is a decent amount of camaraderie because you are training with them and going to orientation, etc." One notes, "There is a lot of contact with other first jobbers here—a lot of things to relate to, but at the same time we do not alienate other employees." New hires appreciate that "everyone seems pretty cool, nice, and laid back" and tell us that "there is an after-hours social scene, [though] not everyone takes part."

MOVING ON

Monster is a relatively new company; it hasn't been around long enough for lots of employees to "move on." The company tells us, "We have a fairly low percentage of first jobbers who stay [fewer] than twelve months. A lot of our employees have been here for a number of years." For the few people who do leave, at least they know where to go to look for their next jobs.

MorNorth
Mortgage Loan Originator

The Big Picture

MorNorth is a leading mortgage lender. First jobbers here sell home mortgage loans and services to homeowners and home buyers and earn a commission on each sale they make. The company's "unique business model" allows its mortgage loan originators to work on their own from their home offices, supported by the lender's "top-of-the-line mortgage technology." *Inc.* magazine recognized MorNorth as "one of the nation's 500 fastest-growing private companies" (it ranked twenty-eighth) in 2004 and noted its annual growth rate of 129 percent between 2000 and 2004.

Stats

Location(s) Where Entry-level Employees Work

Entry-level employees work across the United States.

Average Number of Applications Each Year

MorNorth receives about thirty-six applications each year.

Average Number Hired Per Year

MorNorth hires about twenty-four mortgage loan originators each year.

Entry-level Position(s) Available

Entry-level employees are hired as mortgage loan originators.

Average Hours Worked Per Week

Entry-level hires work about forty hours per week.

Percentage of Entry-level Hires Still with the Company After Three, Five, and Ten Years

Eighty percent of entry-level hires remain with MorNorth after three years.

Average Starting Salary

Entry-level hires earn $30,000 per year.

Benefits Offered

MorNorth offers health and dental coverage, which vests after ninety days of employment. It also offers employees life insurance and a 401(k) plan, both of which also vest after ninety days of employment.

Contact Information

Visit MorNorth on the Web at www.sellhomeloans.com, or contact Anne Chrisinger, Accounting/HR Coordinator at 218-824-5406.

GETTING HIRED

MorNorth looks for "entrepreneurial-minded, motivated leaders" among its new mortgage loan originators; initial screening is handled by a field assistant vice president (FAVP). Applicants may file job applications at the company's website. One successful hire reports, "I just filled out the application as I would for any job. I noted that I am a fast learner and willing to learn new things. A vice president gave me the first interview. The tone was good. He was explaining the company and what jobs they had to offer. He asked me if I had previous experience with the mortgage industry, and I said 'No.' He said that this is good, since I can start fresh and not compare the job with [one I had at] another company." Previous experience is not a disqualifying factor, though; another successful job applicant writes, "I had previous experience in the field and fit the qualifications for the position. The interview, conducted over the telephone by a FAVP, was very short, but thorough. My resume was very detailed about all of my past customer service, sales, as well as civic activities."

MONEY AND PERKS

Mortgage loan originator is a commission position; this means that pay is "determined by performance." First jobbers start earning a 30 percent commission on all revenue generated by the loans they sell; additional money is provided for marketing (the amount of which is based on prior production). Eventually Loan Originators can work their way up to the position of FAVP; individuals in this position earn a 65 percent commission. FAVPs supervise junior loan originators and also earn a 15 percent commission on their subordinates' sales; beyond that, they are given bonuses and a *per diem* stipend. Quarterly sales contests offer such prizes as televisions, trips, and cruises. First jobbers love that they are "in charge of [their] own careers and [their] own destiny."

THE ROPES

Newbies at MorNorth must undergo a "one- to two-day training [session] at the corporate office;" this is followed by "continual training in the field." One loan originator, "The mandatory training session helped me understand the laws and rules of what was acceptable and why things are done [in] the way they are." Another first jobber adds, "It was a lot to soak in, and it's thrown at you all at once." Fortunately, there's plenty of follow-up, as "MorNorth has ongoing training and conventions as well as a very knowledgeable and helpful staff that goes out of their way to answer questions and facilitate the loan process." Field supervision is provided by the FAVP, the "highest level on the tier" for field reps, and the position to which go-getter mortgage loan originators aspire.

Day in the Life

Motgage loan originators spend their days focusing on mortgage marketing and sales. One first jobber reports, "My first responsibilities were to market myself and generate business on my own, though there were some leads that were provided to me." The basic responsibilities of the job remain constant afterward, though the details "change every day with changes in rates, programs, and the law." MorNorth offers a battery of support services, including in-house processing, in-house underwriting, in-house closing, pre-qualification assistance, and loan document preparation. Even so, this job requires a great deal of hard work and even more initiative. One first jobber warns, "This is a stressful occupation, and it's not for everyone."

Peers

First jobbers in MorNorth's home office in Brainerd, Minnesota report that "everybody is friends here. It's like a big family." That camaraderie doesn't extend beyond the confines of the office, though, as "nothing really happens after work." The office's central Minnesota location is certainly a factor there.

Mortgage loan originators in the field generally work on their own, with little or no contact with other first jobbers. One writes, "Primary contact is with field trainers and team leaders. Because most originators work out of their homes in different cities and states, there is not much of a 'social scene.'" Company contacts are "very considerate, generous people," though.

Moving On

Working at MorNorth isn't for everyone. Successful mortgage loan originators have to be highly self-motivated. They also must have the right skills and temperament for sales. To succeed at a top level, they need to recruit other mortgage loan originators, so they can move up in the MorNorth hierarchy. As a result, many here decide to pursue other careers or return to school.

Attrition

Only half the company's first jobbers make it through their first year, and the average tenure of first jobbers is less than two years.

Best and Worst

The best first jobber with MorNorth is one who "makes a six-figure income" due to "high sales volume, a good attitude, strong marketing strategies, and motivation." The less successful new hires are "unmotivated low producers."

NATIONAL CANCER INSTITUTE
Various Positions

THE BIG PICTURE

Come to National Cancer Institute (NCI) and help search for the cancer cure. On the organization's website, the director of NCI writes, "Someday, we will eliminate cancer, but for today our immediate goal is to eliminate the suffering and death due to cancer. I have publicly issued a challenge to the cancer community ot achieve this goal by 2015." Those employed by NCI will help work toward this ambitious and praiseworthy goal.

STATS

LOCATION(S) WHERE ENTRY-LEVEL EMPLOYEES WORK

Entry-level empoyees work in Bethesda and Frederick, Maryland.

AVERAGE NUMBER OF APPLICATIONS EACH YEAR

"NCI has approximately 100 permanent, full-time vacancies per year. The number of applicants for each opening can range from a handful to as many as 300, depending on the position. As many as 1,000 students apply for summer internships annually; as many as 400 students apply for one-year internships annually."

AVERAGE NUMBER HIRED PER YEAR OVER THE LAST TEN YEARS

"[We hire] approximately 600 positions total per year across all levels of the organization, including permanent, full-time federal employees; internships (summer and one-year); and post-doctoral fellows. Currently, this number is lower as parts of the federal government are under a hiring freeze. As a result, employment opportunities are being created at other companies (contractors) that would afford an individual an opportunity to complete work [that is] related to our mission and within our offices."

ENTRY-LEVEL POSITION(S) AVAILABLE

"A limited number of permanent, full-time federal positions are available as we are under a [hiring] freeze at [the time of this writing]. We continue to hire entry-level summer interns (about 250 per year) and entry-level one-year interns (about 100 per year). The following are the [branches and respective areas where] entry-level candidates [can typically find positions]:

"**Sciences:** Biology (biomedical, biophysics, biostatistics, cancer biology, cellular, computational, developmental, etc.), chemistry (analytical, inorganic, medicinal, organic), cytology, epidemiology, genetics (drosophila, functional genomics, molecular), hematology, immunology, mathematics/statistics, oncology, pathology, and pharmacology.

"**Administration/management:** Administrative officer, budget, contracts, grants administration, management/program analysis, project management, public health/affairs, and writing/editing."

Average Hours Worked Per Week

"Most [entry-level employees] work a forty-hour week. Some extra time may be expected in the lab environment."

Percentage of Entry-level Hires Still with the Company After Three, Five, and Ten Years

After three, five, and ten years, the proportion of entry-level hires who remain with the company are 85 percent, 75 percent, and 44 percent, respectively.

Average Starting Salary

New hires who work in permanent, full-time administration/management positions earn from $26,000 to $40,000 (depending on education and experience). Science interns earn from $21,000–$35,000 (also depending on education and experience).

Benefits Offered

"[The company] offer[s] both health and life insurance benefits and long-term care insurance to permanent, full-time employees." Additional benefits for "permanent, full-time positions [include] vacation leave, sick leave, ten paid federal holidays, a wide range of retirement benefits, flexible spending accounts, Transhare (free on-site parking or mass transit subsidies), on-site child care programs, referral services (child care, elder care, legal, financial, housing). [Additional benefits for] science internships [include] ten paid federal holidays, Transhare, on-site child care, [and] referral services."

Contact Information

To apply for a summer internship, complete an online application at: http://generalemployment.nci.nih.gov/. To submit a resume for hiring managers to review, go to the same website.

To review vacancy announcements for federal positions, go to http://reports.cit.nih.gov/jobsnih/advacsearch.asp, and select "National Cancer Institute" in the second drop down window.

Getting Hired

"Each scientific division and program area determines its employment needs individually." NCI recruits at select schools but does not interview on campus. It accepts online applications "for summer science internships and maintains a resume database for permanent, full-time positions; one-year internships; and post-doctoral fellowships." Many first jobbers learn about open positions from professors and research partners. For science positions, "a typical application process involves many steps. Candidates first have to fill out an application online and then submit it. If the candidate qualifies for the position, they will have to go to at least one of three possible interviews, which would include supervisors, administrative officers, and lab managers. After this step is accomplished, the selected candidate will then get an offer letter, which includes a date for an orientation they have to attend, and they will have to fill out a large folder of papers and attend a half-day seminar. So to make a long story short, the application process can take up to three months to complete, if not longer." Examples of typical interview questions include "Tell us about a project or activity where you played a leadership role, and describe your contribution. Describe a challenging experience and how you handled it. Describe a situation or attitude that you would find difficult to work with. What is your approach when presented with [a] new procedure or a problem?"

MONEY AND PERKS

NCI reports that "each employee may be eligible for a raise each year. Permanent federal employees typically get a 3.6 percent raise from Congress and are eligible for a step increase each year. Additionally, permanent employees become eligible for promotions based on performance and employer needs that can result in a substantial raise of $3,000–$7,000 during one year." One current entry-level employee adds, "If you have a previous job before coming [here], your salary might be negotiable, but in most cases you are given a set series and grade, and you have to excel from there." One employee says, "[Top perks include] a flex schedule that allows you to have a compressed work schedule. And don't let me forget the health benefits and holidays. [Those are] the best!" Newbies also love the fact that "being housed in one of the greatest research institutions in the world means [they have] access [to] fantastic conferences and lectures!"

THE ROPES

NCI hires for numerous positions in a wide variety of areas, so specific training regimens vary widely. For all employees, the institution has "a half-day orientation that introduces employees to the agency and the resources available to employees." Officials also point out that "in scientific divisions, mentoring is a longstanding tradition for all employees. Throughout NCI, new hires work under senior managers and should have multiple resources and at least one staff member who is knowledgeable and available to answer questions and address concerns." Most divisions and program areas "have their own orientation process as well." Because most post-doc fellows "are from foreign countries, visa and immigration training is given."

DAY IN THE LIFE

NCI representatives state, "Our array of positions makes [describing a typical day] impossible; however, each position and its responsibilities should be comprehensively explained and on-going guidance provided [by the new hire's supervisor]."

PEERS

One newbie says, "We have a great sense of camaraderie! At NCI, I have gotten along well with other fellows. I spend one-on-one time with other interns about once a week. There's a happy hour once every couple of weeks, but we mostly communicate with [one another] on the job during lunch or on a work break." In most divisions, there isn't much of an after-hours scene, since "many of the employees here have families and live" far apart. Our survey respondents all agree that one major asset of working at NCI is "being around people who are driven by the mission to help others; [they are] truly honored to be associated with [the agency] professionally and [personally]."

Moving On

Many first jobbers leave NCI to return to school; one typical newcomer writes, "I plan to go back to school for a master's degree in nutrition (probably with a focus on health communications)." Other people find related work in the medical field, while employees in administration move onto other, better opportunities within the federal government. NCI does not track data on exiting first jobbers.

Best and Worst

The most successful first jobbers at NCI are "individuals who have a desire to work in public service and who have a passion about the mission of the National Cancer Institute, to eliminate suffering and death caused by cancer. NCI culture rewards collaboration, teamwork, commitment, and an ability to provide leadership within the system. Because NCI is part of a much larger system (one of twenty-seven institutes at the National Institutes of Health, which is one of many operating divisions within the Department of Health and Human Services), ideas, programs, and decisions do not occur overnight. [NCI] is not the best employer for individuals looking to make lots of money quick or [to] be the one individual in the spotlight. While each person is expected to fully contribute and [be] recognized for excellence, there are few individual spotlight moments on the road to curing cancer."

NATIONAL PUBLIC RADIO
Departmental Assistant

THE BIG PICTURE

Welcome to the world of information, music, oddly informative quiz shows, and auto mechanics with infectious laughs. Join what is arguably the nation's best broadcast news organization. "It's where the smartest kids in your class went to work—and what they listen to every day."

STATS

LOCATION(S) WHERE ENTRY-LEVEL EMPLOYEES WORK

Most positions are in Washington, DC. A few are also available at NPR's West Coast facility in Culver City, California.

AVERAGE NUMBER OF APPLICATIONS EACH YEAR

NPR receives 1,500 applications every year.

AVERAGE NUMBER HIRED PER YEAR OVER THE LAST TEN YEARS

NPR hires 150 people per year.

ENTRY-LEVEL POSITION(S) AVAILABLE

Entry-level hires work as production assistants, editorial assistants, research assistants, development assistants, and administrative assistants.

AVERAGE HOURS WORKED PER WEEK

Weekly hours vary by position, but employees work at least forty hours per week.

AVERAGE STARTING SALARY

Production and editorial assistants earn $43,000; research assistants earn $37,000; administrative assistants earn $32,000.

BENEFITS OFFERED

In terms of health care coverage, NPR has a cafeteria-style benefits program that allows employees to customize their benefits selection. NPR offers three medical plans, two dental plans, and a vision care plan. Additional benefits include supplemental life insurance and other optional items. In addition, all employees receive life insurance and long-term disability. New employees receive three weeks of annual leave per year. (After three years, employees receive four weeks of annual leave.) Employees also receive two days of personal leave, three days of bereavement leave, and ten days of sick leave each year. NPR also has ten paid holidays per year. NPR has a 403(b) retirement savings plan.

CONTACT INFORMATION

National Public Radio

Human Resources Department

635 Massachusetts Avenue, NW

Washington, DC 20001

Fax: 202-513-3047

E-mail: employment@npr.org

GETTING HIRED

The best way to get a job at NPR, it seems, is for interested candidates to obtain internships during their college careers, so they can make the contacts necessary to get full-time positions when they open. Many of the employees we spoke with got their jobs this way. NPR posts open positions on its website, and anyone may apply for one; the organization seeks individuals "with journalism and/or media backgrounds and experience. Experience working in and/or knowledge of public radio and the public radio system are preferred." One successful hire says, "The application process was long. I interviewed with a manager and then a vice president. The interviews were professional and conversational. The interviewers mainly focused on why I wanted to work for NPR. It was important that I had a passion for the mission of the organization."

MONEY AND PERKS

Starting salaries at NPR are fixed by job. "Over the first few years, salaries increase based on cost of living adjustments and merit," NPR officials tell us. The best perks, according to first jobbers, include free CDs and books, meeting on-air hosts, frequent travel, and doing a job that they love. One explains: "I am challenged and respected by my coworkers, who I get along extremely well with. The people here are great, [and] they generally want to be here doing what they are doing. NPR can be [a] very meaningful place to work. On a more superficial, image-only level, when I tell people I work at NPR, they always say, 'Oh, I love NPR!'"

THE ROPES

Orientation at NPR is a brief affair—it's a little more than "several sessions regarding general employment practices at NPR (i.e., completing new hire forms, benefits, and IT orientations, etc.). Additional orientations (some optional) can be scheduled to acquaint the new employee further with employment at NPR." After that, most employees receive on-the-job training. A producer for *Day to Day* explained, "I was pretty much thrown in the fire; we were in the piloting process of a brand new show and there wasn't very much time to sit down and learn everything before I started. I sort of learned as I went along. I did receive some training on digital editing software; the other producers helped me with that."

DAY IN THE LIFE

Depending on the area in which you end up working, a typical day at NPR can include "pitching stories, editing sound, writing host leads and questions for interviews; assisting in the overall management of cultivation events and fundraising (a typical day includes menu planning, creating travel and event agendas, writing donor letters, designing invitations, and participating in conference calls with event hosts); compiling submissions to award competitions and just helping out on a variety of projects." There are a lot of different jobs to be done; read thorough descriptions at the job-posting section of NPR's website.

PEERS

The entry-level employees we spoke with at NPR work in areas that lack other first jobbers or have very few of them. They described a comfortable, amiable work environment. One writes, "I am lucky that though I am the only person in my department in my first year of working, I fit in well here for many other reasons." They also express admiration for their coworkers, telling us that they were "amazing; they are intelligent, interesting, genuine, and likeable."

MOVING ON

Low pay is the chief complaint of people who eventually leave NPR. Those who go usually do so to pursue other, more profitable positions in broadcast journalism.

THE NEW TEACHER PROJECT
Operations and Communications Associates

THE BIG PICTURE

The New Teacher Project (TNTP) is "a national nonprofit organization that partners with school districts, states, and other educational entities to develop programs that recruit, select, and train exceptional individuals to become teachers for high-need public schools." It's a great place for people who want to "make a difference." One first jobber explains, "I had left my previous position in entry-level market research because there was no sense of purpose or employee interest, and I also did not feel as though I had much in common with many of my coworkers. When I found the position with TNTP, however, I knew almost instantly that it was an ideal match. I found my coworkers to be driven, intelligent, and genuinely concerned with the work at hand. Also, the organization worked directly to help people, not just help profits and track numbers."

STATS

LOCATION(S) WHERE ENTRY-LEVEL EMPLOYEES WORK

"Our entry-level employees work at various locations, depending on where we have programs and openings. Sites include major metropolitan areas such as New York, New York; Washington, DC; Philadelphia, Pennsylvania; Baltimore, Maryland; Miami, Florida; Memphis, Tennessee; New Orleans, Louisiana; Houston, Texas; and Oakland, California." Additional sites may be found "in states with large rural populations, such as Louisiana and Virginia."

AVERAGE NUMBER OF APPLICATIONS EACH YEAR

TNTP receives 1,000 applications a year.

AVERAGE NUMBER HIRED PER YEAR

TNTP hires six entry-level workers a year.

ENTRY-LEVEL POSITION(S) AVAILABLE

TNTP usually hires operations and communications associates, "and sometimes other positions, as well."

AVERAGE HOURS WORKED PER WEEK

Entry-level workers usually work forty-five to fifty hours per week.

AVERAGE STARTING SALARY

In 2005, the average starting salary was $31,000.

Benefits Offered

TNTP has "a strong medical benefits package that vests on an employee's first day. Medical and vision insurance are fully paid; dental coverage requires a small contribution from the employee." Additional benefits include a 403(b) tax-free retirement plan, paid disability, paid vacation, and personal time off.

Contact Information

The New Teacher Project
304 Park Avenue South, 11th Floor
New York, NY 10010
E-mail: jobs@tntp.org

Getting Hired

The New Teacher Project recruits on college campuses; the specific campuses vary annually "depending on the cities [in which] we have programs and openings." Openings are also posted on the organization's website. TNTP seeks "strong, critical thinkers who are committed to the organization's mission of ensuring that all students are taught by excellent teachers [who are] achievement-oriented, productive, [and] sensitive to others." Communication skills are also considered very important. Interviews here "can be intense. We ask in-depth questions about each candidate's background experiences—including times [he or she has] been challenged or disappointed, not just what [he or she has] achieved, and questions with hypothetical scenarios about situations [that may arise] on the job."

All applications begin with the submission of a resume and detailed cover letter; this is followed by "three interviews and a short project related to the work that we do." One successful hire reports, "I was given about four days to complete the project, which asked me to analyze a set of data and make recommendations based on my findings. Afterward, I was invited for a second-round in-person interview with the director of selection and one of her supervisors. We spent a lot of time discussing the exercise I completed."

Money and Perks

The negotiability of salaries, start dates, and other work-related details vary by position. The organization does lots of contract work; and this often allows for little flexibility in the terms of employment. Raises are awarded annually; while "entry-level employees are generally not eligible for a bonus," occasionally "there are exceptions." TNTP first jobbers love that "the culture here is very results-oriented and flexible, with lots of autonomy for workers. They trust you to do things in the style that makes sense for you, as long as you achieve the desired results in a timely and high-quality manner. Newbies also appreciate that because it is "a nonprofit company, TNTP is very responsive to not having typical work weeks. While some days might be very busy, when it is slow, people are very willing to let you go home early. Also, we get an amazing number of vacation days!"

THE ROPES

Formal orientation at TNTP "occurs over the course of a few weeks [and] generally includes an overview and history of the organization, an overview of benefits and policies, an in-depth overview of the particular program and the employee's job responsibilities, and, as [may be] relevant, an overview of resources available within TNTP to help staff in their new roles (e.g., manuals, contact information for staff with similar roles in similar TNTP programs, etc.)." Training is "ongoing and informal, more a schedule of somewhat informal meetings with managers" and a "learn-as-you-go process."

DAY IN THE LIFE

TNTP hires first jobbers for two key positions: operations associates and communications associates. Operations associates are "responsible for program logistics and materials, entering and maintaining program data, [and] coordinating special program events," while communications associates are "responsible for delivery of accurate, timely, and courteous recruitment and/or program messages by phone, e-mail, and in-person [contact] with candidates, accepted teachers, and teachers already in the classroom." One communications associate reports, "I am primarily focused on dealing with public interest in the program: e-mails, phone calls, public information sessions in the evenings, and creating a database to track all of this. On a typical day I arrive at 9:00 A.M. or earlier and begin by responding to any program e-mails or calls from the day before. This continues throughout the day, but my primary focus eventually switches to sending and tracking correspondence to candidates at different stages of the application process. After lunch, I generally have some candidate screenings to complete, and then I work on building the database needed to house information on selected candidates and [on] completing data requests. Finally, at least once a week, I need to spend an evening assisting or presenting at an information session [at which] the public can get a rundown of the program and ask questions."

PEERS

"The New Teacher Project does not have a 'cohort' of people that comes in every year." As a result, explains one newbie, "there is not much first-job camaraderie here. However, everyone gets along great and tends to socialize with [one another] without the boundary of 'this is my boss/employee.'"

The organization is also a magnet for extremely bright individuals; one first jobber writes, "It can definitely be a bit daunting at times, since everyone was clearly an honors student in the past. However, everyone cares about working together." One employee sums up, "Each person in my organization could be working for a corporation, making a ton of money, but instead [we] choose to work toward this cause. I love going in to work every day!"

Moving On

Those who leave The New Teacher Project generally do so to attend graduate school or to "gain different experiences elsewhere." There is a sense among some here that "there is not much room for growth, and sometimes there is not much interaction between different contracts," both of which present situations that may thwart ambitious careerists in their efforts to advance. The average tenure of a first jobber here is two years.

Attrition

About ten percent of college-grad hires leave The New Teacher Project within twelve months of arriving. Some complain about the "uncertainty" arising from contract-based programs. "Due to the fact that we are often working with the delayed budgets and number projections common in the education world," writes an entry-level employee, "we often have to pull together quickly once our goals are set."

Best and Worst

Among the most successful first jobbers at The New Teacher Project is a woman who "began working as an intern on one of our contracts right after graduation from college. It was clear from the beginning that she was a quick learner and a hard worker and was really inspired by our goals and mission. She took every opportunity to help out when she could. As a result, we offered her an operations associate position in November of that year. In that position, we saw that she consistently produced high-quality work and was highly accountable for meeting her goals and the contract's goals. One year later, she was promoted to recruiter in our largest contract, and less than a year after that, she was promoted to director of placement, [a position in which she was charged with] coordinating a placement process for approximately 2,000 newly-recruited teachers each year."

NEW YORK CARES
Various Positions

THE BIG PICTURE

New York Cares coordinates volunteers for a variety of philanthropic activities. The organization helps "tutor children, feed the hungry, assist people living with HIV/AIDS, revitalize gardens, take homeless children on cultural and recreational outings, visit the elderly, and engage in many other hands-on activities." First jobbers tell us why they find the organization so attractive: "NY Cares's reputation and professionalism precedes it; [we] also believe in their work"

STATS

LOCATION(S) WHERE ENTRY-LEVEL EMPLOYEES WORK

Entry-level employees work in New York, New York.

AVERAGE NUMBER OF APPLICATIONS EACH YEAR

NY Cares receives 300–400 applications each year, and sometimes more.

AVERAGE NUMBER HIRED PER YEAR OVER THE LAST TEN YEARS

The organization hires five to six people per year.

ENTRY-LEVEL POSITION(S) AVAILABLE

New hires work as annual events managers, program managers, and corporate relations managers.

AVERAGE HOURS WORKED PER WEEK

Employees work forty hours per week, including some nights and weekends.

PERCENTAGE OF ENTRY-LEVEL HIRES STILL WITH THE COMPANY AFTER THREE, FIVE, AND TEN YEARS

After three and five years, 30 percent and 10 percent of all entry-level hires remain with the organization, respectively.

AVERAGE STARTING SALARY

New hires earn approximately $31,000 per year.

BENEFITS OFFERED

As far as medical benefits go, individuals "make a modest contribution" to a point of service plan. Additional benefits include flexible spending accounts for qualified transportation expenses, medical and dependent care, a tax-deferred annuity (403(b) plan), vacation and sick days, and ten paid holidays per year.

Human Resources Department
NY Cares, Inc.
214 West 29th Street, 5th Floor
New York, NY 10001
www.nycares.org

GETTING HIRED

With so few positions to offer each year, NY Cares has no need to recruit on campus. Instead, the organization simply "posts job openings on certain websites specializing in nonprofit positions (i.e., www.Idealist.org) where [they] invite interested applicants to send their resumes." Any kind of "in" is valuable. Some people find full-time employment by applying for full-time positions after interning, while others are tipped off by friends who work for the organization. Here's how one worker describes the vetting process: "It was an extended affair (because there were no openings at the time I applied). First, I had an informational interview and spoke with a few former employees who helped me network to find some temporary work. The NY Cares staff and alums were very well connected and had good suggestions for organizations that fit my interests and skills. About a month after my initial conversation, there were job openings in the Program Department at NY Cares, and I was interviewed for two positions simultaneously. The director of human resources and program director interviewed me first, and then I had a second conversation with staff members currently holding the project manager positions. I had follow-up conversations over the phone with the directors to discuss whether I had a strong preference for one position over the other."

MONEY AND PERKS

At NY Cares, "Management determines the maximum annual increase in salaries for all employees. The individual's supervisor determines the actual increase based on [his or her] performance." First jobbers tell us that starting salaries are "somewhat negotiable," though those coming in with little more than a bachelor's degree should expect to be paid an amount near the bottom of the pay scale. The best perks about working at NY Cares, newbies tell us, are "the social atmosphere and the friendships."

THE ROPES

Most of the training at NY Cares happens on the job. Preliminary orientation lasts a day or two and consists primarily of "meeting with various staff members, including the finance and operations officer, office coordinator, and other members of their department to understand office procedures and job specifics." After that, it's time to work. Fortunately, there's lots of mentoring for new hires. A newbie recalls, "I was constantly in touch with my boss. She really helped me to get oriented and come along." Another newbie adds, "NY Cares really had a commitment to sending me to workshops and trainings. This helped a lot. In looking back, I am grateful that I came to a place that really had such a nurturing environment."

Day in the Life

Starting positions at NY Cares fall into three categories. The organization describes each position this way: "Program managers work directly with agencies to design meaningful volunteer projects. Our annual events staff runs four different events: a coat drive, a holiday gift exchange for needy children, and two citywide volunteering events in the public schools and parks. The staff is responsible for a multitude of tasks relating to the particular events' execution. Our corporate relations managers are responsible for maintaining the relationships with our corporate donors, mainly through enlisting their support for our annual events and other service projects." First jobbers find themselves handling a tremendous amount of responsibility early on in their tenures, and most find it gratifying. As one former employee explains, "One of the great things about NY Cares is that it is a relatively small organization; roughly thirty-six people were on staff when I was there. Everyone was close, and the executive director always had me [sit] in on important meetings. I was also expected to give my viewpoint."

Peers

The environment at NY Cares, workers tell us, "is incredibly friendly." As one employee describes it, "the social scene is such an integral part of the culture here; we work hard all day and then socialize in the evening. Many of us go to local bars regularly to play pool and drink beer after work; many people date colleagues. We (the younger staff) eat lunch together all the time." Another approvingly adds, "The culture of NY Cares is one where there's an accepting spirit. It is full of smart, energetic, idealistic, and committed people—how could you not make friends in that environment?"

Moving on

Most people who leave this small organization do so because "it does not have a great amount of opportunity for advancement. While you can take on additional projects and responsibilities, there aren't many opportunities for promotions." Mostly they find jobs with other nonprofit organizations, though some proceed to graduate school. The average tenure of a first jobber is two to three years, organization representatives report.

Attrition

NY Cares does not offer a fixed-term first job program, so there is no attrition *per se*. Employees most often leave, as noted above, because the chances for career advancement are minimal. Some people say they leave because the pay is too low, especially given the cost of living in New York City.

NEW YORK CITY TEACHING FELLOWS
Fellow

THE BIG PICTURE

If you like the idea of "leaving corporate America" for the opportunity to make a difference and help shape the lives of young people, the New York City Teaching Fellows program may be just the thing for you. A commitment of approximately two years to the program puts you in front of one classroom and makes you a student in another, so you can earn your master's degree in education.

STATS

LOCATION(S) WHERE ENTRY-LEVEL EMPLOYEES WORK

All teaching positions are located in New York, New York.

AVERAGE NUMBER OF APPLICATIONS EACH YEAR

The NYC Teaching Fellows receives 16,000–20,000 applications each year.

AVERAGE NUMBER HIRED PER YEAR OVER THE LAST TEN YEARS

The organization hires about 2,000 people each year.

ENTRY-LEVEL POSITION(S) AVAILABLE

New hires work as teaching fellows.

AVERAGE HOURS WORKED PER WEEK

Fellows work forty hours per week.

AVERAGE STARTING SALARY

Fellows who have bachelor's degrees earn $39,000; for fellows with additional course work, the salary can be higher. For more information, visit www.teachny.com/salary_calc.asp.

BENEFITS OFFERED

Fellows have a choice of health insurance plans, including medical, dental, prescription, optical, and hearing. Additional benefits include a subsidized master's degree, disability insurance, mortgage programs, special discounts, a pension plan, TransitChecks, and flexible spending accounts.

CONTACT INFORMATION

Apply at www.nycteachingfellows.org.

GETTING HIRED

Teaching fellows tell us that the program has "a reputation for being very selective. The process of applying is more rigorous than graduate school applications." Applications are accepted online; they require "basic" essays that "require thoughtful answers outside of the typical 'I want to be a teacher because I love children.'"

Those who make the first cut are called for an all-day interview session. One fellow reports, "The interview started in a group format. I had to prepare a five-minute lesson (which, by the way, is not much time at all!). All of us were nervous, and the best thing I can recommend to anyone going through the process is to make friends with the other interviewees before the process begins. This puts everyone at ease, and, more likely than not, these are not the people you will be competing with, since there are many subjects areas for which qualified teachers are sought." The next part of the process is a one-on-one interview, which "consists of pre-written questions. The questions are read, and then the responses are written down word for word. The questions are mostly what-if situations: 'If you were teaching and blank happened, what would you do?' The woman who interviewed me was helpful, kind, and patient. She made me feel comfortable. She explained that later that evening she would meet with another group to review the results of the interviews and then make her recommendations. After spending the entire day (six hours) interviewing, I was told that I would have an answer within the month. I was accepted into the program five weeks later."

Money and Perks

Teaching fellows belong to the teachers' union, so their salaries are determined by the union contract. Because of the program's prescribed training program, starting dates are also nonnegotiable. Regarding placement, "The NYC Teaching Fellows program places teachers in high-need areas. We were given an opportunity to state our preferred borough and region, but the point of the program is to assist schools and children [with] the greatest need; the needs of the program come first. The desired subject [and] grade level was also needs-based, but we were given a chance to state our preference." Union membership ensures a solid benefits package. Teaching fellows are also eligible for a subsidized master's degree in education; in 2005, teachers were required to cover $4,000 in master's-related expenses over two years, with the city picking up the rest of the tab. Other fringe benefits of the job include "great vacations." One teacher writes, "I hate it when people say the best part about being a teacher is the summers off! This is the most demanding and difficult job I have ever held. If we didn't have vacations, I would burn out within a year. Besides, the next two summers of my life will be spent in graduate school classes!"

The Ropes

Pre-service training, a seven-week program that begins in the middle of June, is required of all fellows. Referred to by many as "summer boot camp," it is "consuming, exhausting, and demanding" but ultimately "a very positive experience." Here's how one fellow describes it: "It takes place in the college where you will be doing your graduate work (you need to get a master's degree to become a teacher). You get both academic classes and the 'straight dope' from actual New York City teachers called 'fellow advisors' who give you the lowdown on what to expect in the classroom. My fellow advisor was cool, and I was very impressed with that aspect of the program. Halfway through the summer, we were placed in a school in our district to assist another teacher teaching summer school. We assistant taught in the mornings, then went to grad school in the afternoons." Although teachers are usually required to hold a degree in their area of specialization, New York makes an exception for math teachers (because they are in such short supply). A rigorous math-immersion program, in addition to the above-mentioned training, is required of prospective math teachers who do not qualify to teach under the standard guidelines.

DAY IN THE LIFE

Teaching is a demanding job, and the fellows we spoke with describe filled-to-bursting work days. According to one fellow, "My days typically started at 5:30 A.M. at home doing planning and correcting papers and homework. At school by 7:30 A.M. Teach until 3:00 P.M. or 4:00 P.M., depending on the day. Three days a week at college until 7:00 P.M. Home by 8:30 P.M. Planning, paperwork, studying, etc. until 10:00 P.M." Lather, rinse, repeat—no wonder teachers are so effusive about their summer vacations! There's also once-a-month after-school faculty meetings, professional development sessions, and occasional teacher-parent meetings. It's a grind for sure, albeit a fulfilling one for the right individual. The job doesn't evolve over time, but the teachers do; one explains, "My job has not changed, but I have. I started the school year clueless as to how to reach and teach the children. I believe I have grown as an individual and as a teacher through this experience, and not," she adds pointedly, "through my college courses."

PEERS

Between teaching, grading assignments, and studying for a master's degree, most fellows have precious little time to hang with peers. "There was more camaraderie with my NYC Teaching Fellows classmates this summer," explains one teacher. "I find it difficult to maintain an active social life while teaching and attending college simultaneously. I keep close phone contact with several classmates, and we have a mass e-mail system set up for our group, which we use regularly." Most understandably admire their peers, since they know exactly how heavy a load they are shouldering. One writes, "I like most of my fellow fellows and genuinely admire many. They are mostly committed and intelligent people. It is unfortunate that the program is designed so that making friends is not really possible."

MOVING ON

The program is designed to generate career teachers; the master's degree in education is a huge incentive to remain in the school system, since it translates roughly into a 10 percent pay hike. Thus, many of those who complete the program continue to teach in the city-school system. Other people move elsewhere in the state and continue teaching. More than a few teachers, however, get burned out by the demands of the job and seek employment outside the education world.

ATTRITION

Teachers who leave the program early receive no tuition compensation for their master's work, so the incentives to tough it out, regardless of how difficult it may be, are great. Even people who complain most bitterly about incompetent administrators, unreasonable demands and standards, the challenges of teaching in the city-school system, and the superfluity of some graduate courses in education tell us they planned to remain in the program to the end. Retention after the two-year commitment is also very high. More than 80 percent of those who complete two years of teaching return for a third.

THE NEW YORK TIMES
Columnist Assistant/Editorial Assistant

THE BIG PICTURE

The public image of the newspaper columnist is that of the solitary scribe, but in fact they're not solitary at all—they have assistants to keep them company! Their assistants also fulfill a wide range of duties, including interviewing experts, checking facts, and—if their relationship with their mentors grows strong enough—offering feedback and criticism for their columns.

STATS

LOCATION(S) WHERE ENTRY-LEVEL EMPLOYEES WORK

Entry-level employees work in New York, New York.

ENTRY-LEVEL POSITION(S) AVAILABLE

Entry-level hires work as columnists or editorial assistants.

AVERAGE STARTING SALARY (BY POSITION)

Starting salaries range from $40,000–$45,000.

GETTING HIRED

"It's been a word-of-mouth position," say all the researcher/assistants we spoke to with the *New York Times*; everyone we contacted either knew his or her predecessor or knew someone who helped him or her find another position at the paper, then luckily snatched the assistant's job. As a result, the application process is much less formal than at most other jobs. One writes, "My resume was unformatted, just a summary job history, very informal. This is where knowing people and being recommended goes further than anything you'd imagine. When I got this job, my first job was to reject all the applicants. There were great resumes—people applying right out of college, people who had lots of experience. It's hard; people [are lucky to get] these columnist jobs." Even so, the interview process can be grueling. One assistant, "My initial interview was with my predecessor, who informally described the responsibilities of the job. In the second interview, [the columnist] and my predecessor further described the work involved, then engaged me in a discussion of the current events and potential topics for [the columnist]'s next column. The final interview was something of a death match between me and two other candidates: Each of us was called upon to meet separately with [the columnist] and offer more developed ideas for his next column."

MONEY AND PERKS

Union rules strictly limit the negotiability of many jobs at the *New York Times*, editorial assistantships among them. First jobbers are occasionally able to negotiate start time and may even win some small concessions on salary; most, however, are more interested in the experience than the pay, so they don't push too hard on their initial terms of employment. Once here they find that "there are a lot of perks, which is one reason it's hard to leave the *Times*. I've written for other publications, and I've called and called and they're not interested because you need a contact there. Not so here." There's also "a lot of free stuff that comes in: books, tickets to premieres, CDs, that sort of thing." Finally, "there's a lot of respect that comes from calling from the *New York Times*, even if you're not a big person, and that's nice. I used to work in a nonprofit, and I didn't get any of that then."

THE ROPES

Training at the *Times* begins with orientation, "a couple of hours around a table. They basically gave us a handbook and a little union talk." And that's about it for formal training mechanisms here. Lucky assistants learn from their predecessors and their peers. Unlucky ones replace fired predecessors and have only their peers to fall back on. They also generally lose access to their predecessor's files. One such ill-fated assistant wrote, "I had to start without even a Rolodex, which was hard. But I used common sense, figured out who to call to get info and check things, that sort of thing. It would have been nice to have a Rolodex of experts on gun control and bulimia in Zanzibar because it's hard to find them on your own, even for the quicky stuff." Overall, though, "it's not a hard job to learn. Any questions I had, I could ask other assistants. This is a friendly place, and there's always somebody there to help you."

DAY IN THE LIFE

Editorial assistants do everything their bosses don't have time to do. One explains, "It would be difficult for [the columnist] to do as much as he does without an assistant. These guys, they do a lot of public stuff. They go on television shows, they work on books, and they get so much feedback because they're the opinion people here. They have a lot of stuff to deal with that a reporter doesn't, and they wouldn't be able to put out a column every week without an assistant." In addition to administrative duties "such as answering the phone, opening the mail, [and] arranging logistics of travel and media engagements," assistants serve "as another set of eyes and ears for [the columnist]. That means reading newspapers, magazines, online sources and the occasional book; watching/listening to cable and network news, entertainment TV, radio, and the occasional film; and generally keeping abreast of the news of politics and culture. A typical day begins with reading newspapers and checking several regular websites for string on subjects relevant to the column. I'll gather a number of news stories, transcripts of speeches or news shows, and organize them into files based on subjects of immediate and ongoing interest. I'll field several calls from publicists pitching stories, news program producers requesting interviews, and friends and colleagues."

PEERS

"Everyone here is smart and talented" is the unsurprising consensus among assistants at the venerable Gray Lady. One writes, "First when I got here, I felt like the only non-Ivy Leaguer. That's true to a certain extent, but it's not really like that. There's a mix of people." While there's not a big after-hours scene, "there are efforts among young staffers to connect with one another, including a writers group that organizes lunches/talks with senior reporters and editors." Also, "one of the guys on the editorial board decided to give us a once-a-week writing class. He used to teach at Harvard. That's amazing. Oh, and we have a softball team. That's a great way to meet nonwriting people."

NEWELL RUBBERMAID
Phoenix Program

THE BIG PICTURE

Participants in the Phoenix Program serve as liaisons between Newell Rubbermaid—which produces kitchen storage containers, high-end cookware, writing instruments, home-improvement tools, and accessories—and the stores that sell its products. The Phoenix Program, Newell Rubbermaid's entry-level recruiting initiative, is "the launching pad to unlimited career opportunities." The company "shapes future leaders by hiring top talent in areas [such as] sales, marketing, operations, purchasing, engineering, finance, and human resources." The Phoenix Program has "a successful track record of developing individuals' business acumen and skills and rewarding them for their results."

STATS

LOCATION(S) WHERE ENTRY-LEVEL EMPLOYEES WORK

"Nationwide. We have reps in cities across the United States," as well as "several in Canada and Mexico."

AVERAGE NUMBER OF APPLICATIONS EACH YEAR

The company receives more than 7,500 applications per year for the Phoenix Program.

AVERAGE NUMBER HIRED OVER THE LAST TEN YEARS

Newell Rubbermaid hires about 250 people per year for the Phoenix Program.

ENTRY-LEVEL POSITION(S) AVAILABLE

Entry-level hires in the sales and marketing Phoenix Program "have the opportunity to work with multiple Newell Rubbermaid divisions and key accounts in a variety of functional areas."

AVERAGE HOURS WORKED PER WEEK

The number of hours that entry-level employees work varies per week. Representatives work the hours necessary to accomplish their goals; for example, a sales and marketing representative will work longer hours during a store opening.

PERCENTAGE OF ENTRY-LEVEL HIRES STILL WITH THE COMPANY AFTER THREE, FIVE, AND TEN YEARS

Approximately 75 percent of all entry-level hires remain with the company after four years, which is the age of the Phoenix Program.

AVERAGE STARTING SALARY

Entry-level hires earn a salary of $37,000.

Benefits Offered

Newell Rubbermaid offers competitive benefits to individuals in the Phoenix Program. These include medical, dental, and vision coverage; prescription drug plans; disability coverage; life insurance; a company-matched 401(k) plan; flexible spending accounts; employee counseling; and vacation.

Contact Information

Candidates may apply online at www.newellrubbermaid.com/campusrecruiting.

Getting Hired

Successful hires in the Phoenix Program have many gatekeepers to impress; the application process includes three separate interview sessions, the third of which is a three-parter. One employee who made it all the way through explains, "The first [interview] was held on campus (at Eastern Illinois University) and was essentially a screening interview. I was asked about my involvement in college, career goals, and overall interests. An alumna conducted this interview. My second interview was also on campus and was with a different alumna of Eastern Illinois University. During this interview I was asked how I would react in different situations; it was a much more in-depth interview and covered a significant amount of information. The third [interview consists] of three rounds of interviews with different employees of different divisions. Here they asked about my relocation preferences, what I knew about the company, and why I thought I would be a [good] match. I received my offer letter about five days later in the mail." Undergraduates may also apply online; typically, those culled from this batch have their first two interviews with Newell Rubbermaid managers. According to company officials, "Newell Rubbermaid looks for candidates who have leadership skills. We need leaders at all levels in our organization, and we want to recruit only those applicants who have shown that they are leaders. We also look for team-oriented, driven, and results-focused applicants."

Money and Perks

All sales and marketing Phoenix Program hires start at the same salary; one explains, "The job offer was negotiable in terms of when I started but not where I was going to be positioned or salary." The company "conducts reviews and [awards] merit raises once a year. Promotions result in a 10 percent salary increase with bonus potential or a 15 percent raise and no bonus potential depending on the role." Another perk is a company branded vehicle (decorated with the logo of whichever product the representative promotes). "It saves you so much money [when you don't have] a car payment and insurance payment every month," explains one field representative. Additionally, "the freedom in this job is incredible. Every Phoenix employee in the field is in charge of maintaining his or her own territory, and this work is not done the same by any two employees."

THE ROPES

The sales and marketing Phoenix training differs depending on the division in which the hire is placed. Some trainees start their tenures at one- or two-week orientation trainings. Other trainees work in the field for a while with a mentor before attending formal training sessions. According to company officials, "Our new hire orientation classes cover a variety of topics. The sessions start with corporate information, including a strategy talk from the chief executive officer, an event-marketing overview, professional presence, human resources benefits and policies, career paths, who's who at Newell Rubbermaid, and world-class marketing, to name a few. We then go into sales process training, which covers the steps in our sales process and role-playing for practice. The sessions conclude with division-specific breakouts to cover product knowledge and hands-on demonstrations." Trainees in all divisions agree that the formal orientation "consists mainly of product knowledge." One Calphalon representative reports, "We cooked with our products to see the differences between them and also to learn how to do [the] demos that we perform at store level."

A DAY IN THE LIFE

Once established in their jobs, sales and marketing Phoenix hires "work in the field on a daily basis [and are] responsible for all of Newell Rubbermaid's product lines in their stores." They "merchandise our products, sell orders, obtain extra shelf and endcap space [an end-of-the-aisle display], and plan and execute special store events such as grand openings or sales events." An average day, writes one Sanford pen representative, "would be to greet the managers and employees, give them a sample pen, and train them about the benefits of the pen, then complete a store walk-through and write down any Sanford product placement or competitors' placement. I would also look for possible product placement and cross-merchandising opportunities. Then, I would make sure that any promotional displays from corporate were placed on the floor, labeled, and filled. Finally, I would go to the pen aisle and make sure that our products were correctly placed in the Plan-O-Gram [display], down stock the pens to make sure that the pen aisle is full, and label any spots that do not have a label. Then I would go to my home office and enter my daily activities and any expenses that need to be reported to corporate." As far as access to higher-ups goes, "there are no barriers at Newell Rubbermaid. Each employee has direct contact with every other employee in the company, regardless of rank. I have the cell phone number of the president of my division and have used it several times. All calls were received with enthusiasm and were valued for what they had to offer."

Peers

Unlike many other entry-level positions profiled in this book, Phoenix representatives have little face-to-face contact with one another after initial training. That's because most of their work is done in the field on their own. One notes, "I have formed very close relationships with many of my peers at work, but we do not always get to spend a ton of face time working together because many of us live in different states. We do communicate by phone, Audix [the company's voicemail system], and e-mail very frequently." Another agrees: "Aside from direct contact, we all leave 'successes' on voice-mail. The success stories help others to hear what other people are doing in the field to generate sales." When they do get together, Phoenix representatives enjoy one another's company in social activities outside of work. One tells us, "My friends comment that I am lucky to have a network of young coworkers [who] are so outgoing and fun. They are jealous that we have so many great people in the company."

Moving on

Because the Phoenix Program is relatively new, Newell Rubbermaid officials report that data on trainees who choose to move on is insufficient.

Attrition

According to a Newell Rubbermaid representative, "By far, the most common reason people resign from the Phoenix Program is because of location. We ask these individuals to be very flexible in their first few years of employment [because] when they get promoted they will most likely be asked to move. In many cases, they aren't able to leave the city they are in for personal reasons and instead resign from Newell Rubbermaid. After that, the reasons given are too [few] to track."

Best and Worst

Great Phoenix representatives "are defined as such by their sales numbers, improved year[ly] store numbers, innovative merchandising ideas, and leadership."

NORTHROP GRUMMAN

Integrated Systems and Other Entry-level Positions

THE BIG PICTURE

Air defense systems, such as the unmanned Global Hawk, and airframe subsystems for surveillance, battle management, and warfare are the order of the day at Northrop Grumman's Integrated Systems sector. Tech-savvy job seekers could well find a happy home at Northrop Grumman, which offers a generous benefits package and job security.

STATS

LOCATION(S) WHERE ENTRY-LEVEL EMPLOYEES WORK

Entry-level employees work all across the country.

AVERAGE NUMBER OF APPLICATIONS EACH YEAR

Northrop Grumman receives thousands of applications every year.

AVERAGE NUMBER HIRED PER YEAR OVER THE LAST TEN YEARS

"Prior to 2001, Northrop Grumman's Integrated Systems did very little college hiring. Over the last two years, we have been hiring about 250 full-time college students and seventy-five interns."

AVERAGE HOURS WORKED PER WEEK

New hires work forty to fifty hours per week.

PERCENTAGE OF ENTRY-LEVEL HIRES STILL WITH THE COMPANY AFTER THREE, FIVE, AND TEN YEARS

"Over the last three years, we have averaged a 4 percent attrition rate with our entry-level hires."

AVERAGE STARTING SALARY

"Salaries [are] based on co-op/intern experience, GPA, major, research work, and leadership and club participation."

BENEFITS OFFERED

All benefits begin on the first day of work. Benefits include health insurance coverage, a 401(k) and pension plan, results sharing, education reimbursement, pet insurance, gyms, clubs, organizations, and volunteer opportunities.

CONTACT INFORMATION

Visit the website at www.definingthefuture.com.

Getting Hired

Northrop Grumman recruiters visit select colleges that they determine to "have the necessary programs, research, etc., that will help meet our needs." Students from other schools "can apply by going online at www.definingthefuture.com and applying for a position through our college website." The company attends "career fairs, on-campus student events, information sessions, and other [places that have] opportunities for involvement with students and faculty. All of the resumes that come from these events are sourced against openings. When [Northrop Grumman] find[s] a match, [the company] brings that student in-house for an interview." According to company officials, interviewers "use a combination of behavioral and technical interviewing questions. We are trying to see if candidates would be a [good] fit for the group, [if they have] interest in the position, [and] if their background and qualifications meet the job requirements." Successful hires tell us the interview process is "friendly and comfortable." One explains, "I was a little overwhelmed with all the information that I was given about the company. The interviewer informed me of the direction the defense industry was taking and how this was going to be a great opportunity for me. I was very excited about possibly getting a job at [Northrop Grumman Corporation] but nervous at the same time because I didn't have any background in the defense industry. A week after the interview, I received a job offer."

Money and Perks

The first jobbers we spoke with tell us that their start date was negotiable. Some new hires tell us that salary is negotiable, while others say that the job offer carries with it a specific, nonnegotiable salary. Salaries increase as a result of "a performance review every year, as well as an equity adjustment review for the first three years." An employee describes the one top perk of the job: "frequently being able to see the flights of the plane I'm working on. It makes all of the hard work seem much more substantial and meaningful when you actually see the results." One newbie cites "going to a very important conference free, and getting to be involved in organizations that mean a lot to me, and [having] my company support it" as other extras that nicely round out professional life at Northrop Grumman.

The Ropes

Employees say that orientation at Northrop Grumman focuses on "the nature of work for this company, which is very delicate; there was a lot of emphasis on security issues, which is natural" given the fact that much of Northrop's business comes from the United States and foreign militaries. Beyond that, orientation "is about the company in general, the business areas, how the company works, ethics, pay, benefits, savings plans, vacation time, commuter services, gym facilities, etc." The program lasts a full day; a second day of orientation "is conducted by the actual projects and can run from one hour to all day." Subsequent training occurs primarily on the job, "provided by other engineers, managers, etc." There is some training offered "through human resources for presentations and business writing. There is also ethics training available online."

DAY IN THE LIFE

Northrop Grumman hires entry-level employees for many different positions; most positions, judging from our respondents' surveys, are "challenging, detail oriented, and sometimes a little stressful." Because there is so much to do, a first jobber can gain a broad range of work experience relatively quickly. One engineer who works in unmanned systems writes, "My job has actually not stayed the same for more than a few months at a time. It has been constantly changing. This I attribute to the people I have worked for, who have made certain that I had very diverse experiences. I have gone from testing production parts to design qualification to working in the factory to laying the groundwork for new designs to managing spending time at the factory to running my own little test and integration projects. The common thread between all of these various experiences is that I have gotten to work with really wonderful teams and that my manager always sought out new challenges for me."

PEERS

First jobbers tell us, "There is quite a bit of camaraderie among new hires at work. We have all formed good friendships and enjoy spending time together outside of work." Some tell us that "there is a good after-hours social scene as well as a lot of weekend activity," while others think that "there's really no after-hours scene." In a company as large as Northrop Grumman, the amount of peer networking first jobbers enjoy depends largely on their assignments. Regardless of the degree of contact outside the office, most agree that their peers are "smart and ambitious." It is a diverse workforce, a fact that appeals to many. One newbie writes, "It is always nice to meet new people who have had experiences different [from] your own [because it allows you] to gain a new perspective on the world."

MOVING ON

When first jobbers leave "some [go] to work in other sectors of Northrop Grumman Corporation, some go back to graduate school, [and others] leave the defense industry as a whole."

ATTRITION

More than 95 percent of new hires last more than a year with Northrop Grumman; the few who leave often complain that the company is "too political and too bureaucratic." First jobbers tell us that the quality of one's first assignment is pretty much the luck of the draw; one says, "People who are less fulfilled than [me] usually cite feeling isolated, bad management, and excessive bureaucracy as primary criticisms. I feel like these are all very real problems at the company, but I have been particularly lucky in terms of not having to deal with [them] too much."

NORTHWESTERN MUTUAL

Financial Representative

THE BIG PICTURE

Northwestern Mutual Financial Network, the marketing name for the sales and distribution arm of the Northwestern Mutual Life Insurance Company, provides "expert guidance on insurance, investment products and services, retirement and estate needs, education funding, and employee benefits." Among its affiliated companies are those that comprise the Russell Investment Group; Northwestern Mutual Investment Services, LLC (NMIS); Northwestern Mutual Wealth Management Company; and Northwestern Long Term Care Insurance Company. Financial representatives with the Northwestern Mutual Financial Network provide access to these products and services; their compensation is based entirely on commission. The job provides a great opportunity for self-motivated individuals who want to make their own hours and set their own achievement goals; as one rep puts it, "The opportunity has no ceiling on income potential or growth potential. The more I work and the more efficiently I work, the higher my income potential."

STATS

LOCATION(S) WHERE ENTRY-LEVEL EMPLOYEES WORK

Entry-level employees may contract with more than 350 offices nationwide.

AVERAGE NUMBER OF APPLICATIONS EACH YEAR

Northwestern Mutual receives 40,000 applications per year.

AVERAGE NUMBER HIRED PER YEAR

The company hires 1,400 entry-level employees each year.

ENTRY-LEVEL POSITION(S) AVAILABLE

Entry-level workers are hired as financial representatives.

AVERAGE HOURS WORKED PER WEEK

"As independent contractors, our financial representatives set their own working hours per week. In the early building years, financial representatives may work longer hours" but "still maintain some flexibility with their schedules."

PERCENTAGE OF ENTRY-LEVEL HIRES STILL WITH THE COMPANY AFTER THREE, FIVE, AND TEN YEARS

Seventeen percent of financial representatives remain with the company after five years. According to a company official, "Once a financial representative reaches the fifth year and beyond, the retention rate is 95 percent."

Mutual Financial Network financial representatives are not paid on a salaried basis, but
ᴍmissions that are based on the productivity of each financial representative. First-year
ᴄᴄᴄᴏns in 2004 averaged $40,400 and increased to an average of $86,600 in five years."

ᴄᴇɴᴇFITS **OFFERED**

"Northwestern Mutual contributes to a very competitive benefits program for financial representatives.
The medical benefits program includes comprehensive medical coverage, pre-tax group medical and group
life, a tax-free medical reimbursement account, and a health reimbursement account."

Additional benefits include group life insurance, long-term disability, errors and omissions insurance,
retirement plans, commission spread-out plans, and income deferral plans.

CONTACT INFORMATION

Prospective applicants are encouraged to visit www.careers.nmfn.com.

GETTING HIRED

Northwestern Mutual recruits its financial representatives "on college campuses and at career fairs
nationwide. We also rely on referrals from a vast network of people, including professors, career advisors,
community leaders, and other professionals." All candidates should apply online. Screening and hiring are
handled by a local office (Northwestern Mutual has more than 350 such offices in the United States), so the
process may vary. Typically, "candidates meet multiple times with various members of an office, from the
recruiter to members of the leadership team and other financial representatives. A career as a financial
representative is not right for everyone, so our selection process is designed to determine if there is a mutual
fit." According to company officials, the best fit is someone "with a history of success, both academic and
in previous work experience. Strong candidates are self-starters [who are] motivated to achieve and have
an entrepreneurial spirit. They also have a solid work ethic, strong relationship-building skills, and a high
level of professionalism." Most offices "use a behavioral interview process designed to discover themes and
patterns in a candidate's background that would suggest if this career is a fit for them." One successful
candidate describes the interview this way: "The interview process was about having them learn about me
as well as having me learn about them. At the end of the process, the decision was mutual that the job was
a good fit."

MONEY AND PERKS

Financial representatives "receive commissions that are based on the productivity of each individual.
Therefore, as the financial representatives continue to grow and develop within the system, they become
more productive and are compensated accordingly. In essence, they control the frequency and amount of
their [own] raises." There is no bonus system here, but "some financial representatives are eligible to receive
stipends that can be applied toward continuing education and training." The best perk of the job, explains
one rep, is "the freedom. I don't have set hours. I don't have a boss micromanaging every move I make. I

have the ability to use that freedom to my advantage. I work on 100 percent commission and love it because I know that how hard I work [has a direct] impact [on] my income."

THE ROPES

Northwestern Mutual "provides a wide variety of training vehicles for its new financial representatives, in the areas of both product knowledge and selling. New representatives [undergo] several weeks of formal training on products and sales skills. After this initial phase, network offices provide one- to two-hour training sessions each week for approximately two years. After that, training is ongoing through a combination of online learning and classroom training." One financial representative writes, "The orientation process started with the state [insurance] licensing classes and then [developed] into training at our [network office]. The state [insurance] licensing [required] four days of studying and classroom time to prepare for the state exam that one needs to pass to accept the position at Northwestern Mutual. The training was also four days of intense product knowledge and information gathering. It also [provided] a lot of hands-on [experience], as well." The most valuable learning opportunities, though, are achieved by "shadowing fellow representatives, having mentors, and by actually going out and learning on the job."

DAY IN THE LIFE

The financial representative's job is "to develop relationships with clients to provide expert guidance for a lifetime of financial security. Once a new financial representative is fully licensed and trained, he or she is responsible for identifying prospective clients and meeting with them. He or she will talk with potential clients about their financial needs and goals and conduct a needs analysis." A financial representative writes, "During [a] typical day, I make calls, set up meetings with individuals, and meet those individuals to [offer guidance] about their financial [futures]. I fulfill these responsibilities by actively using what I learned in training. [In a nutshell] a typical day [consists of the following schedule]: 8:00 A.M. to 8:30 A.M.—review of previous day; 8:30 A.M. to 10:00 A.M.—phone calls; 10:00 A.M. to whenever—going out and seeing the people you set up meetings with."

PEERS

The financial representative position with the Northwestern Mutual Financial Network attracts like-minded people who bond easily. One writes, "My peers are wonderful. They all seem to have the same characteristics: an entrepreneurial spirit, good communication [skills], and the desire to succeed." Those who interact regularly with their regional office enjoy "a lot of camaraderie with not only new financial reps, but also with veterans. Everyone gets along. It's like a family."

MOVING ON

Financial representatives leave Northwestern Mutual Financial Network "for a variety of reasons. Many of them find their next opportunity by leveraging their career connections from their work with Northwestern Mutual." Some find sales and marketing positions with other companies; an HR official writes,

"Because we contract new representatives from a large variety of backgrounds and college degrees, their subsequent positions when they leave Northwestern Mutual vary greatly."

ATTRITION

Northwestern Mutual officials note that "the financial representative career is a challenging one, and that challenge is reflected in the retention rates of our newest financial representatives. For those representatives in their first five years in the business, our retention rate is 17 percent (while the industry average is less than 10 percent)." At the fifth year and beyond, "our retention rate is 95 percent; [and this figure] is comparable to the industry average." As far as those who do leave are concerned, some simply can't handle "the ups and downs in the first few years of the business. It's kind of a rollercoaster. The longer you stay in it, the easier it becomes."

OAKLAND TEACHING FELLOWS
Teaching Fellow

THE BIG PICTURE

The Oakland Teaching Fellows program is designed to recruit talented teachers in math, science, and special education; applicants need not have teaching credentials or even prior teaching experience to be hired. A "streamlined application and selection process" allows candidates to learn of their status relatively quickly. Comprehensive training prior to entering the classroom prepares fellows to teach; and coordination with area colleges allow fellows to earn their credentials while they work. The organization's website notes, "As a teacher, you can be the single most important factor in raising student achievement. As a teaching fellow, you will join a network of like-minded professionals dedicated to improving public schools." A current fellow adds, "Teaching is very rewarding, and the pay is excellent for entry-level work in public service."

STATS

LOCATION(S) WHERE ENTRY-LEVEL EMPLOYEES WORK

Jobs are located in Oakland, California.

AVERAGE NUMBER OF APPLICATIONS EACH YEAR

The Oakland Teaching Fellows Program receives about 750 applications each year.

AVERAGE NUMBER HIRED PER YEAR

The program hires about forty fellows each year.

ENTRY-LEVEL POSITION(S) AVAILABLE

Available positions are for "first-year teachers in the Oakland Unified School District (OUSD) [who] enter through a highly selective program and teach in the high-need subject areas of special education, science, and math. Fellows earn a California Credential while teaching full-time."

AVERAGE HOURS WORKED PER WEEK

Fellows work about fifty to sixty hours per week.

AVERAGE STARTING SALARY

Starting salaries range from $37,090–$43,980, "depending on education level and related coursework. Fellows with previous teaching experience may start at a higher rate. Additionally, fellows receive a stipend for completion of the Fellows Summer Training Institute, which they finish prior to entering the classroom."

BENEFITS OFFERED

"Teachers in OUSD have a choice of medical, vision, dental, and life insurance coverage; [these] begin at the start of the school year. The district pays for full benefits for the employee as well as eligible dependents."

Additionally, "fellows benefit from an intensive pre-service Training Institute, which prepares them to enter the classroom successfully as first-year teachers. Fellows receive a transitional living stipend for this training. [During] the first two years in the classroom, OTF also coordinates regular events and communications for all fellows. The program offers the opportunity to earn a credential while teaching full-time and earning a regular teacher's salary and benefits." Teachers may also participate in a 403(b) program and are eligible for the California State Teachers Retirement System.

CONTACT INFORMATION

Oakland Teaching Fellows
1025 Second Avenue, Room 217
Oakland, CA 94606
Tel: 510-879-8087
E-mail: info@oaklandteachingfellows.org
www.oaklandteachingfellows.org

GETTING HIRED

Those considering applying to the program should read all the information on the program's website to ensure that they meet eligibility requirements. Provided they do, they should then submit an online application form, including a resume, personal statement, and copies of all academic transcripts. Those who pass this level of screening are interviewed. For one component of the interview, candidates must prepare and teach a five-minute lesson. Before the Fellows Summer Training Institute begins, candidates must also pass "all required California teaching tests to finalize enrollment in the program."

One fellow reports, "A teacher in Oakland Public Schools interviewed me. The tone was very cordial. She asked me why I wanted to teach; what led me to apply; how I would implement high expectations in my classroom; what my behavior management style was; what I would do if nothing seemed to work. It was clear to me [from the interview] that [the Oakland Teaching Fellows program] sought creative and resourceful individuals who wouldn't give up. They wanted people to be mentors and leaders."

MONEY AND PERKS

Teaching fellows are paid on a fixed scale that "determines an individual's salary according to years of classroom experience and units of related coursework." The organization notes that "bonuses for specific subject areas or contract signing vary from year to year and depend on an individual's qualifications." Top benefits include participation in the California State Teachers Retirement System (STRS), "financial planning assistance through the option to establish a 403(b) account," and "home-buyer assistance programs for Oakland teachers." Teachers also love "having the summer off" and "knowing that you are making a difference in someone else's life."

THE ROPES

All candidates "begin their participation in the Oakland Teaching Fellows through a rigorous six-week training program generally beginning in June and aligning with the district's summer school calendar." During the program, "fellows build a solid foundation and skill set through curriculum sessions led by successful teachers in target subject areas;" they also benefit from the "experience of observing and lead-teaching in summer school classrooms. Fellows learn how to succeed as newcomers in their first year of teaching, and benefit from research on the factors that have contributed to success for other first-year teachers in urban settings." A typical training day "begins with four hours of observation, practice teaching, or small-group work in summer school classrooms. During the hour-long lunch break, fellows may discuss lesson plans or reflect on teaching practices with an experienced teacher or other fellows. The afternoon consists of around three hours of curriculum sessions with their fellow advisor groups; during these, they build on skills related to practice teaching and plan for the year ahead. At the end of the day, they may attend a workshop on a specific teaching topic or meet with colleagues to plan upcoming lessons."

DAY IN THE LIFE

Teaching fellows have "the responsibilities of any teacher running a classroom." They spend their days "meeting the needs of their students; ensuring high standards for success in their classrooms; working with struggling learners; and building relationships with families, colleagues, and administrators important to the success of any student." One fellow observes, "One can never be bored in this profession. I find that when I feel slightly 'overwhelmed,' I then know that I have met an appropriate challenge. This is why I chose this profession in the first place."

PEERS

First-year teachers are incredibly busy managing their classrooms and preparing lessons; one fellow explains, "I don't socialize that much with the fellows because we are all swamped with work—but we have a great time when we do get together." When they can spare a minute to converse, fellows find that they have a lot in common with one another. One writes, "I have found everyone to be very bright, motivated, and wanting to make a difference in students' lives as well as in their own lives. You have to be smart, flexible, and self-motivated to be able to do this job."

MOVING ON

Oakland Teaching Fellows is "a relatively young program," too new to have collected significant quantities of data on former fellows. The organization notes that "to date, individuals who have not completed commitments to the program state personal reasons as the primary basis [for leaving]." Some find the job too arduous; one fellow notes, "There is a big learning curve as a new teacher, and there is no way to avoid that. Different people react differently to that type of situation—whether they rise to the occasion or complain is all up to the individual."

BEST AND WORST

According to the organization, "The most successful first-year Oakland Teaching Fellows and teachers show a relentless drive for holding themselves and their students to the highest standards and overcoming obstacles to meet classroom goals. Successful teachers reach out to people and resources that will [have an] impact [on] the success of their students." They also "build relationships with other successful teachers, with the families of students, and with colleagues at their school site or in the Teaching Fellows Program. These individuals continually reflect on their teaching practices, actively seek ways to improve, and maintain a sense of perspective in the face of challenges."

OGILVY AND MATHER

Assistant Account Executive and OgilvyOne Associate

THE BIG PICTURE

First jobbers at Ogilvy and Mather, "one of the most prestigious firms on Madison Avenue," enjoy "the opportunity to work with blue-chip clients." One newbie notes, "It's fun to watch television with your friends and have every third or fourth commercial be an Ogilvy-created advertisement." Employees say they also benefit from "a training program that demonstrates Ogilvy's investment in its people . . . even contacts who had started at Ogilvy and moved to other agencies declared the excellence of training programs at Ogilvy and Mather. It didn't make sense to start anywhere else."

STATS

LOCATION(S) WHERE ENTRY-LEVEL EMPLOYEES WORK

The company's headquarters are in New York, New York; about 450 offices are located worldwide. Regional offices hire on-site.

AVERAGE NUMBER OF APPLICATIONS EACH YEAR

Ogilvy receives 5,000 applications each year.

AVERAGE NUMBER HIRED PER YEAR OVER THE LAST TEN YEARS

The company hires seventy people every year.

ENTRY-LEVEL POSITION(S) AVAILABLE

New hires work as assistant account executives and OgilvyOne associates.

AVERAGE HOURS WORKED PER WEEK

New hires work forty hours per week.

AVERAGE STARTING SALARY

Employees earn a little over $34,000 per year.

BENEFITS OFFERED

The company offers "full medical" coverage. Additional benefits include company vesting, dental benefits, WPP stock ownership, life insurance, a 401(k) plan, and long-term disability.

CONTACT INFORMATION

Job Hotline: 212-237-5627

GETTING HIRED

Ogilvy "accepts and welcomes students from all schools, disciplines, and majors. All candidates can call the Ogilvy job hotline or, if applicable, their campus' career services office. Human resources representatives from Ogilvy travel across the country to different schools, promoting Ogilvy's entry-level positions and training programs." Successful applicants generally "are driven by a desire to succeed, show leadership skills, and have a passion for advertising, which can be demonstrated through prior work experience, classes, and activities." They are also the kind of people who demonstrate an ability to "work hard, have high energy, [and] are flexible yet detail-oriented." According to one first jobber, "Ogilvy has two different rounds of interviews. The first round is with a human resources representative. If they like you and feel you will be a good fit with the culture of Ogilvy, then [they bring you] back for second-round interviews with the teams you will be working with." During the interviews, recalls one assistant account executive, "I was asked questions about why I was interested in advertising, what my favorite ads were and why, and, the most intriguing question: If I had a full page ad in the *New York Times* to sell myself to Ogilvy, what would it say?" The process can be arduous; "In my case," offers one successful applicant, "it took three months and probably a total of twelve different interviews." One entry-level employee offers the following advice: "Before applying for any position at Ogilvy, I strongly recommend you read David Ogilvy's book, *Ogilvy on Advertising*. The book has many useful insights about the agency and how to get a job here."

MONEY AND PERKS

"Most assistant account executives are paid the same amount of money" at Ogilvy, and it's not much, but that's fine with most first jobbers because the job is a foot in the door at a preeminent ad agency. Salaries increase "based on performance; Ogilvy is a meritocracy." The best fringe benefit, some employees tell us, is "lots of free products. Ogilvy has tons of well-known clients [who manufacture] well-known products. If you work on Kraft Foods, it's a good bet you'll get a lot of food free or at a severely discounted price. If you work on Miller Lite, getting free beer shouldn't be a problem. The same goes for many of our other clients as well." Others love the half-days on Fridays in the summer and the paid Christmas-week vacation.

THE ROPES

"Ogilvy's heritage in training is immense, stemming back to the days when David Ogilvy ran the agency," company officials note, adding that "it is what differentiates [us] from any other agency." In the account management training program (AMTP), "between thirty and forty-five of the participants spend three-and-a-half months learning the ins and outs of the business. They spend five to eight hours a week in seminars hosted by senior management specialists. The assistant account executives and associates apply their learning from each of the seminars to the most important component of AMTP, the client case study." The client case study is the mother of all senior projects, undertaken with a real Ogilvy client; in it, "the trainees are grouped into competing 'agencies' to pitch against [one another] in the final presentations. The clients truly value this initiative and in the past have implemented some of the presented solutions and ideas into their brand strategies." One graduate of the program notes, "During the project, your team is assigned a coach who is typically a very senior executive. My team's coach was the president of the New York office. It was fascinating to learn and discuss ideas with the head of Ogilvy's flagship office. It really shows how important this training program is to Ogilvy and its leadership." Indeed, first jobbers tell us that they love how Ogilvy "always puts training ahead of [their] daily responsibilities. The company's focus [is] on investing in long-term solutions as opposed to short-term fixes."

Day in the Life

One entry-level employee cautions, "As anyone who works in advertising will tell you, there is no typical day. Chaos is the norm at any advertising agency, and Ogilvy is no exception. Things change at the drop of a hat." That's why "it takes a certain disposition to work in advertising. Your ability to manage the chaos is one of the marks of a good account manager. I never get bored working at Ogilvy. Every day there is a new problem to solve and a new challenging experience to grab hold of." Interaction with top executives is often a part of a first jobber's day; one writes, "I spend an immense amount of time with high-level people at Ogilvy. I am invited to virtually every important meeting for my account (except for the most senior meetings, naturally), and I feel totally comfortable strolling into the office of an executive creative director or client services director [to] bring up an issue. This place has very few ageists and very few people who care a lot about titles." The job is tough; as one assistant account executive tells us, "There are times when things are just overwhelming. In these economic times, there are fewer people to do the same amount of work. But if you are diligent in managing your time and using it effectively, there is more than enough time to get the job done. Advertising is an industry where you have to put in the hours to get the results. It's certainly not a nine-to-five job."

Peers

First jobbers at Ogilvy usually grow close during the intensive AMTP period. "For the first three months on the job, I had lunch with my entry-level companions every day. We went out at night, introduced [one another] to other entry-level employees, etc. There is quite a lot of camaraderie here, especially amongst the associates because all of us experience similar things," notes one entry-level employee. Another newbie adds, "Making friends was very easy. All of us share similar types of personalities, and all of us get along very well. Those that interviewed us made sure that all of us would fit within the Ogilvy culture, and those that do shouldn't have any problem getting along."

Moving On

When first jobbers leave the firm, it is most often to go back to school, to pursue another opportunity in advertising, or to switch careers entirely.

Attrition

Very few people—less than 1 percent, according to Ogilvy—drop out of AMTP, in which both Assistant Account Executives and OgilvyOne Associates participate as entry-level employees. Some in the Associates program criticize its rotational nature. They feel that it's a "negative to spend three to four months learning an aspect of the business only to be moved off and have to begin from square one somewhere else." Those who praise the Associates program, ironically, also focus on the rotations, noting that it is designed "to cultivate Ogilvy's next generation of leaders in the long-term." Those who know that they want to focus on the business aspect of the industry tend to seek out positions as Assistant Account Executives, and members of this group praise the valuable work experience that they receive from the outset.

OXYGEN

Various Positions

THE BIG PICTURE

Once upon a time, aspirants to the television industry had to break in through one of the Big Three networks or one of their local affiliates. Now, thanks to digital cable, there are literally hundreds of television networks out there that serve every conceivable demographic. Oxygen is an "edgy" network for women that was co-founded by Oprah Winfrey, Geraldine Laybourne (formerly a big player at Nickelodeon), and the Carsey-Werner-Mandabach juggernaut (responsible for *Roseanne*, *Third Rock From the Sun*, *That 70's Show*, and *The Cosby Show*).

STATS

LOCATION(S) WHERE OXYGEN HIRES ENTRY-LEVEL WORK

Headquarters are in New York, there are small offices in Los Angeles, Detroit, Chicago, and Dallas.

AVERAGE NUMBER OF APPLICATIONS EACH YEAR

Oxygen receives about 1,000 applications each year.

ENTRY-LEVEL POSITION(S) AVAILABLE

Entry-level employees are hired as business and legal affairs assistants, community affairs associates, public relations assistants, research assistants, sales assistants, development assistants, marketing assistants, production assistants, department assistants, desktop support techs, and administrative assistants.

AVERAGE HOURS WORKED PER WEEK

Entry-level hires work an average of forty hours per week.

BENEFITS OFFERED

Oxygen offers medical and dental coverage, as well as flexible spending accounts, life insurance, short-term and long-term disability, TransitChek, and 401(k) plans.

CONTACT INFORMATION

E-mail your cover letter and resume to jobs@oxygen.com or call the job hotline at 212-651-5687.

GETTING HIRED

Connections are critical in the entertainment industry, so it comes as no surprise that all the first jobbers we spoke with at Oxygen utilized previous contacts in the business to land their jobs. For some, the contact was someone met during an Oxygen internship, but just as many found their current positions because a family member or friend knew someone and was able to put in a good word. One first jobber explains, "I heard about it through a friend. It sounded like the perfect position to get started in the television industry."

Because most hires arrive with a recommendation, the interview process is less grueling than at most places of employment. "I was interviewed by the vice president of Consumer Marketing and Affiliate Marketing," writes one marketing assistant, who continues, "The interview was very relaxed. Both sides were very excited to explore what [one another] had to offer. The first interview was very exploratory while the second was more finances and benefits."

MONEY AND PERKS

Start dates and salaries may vary, depending on the urgency to fill the position and the unique qualities the hire brings to the job. One newbie reports, "For me, the salary wasn't negotiable at all. I was told that I would have some influence over my job duties, but for the most part, that has yet to happen." Fringe benefits include four full weeks of paid vacation and "the CDs that you can take from the bin of unwanteds."

THE ROPES

New hires can start at Oxygen any time, and for the most part, they learn as they go, watching their bosses and trying not to foul things up too much until they master their jobs. Formal orientation occurs on or near the first day of work, "is three hours long, and features guest speakers from various departments throughout the company to provide new hires with an overview of Oxygen. The company mission statement is presented, and the group is also addressed by our CEO and COO." First jobbers also receive harassment training and a review of their benefits package during orientation. After that, "Your boss trains you. In my case, whenever I had a question she would sit with me until I figured it out. She was very patient. It probably took about a month to get acclimated and learn most of the ins and outs, which was mostly done by asking as many questions as possible."

DAY IN THE LIFE

Oxygen hires first jobbers for a broad range of functions. What they do on a daily basis, how much autonomy they exercise over their work, and how likely they are to advance within the company all depends on where and for whom they work. First jobbers in small departments, for example, may enjoy a congenial work environment but have little chance for advancement, since few higher-ups leave the company. Among our survey respondents was a program coordinator who is "in charge of making sure that the correct episode or movie goes on the air at the correct time. I program them into the computer and keep the system updated with the correct series and their descriptions. I also keep track of what is going on at other networks and answer the viewer services line." We also heard from a marketing assistant whose responsibilities "are mostly administrative with some conceptualizing for consumer and marketing plans." A community affairs associate told us that "a typical day involves a lot of calls with nonprofits, note taking, arranging budgets, and transferring information from outside organizations within various company departments. Brainstorming and communication are always a big part of my day." All Oxygen employees benefit from an extensive formal mentoring program as well as a variety of informal mentoring apparatuses.

Peers

At Oxygen "there are opportunities for socializing after work," facilitated in part by "a bar downstairs from the office," but "it is mixed with all levels of employees," not just first jobbers. It's not a wild social scene, though, "because most of us are dead tired." Employees tell us that "the company is fairly relaxed and the people are easy to get a long with," and "it's a company mostly made up of young women, and it's great."

Moving On

According to Oxygen, "Entry-level employees who leave the company do so for another job opportunity or to switch career paths. For the most part, our entry-level employees do not leave but are promoted to other positions in the company." Some here complain that "it is hard to move up the corporate ladder because the company is so small and no one wants to leave their job." That drives some first jobbers to leave. Others "don't like the programming choices we put on air or are afraid we will become too corporate some day." Most, however, recognize that Oxygen is a pretty good gig and hope to stay on long-term.

PEACE CORPS
Volunteer

THE BIG PICTURE

Travel the world and see developing countries without having to carry a machine gun. Help people help themselves. Broaden your horizons. The Peace Corps: the perfect organization for the globe-trotting idealist.

STATS

LOCATION(S) WHERE ENTRY-LEVEL EMPLOYEES WORK

Peace Corps volunteers work "in more than seventy developing countries in Africa, Asia, the Caribbean, Central and South America, Europe, and the Middle East."

AVERAGE NUMBER OF APPLICATIONS PER YEAR

Peace Corps receives approximately 9,700 applications per year.

AVERAGE NUMBER HIRED PER YEAR OVER THE LAST TEN YEARS

Approximately 36,500 Peace Corps volunteers have served in the last ten years.

ENTRY-LEVEL POSITION(S) AVAILABLE

"Peace Corps assignments are tailored to each volunteer's primary skills sets, as volunteers are given the opportunity to use their classroom knowledge to develop real-world skills. Positions are available in a variety of areas including education, agriculture, community development, information technology, health education, HIV/AIDS education and awareness, environmental awareness, or businesses development."

PERCENTAGE OF ENTRY-LEVEL HIRES STILL WITH THE COMPANY AFTER THREE, FIVE, AND TEN YEARS

"Peace Corps volunteers serve for a twenty-seven-month term overseas, which includes a three-month training session. Many often extend their two-year terms or apply to serve in a new country."

AVERAGE STARTING SALARY

Volunteers receive "a living allowance that enables [them] to live in a manner similar to the local people in their community. Volunteers also receive $225 per month toward a 'readjustment allowance' that they receive on completion of their two years of service."

BENEFITS OFFERED

Volunteers receive comprehensive medical and dental coverage, plus a health insurance plan for eighteen months following the completion of service. "In most cases, [volunteers receive a] deferment of Stafford Loans, Perkins Loans, Federal Consolidation Loans, or Direct Loans [and] a 15 percent cancellation of their outstanding [Perkins Loan] balance for each year of their two years of service. Deferment does not happen automatically; the volunteer must apply for the deferment."

Talk to a Peace Corps recruiter at 800-424-8580, or visit www.peacecorps.gov.

GETTING HIRED

The application process is "pretty long," according to one volunteer. "I applied in December, had my interview in January, and then did not hear about my actual assignment until May." Volunteers suggest that you "take the interview seriously. Although it is a volunteer position, treat the job application process as you would any other job. It is competitive, and Peace Corps attracts a high caliber of people. My interview lasted over an hour, and they asked a lot of questions about past experiences and interests of mine." Peace Corps representatives add, "Applicants may be surprised that a recruiter asks personal questions during the interview. But it's important to us that all prospective Peace Corps volunteers consider the impact that service will have on their professional and personal lives." After the interview comes medical and legal screening, a step that eliminates a surprising number of potential members. "It's the most frustrating step for many because the exams are so thorough," one successful applicant reports. Finally, people who are accepted are matched with an area needing their skills; orientation commences pretty soon thereafter.

MONEY AND PERKS

The word "volunteer" figures prominently in the position you'll be seeking and for good reason; as the recruiters explain, "Peace Corps volunteers are not employees of the federal government and therefore do not receive a salary. However, Peace Corps provides volunteers with a living allowance and a 'readjustment allowance' that they receive on completion of their two years of service. It is often used for a rent deposit, groceries, and other living expenses when the volunteer returns to the United States." Volunteers join for the experience, not for the money, and the experiences they have, they say, are the big perks. "The best fringe benefit was getting to live in a village in Africa for two years," writes a typical volunteer. "There is no other entry-level job that will give you such an amazing and life-changing experience."

THE ROPES

There are two phases of Peace Corps training: a brief, pre-departure orientation called "staging," and a three-month in-country immersion training in the language and culture of the host town or village. During staging, "Applicants meet their fellow trainees and begin to identify personal and cultural adjustments that will help them to promote their successful service." They fill out forms, get vaccinated, and learn Peace Corps policies and procedures, study risk identification and management, and adjust to life on a Peace Corps post. Immediately following staging, volunteers depart on their assignments for in-country training. Here's how one volunteer describes the experience: "Your first three months in-country are taken up by training. During this time you are taught the local language, local culture, safety and security, and medical training. Training is extremely overwhelming. During the first three months, you also live with a host family, which adds another dimension [to] your experience."

Day in the Life

There is no typical day in the life of a Peace Corps volunteer. As one volunteer puts it, "I never knew what was going to happen that day when I woke up in the morning. Sometimes school would be closed, or there would be a big celebration. I loved that! Basically, I ran in the mornings, spent all day at school teaching, planning lessons, working with other teachers, and socializing with teachers. Then I would come home and help my host mother with dinner for a couple hours, eat for a couple more hours, drink tea for a couple more hours, and then read and [plan lessons]. Even though I was only actually working for six hours, I felt like it was a twenty-four-hour job because you always had to be 'on' and teaching and learning, even while [washing] the dishes." Another volunteer adds, "You cannot go into your village with a set idea of what *you* think needs to be accomplished. You need to spend time getting to know people and the realities on the ground and then work with people to do projects. For me, tasks in Peace Corps were much more long range. There were things I wanted to accomplish each month, but on any given day, I did not have definite things to do. It is such a different pace of life—without 'to do' lists, PDAs, cell phones, and endless meetings. You are really on your own schedule and [create] your work."

Peers

"There is a huge sense of camaraderie among the Peace Corps volunteers I served with," enthuses one volunteer. "One of the greatest things about Peace Corps is the people you meet." They see [one another] "at big gatherings, go to [one another's] villages to work on projects together, [and sometimes] travel to the capital city and meet other volunteers for a movie, dinner, etc." Not all volunteers seek out fellow Peace Corps members, however. Some "want to focus on building relationships with the local people and do not want to socialize with other Americans. In general, Peace Corps can be very social, or you could totally immerse yourself into your own community."

Moving on

Some Peace Corps volunteers continue with the organization after their two-year term is up; several of our survey respondents, in fact, now work as Peace Corps recruiters. Others parlay their experiences in the Corps into springboards to graduate school or interesting job offers. One former volunteer writes, "I now work for a consulting firm that does international development work. The fact that I had Peace Corps experience was a big reason why I was hired. This company values the skills and experience you learn in Peace Corps." As organization representatives put it, "The Peace Corps experience enhances long-term career prospects, whether a volunteer wants to work for a corporation, a nonprofit organization, or a government agency. The Peace Corps can even open doors to graduate school."

Attrition

"You have to go into Peace Corps for the right reasons, or else you will be disappointed," explains one volunteer. Those who are disappointed are often those who are "upset about the lack of direction Peace Corps gives you with what you're supposed to do in your projects." As one volunteer puts it, "If you are a person who likes to have exact direction and guidance to what you're supposed to be doing and when it needs to be done, Peace Corps may not be a good job decision for you."

PHILADELPHIA TEACHING FELLOWS
Teaching Fellow

THE BIG PICTURE

The Philadelphia Teaching Fellows (PTF) program is in its second year, having just been launched for the 2004–2005 school year. The program seeks to recruit "a cohort of full-time new teachers in the school district of Philadelphia who fill high-needs vacancies in special education, math, science, English as a second language, and middle school subjects while working toward [obtaining] Pennsylvania [teaching] certification."

STATS

LOCATION(S) WHERE ENTRY-LEVEL EMPLOYEES WORK

Jobs are located in Philadelphia, Pennsylvania.

AVERAGE NUMBER OF APPLICATIONS EACH YEAR

In 2005–2006, the first year of the program, 705 individuals submitted applications.

AVERAGE NUMBER HIRED PER YEAR

The program hired sixty teachers to fill midyear teaching vacancies in February of 2005, and program officials now hope to recruit "seventy-five to one hundred teachers to fill vacancies at the beginning of the school year" and "fifty to seventy-five teachers to fill midyear teaching vacancies."

ENTRY-LEVEL POSITION(S) AVAILABLE

New hires work as teaching fellows.

AVERAGE HOURS WORKED PER WEEK

Teaching fellows work more than thirty-five hours per week.

AVERAGE STARTING SALARY

The base starting salary is $37,622, but "fellows with a master's degree and those teaching certain subject areas receive additional pay. Bonuses and incentives may also be available."

BENEFITS OFFERED

Teaching fellows have a choice of health insurance plans; they also receive dental, prescription, and vision coverage. Additional benefits include a pension, a 401(k) plan, and a pre-service Training Institute for which "fellows are paid a stipend [to cover] living expenses."

Philadelphia Teaching Fellows
440 North Broad Street, 2094-1
Philadelphia, PA 19130
Tel: 215-400-8687
www.PhiladelphiaTeachingFellows.org

GETTING HIRED

Applicants to the PTF program must apply via the organization's website; a completed application includes a resume, a personal statement, and official academic transcripts for all college and university work. Applications are screened and notified of their status within two weeks. Those who clear this hurdle are invited to interview. One fellow reports, "I was interviewed by current school staff and the PTF recruiters. The thought of the interview was nerve-wracking to me, since I had to prepare and present a class lesson to not only my interviewer, but also my fellow [interviewee] group. However, it wasn't as bad as I had anticipated. The interviewer and my group were all welcoming and friendly and made me feel at ease throughout the whole process. After the group interview, we returned to speak with a PTF recruiter for a question-and-answer session at which all our concerns were addressed. Next, we met with a PTF recruiter one-on-one to talk about our interests specifically within teaching. I ranked my top three areas of interest, with computer science at the top." Applicants are informed of their status within three weeks of the interview. Those selected to teach "are supplied with an enrollment package." To finalize the process, candidates must pass state teacher tests (Praxis examinations) before entering the classroom as teachers."

MONEY AND PERKS

Teacher salaries are determined by strict schedules that vary slightly by district. Bonuses "may be offered for teaching in specific subject areas or schools. If this is the case, it will be clearly stated during the application process." Fellows love the work calendar, with its "many vacations, summers off, weekends off, and an early end to the work day."

THE ROPES

Fellows enter orientation during two periods. The midyear replacement program begins in January; the summer program starts in June. Both training sessions consist of two parts: morning classroom teaching and observations and afternoon sessions led by a veteran teacher that cover "teaching strategies, managing student behavior, and understanding the diversity and culture in your school." One fellow explains, "The month-long orientation process is very informative, yet at the same time very exhausting. The days are long. Every day I would wake up at 6:00 A.M., leave my house by 7:00 A.M., get to my cooperating school at 8:00 A.M. for student-teaching sessions, [eat] lunch from 12:00 P.M. to 1:00 P.M., then head over to the training institute for training from 1:30 P.M. to 7:00 P.M. Most of the training I received dealt with working in an inner-city school, working with inner-city students/administrators/parents, and class management. By the time I got home, ate, and did some of my homework, I was exhausted and ready for bed." In their first year as teachers, "fellows begin a course of study for their Pennsylvania teaching certificate. Fellows are responsible for the cost of tuition for certification coursework."

DAY IN THE LIFE

Fellows are full-scale teachers whose responsibilities "are those of a classroom teacher." One fellow reports, "A typical day begins at about 7:30 A.M., when I first get to school to begin setting up for the day. The kids come in and are picked up in the playground at 8:30 A.M., and classes begin by 9:00 A.M. Each fellow teaches six periods a day, with one period for prep and one for lunch. The school day ends at 3:00 P.M., but most teachers stay in the building until at least 4:00 P.M.." Another adds, "The School District of Philadelphia has so much that needs to be done within each and every school [that] there is definitely no extra time for boredom. If you really enjoy what you are doing and want to help, you will find something or another to occupy your time."

PEERS

Friendships are forged during the PTF orientation period, a time when fellows are all together in one place. One fellow observes, "I probably made more friends with members in my PTF cohort [than with members of] the staff at my school." In "high-needs" schools that are "largely staffed by Teaching Fellows, Teach For America [volunteers], and alternative certification teachers," the faculty is "largely young and idealistic," and "there is a lot of camaraderie. Collaboration and supporting [one another] is essential for survival." Most fellows are too busy to enjoy a robust after-hours scene; when they do socialize, however, they find it "a good way to unwind, relax, and be yourself."

MOVING ON

The Philadelphia Teaching Fellows program is brand new, so relatively few fellows had left the program as of the writing of this profile. Those who had left "cited personal reasons (moving from the city) as well as challenges [to] their school placement." One fellow writes, "some of my peers came to quick conclusions that teaching wasn't for them after all. [This job] definitely opens your eyes and makes you realize whether or not [teaching] is for you."

BEST AND WORST

A successful fellow is "intentional and reflective on his or her own professional growth. A successful employee is continually focused on the goal of increasing student achievement and takes responsibility for developing his or her craft to ensure success with regard to this goal. The successful employee welcomes feedback, seeking mentors in his or her school and beyond; seeking opportunities to observe and be observed; and constantly measuring the success of his or her strategies in terms of their ability to concretely raise student achievement in the classroom. This teacher is disciplined, consistently prepared, and is able to persevere when times are tough. This teacher fosters positive relationships with his or her principal and colleagues. This teacher is inspired by the students in his or her classroom and looks for opportunities to build meaningful connections with them, their families, and their communities."

THE PHOENIX COMPANIES, INC.

Various Positions

THE BIG PICTURE

The Phoenix Companies, Inc., "a leading life insurance, annuity, and asset management products provider for the affluent and high-net worth," is a heavy hitter; the company ranks a spot on the Forbes Global 2000. The company's two main subsidiaries are Phoenix Life Insurance Company and Phoenix Investment Partners, Ltd. Phoenix's efforts to create a family-friendly, diverse work environment have been praised by *Working Mother Magazine*, the National Association of Female Executives, and the Anti-Defamation League.

STATS

LOCATION(S) WHERE ENTRY-LEVEL EMPLOYEES WORK

Entry-level hires work at the company headquarters in Hartford, Connecticut and at offices in Albany, New York and Greenfield, Massachusetts.

AVERAGE NUMBER OF APPLICATIONS EACH YEAR

The Phoenix receives approximately 1,400 applications for five of their key entry-level positions: actuarial assistant, client services representative, internal wholesaler, life new business account manager, and new business representative. An additional 1,000 applications are reviewed annually for a variety of other entry-level positions.

AVERAGE NUMBER HIRED PER YEAR

During the past year, the Phoenix hired approximately sixty entry-level employees for the five positions listed above and an additional seventy-five employees for other entry-level positions.

ENTRY-LEVEL POSITION(S) AVAILABLE

Five key entry-level positions available for recent college graduates are: actuarial assistant, client services representative, internal wholesaler, life new business account manager, and new business representative. A variety of other entry-level positions are also available; among these are internal investment consultant, internal sales support representative, and sales completion specialist.

AVERAGE HOURS WORKED PER WEEK

Full-time employees work forty hours per week.

AVERAGE STARTING SALARY (BY POSITION)

In 2005, actuarial assistants earned $50,000–$70,000 per year; client services representatives earned $32,000–$38,000 per year; and new business representatives earned $36,000–$45,000 per year.

Benefits Offered

Phoenix Companies offers "a generous benefits package" that includes "medical, dental, vision care, and prescription benefits, with a range of medical care provider plans." These are available "for the individual, family, or same-sex domestic partner. New hires have thirty-one days from date of hire to enroll in benefits that are retroactive to the date of hire."

Because "at Phoenix, we recognize the need to balance work and personal time," the company offers "flexible work arrangements, work-life programs, and policies and services aimed at helping employees maximize their time at work and outside of work." In addition, the Phoenix offers "a wide range of company-sponsored pension plans, a 401(k) plan with company match, disability management and insurance, life insurance, a dependent care spending account match, adoption assistance, tuition assistance, and an on-site credit union!"

Contact Information

The company encourages prospective candidates to apply online "through our website: www.PhoenixWM.com. Click on "My Career," "Career Center," and "First-Time User" to access the job posting database or set up a job agent." Interested applicants may also access the Career Center directly by visiting http://secured.kenexa.com/phoenixv36/external.

Getting Hired

Phoenix requires all job seekers to submit applications online. After that, "a corporate recruiter reviews candidate resumes and selects individuals to call who appear to be a strong fit with position requirements. Candidates are assessed by phone and in person." The company also recruits on many campuses and accepts applications from students at all colleges and universities. The company notes that "technical skills for specific professions may include strong math ability for actuarial students and finance/accounting for other disciplines. Excellent written, verbal, and interpersonal skills are necessary to partner with other professionals, departments, and customers. A strong focus on customer satisfaction is a plus." One successful hire describes the on-site interview process: "There was a dinner interview on the night I arrived in Hartford. It was quite informal but gave me an opportunity to learn more about the company. It also gave me an idea about the skills they require for the position. The next morning, I had a series of five interviews. Each interview focused on a different aspect of my resume. There were a few technical questions based on my finance background, but in general, the interviews were very friendly and relaxed."

Money and Perks

"Job offers are competitive within the industry," company officials note. That said, initial offers are not always negotiable. One recent hire explains, "When I started may have been negotiable, but the offer worked well for me, so I never tried to negotiate." One employee reports having been unsuccessful in trying to negotiate a higher starting salary. But fear not: Regular salary reviews and increases "coincide with performance reviews." Those in the Actuarial Development Program also earn raises "as a result of passing rigorous actuarial professional exams." One ADP participant notes, "The exam raises and exam bonuses are liberal. The pay package is attractive to begin with and keeps getting better with the exam raises." The company also notes that "a few entry-level positions are eligible for a 5–10 percent bonus." Some employees consider the job location a big perk; one such employee writes, "Phoenix is located in Hartford, the insurance capital of the world. The kind of actuarial exposure and opportunities available here are incomparable." Another plus: The Asset Management and Life Operations "work closely together. This gives [employees] the opportunity to work in a life insurance company with a very strong investment side. Actuaries are ultimately financial professionals. Hence, having access to a complete investment branch within the company inevitably expands one's fiscal knowledge base."

THE ROPES

An orientation kit is given to new hires before they start working. One first jobber writes, "Orientation lasted about two hours, [during which] they informed us of all the benefits offered by the company and [of] how to register/sign up for our selections. They also reviewed the office tools employed by the company and how to navigate them. After orientation, my boss was called to come get me." And that's it; after that, it's time to get to work. A series of one-on-one trainings follow [during] the subsequent weeks and months; the specific training content depends on the employee's job functions in the company.

DAY IN THE LIFE

Phoenix brings new hires on board in a number of areas. Noteworthy positions include actuarial assistant, internal wholesaler, and client services representative. Actuarial assistants are part of an elite "intensive development opportunity" that "seeks to recruit, train, and develop business professionals with strong actuarial aptitude for a progression into technical and managerial roles at Phoenix." Daily life involves "interdepartmental rotations generally lasting eighteen to thirty months;" these may include work in life and annuity pricing and product development, individual financial reporting, investments, strategic planning, investor and rating agency relations, underwriting, corporate finance, and enterprise risk management. Internal wholesalers "partner with and support the external sales team to distribute and sell individual annuity products to independent financial planners, regional brokerage firms, and banks. [They must be able] to develop strong interpersonal working relationships with wholesalers and advisors. Candidates must be able to multitask and produce results," as well. Client service reps handle client inquiries on annuities and life insurance; they also "assist advisors and clients through education of products and by resolving problems."

PEERS

It's easy for first jobbers here to make "some very good friends" among their peers because of the "great camaraderie," which is bolstered by "social events, happy hours, etc. that allow us to spend time with [one another] outside the office." One actuarial newbie reports, "We sometimes plan out something to do over the weekend. Since there are only fourteen actuarial students, it's a close-knit community. The fact that we are all going through the same exam process automatically makes people connect. We often eat lunch together at the cafeteria; it's a great way to get to know everyone on a personal level." Human resources "organizes various events from time to time;" for example, "recently we had the whirly ball event that was a lot of fun." First jobbers also report that "the work environment is great. It's relaxed, and everyone is willing to help you."

MOVING ON

Company officials tell us, "When employees leave Phoenix, most often it is for a new job or to relocate to another area of the country. Other reasons are too diverse to categorize." The Phoenix has undergone a structural change over the course of the past three years, during which it morphed from a mutually held company into a stockholder entity. This, too, "has led to a change in workforce composition." "Company statistics suggest that about one-third of Phoenix's work force has been with the company for fewer than two years, and another third have been with the company for [a period of] three to five years."

ATTRITION

Of the 190 college graduates Phoenix hired in the year prior to our survey, 177 were still with the company. Current employees explain why some leave: "Most people are concerned with the current environment of corporate change and consolidation happening within the industry."

BEST AND WORST

The best example of a successful entry-level employee who has advanced within the company is "Dona Young, Chairman, President, and CEO," who "has been with The Phoenix for twenty-five years. She began as a summer law intern and has risen steadily the top of The Phoenix!"

PIER 1 IMPORTS
Various Positions

THE BIG PICTURE

Pier 1 Imports, a specialty retailer of imported decorative home furnishings and décor, does not have a structured college-hire program; but the company "does hire candidates directly out of college for positions based on their academic background and internship/work experience." Many begin their Pier 1 careers as sales associates in stores, an experience that provides them with "valuable knowledge to bring to the corporate home office," at which they may ultimately end up working in allocations and logistics, human resources, finance, customer relations, ISD, marketing, merchandising, or store operations. There are also significant growth opportunities within the organization's retail stores and distribution centers.

STATS

LOCATION(S) WHERE ENTRY-LEVEL EMPLOYEES WORK

Pier 1 has its corporate headquarters in Fort Worth, Texas. There are distribution centers in Savannah, Georgia; Ontario, California; Mansfield, Texas; Baltimore, Maryland; Columbus, Ohio; Chicago, Illinois; and Dupont, Washington. Pier 1 has more than 1,200 stores nationwide.

ENTRY-LEVEL POSITION(S) AVAILABLE

Pier 1 has various positions available for entry-level hires.

AVERAGE HOURS WORKED PER WEEK

Employees work an average of 37.5 hours per week (at the home office).

BENEFITS OFFERED

Pier 1 offers a medical PPO as well as dental and vision coverage. Additional benefits include a 401(k) program, stock purchase program, paid time off, associate discounts, flexible spending accounts, educational assistance, and holiday gift dollars.

CONTACT INFORMATION

Learn about job opportunities at Pier 1 by visiting www.pier1.com/jobs.

GETTING HIRED

Many first-jobbers come on board at Pier 1 via the company's retail outlets. A large proportion of the first jobbers we contacted at the home office had begun their careers as sales associates; they frequently checked the job postings at the Pier 1 website until they found an opening that suited their talents and goals. The company tells us that it seeks candidates "who are customer- and solutions-oriented, collaborative, enthusiastic, and flexible. We look for effective communication skills, strong interpersonal ability, and passion and excitement for the work that they do." The standard interview consists of behavioral-based questions. These are intended to elicit the past successes of candidates and in turn, determine their potential for success in the future. "We focus on customer orientation, problem solving, teamwork, communication skills, business knowledge, and questions that are technically specific to the position for which they are interviewing."

One first jobber hired in allocations explains, "Two managers interviewed me for the position. Since it was obvious that I had no previous allocations experience, the questions were more related to my work ethic, ability to learn, etc. There were some behavioral questions (e.g., 'Name a time when…') and some questions about my school experiences and how I handle certain situations. I was told that I would be informed within a week or so, and several days later I was offered the job by the staffing department."

MONEY AND PERKS

For most starting positions at Pier 1, "salaries/wages are nonnegotiable and work off a tight job grade/ pay scale." Raises are "merit- and equity-based" and are awarded annually. Major perks include a benefits package with a 401(k) plan, medical benefits, stock purchase plans, stock options, associate discounts, and vacation time. One first jobber writes, "The coolest thing about this company is that they offer so much to their employees. It is hard to pick one, but the employee discount is probably the best fringe benefit." Workers also love "Holiday Dollars," which are distributed to associates every November and may be spent at Pier 1 and Pier 1 Kinds stores. For many, "the biggest benefit of working for Pier 1 [is] the atmosphere and environment." "After eighteen years," writes one veteran employee, "I still enjoy coming to work every day. The environment is positive, enthusiastic, and motivational."

THE ROPES

New hires at the home office undergo a half-day orientation that "covers company policies, new hire paperwork, employee relations issues (such as drug abuse policy, sexual harassment, etc.), the Employee Assistance Program, and building and systems security." Subsequent training occurs on the job. One allocations analyst reports, "I received training first from my manager. She got me on my feet so I could start doing daily tasks. Over the next twelve weeks, I received training with many different analysts, each focusing on a different part of the department functions. By the end of the twelve weeks, I had some familiarity with everyone's job functions and a more in-depth representation of our department." Since so many first jobbers enter the company as sales associates, they literally learn the business from the ground up. One first jobber who worked his way up from floor sales notes, "training lasted about a month. It involved every aspect of my job, from receiving freight to processing the shipments, merchandising, and customer service. I was given feedback on a daily basis."

DAY IN THE LIFE

Day-to-day responsibilities at Pier 1 vary considerably among first jobbers, who are brought into all areas of the company. Most enter positions with few important responsibilities; they learn, they watch, they network, and ultimately they parley their time and efforts into a better job with more responsibilities—sometimes within the same area of the company, sometimes not. One first jobber who began as a help-desk specialist (i.e., telephone support contact for stores and customers) "gradually worked up to a morning shift (preferred shift for me) and was then promoted to supervisor of the team. I supervised the group for just over one year, and I then applied for a position in a different group of IT—the backup and recovery group. I have been working with the business continuity group for almost one year now."

PEERS

First jobbers can be found throughout the Pier 1 empire, so there's not a well-defined first-jobber network here. One newbie writes, "There is a lot of diversity with my peers. We're similar in some respects, but very different overall. I think this has been helpful for me; it's kept me open to others' ideas and perspectives." Another reports, "There are often after-hours activities available, but first jobbers here at the company must be socially active and forward to be included in these activities."

MOVING ON

Ironically, one of the problems with working at Pier 1 is that employees like the place a *lot*. "There's a lack of upward movement due to the fact that so many people are happy here; and management jobs do not open up that often," explains one first jobber. This sends some ambitious career-seekers off in search of employment elsewhere. Most, however, stay. They appreciate that "the company is wonderful about taking care of its employees. The company provides a great work-life balance, and most people are satisfied with this."

BEST AND WORST

Pier 1 sent us typical success stories rather than a best or worst. Here's one: "P. B. began her Pier 1 career in the stores, working as a Pier 1 store associate in Texas. After a year, she was promoted to assistant manager, and about two and a half years later, she moved on to the corporate office as a customer relations representative. After a year as a customer relations representative, armed with her advertising/marketing degree from the University of North Texas, P. B. moved into the marketing department." "My job is incredibly fun," she reports. "I have been able to apply my knowledge from the store and from the call center to about every decision I have had to make."

PRICEWATERHOUSECOOPERS
Associate

THE BIG PICTURE

Whether PricewaterhouseCoopers (PwC) really is "the best of the big four accounting firms," as one first jobber tells us, is open to debate. However, this is certainly a great place to start a career in the high-powered fields of assurance, tax, and advisory services. PwC was nominated one of *Fortune*'s "100 Best Companies to Work For" in 2005.

STATS

LOCATION(S) WHERE ENTRY-LEVEL EMPLOYEES WORK

The company has offices in 144 countries.

ENTRY-LEVEL POSITION(S) AVAILABLE

New hires work as associates.

AVERAGE HOURS WORKED PER WEEK

New hires work from forty to sixty hours per week.

BENEFITS OFFERED

The company offers a choice of health plans, prescription plans, hearing/vision/dental coverage, and flexible spending accounts. Additional benefits include paid holidays; vacation; sick days; disability, life and accident insurance; mortgage program; savings and retirement plans; and adoption assistance.

CONTACT INFORMATION

"Apply for a job on our website at www.pwc.com/lookhere."

GETTING HIRED

PricewaterhouseCoopers has appeal to business students at top campuses. "For the last four years [the company has] been recognized as being the number one ideal employer in its profession among business students, according to the Universum American Undergraduate Survey." PwC "has an extensive campus-recruiting program across the nation and visits several schools with accredited accounting-business programs to staff their offices around the country." Undergraduates may also apply for associate positions online at the PwC website. One associate explains, "The big four are actively recruiting. Once you choose the accounting major, there's only one goal, and that is to get an internship or associate position with a big four firm." PwC seeks candidates who "demonstrate the ability to work in a team, be organized, be [good at multitasking], work under pressure, and be willing to learn. A person's resume should not be longer than one page and should be concise, detailing [his or her] education, past work experience, and extracurricular activities. Although it is definitely helpful to have an accounting background, it is not mandatory, and, if qualified in other areas, PwC may still hire someone without the requisite accounting skills." A successful candidate advises that "it helps to follow up with someone in recruiting to make sure that [your] resume [and] cover letter [are] received and to establish a rapport with the recruiter. Because the firm receives so many resumes for positions every year, having a quick conversation with the recruiter and demonstrating your interest could make a difference in getting an interview." People who secure interviews tell us that the recruiters "ask a lot about working in teams [and] how you react in difficult situations. They want to find out what type of person you are." First jobbers also note that "a lot of juniors in college do the internship. The majority of hires are through the summer internship program."

MONEY AND PERKS

Although "salary isn't really negotiable—the current market situation determines your starting salary"—many PwC employees are content with their compensation. Other aspects of the PwC job offer are negotiable. Associates tell us that "rather than give you one start date, PwC gives new hires certain date options of when they can start. Most new hires either start at the beginning or end of September or the beginning of January. The start dates usually coincide with the orientation/training programs PwC offers." They also report that "because PwC has offices around the world, location is negotiable, depending on the needs of that office location."

PwC offers a generous benefits package, "comprised of a 401(k) plan with company matching, health care plans, paid time off, meals for overtime, travel reimbursement, corporate discounts on various products and services, and other perks, including exposure to other companies. If somebody ever wants to leave public accounting field, you've worked with fifteen to twenty different clients, the contacts that you make definitely come in handy in the future." Associates also love the Spot Bonus Program, which "gives partners and managers the opportunity to recognize hard work or exemplary performance by members of their team by giving them bonuses in their paychecks at random points throughout the year. As an associate, it's a great feeling to know that your hard work [does] not go unnoticed." According to PwC officials, "People are the number one strategic priority."

THE ROPES

First jobbers at PwC tell us that "depending on what industry group a new hire starts in, the orientation program varies." One associate writes, "It's a two-week program. Depending on what line of service you're in, they send you somewhere in the country—New York or Boston—[for] regional training. Mostly they go over the basics of when you start a new job, exactly what you're doing, [and] how you'll be doing it, and they show you how to use the technology." Subsequently "you do a lot of icebreakers. Also, once you come to the office, they send you a lot of e-mails about online courses [and] try to get you familiar with things before you get into it. Basically everyone that works here is very friendly. They emphasize not to be afraid to ask questions when you have them." No matter how good your undergraduate program was, you'll have to be prepared to learn most everything from scratch at PwC; one associate advises, "The thing about the undergraduate accounting programs is that they expose you to financial statements and policies and techniques, but they don't teach you auditing. You don't know what you're really doing until you show up and actually do it for a while. Even [during] the first two weeks of training, I didn't know exactly what the process was. Until you actually do it, there's only so much you can know."

DAY IN THE LIFE

"Typically what you do as a first-year associate is a lot of auditing of [easier] accounts," explains one PwC first jobber. "I do cash, fixed assets, accounts payable, [and] accounts receivable. They start you out with something you can succeed in." Young associates "travel out to the client site; the majority of work is there, not in the PwC office. You get there and [may] have two or three meetings a day to get information, ask questions, and get a feel of the account you'll be auditing. Then you go back to the audit room, evaluate the information you have, compare what you have with what they have, and then when you're finished, the senior will review your work. At the end of each engagement, the manager and partner will review everything, bringing you in as well." It isn't long before new hires are taking on increased responsibility, accountants tell us; one says, "One of the great parts about working at PwC is the amount of responsibility a new or experienced associate can have. Over time, associates are given more responsibility, have the opportunity to take control over more complex areas, and play an integral role in completing each audit." Another notes, "It is a rapid succession, a pretty quick learning curve. Most individuals make senior [associate] within two to three years."

PEERS

"At PwC, we work hard, but we like to play hard, too," first jobbers report, and "with everybody being the same age and everybody being in Boston, New York, etc., it fosters an atmosphere of going out every night." It all starts in training. One associate writes, "I was able to develop friendships with other new hires at training, and I still talk to several of them regularly. Because we all are at client sites on a regular basis, we rely on other social activities to see [one another]. The firm organizes several events for employees to mingle, network, and socialize including monthly 'hangouts' at the office, industry group social events (such as bowling), or happy hours. Teams also have their own happy hours, dinners, and events on a regular basis." First jobbers are "very impressed with how 'smart' and 'cool' PwC employees are. As a stereotype, accountants are supposedly quiet, nerdy, and unsocial. The people I work with are definitely a fun group of people who don't fit the stereotype. Everyone is here to challenge themselves, learn, work hard, and make the best of their experiences."

Moving on

First-jobbers come to PwC with the goal of building a career at a big four accounting firm. Still, "PwC gives you the opportunity to develop and hone skills that you can apply at many other jobs. Your skills are highly sought after by all companies who have accounting, finance, and risk-management departments, and you can easily move to a job in any industry that interests you."

Attrition

The most common reason folks don't last at the company is "the incredible volume of work." The hours are long. "It's a pretty constant fifty-hour workweek," writes one associate. Another adds, "People who are going through rough times often attribute it to having too much to do and working long hours. Working for PwC is not a nine-to-five job, and you have to be willing to put in some days with long hours to succeed." HR officials note, however, that PwC is "flexible and will allow you to work longer some days [to be able to leave early on others] and even take off [some] Fridays without using vacation."

THE PRINCETON REVIEW

Various Positions

THE BIG PICTURE

It's the best company ever! But seriously, folks, for many, The Princeton Review (TPR) offers the ideal entry-level job, one that offers diverse work experience, unusual amounts of responsibility, and plenty of opportunities for advancement. The workforce is unusually young, so the company's offices support an active, fun social scene that will probably remind you (at least a little) of your college days.

STATS

LOCATION(S) WHERE ENTRY-LEVEL EMPLOYEES WORK

TPR has nearly sixty offices across the country.

AVERAGE NUMBER OF APPLICATIONS EACH YEAR

The company receives 2,500 applications every year.

AVERAGE NUMBER HIRED PER YEAR OVER THE LAST TEN YEARS

The company hires 150 people per year.

ENTRY-LEVEL POSITION(S) AVAILABLE

New hires work as assistant marketing managers, research assistants, call center representatives, help desk assistants, production editors, and department coordinators.

AVERAGE HOURS WORKED PER WEEK

New hires work forty-five hours per week.

PERCENTAGE OF ENTRY-LEVEL HIRES STILL WITH THE COMPANY AFTER THREE, FIVE, AND TEN YEARS

After three years, 15 percent of entry-level hires remain with the company.

AVERAGE STARTING SALARY

New hires earn $28,000–$32,000 per year.

BENEFITS OFFERED

The company offers a full medical coverage package. There is also an optional dental plan, a 401(k) plan with company matching (after one year of employment), tuition reimbursement of up to $1,000 per six-month period ($2,000 per year) after six months of service, pre-tax flexible spending accounts for transportation, and dependent and nonreimbursed medical costs. As a full-time employee, you (and members of your immediate family) may also take any of TPR's test prep courses free.

CONTACT INFORMATION

Visit the company's website at www.PrincetonReview.com.

Getting Hired

There are several ways to land full-time employment at TPR. The company posts positions on its website and on www.monster.com. Many start with the company as part-time teachers for its test preparation courses, then apply for office positions as they become available. The company reviews all candidates for "excellent academic background and internship experience. Soft skills we look for include high energy, excellent communication skills, enthusiasm, excitement about the product, [and] passion to learn." Consistent with the company's approach, the interview process is serious but informal. As one recent hire explains, "I was familiar with TPR's casual approach to business and decided that the tone of my e-mail should be light, yet professional. I wanted to distinguish myself from other candidates, and my previous job in a similar field certainly helped land me the interview. I was interviewed by my current boss, who insisted that I come to chat wearing jeans. The interview was incredibly laid-back; I felt right at home and very comfortable. I remember on my second interview being asked by my boss' boss if I had $100 dollars, how I'd spend it. It was a great little ice-breaker, and it helped me open up some more. I knew that if I were hired, these were the two people I'd be working with closely, day in, day out, and no one else in such near proximity."

Money and Perks

Those who bring valuable prior experience to their jobs find that their salaries are negotiable; others may find less flexibility. Most people here "aren't in it for the money. I was more interested in landing a position with a company where I'd always wanted to work—a company that best represented my outlook on life—a casual approach and a young, energetic, palpable vibe that ran throughout." Others tell us that "the fact that the company is based in the academic world was also a big draw." What are the best perks here? "It's a tie between all the social events TPR sponsors and the tuition reimbursement," agree many. "Getting the company to help pay for the next stage in my education will be of immense benefit to me," writes one first jobber.

The Ropes

The Princeton Review offers a brief orientation to new hires ("[at which they] go over the company history, benefits, and our intranet. They also meet senior members of the company."), then sets them to work immediately. One first jobber writes, "It was on-the-job training. The first kick I took was from the moment I stepped into the office. It was a Monday, it was summer, and there were forty sets of student materials that had to go out. I was processing enrollments within my first three hours, and I probably handled my first phone call by day number two. Training was ongoing; I'd learn how things were done and then develop my own system based on what I'd learned." Another adds, "As I have encountered situations for which I don't have the experience or am not familiar with procedure, I have been able to ask other members of the office staff for help. Everyone has been great about helping to get me oriented and functional."

DAY IN THE LIFE

TPR offers a variety of positions to entry-level workers, and "there is no such thing as a typical day." Many people start out as assistant directors of an office. Here's how one person describes the position: "From day one, I was doing it all, helping run a small business. You want stress, you've got it. Everything falls into your hands—phone calls, e-mails, enrollments, ordering supplies, and getting office machines fixed. This isn't a cushy job; I had no idea I'd be getting my hands dirty, lifting packages and such. Here, from the moment I walked in the door, they sat me down at my desk, gave me a training schedule, and forced me to be their assistant director. We work hard, we drive for results, and we want the customer to recommend us." There's a lot of leeway in how you get your job done, as long as it gets done on time. One employee in computer support states, "As someone with a vested interest in the Internet, I felt this job would be a perfect match for me. It combined both my love of education and the Web, along with a casual work atmosphere. Where else can I grow a beard, wear shorts, surf the net, and get paid for it?"

PEERS

There's always been a youngish vibe in The Princeton Review offices; one employee notes, "We're an office with a mean age of about twenty-three, so it's nice to be around so many people my age." Nearly everyone agrees that "there is much camaraderie at the office. Although I am the only first jobber in my division, we're all really close, and sometimes it seems as though we work in a sitcom. We interact twenty-four hours a day, seven days a week. I'm serious. There's no getting away from these people." Fortunately, "these people" are "a very cool group."

MOVING ON

For some people, jobs at The Princeton Review become careers, and they tend to remain with the company. For many others, TPR is like the old television show *Taxi;* people work at the company, but their *real* gigs are acting, music, writing, art, and other such creative ventures. A number of these folks have moved on to successful careers in their chosen fields.

ATTRITION

People who leave the happy fold cite "overwork, with too many expectations being put on one person for the time allotted." One employee says it is not uncommon to hear "complaints about unrealistic expectations being put on us, particularly from national marketing. However, with that said, what I mostly hear [are] positive comments. People are happy to be working for a company that allows them to be who they are without laboring under massive corporate structures. Also, there is pride in serving students well and delivering a quality educational product."

PRINTING FOR LESS
Technical Service Representative

THE BIG PICTURE

Printing For Less (PFL) is an online seller of full-color printing products; their product line includes brochures, catalogs, cards, newsletters, and stationery. The primary entry-level position at PFL is that of technical service representative (TSR). This job offers many opportunities to advance; a company rep notes, "Some entry-level TSRs have moved quickly into leadership roles on our three-person self-directed teams within a few months of graduating from the training program. TSRs also may assist on project work in developing new products and services."

STATS

LOCATION(S) WHERE ENTRY-LEVEL EMPLOYEES WORK

The headquarters are in Livingston, Montana.

AVERAGE NUMBER OF APPLICATIONS EACH YEAR

Printing For Less receives 250 applications each year.

AVERAGE NUMBER HIRED PER YEAR

Printing For Less hires thirty entry-level employees per year.

ENTRY-LEVEL POSITION(S) AVAILABLE

Entry-level workers begin as technical service representatives (TSR).

AVERAGE HOURS WORKED PER WEEK

Entry-level employees work forty-five hours per week.

PERCENTAGE OF ENTRY-LEVEL HIRES STILL WITH THE COMPANY AFTER THREE, FIVE, AND TEN YEARS

Eighty percent of entry-level employees remain with the company past the three-year mark.

AVERAGE STARTING SALARY

Entry-level hires earn $28,000 per year.

BENEFITS OFFERED

"All regular full-time employees [have] the opportunity to obtain major medical insurance coupled with a health savings account" as well as "dental, vision, accident, disability, and life insurance" coverage, all of which vests after thirty days of employment. Additional benefits include paid time off, matching IRA contributions (up to three percent of employee's income), a stock option plan, and subsidized childcare.

Human Resources
211 East Geyser Street
Livingston, MT 59047
Fax: 406-222-4990
E-mail: employment@printingforless.com
www.printingforless.com

GETTING HIRED

The vetting process for new hires at PFL is "very rigorous," according to those who have successfully navigated it. It begins with an online application; those deemed worthy of further consideration undergo a "top-grading" interview approach, which begins with a forty-five-minute, four-question prescreening interview (which may include questions such as: How did you learn about our company? What are your career goals? What are you good at? What are you not good at?). Next comes "the first structured interview process," a three- to four-hour ordeal in which candidates review their past successes and failures. Then comes "the assessment and reference phase, which includes a personality assessment, a math test, technical evaluations, and reference checking (references must be previous supervisors or managers)." Then you're done, right? Not quite. Finally, "HR schedules the second round of interviews, [in which] the candidate meets with several department and senior managers and observes a TSR at work." One successful applicant writes, "The process was very rigorous. I spent two hours with the HR department during my first interview. We took a tour of the facility, and the HR director sat down with me to explain the extensive database and the roles and responsibilities of the position that I was applying for. My second interview lasted a total of seven hours. I met with everyone from the HR department and the president of the company, the VP of business development, and executive members of the IT department and management team. The whole thing was very thorough. What I really liked about all of this strenuous interviewing is that each person made sure to give me [a] personal testimony about why he or she liked PFL and what makes him or her excited about coming to work every day."

MONEY AND PERKS

Most first jobbers at PFL agree that their job offers were at best marginally negotiable. They felt they had little leverage to negotiate salary; start dates here are largely determined by the company's orientation schedule. All employees "are eligible for company bonuses. Bonuses may be earned quarterly and are based on overall company performance in meeting sales revenue and other performance goals for the quarter." One employee notes, "The best benefit is having the chance to gain experience and have a successful career while living in a place like Bozeman, Montana. This area offers skiing, hiking, hunting, and some of the best fly fishing in the world. PFL pays me a salary that lets me enjoy all of this. They also offer discounts on lift tickets at the local ski hills and host an annual company whitewater-rafting trip and a golf scramble. This is a great place to live."

THE ROPES

PFL starts new hires with a four-month training program; new cohorts are initiated every three or four months. One first jobber reports, "The program included instruction on customer file processing, customer relationship management, phone sales and skills, and database navigation. Plus, we all learned about twelve new high-end design programs used by graphic designers around the country. The training was presented by current and former TSRs who had been successful in their positions and knew the material well. This was great because they also gave us insight [into] what we would experience when we were actually on the job."

DAY IN THE LIFE

Entry-level TSRs at PFL handle "customer service and sales via phone and e-mail, digital file processing using graphics software applications, order processing, and quality control." One TSR writes, "The job is very different [from] any other job that I know of. PFL has basically rolled customer service, commercial pre-press, graphic design, consulting, and business management into a single position." A typical day for a TSL "includes coordinating with teammates to strategize [about] how we could best handle forty or more customer phone calls and the same volume of customer e-mails; process twenty or so customer orders from beginning to production; and meet all of our high-level objectives, which typically included something like 'increase our customer conversion rate' or 'reduce latency between order entry and order approval.'"

PEERS

PFL "doesn't hire anyone [whom supervisors] wouldn't want to be friends with," and "as a result, we have a great corporate culture." PFL first jobbers are "smart, cool, highly motivated, and high performing. They are great to hang out with at work or on the weekends." There is an especially strong bond among workers who went through training together; explains one, "You spend four months together training, and a lot of the time, you do social activities such as lunches, dinners, weekend activities, etc."

MOVING ON

PFL is "a young company that has only been hiring entry-level technical service reps for their first post-college job for three years." The company reports that more than "90 percent of those are still with the company," a solid record of employee retention. The low turnover rate is attributable to the "many growth opportunities within our company. The few [who] have left accepted jobs in other industries or pursued other educational opportunities."

ATTRITION

About one in twenty first jobbers leaves PFL before finishing at least one year with the company. An HR rep writes, "The most common reason for turnover at PFL is [the] pace. We are operating a high-growth, fast-paced company with virtually no downtime. While [PFL] provides employees [with] plenty of excitement and opportunities for career development, not everyone can consistently and effectively function at that pace at all times. Second to that would be just a change in lifestyles and personal plans, i.e., moving out of the Montana area, going back to school, [attending to] family needs, etc."

Best and Worst

The company reports, "One college grad we hired showed such competence and drive that he was able to catch up and graduate with a training class one month ahead of him; was placed on a front-line team immediately after training; became a highly successful team lead; and was promoted to production manager and later marketing manager in less than two years."

The worst first-jobber ever "did not complete the training program. The biggest challenges she had here were the demands for excellent listening (both to customers and team members), coachability, and reliability. Employees who are not team-oriented and motivated for personal and professional growth have difficulty fitting in and are not well suited for our company culture."

Proctor and Gamble
Various Positions

The Big Picture

Proctor and Gamble (P & G) is one of the nation's corporate giants and makes products for personal care, beauty, health, house cleaning, and baby care. The company offers entry-level positions in just about every area essential to its business.

Stats

Location(s) Where Entry-level Employees Work

"P & G is a promote-from-within company; [this] means that we hire almost exclusively from college campuses for both commercial and technical functions. Depending on the year, we will hire between 1,000–3,000 [entry-level employees] globally, of which about 50 percent are located in the United States. Of the people hired in the United States, about half are based in the greater Cincinnati area and half in subsidiary company, plant, or field sales locations throughout the country."

Average Number of Applications Each Year

"We typically receive [more than] 100,000 applications each year, all of which are electronically processed via our online application system."

Average Number Hired Per Year over the Last Ten Years

"P & G has averaged 725 management hires per year over the last ten years with a high of 1,100 and a low of 450."

Entry-level Position(s) Available

"Entry-level positions typically exist across all functional areas, including marketing, finance, accounting, [taxation], legal, marketing research, sales, engineering, purchases, PhD scientists, human resources, etc. In addition, we have a large number of nonmanagement positions in administrative and technical areas, most of which require college-level educations. For example, we hire a significant number of research associates who are four-year degreed people with majors in the natural science areas."

Average Hours Worked Per Week

"Average workweek varies by function within [the] business unit. The company uses flex time and other flexible work arrangements to help people maintain balance in their lives. Managers typically work about fifty hours a week with variation to meet important deadlines."

Percentage of Entry-level Hires Still with the Company after Three, Five, and Ten Years

"P & G hires for the long term. Our entry requirements are very high, and we use a rigorous assessment process to select the best people we can find. Once in the company, many people choose to stay for their entire careers, often working in different locations (domestic and international), different business units, or [different] functions. Early turnover is relatively low across all functions. Overall turnover is about 8 percent per year [of which] 3 percent are people who are retiring, so the three, five, and ten year turnover figures are roughly the same and stay in the 3–5 percent range."

AVERAGE STARTING SALARY

"We know from survey comparisons that our starting salaries are highly competitive [as compared with] a very strong competitor group of companies."

BENEFITS OFFERED

"Employees have a choice of medical plans designed to meet individual needs and preferences. Overall cost sharing is about 75 percent company, 25 percent individual. The plans are designed to provide broad coverage and have reasonable co-pays, out of pocket maximums, and premiums. Coverage is available for individuals and families including domestic partners or legal dependents." Additional benefits include profit sharing, retiree health insurance, flex comp, pre-tax credits for various services and insurance, and paid holidays.

CONTACT INFORMATION

Director, College Relations
Tel: 513-983-3788
www.pg.com

GETTING HIRED

P & G takes the scientific approach to hiring; company representatives note, "The criteria we use for hiring is directly linked to our competency model that was developed by interviewing our top management, a sample of 1,600 employees from every region of the world in which we operate, [and] a sample of our alumni, customers, and investors. This effort is sponsored and led by our Global Talent Supply organization." The model calls for candidates who have "integrity, brainpower, and demonstrated leadership. They should be collaborators [and] embrace change. They must communicate persuasively and clearly. They must have an appetite for results and a flare for innovation. We expect mastery of their learned discipline." Applications are fielded online on the corporate website and supplemented by recruiting trips to thirty-five campuses; top applicants "are invited to [visit] with the company [for a day]," during which they "tour the city, tour the facility, and have the opportunity to meet with new hires (one to three years) during lunch and in one-on-one situations." During the visit, applicants also "have a behaviorally-anchored interview by a panel of three people and go through some form of cognitive assessment." One first jobber cautions, "The tone of the interview was intense and serious. They wanted specific examples of how I was successful in previous roles that I have been in." Those who make it through the intense interview process tend to be very happy with the offers they receive.

MONEY AND PERKS

P & G offers solid starting salaries; one first jobber reports, "Their offer was much higher than the other offers I had." The same first jobber especially appreciated the company's flexibility: "At the time I was brought in, the business unit recruiting me was looking to fill several positions in engineering. My initial offer was for a position in a field that did not interest me. I made my hiring department aware of my preferences, and they were able to place me in one of the departments that appealed [more] to me." Other perks (which may vary widely by department and function) include flex time, travel opportunities, and discounts.

THE ROPES

The company has "an extensive [orientation] process that starts [on] acceptance of our offer, utilizing a new hire pre-start website. Once a new hire is in the company, the join-up period lasts for one year and is centered around three major training events that give people exposure to [one another], top management, functions, business units, company history and principles, and more. The events are fun, interactive, and thorough." Training sessions range from "one-day to one-week programs on such topics as company policy, inclusion training, women in engineering, or technology-related training." Subsequent training "is both formal and informal, offered by outside vendors, agencies, and upper management. All focus [is] on building business understanding early to help make an impact."

DAY IN THE LIFE

First jobbers at P & G often find themselves waist-deep in responsibility almost from the get-go. As company officials put it, "New hire roles vary according to function, but all have tremendous early responsibility built into their work." Our survey respondents confirm this assertion; one writes, "When I was first hired, I was given three different projects to work on, each on a different product. This allowed me to know three different product lines very quickly. I was given clear direction and full reigns and was responsible for all results. My manager wrote a work plan with me that described my responsibilities. This work plan included a list of key contacts, in my own and other functions, for each project that he suggested I meet with for join-ups. These contacts became an integral part of the project team, and their collaboration helped to make me succeed. Essentially, I was given the tools and the contacts to get the work done and the rest I was responsible for."

PEERS

For most first jobbers at P & G, there's "tons of interaction with new hires, including training and social events (informal and formal) on a weekly basis." One newbie reports, "About once a month there would be a happy hour or other event that allowed us to interact with others in their first year. There is also a sense of camaraderie within my group. I enjoy working with the others in my group, and occasionally we meet up outside of work." In the larger offices, "it is difficult not to run into others and have a quick chat in the halls because of the cubicle environment," while engineers in the field tell us that "during plant visits, experiments comprise long days and sometimes long weeks, so [people] get to know [one another] very well while traveling. During these trips [people] eat all meals together and often have long commutes to and from work."

MOVING ON

Although "many stay for a career" at P & G, occasionally workers do move on. The Cincinnati location in particular sees some workers move on. "It's a conservative, family-oriented city with employment opportunities [that] are less robust than [those in] Chicago or New York. This is sometimes an issue," company representatives inform us.

ATTRITION

Less than 1 percent of first jobbers leave P & G within twelve months of being hired, according to company officials.

BEST AND WORST

"All of our CEOs started as first jobbers," P & G representatives tell us. "We have had many great leaders. We believe our current CEO, Mr. A. G. Lafley, is an example of the kind of leader we produce, and [that he] will be one of the very best we have ever had." The worst first jobbers were "the people who joined P & G with skills, capabilities, and values that were not consistent with the culture of the company."

QUALCOMM

Various Positions

THE BIG PICTURE

You may know them as the company "that pioneered Code Division Multiple Access (CDMA) technology, which is now used in wireless networks and handsets all over the world." You may also know them as the purveyors of your e-mail software (Eudora) or as major players in the world of digital imagery. They are also major players in today's wireless industry, and they just may have a position for you.

STATS

LOCATION(S) WHERE ENTRY-LEVEL EMPLOYEES WORK

QUALCOMM employees work in offices located around the world, but the majority of positions are at company headquarters in San Diego, California.

ENTRY-LEVEL POSITION(S) AVAILABLE

Various positions are available to new hires: 70 percent engineering/technical and 30 percent business, finance, and other.

PERCENTAGE OF ENTRY-LEVEL HIRES STILL WITH THE COMPANY AFTER THREE, FIVE, AND TEN YEARS

"QUALCOMM has been ranked by *Fortune* magazine as one of the 100 best places to work in the United States for seven consecutive years, so we have a very low turnover rate."

BENEFITS OFFERED

The company offers a medical, dental, and vision PPO for employees and their spouses or partners. Additional benefits include a 401(k) plan, stock options, three weeks of vacation per year, an on-site fitness center, income protection, survivor protection, and tuition reimbursement.

CONTACT INFORMATION

Visit the website at http://jobs.qualcomm.com.

GETTING HIRED

Many first jobbers begin their tenure at QUALCOMM in the summer, either through the company's summer internship program or as new hires. The company posts open positions on its website, and they are open to all applicants. The advantage of interning, obviously, is that it allows people to establish connections with others at the company; this in turn makes the interviewing process much smoother. It also allows young job seekers to explore the company to determine the area that is best suited to their goals and talents. Most of our survey respondents describe their interviews as relaxed and very California style; one new hire writes, "It was more like a conversation than an 'ask/answer' session. My interviewer was interested in what I had to ask and say as well, and although there were also technical questions, my interviewer helped ease the stress I was feeling so that I could better answer the questions. It seemed as if my interviewer remembered what it is like to interview and empathized with the nervousness and occasional 'blank mind' that occurs during a technical interview." Even so, interviews at QUALCOMM sometimes resemble final exams. One hardware design engineer writes, "Each of my interviewers had his own style. One interview included worksheets of binary logic, circuit analysis, and C code. The interviewers were relaxed and friendly, but it was obvious they took the screening processes very seriously."

MONEY AND PERKS

QUALCOMM hires first jobbers in a number of different areas, and the negotiability of the offer depends on where they will ultimately work. Most of our respondents say that only the start date was negotiable. One engineer, however, reports that "the job offer was negotiable. QUALCOMM was able to match and beat offers from other companies." All jobs come with "lots of fringe benefits," including "fitness centers, free dinners Monday through Thursday, the lack of a dress code, the employee stock purchase plan, and flexible hours—[employees] can pick [their] own hours and take time at any time during the day to take care of life. The only expectation is that you get your work done, and you allow others to do the same." And don't forget "the QUALCOMM yearly party. What an event! Each department within QUALCOMM holds some sort of celebration about once a year during the winter season. QUALCOMM really goes 'all-out,' and it is a great excuse to dress up, be elegant, and have a blast!" Money-wise, QUALCOMM representatives say that "employees are eligible for two merit increases each year. Performances are evaluated, and depending on how well they met their goals, [they] may receive a salary increase, a bonus, and stock options." Also, "some employees may be eligible for relocation assistance, and we have a generous tuition-reimbursement program and on-site professional-development curriculum."

THE ROPES

QUALCOMM orientation is "very welcoming and informative. Employees learn about the policies, culture, and computer programs that are used at QUALCOMM." One first jobber writes, "At orientation, we got a packet of information that included two tickets for free lunch at the company café. It lasted an entire morning. I met my boss after the orientation, and we went to lunch [with the lunch tickets]." For many employees, subsequent training occurs on the job, mostly from coworkers and managers, and with occasional formal training sessions. The company offers engineers "a wide range of technical and management courses to get you up to speed with the technology."

Day in the Life

Our respondents at QUALCOMM included engineers, financial analysts, and designers. The majority of positions available are for engineers who begin their tenures by "following other engineers and learning from them. . . . If they needed help, they would show me how, why, [and] what to do, and I would go ahead and work on the assignment. As I grew more familiar with the process, they would then assign more challenging tasks, without going into every detail of the task." Engineers tell us that you can't just sit around waiting for an assignment; one writes, "If I don't ask around and talk with my fellow engineers, I [may] not find out about key things that are going on. I have to make sure I move around every now and then so I can find out about any projects going on that I [may] have fun participating in or that will give me added valuable knowledge and experience. People don't chase you around here, so you have to be motivated to keep yourself in the loop."

Peers

QUALCOMM is a big company, and the degree of peer networking first jobbers enjoy varies from area to area. Some tell us that "there is a pretty decent social scene here. There are a lot of young people at this company who are very active, and various clubs and teams seem to form each year. For example, I am on a softball team now that is mostly Q-Commers." Others report that there's "not a big after-hours social scene, but every now and then on weekends, Super Bowl, etc., people have parties or even just hang out and play basketball or soccer." Most employees agree that "QUALCOMM attracts great people who are all well-rounded and fun. They have open personalities and are very friendly."

Moving on

Most first jobbers at QUALCOMM have a hard time imagining a better work situation, telling us that they love "the trust management puts into its employees. My manager trusts that when I am at work, I am working and on top of things. It is this absence of 'micromanagement' that motivates me to put 200 percent into my work and overtime if I need to." One employee says, "When I talk to people outside of QUALCOMM, I realize just how good we have it."

QUICKPARTS
Various Positions

THE BIG PICTURE

Quickparts is a business-to-business e-vendor that uses proprietary software to custom-generate price quotes on parts production. In other words, if your business needs a machine part custom-made, Quickparts can find the producer for you and get you a good price on it. First jobbers work in a variety of areas for this up-and-coming company, whose Atlanta location is a definite plus for many city lovers.

STATS

LOCATION(S) WHERE ENTRY-LEVEL EMPLOYEES WORK

The company has offices in Atlanta, Georgia and Huntsville, Alabama.

AVERAGE NUMBER OF APPLICATIONS EACH YEAR

Quickparts receives 1,600 applications per year.

AVERAGE NUMBER HIRED PER YEAR

Quickparts hires fourteen entry-level employees per year.

ENTRY-LEVEL POSITION(S) AVAILABLE

Entry-level hires work as software developers, inside sales representatives, project managers, and territory accountants.

AVERAGE HOURS WORKED PER WEEK

Entry-level hires work an average of forty-five to fifty hours per week.

PERCENTAGE OF ENTRY-LEVEL HIRES STILL WITH THE COMPANY AFTER THREE, FIVE, TEN YEARS

Twenty-five percent of entry-level hires are still with Quickparts after three years.

AVERAGE STARTING SALARY (BY POSITION)

Software developers earn $38,000–$42,000; inside sales representatives earn $35,000–$40,000; project managers earn $38,000–$42,000; and territory accountants earn $28,000–$32,000.

BENEFITS OFFERED

"All Quickparts team members are eligible to join our group benefits plans on the first day of the month following sixty days of full-time employment. Currently, we offer medical, dental, vision, short-term disability, and long-term disability insurance." Additional benefits include a 401(k) plan and life insurance.

CONTACT INFORMATION

The Human Resources Department can be reached by telephone at 770-901-3200 and by e-mail at resume@quickparts.com. Jobs are posted at www.quickparts.com/info/job.asp.

GETTING HIRED

Quickparts posts job openings online, both at its own website and at various internet job sites (e.g., monster.com and ajcjobs.com). The Human Resources Department here "practices a process called Topgrading, which focuses on filling all open positions with an 'A' Player. Our hiring manager (the future team member's supervisor) and human resources work closely together to make sure that the position is clearly defined and candidates are evaluated accordingly." After screening resumes, HR conducts a brief telephone interview with likely candidates; if that goes well, "we have them fill out an employment application in preparation for on on-site half-day interview. During this step, the candidate interviews with several members of our team, covering everything from high school to college to work experience (even if it is unrelated to the position) to future plans and goals. Also during this step, the candidate will take several assessment tests (personality, computer skills, verbal, and quantitative tests)." The process is designed to yield "future leaders who are aligned in positions that correspond with their passions and goals."

MONEY AND PERKS

Terms of employment at Quickparts are negotiable "to a small degree," first jobbers tell us, especially with regard to start time. Salary and job description are far less negotiable, our survey respondents agree. Quickparts "conducts salary reviews on an annual basis. We don't believe in giving team members raises based on tenure. We are strong believers in pay for performance." To that end, "All team members are eligible for bonuses, depending on which department the team member is in. All bonuses are based on exceeding the performance goals of the department and are clearly outlined at the beginning of the year."

New hires agree that "Quickparts University is the best benefit to the employees now and in the future inside or outside of Quickparts. QPU is a program by which we continue learning about business and technology through a set curriculum, and in doing so, [earn] raises on top of our normal increases." Sample courses include Telephone Customer Service, Negotiation Skills, Marketing Strategies, "A" Player Attitude, Dealing with Change, Personal Finance, Delegation, Open-Book Management, and Stress Management. "Upon completion of each degree, the team member receives a $2,000 salary raise," the company reports. Employees also love the "many company events, parties, and free lunches" that Quickparts provides.

THE ROPES

Orientation at Quickparts begins at HR, where "the team member learns about the company's history, culture, and expectations and is free to ask any questions about his or her role in the company. This part of orientation typically lasts one to two hours. The remainder of the day is spent with the team leader, who takes the new team member around to personally meet everyone. The team member then finds out in more detail the requirements and expectations for his or her role and will [then] begin a two-week extensive training period."

Day in the Life

Many first jobbers begin at Quickparts as sales representatives. One writes, "My responsibilities entailed engaging new customers for the first time and working on the smaller projects as they came up, as well as assisting the area manager with his duties." For another, a typical day consisted of "calling and working with prospective customers to see how we could better fit the needs that they have for projects. I was also tasked with follow-up on old quotes and [with] helping customers [who] had questions [about] our online store." Others enter via the finance department; one such first jobber writes, "My responsibilities were to reconcile vendor bills, input invoices, and manage projects financially. A typical day would include entering twenty to thirty-five invoices, followed by reconciliation of vendor bills, and ending with reviews of projects."

Peers

Quickparts "is a very young company" with "a lot of camaraderie among young workers, but without excluding older employees." First jobbers are impressed with how "smart, interesting, and different" their peers are; one area rep writes, "I have very intelligent team members, and several are friends I spend time with outside of the office on a regular basis. Even my direct boss is a friend with whom I have developed an extremely close mentor-type relationship." There isn't much of an after-hours scene here, though, since "some of the new people are married and have kids," explains one first jobber.

Moving On

When they do leave Quickparts, first jobbers cite their desire "to pursue a passion that could not be fulfilled at Quickparts." A company representative notes, "Given our company's size, we have only had a few team members decide to leave our company. They left to pursue professional and educational aspirations in financial services, acting, law, and entrepreneurship."

Attrition

About 15 percent of first-jobber college grads remain with Quickparts for fewer than twelve months. Because the company is relatively young, the average tenure of first jobbers here (1.52 years) does not accurately reflect the company's turnover rate. In fact, a substantial number of first jobbers who started their careers with Quickparts are still with the company. There are compelling reasons to stick around. As one employee notes, "Because this is a small, growing company, I feel there is plenty of room to grow and develop. Since we are still growing, there is a flexibility to create new procedures and programs that allows for lots of room for growth."

Best and Worst

The director of HR at Quickparts tells us that "We have a team member who has been a star in our finance department and on his most recent performance review expressed his desire and goals to do more analysis work. When an opening for a business analyst position was available, we promoted this team member to this opening. He didn't have the education we required for the position (MBA), but he has expressed a desire to go back to school to get his MBA. He also has a track record at Quickparts of excelling and being a leader in finance."

RANDOM HOUSE

Various Positions

THE BIG PICTURE

Find, develop, edit, print, and market books just like the one you're holding now! Entry-level positions in all facets of the publishing industry await you at Random House, a bellwether of the world of book publishing.

STATS

LOCATION(S) WHERE ENTRY-LEVEL EMPLOYEES WORK

Jobs are available primarily in New York, New York; the company also hires for individual publishing imprints in Colorado Springs, Colorado and Roseville, California. "Additionally, we have operations centers in Westminster, Maryland and Crawfordsville, Indiana; these handle distribution and other critical support services. Entry-level employees are hired at all of these locations," company officials report, adding that "as the world's largest trade book publisher, Random House also operates in Canada, the United Kingdom, Germany, Spain, South Africa, Australia, New Zealand, Mexico, Argentina, Chile, Venezuela, and Japan."

AVERAGE NUMBER OF APPLICATIONS EACH YEAR

Random House receives 25,000–30,000 applications in the United States per year.

AVERAGE NUMBER HIRED PER YEAR

The company hires about 200 people per year in the United States.

ENTRY-LEVEL POSITION(S) AVAILABLE

The company tells us that "for college grads interested in a career in book publishing, Random House offers an enormous range of opportunities. Entry-level employees usually start out at the level of 'assistant' and not only work in traditional publishing areas such as editorial, marketing, and publicity, but also in production, sales, information technology, finance, human resources, subsidiary rights, new media, and other areas." A one-year associate program "for entry-level hires who are uncertain as to which area they want to join but are committed to publishing" is also available. In this program, associates rotate among various departments for one year; after that period, most stay on to take a permanent position at the company.

AVERAGE HOURS WORKED PER WEEK

Entry-level hires work thirty-five hours per week.

AVERAGE STARTING SALARY

Starting salaries are competitive by publishing industry standards.

BENEFITS OFFERED

PPOs, EPOs, and HMOs are offered; employees must contribute, "but the company pays the majority of the cost." There are also options to participate in dental, disability, life insurance, flexible spending accounts, the 401(k) program, pension program, tuition reimbursement, and profit sharing. Additional benefits include a *very* generous vacation benefit (four weeks per year after your first year!), paid parental leave, child care benefits, physical fitness reimbursement, a pre-tax account for transportation expenses, and a work/life assistance program.

CONTACT INFORMATION

To apply for a job, visit www.careers.randomhouse.com.

GETTING HIRED

Random House officials note, "Most obviously, we look for employees in our publishing and sales divisions who are passionate about books. Beyond that, we also look for individuals who take initiative, possess strong communication skills, and work effectively with others." The company recruits on campuses at certain colleges and also accepts applications via its website. Some new hires attribute their employment success to a post-college publishing course experience; one such employee writes, "I definitely think that having my resume come from the director of the Columbia Publishing Course was crucial in helping me to get an interview." That said, a substantial proportion of entry-level employees have not taken a publishing course. The vetting process includes a two-stage interview. One associate recalls, "My first interview was with human resources. The tone of the interview was very positive and friendly. I was asked about my educational background as well as my work experiences. I was then invited for further interviewing. I interviewed with several people, one from editorial and others from sales and marketing. All of these meetings were very informative and confirmed the positive impression of the company that had been established earlier." After that, it's a waiting game. According to one newbie who cleared the interview stage, "When a position became available that would allow me to utilize my major, I was asked if I'd be interested, and I was. I was hired about six months after my initial contact."

MONEY AND PERKS

Starting salaries at Random House are "the most competitive in the industry," according to one employee. Still, this is publishing, which is "by no means a gold mine," jokes one worker. Avid readers and others will enjoy the many perks of working at Random House. These include "getting to read interesting books months before they come out. It's entirely energizing to stay ahead of trends and get a glimpse at innovative writing as authors are creating it and as it winds its way into the mainstream. Getting to go to book events and movie premieres and meeting literary greats is also wonderful." One boasts, "Since I've started working here, I've encountered Joan Didion, John Updike, and Billy Collins [and many other important authors] who help shape our culture." Random House employees also enjoy "incredible" medical coverage and "unparalleled" vacation time—including the week off between Christmas and New Year's. Employees praise the physical fitness reimbursement program as "generous." Company representatives report that "many entry-level employees benefit from Random House's highly decentralized organizational structure. This enables each of its publishing divisions to maintain the ambience and creative and entrepreneurial autonomy of a small company, while enjoying all the resources and operational support of a market leader."

THE ROPES

Orientation at Random House is a relatively brief affair. One employee explains, "The orientation process was quick—just one morning, [for] about three hours." Another reports that the orientation session gave "a very general overview of all our benefits, vacation policies, sick days, etc." Beyond that, this employee writes that she "received a half-day computer session [in which she learned] how to use a complicated program designed for our contracts system." Most agree that the bulk of training takes place on-the-job "on an as-needed basis." One notes, "my managers went out of their ways to give me varied tasks so that I could learn new systems." Another newbie reports that "come lunchtime [on the first day], I was already in my office, reading manuscripts and answering the telephone and communicating with authors. Publishing moves so fast that it is necessary to hit the ground running and learn as you go." Random House also has a weekly Luncheon Seminar series, in which executives from various departments share information about their areas of expertise, their career paths, and their workgroups. The series typically concludes annually with a talk by Peter Olson, chairman and chief executive officer.

DAY IN THE LIFE

Random House offers entry-level jobs in editorial, production, publicity, marketing, sales, rights, HR, finance, customer service, and warehouse operations, so the daily experiences of new hires vary greatly. Those who enter through the associates program rotate among various jobs within a particular division. This path has its plusses and minuses; one employee who took this route explains, "As an associate, I was placed in an entry-level position for a period, after which I would move to a new position. At the end of the one-year program, I was expected to select a permanent position. The program's goal is to give a new employee a better understanding of the different work environments within a single publishing house." Associates praise the variety of their positions, though one cautions that it "could have been very boring if I had not been assertive about getting new jobs and tasks." That said, the Associates Program positions new hires well for permanent positions; in the words of one former associate, "It was definitely a great advantage to already be sitting on the bench versus still trying to get into the stadium."

Even for entry-level hires who start out as assistants, many note that they "don't really have a typical day." One editorial assistant writes, "When I first started, my responsibilities leaned more toward clerical work—copying, writing up rejection letters and reader reports, reading lots of slush submissions, answering phones. However, I also took my downtime during this slower period to ask lots of questions of the other assistants, read up on industry news, and read my bosses' previous titles to find out what types of books they were interested in." Another notes that there was some flexibility for her to plan her days: "I was able to organize my time myself, when I wasn't scheduled for a meeting, as long as I completed my projects on time."

PEERS

"There is tremendous camaraderie among first jobbers at the company," writes one newbie. "From the minute I walked to my new desk, people came to introduce themselves and offer help in my settling in." Another newbie writes, "I have made quite a few good friends within the company, and they are a lot like me—outgoing and social, but still really interested in books, literature, current events, and the like." Another chimes in, "Because the industry has an apprenticeship culture ('everybody started as somebody's assistant' is a favorite axiom), it often feels like half the company is under twenty-five. I have lunches or happy hours with other twenty-somethings almost daily." In particular, "the Associates Program offered a ready-made group of people to become friends with, and by rotating, I met most of the first jobbers in the imprint."

MOVING ON

Entry-level jobs at Random House are designed to lead to better positions within the company. Many young workers stay to pursue their careers in publishing. "A major reason for voluntary departures is often to attend graduate school," note company officials, who also cite "relocation, career change, and personal reasons" as reasons why some employees leave the company. One entry-level employee notes that "there is plenty of room to grow in terms of pay and responsibility," though some report that promotion occurs faster in some imprints than in others. While "people complain about the workload and relatively poorer pay of publishing," they "also love the culture."

ATTRITION

Personal relationships are important in publishing, and many who leave do so because they don't enjoy working for their superiors. "Enjoyment of one's entry-level job is directly proportional to how much one enjoys one's supervisor, professionally and personally," points out one successful entry-level employee. Other people leave because they are "not satisfied with the level of responsibility allocated to them." Still others note a publishing industry trend: "Sometimes a move is necessary after a few years (generally four to five) in order to progress. As there is generally little movement once you reach the higher positions in editorial, it is often beneficial to move in order to be promoted, no matter how much you enjoy your current company."

RAYTHEON COMPANY
Engineer

THE BIG PICTURE

In today's world, you can't really ask for a bigger potential growth industry than defense. Raytheon is one of the world's biggest defense and aerospace systems suppliers in the world, and its vastness allows engineers to work in virtually any area that interests them. In the process, as one engineer reports, they also get "to provide countries like the United States with products that help maintain peace."

STATS

LOCATION(S) WHERE ENTRY-LEVEL EMPLOYEES WORK

"Nationwide. Our fifty-five locations that hire co-ops/interns and full-time entry-level employees include the following metropolitan areas: Boston, Massachusetts; Falls Church, Virginia; Los Angeles, California; Southern California; Dallas, Texas; Tucson, Arizona; Denver, Colorado; St. Petersburg, Florida; Ft. Wayne, Indiana; and Indianapolis, Indiana."

AVERAGE NUMBER OF APPLICATIONS EACH YEAR

"Our electronic resume process logged 23,000 domestic United States entry-level candidates in Fall 2004 and Spring/Summer 2005."

AVERAGE NUMBER HIRED PER YEAR OVER THE LAST TEN YEARS

"Raytheon grew to its current state through mergers and acquisitions in the late 1990s. The average number of entry-level hires for recent college graduates has been over 1,000 per year since then."

ENTRY-LEVEL POSITION(S) AVAILABLE

"[There are from] 700–1,000 new positions for full-time, entry-level openings. Predominately, openings are for engineering positions in hardware, software, and systems designs of large, complex defense and commercial electronic systems. Raytheon fills the greatest number of openings with candidates who majored in electrical engineering, computer engineering, and computer science. [They] also hire graduates with the following majors for technical positions: mechanical engineering, math, aeronautical/aerospace engineering, physics, [and] material science. Raytheon recruits graduate engineering degree candidates from select universities to participate in a rotational engineering leadership development program. Finally, [they] hire candidates with majors in human resources, marketing, and finance/accounting/business for leadership development programs in support [and] functional organizations such as business development, communications, contracts, finance, human resources, information technology, and supply chain management."

Average Hours Worked Per Week

"Most recent college graduates are [placed in] salaried positions. Hours worked vary according to individual program and phase [of project]. Employees average forty to fifty hours per week, but the greater focus is doing what is required to get the job done. Many employees enjoy a flexible work arrangement and are on a 9-80 workweek (nine-hour days for eight days and one eight-hour day in a two week period with every other Friday off)."

Average Starting Salary

"Raytheon offers competitive salaries for new college graduates based on a number of criteria, including work location, degree level and major, academic qualifications, and work experience. Recent salary offers were $53,000–$59,900 for technical [bachelor of science] degrees and $42,900–$53,000 for nontechnical [bachelor of science] degrees."

Benefits Offered

"At Raytheon, we understand the importance of rewarding our employees for all they bring to the table. For a general overview of the health care, income protection, investment/retirement, and work/life benefits as well as some of the extras available to eligible Raytheon employees worldwide, please refer to our recruitment website at www.rayjobs.com/campus." Additional benefits include income protection (disability coverage, basic life insurance, accidental death and dismemberment insurance, and business travel accident insurance), investment/retirement plans (pension, savings, and investment plans, and [a] stock program), work/life (flexible work schedule, paid time off, holidays, dependent care reimbursement account, adoption assistance, employee assistance program, and business casual attire), and extras (educational assistance, internal job transfer system, relocation assistance, home and auto insurance, matching gifts, Raytheon Scholars Program, same-sex domestic partner benefits, and discounts).

Contact Information

Visit the website at www.rayjobs.com/campus. Candidates are asked to submit their resume online.

Getting Hired

Raytheon recruits most aggressively at "twenty-three universities nationwide; these 'strategic schools' are valued [because of] our hiring history, potential to produce numbers of targeted graduates, and potential to produce females and minorities in our targeted degree majors. They also have research capabilities in technologies of interest to our businesses. We actively recruit on campus at approximately 100 schools. All candidates are referred to our campus recruitment website, where they can search for opportunities, complete a profile, and attach their profile to the jobs of greatest interest and match for them. This would include any candidates from schools where we may not actively recruit." One engineer who landed a job explains how he did it: "I submitted a resume at the job fair and then was contacted by Raytheon for an on-campus interview. The on-campus interview was done with one interviewer, and it lasted about twenty minutes. It was a scenario-based interview; the interviewer would ask 'what would you do?' questions based on scenarios. Also, there were questions about my greatest accomplishments in college and what specifically useful classes/projects I [completed] in college. After the on-campus interview, which consisted of thirty-two people from every department at the school, Raytheon invited four of us to a second round of interviews at Raytheon. In addition, there was a 'get acquainted' dinner the night before, a plant tour, and an information session before the interviews [at which] we were given an overview of Raytheon, and the initial work for our security clearances was begun. After the plant tour and lunch, a second interview was held. There were two interviewers in this session, but the questions were basically the same as the on-campus interview. The interview was longer, approximately forty-five minutes, and more time was set aside to allow me to ask any questions that I had. About three weeks later, I received a job offer from Raytheon. My later understanding was that the second interview was more of a formality, and that the real cut point for getting a job offer was made during the on-campus interviews."

MONEY AND PERKS

Raytheon offers competitive salaries, so the first jobbers we surveyed saw no need to negotiate pay; they also tell us that start time and location are sometimes negotiable. One writes, "I was given a six-month time window for when I wanted to start. The salary was not negotiable. However, the salary I was offered was $5,000 higher than any other offer I received, so there was no incentive for me to try to negotiate a higher salary. I felt the offer I was getting was more than fair." Company officials note that "salary increases are an integral part of an annual performance evaluation process. Increases are based on individual performance and company factors." Top perks include relocation allowances and the flexible work schedule.

THE ROPES

Raytheon newbies are introduced to their new workplace through a brief orientation, which lasts anywhere between half a day and two days, depending on their placement in the company. One entry-level employee writes, "The initial orientation was an introduction to the company, company policies, security polices, and so on. Although it was necessary, it was no fun." Some engineers report subsequently taking formal classes, but most of them tell us that the majority of their training came from their bosses. One engineer explains, "I didn't receive any streamlined training. I was assigned to work on a project with another engineer the afternoon of my first day at work. He told me what we were working on and what he thought the next steps should be, and I basically jumped right in. I had enough theoretical and practical experience that a few questions were all I needed to be helpful. After a few days my boss and coworkers trusted that I knew what was going on, and they started to let me suggest ideas and initiate experiments." Another engineer agrees: "Aside from a few training classes, all of which took place months after I started working, all of my training has been informal, 'ask-my-mentor' type training."

DAY IN THE LIFE

Raytheon hires engineers and support staff in a variety of areas. Company representatives tell us that "New technical hires work in a wide variety of assignments ranging from production support, design upgrades, full-scale program design and development, advanced developments for concept demonstration, and pure technology development. In all cases, new grads work with experienced lead engineers, and it is common to have an additional senior engineer designated as mentor." Engineers must also be prepared to work independently; as one tells us, "When I was first hired, I had to design a graphical user interface in Matlab. I had absolutely no idea how to do this, so first I had to gather as much info as I could from the Web and books. Not many people I asked had any experience with it, so I basically had to teach myself how to do it, but that was probably a good first experience because I learned that I could do something on my own with minimal help from others." Company representatives point out that engineers have responsibilities that people may not normally anticipate, such as "the requirement to present and defend designs at a design review, develop documentation, work with tenured technicians, source parts and deal with vendors, workout at one of our 'on-site' athletic facilities, participate in a community affairs/outreach events at a local school, etc. The ability of new grads to perform well in these additional tasks is what separates successful engineers from those who become disenchanted with their role and/or Raytheon in general."

PEERS

Most of the new engineers we spoke with tell us that there were "very few entry-level engineers" in their particular area, making it hard to develop a peer network. One first jobber found a solution: "A small unit of young engineers had posted e-mails and established a company-sponsored social group, which did help me get acquainted with other new hires. This enabled me to increase social interaction after-hours." Those who do have contact with other newbies enjoy the experience; one writes, "All of us play sports and drink together. I still have lunch every week with some of the other new guys at the other two facilities."

MOVING ON

Raytheon at one time lost a substantial number of first jobbers, but that has changed in recent years. Company representatives explain, "Early this decade, Raytheon lost many recent hires to the lures of very large salary increases and stock option hiring bonuses from now-defunct high tech companies." These days, most Raytheon workers are in it for the long haul. One veteran writes, "While twenty-seven years sounds like a long time, it would place my tenure at third of four people in a small row of offices in the staffing systems and university programs office in Dallas. I've had the opportunity to do many different things during my career, from marine data collection on a seismic survey vessel in the North Sea to technical writing, training and development, and staffing. This becomes one of the greatest strengths of a corporation the size of Raytheon: the ability of its employees to use internal job mobility to change assignments and even locations to facilitate personal career vitality. For many years, I have listened to experienced line workers, whom we have assembled to share meals with new hire candidates, remark that once they had decided what they really wanted to do, all they had to do was ask."

BEST AND WORST

The best first jobber, Raytheon tells us, was "a guy hired from California Polytechnic University—San Luis Obispo, with a bachelor of science degree in industrial engineering, named William Swanson. Why? He is now Raytheon chairman and chief executive officer."

REPUBLICAN NATIONAL COMMITTEE
Various Positions

THE BIG PICTURE

As an employee of the Republican National Committee (RNC), you will help solicit political donations, coordinate "get out the vote" drives, formulate the Republican platform, produce issue advertising, and devise election strategies.

STATS

LOCATION(S) WHERE ENTRY-LEVEL EMPLOYEES WORK

Employees of the RNC work in Washington, DC.

ENTRY-LEVEL POSITION(S) AVAILABLE

Various support staff positions are available to entry-level hires.

AVERAGE HOURS WORKED PER WEEK

New hires work forty or more hours per week.

PERCENTAGE OF ENTRY-LEVEL HIRES STILL WITH THE COMPANY AFTER THREE, FIVE, AND TEN YEARS

First jobbers typically stay for one election cycle, then use contacts made during their tenure to find other party/political jobs.

CONTACT INFORMATION

Contact your local Republican party office, via www.gop.com/contactus.

GETTING HIRED

You've got to hang around the grapevine to get a job at the RNC. All but one of the employees we spoke with told us that they learned about their jobs through personal contacts (the remaining first jobber, who works at GOP TV, was recruited). If you're active in the College Republican National Committee or with your state party organization, you're probably connected enough to find out about job opportunities at the RNC. One newbie writes, "I found out through the Wisconsin state party. It was the perfect job for me—I wanted to move to DC to work in press and for a Republican. It had all three. Initially I passed my resume to everyone I knew at the state and national party. It was more word of mouth that helped me get the initial interview. The interviewer just asked [about] my background [and] told me what the job entailed, and I told them how I could carry out the necessary tasks. I called two weeks later to follow up, and we scheduled another meeting two days later [during which] I was hired."

Money and Perks

New hires at the RNC have some flexibility in defining their roles in the organization but find little wiggle room in negotiating start time, location, or salary. Most don't care; one writes, "I didn't put up much of a fight about anything because the job was what I wanted." Perks include "getting to help with all of the political aspects in Washington: campaign, convention, and other events," and the "exposure and contacts" employees make.

The Ropes

"There is no specific orientation process" at the RNC; it varies from hire to hire. For one newcomer, it was "one afternoon during my first week, mostly 'company' policy and insurance issues." For another, it was "a couple of hours on the first day," mostly just meeting the other staffers and getting settled in. Subsequent training is similarly informal. "I was shown around and trained by my boss's assistant, and it was 'learn as you go,'" explains one first jobber. "A guy who had held the position a year ago was very helpful," offers another. A third advises, "Learn quickly!" The reason for this apparent lack of structure? One fresh hire opined, "Obviously everything moves very quickly right now, including hiring and placement. Jobs develop because there is a need for the function, not because a title is empty."

Day in the Life

Support staffers at the RNC often find their days filled with administrative duties; they "answer phones, make copies, put press releases up on newswire, and handle any additional administrative tasks people have in the office. [They] also help plan events and communication in the office." Those who make a solid impression quickly gain more responsibility and eventually move up the organization's hierarchy. While they "spend very little time with high-level executives personally, it's not uncommon to see the chairman roaming around downstairs talking to my bosses." Our first jobber at GOP TV has a radically different itinerary; he "coordinates reporters and crews, daily news feeds, and live-shot requests, liaises with capitol and presidential administration officials to plan and set up interviews for news and special feature programming, and creates pitches and coordinates outreach and pitching efforts on behalf of GOP TV with national and local media."

Peers

RNC staffers tell us that "there are many opportunities to meet other coworkers. We do have happy hours, for example." One entry-level employee writes, "There is a good social scene and overall respect and camaraderie. RNC staff members are wonderful people!" They don't distinguish between first jobbers and more senior staff, though; there's "nothing special because we are first jobbers."

Moving On

RNC staffers tend to move on after the given election cycle during which they were working ends. All of them will try to move onto other jobs within the world of party politics.

RESULTÉ UNIVERSAL
Recruiter and Account Manager

THE BIG PICTURE

Resulté Universal is a Texas-based consulting and staffing services firm that "helps clients achieve their business goals through strategic investment in human capital." According to Resulté's website, the firm's consulting services division "deploys tactical teams to solve clients' critical business problems." Its staffing services division allows the company to deliver "top talent for contract, contract-to-hire, and direct-hire opportunities." First jobbers here recruit candidates to meet both client staffing and internal needs and help develop the firm's relationships with current and future clients.

STATS

LOCATION(S) WHERE ENTRY-LEVEL EMPLOYEES WORK

Employees work in Dallas and Houston, Texas.

AVERAGE NUMBER OF APPLICATIONS EACH YEAR

Resulté receives 1,000 applications each year.

AVERAGE NUMBER HIRED PER YEAR

Resulté currently hires just five entry-level employees each year, but the firm plans to increase the program size in the near future.

ENTRY-LEVEL POSITION(S) AVAILABLE

Resulté hires entry-level employees as recruiters and account managers.

AVERAGE HOURS WORKED PER WEEK

Entry-level hires work fifty hours per week.

AVERAGE STARTING SALARY

Recruiters and account managers earn $30,000–$35,000, plus commission.

BENEFITS OFFERED

Resulté offers health and dental coverage as well as life insurance. Disability is paid at 75 percent after ninety days of employment. Additionally, employees are eligible to contribute to the 401(k) program after one year of employment.

Resulté Universal

5151 Belt Line Road, #455

Dallas, TX 75254

Tel: 972-448-7070

Fax: 972-448-7059

E-mail: jobs@Resulté.com.

GETTING HIRED

Resulté "has an entrepreneurial environment." "If you work hard and produce, you have a lot of personal freedoms," reports one first jobber in recruiting. The firm seeks candidates who are a good fit for its corporate culture—people who are "competitive, intelligent, creative, and driven. They are people who can separate themselves from the crowd. An ideal employee at Resulté needs to be flexible, motivated to overcome obstacles, and great with people to get the job done successfully." Resulté "generally posts jobs online;" after all, "the type of candidate we are looking for needs to be well versed [in] computers to effectively use our patented system for qualifying, delivering, and managing contingent resources. Our internal recruiters, who are usually searching for qualified IT and accounting/finance professionals, use their skills to find the best prospects for their new coworkers. Once the prospects are narrowed down, the candidates are brought in first for a face-to-face interview with two to three recruiters or account managers in the division for which they are applying. The candidates who pass that round will interview with the division recruiting and account managers. Finally, a select few will meet with the three company partners, and the entire group decides which person will be the best fit for the organization." One successful hire notes, "Resulté Universal has a long interview process that allows everyone on the team to make a decision on a prospective employee."

MONEY AND PERKS

Starting salaries and wages are "somewhat negotiable" at Resulté, first jobbers here report. In addition to base pay, "entry-level recruiters and account managers are eligible for commissions at the same rate that the more senior employees earn. There is literally unlimited earning potential for new employees. The more job orders they fill and the more clients they satisfy, the more money they make." Raises "are given annually based on revenue and activity and quality goals, [such as] number of interviews, number of filled job orders, and customer satisfaction level. Teamwork, mentoring activities, and volunteering for special projects are also taken into consideration for raises."

Top perks include "a great Christmas party and an annual trip for high performers," plus quarterly events called "Gold Club outings." Gold Club events may include "racing Mustangs on a professional track, visiting an amusement park, or taking a helicopter tour of the city." Finally, "employees who meet certain requirements get to attend the annual company trip, which in the past has included a cruise to New Orleans and Cozumel, a trek through the Costa Rican rainforest, and lounging on the beach in Cancun."

The Ropes

Orientation at Resulté "typically lasts a week. It starts with a tour of the office and an introduction to all of the new employee's coworkers. Next, the employee will be introduced to Resulté, and one of the partners will present the state of the company and explain our history, our patented methodology, and where we fit [into] the marketplace. Then, a representative from the IT department will demonstrate how to use our proprietary systems for general tasks like scheduling appointments and e-mail and provide the new employee with all of the technology he or she will need, such as a laptop and a Blackberry. The majority of the first day is spent in formal training on the new employee's role—what's expected, the processes for achieving goals, and the Resulté way of doing things.

The rest of the week consists of attending short team meetings every morning to discuss the focus for the day and job shadowing." During the shadowing period, the new hire "spends several hours with each of the team members in the same position, so account managers will shadow all the other account managers in their division, and recruiters will shadow all the other recruiters in their division. This allows the employee to get different perspectives and form a more complete view of his or her role and the company while getting to know team members. Because recruiters and account managers work as a team to provide skilled employees to the clients, new recruiters will spend a day with the account manager division lead, and new account managers will spend a day with the recruiter division lead."

Day in the Life

Account managers work with current clients and also seek out new ones. Job duties include creating and implementing a successful sales plan, maintaining positive relations with current and prospective customers, and seeking new opportunities for Resulté to expand the services it provides to current clients.

Recruiters "source, screen, and evaluate candidates." One recruiter writes, "A typical day entails routine follow-up calls and check-up calls to ensure that all candidates are aware of where they are in the process. [We are also responsible for] calling new candidates, interviewing them, and submitting them [as applicants for] various positions, as well as setting up any interviews between the candidates and clients. Finally, [we receive] feedback about candidates and from candidates about their feelings on an opportunity."

Peers

"There is a big after-hours social scene among all employees" at Resulté, and this provides "a good and popular way to get new people to come out and meet their coworkers. Many people even hang out on the weekends." First jobbers feel their peers "are a lot alike in terms of their personalities and general attitude. We work well together because the atmosphere allows people to ask questions and be open."

Moving On

According to Resulté, "Few employees leave voluntarily, but many of those who have [done so] have gone on to start their own staffing companies."

ATTRITION

Resulté loses less than 10 percent of its college-grad first-jobber population within twelve months of hiring. Most who leave do so "because they were not able to meet our performance requirements." The firm tells us that such employees "generally go to work for a competitor." The average tenure of a Resulté first jobber is three years.

BEST AND WORST

Resulté identifies IT Recruiting Manager K. S. as an exemplar of a successful first jobber, reporting that she "was hired straight out of college with no experience in the industry. Because of her willingness to learn and her competitive drive, she quickly moved up the ranks and was promoted over more senior recruiters. In just a few short years, she has gone from knowing nothing about staffing to managing a team of eight responsible for more than $7 million in revenue in 2004 and has consistently exceeded her stated individual and team goals."

Unsuccessful first jobbers "are the ones who don't seem to have the ability or the initiative to solve problems and come up with answers and solutions on their own. A Resulté employee has a high degree of control when it comes to taking action to satisfy a customer. A new hire needs to be able to make decisions, defend those decisions, [be accountable] for mistakes, and do whatever is necessary to correct any mistakes that are made."

SCHLUMBERGER

Field Engineer and Research, Development, and Manufacturing Engineer

THE BIG PICTURE

Are you an engineer seeking entry into the world of bubblin' crude? You know, black gold? Texas tea? If so, here's your invite. Join Schlumberger, "a recognized technology leader providing products, services, and solutions to the oil and gas exploration and production (E&P) industry."

STATS

LOCATION(S) WHERE ENTRY-LEVEL EMPLOYEES WORK

"We recruit where we work worldwide, in approximately 100 countries, virtually everywhere you find oil and gas. In the United States, approximately 30 percent of the field engineers (FE) hired will start employment in an international location. Most research, development, and manufacturing engineer (RPM) hires work in one of the United States facilities."

AVERAGE NUMBER OF APPLICATIONS EACH YEAR

The company receives roughly 4,000 applications for the field engineer position and 1,500 for the RDM position (both in the United States).

AVERAGE NUMBER HIRED PER YEAR OVER THE LAST TEN YEARS

The company hires 200 FEs and 50 RDMs, yearly.

ENTRY-LEVEL POSITION(S) AVAILABLE

"Schlumberger mostly hires engineers and technical professionals. The two main types of positions are for field engineers and research, development, and manufacturing engineers."

AVERAGE HOURS WORKED PER WEEK

"Field engineers do not work a typical eight-to-five office schedule; the jobs often have long shifts (more than twelve hours per day) and/or odd hours. Time off is not on the normal weekend cycle; there is either a planned schedule (something like nine days on, three days off) or a minimum amount of days off per month (four). Research, development, and manufacturing engineers have a more typical schedule, with longer hours during peak project times, an average of forty to sixty hours per week, with weekends off."

AVERAGE STARTING SALARY

FEs earn $52,000, plus operating bonuses. RDMs start at $50,000, and MS Design Engineers average $55,000.

BENEFITS OFFERED

For health care coverage, Schlumberger offers flexible spending options for medical, dental, and vision care. Additional benefits include 401(k), pension, retiree medical, discounted stock purchase plans, and annual vacation time.

CONTACT INFORMATION

Visit the website at www.slb.com/careers.

GETTING HIRED

Schlumberger recruits "on forty-nine United States campuses, including most of the top engineering schools. Students from other schools are open to apply through our online system, and many come to us through the referrals of current employees." The company seeks a complement of skills in its new hires, including technical aptitude, problem-solving skills, self-motivation, and interpersonal skills. First interviews are conducted by phone or on campus; subsequent interviews are held at company offices. The company notes that "because the FE job especially is quite different than the average engineering job on offer, attendance at the pre-interview information session the night before is critical." A field engineer reports that her first interview was with a recruiter on campus: "Questions asked ranged from how I handle stress to what activities I was involved in. About a week after the initial interview, I was contacted [and told] that I was a candidate for a second interview. Two months later, I was given a list of interview dates, and asked to pick the most convenient ones for me. It was a two-day interview, including a tour of one of the training centers, an overview of the company and positions available, and all of it was done in a relaxed manner."

MONEY AND PERKS

Field engineers "are promoted two separate times [during the training program] before finally being promoted to general field engineer. Each time the base salary increases incrementally. Each service segment also has an operational bonus structure based on its service delivery model. It can be highly dependent on work location and operational activity, but in general, there is extremely high growth potential in the second and third years as the engineer assumes higher levels of responsibility." Research, development, and manufacturing engineers receive "bonuses and promotions linked to performance." New recruits tell us that "the job offer is generally negotiable in terms of start date. However the actual location, salary, and position are set." Perks include a new laptop, extra allowances for engineers placed overseas, and bonus pay.

THE ROPES

Orientation at Schlumberger lasts for ten days. Here's how one engineer described the experience: "The orientation process began in Houston for initial training into the Schlumberger lifestyle. Beginning on a Tuesday, the new hires spent five days covering company history, IT issues and setup, introductions to available resources for seeking help in anything, an introduction to the oil-field setup, and issued proper personal protective equipment and a drug test. The next five days were spent in driver training near Tulsa,

Oklahoma." Other components of orientation include "health and hygiene training from a certified Schlumberger instructor and alcohol and drug awareness training from an outside contractor." Training is an ongoing process throughout an engineer's tenure with the company; one worker offers, "I have spent [more than] nine months in Schlumberger training schools since coming to work for the company."

DAY IN THE LIFE

Research, development, and manufacturing positions frequently require an advanced degree; most offer entry-level positions as "sustaining engineers, responsible for sustaining and improving a variety of projects," gradually earning more responsibility and gaining more independence over time. For field engineers, the position that is more often available to recent college grads, "there is not much of a typical day." One new hire reports, "When I was first hired, I was assigned a supervisor to shadow and learn from, so I was on call with his schedule, which meant working about seventy hours a week. On any given day, I would be on call. When I was called in, I had an hour to report to the office and prepare for the job. Over time, I have been given an exponential amount of responsibility. In four months I've progressed from being an observer on the job to nearly running the entire job when on location." Another FE adds, "I had to get dirty (every day!) with the operators and work like an operator to learn and appreciate the equipment and the operators' job responsibilities before I could sit in the big seat and run a job (you don't get as dirty there)." Field engineers love "the early responsibility, in-depth training, and the ability [really to] put engineering theory into application. And over the longer term, the diversity of career opportunities is really the most attractive aspect. We call it 'borderless careers,' and it means people have the option to move fairly fluidly between businesses, functions, and locations."

PEERS

Contact with other field engineers is inevitable, given the isolation of some work environments. One writes, "I work offshore; therefore I live, eat, sleep, and work two weeks at a time with the same people. They become family and great friends." Another agrees: "There is a good amount of contact with other first jobbers. There are two other people who fall into this category [where I work]. As far as after-hours social interaction, we get together when we can, but that time is limited. At work, we spend some time together depending on how the rotations work out." Off the rigs, peer-to-peer contact at Schlumberger "depends on the location. Some new hires spend a lot of time together at work and outside of work, and some do not. I [seldomly] spend time with peers outside of work. We spend so much time together at work that I try to spend time with other friends or family [on] my off-time."

MOVING ON

Those who leave Schlumberger early "will [most likely enter] completely different industries. Those who stay on and gain a bit more experience will often go to operators (oil and gas companies) and to a lesser extent our competitors and other oil field services companies." Most people view Schlumberger as a good place to build a career. As one field engineer tells us, "If I have the opportunity to leave the company for an interesting position [that] I feel I can do well in, then I will. However, I will not leave intentionally to work for another service company. I would like to continue my career here if the opportunities within the company allow me that opportunity."

ATTRITION

Attrition rates are relatively high for field engineers; about one in five can't handle the long hours, the stress, and the separation from family and friends. As one field engineer puts it, "The first few [reasons for leaving] that come to mind are the hours, schedules, and locations. We work twenty-four hours a day, seven days a week, and we do not stop for holidays. You do *not* have a schedule to follow and almost all locations are remote. You don't see many oil rigs in tourist-type locations." Research, development, and manufacturing engineers, who work under more conventional conditions, are much less likely to quit.

BEST AND WORST

Good first jobbers "learn early on how to strike a good balance between their work lives and their personal lives. A candidate who thrives in the face of challenge and takes an objective view of the long-term prospects will generally do very well." Less-than-ideal new hires "tend to be those who are less prepared for the transition into full-time job independence."

SeamlessWeb

Various Positions

The Big Picture

Those looking for opportunities in "an extremely fast-paced and growing company, as opposed to a large established corporation," should seriously consider applying for a position at SeamlessWeb. SeamlessWeb provides companies and individuals with a Web-based system for ordering from restaurants, caterers, florists, gift-basket purveyors, and other local vendors. In fact, the service was so well received that SeamlessWeb launched a consumer site for individuals to order at home or anywhere. The company serves individual customers and corporate clients in New York City; Washington, DC; Chicago; San Francisco; Los Angeles; Philadelphia; Stamford; Greenwich; and Jersey City and is rapidly expanding to serve corporate clients in other major cities. Not surprisingly, SeamlessWeb was ranked the number four fastest-growing privately-held company in the country by *Inc.* magazine. According to one employee, SeamlessWeb "has literally tripled in size in the last year."

Stats

Location(s) Where Entry-level Employees Work

SeamlessWeb's headquarters are in New York City; the company also has several regional offices.

Average Number of Applications Each Year

SeamlessWeb receives 4,000 applications each year.

Average Number Hired Per Year

SeamlessWeb hires fifteen entry-level employees each year.

Entry-level Position(s) Available

Entry-level employees start as inside and outside sales associates, junior account managers, marketing associates, member support representatives, and accounting/human resources assistants.

Average Hours Worked Per Week

Entry-level employees work forty hours per week.

Percentage of Entry-level Hires Still with the Company After Three, Five, and Ten Years

More than 85 percent of entry-level hires remain with the company after the three-year mark, and just about 85 percent stay on past five years.

Average Starting Salary

Entry-level employees earn $30,000 per year.

BENEFITS OFFERED

SeamlessWeb offers health and dental coverage, both of which vest after one month of employment; it also provides FSA, which vests after one year of employment. Additional benefits include a 401(k) plan with employer matching, which vests after one year; a monthly MetroCard (for NYC employees); and a discounted meals program.

CONTACT INFORMATION

Interested applicants may send e-mail messages to jobs@seamlessweb.com.

GETTING HIRED

SeamlessWeb reports that successful applicants "must be enthusiastic and have a desire to succeed as well as exhibit strong communication and follow-through skills. We try to avoid applicants who are not passionate about our product and the growth potential of SeamlessWeb." As at many small, nascent companies, the application process is relatively informal. One successful applicant recounts, "My initial interview was held in one of the VP's apartment in NYC. The VP was in sweats and a T-shirt when he interviewed me. Some [may] have seen this setting as a negative when reviewing a potential employer, but I saw it as the sign of a company that knew it was going places and didn't feel the need to impress anyone. [There] was very much a 'You'll be lucky to join us' attitude, [and] I appreciated [that]. I was brought back for a second round of interviews with the VP of firm sales, the department [within which] I was applying for a job, and [also with] the CEO. Both these individuals were founders and had gone to law school together. They were young, motivated, and demonstrated tremendous vision and sheer brilliance in answering my onslaught of questions about the company, its history, and its path for the future."

MONEY AND PERKS

Starting salaries are negotiable, first jobbers here tell us, and can be augmented with performance-based raises and performance-based bonuses. Some sales positions are commission-based. Perks include "free samples from New York City's finest delivery restaurants," a 401(k) pension plan, the "relaxed dress code," and "the chance to work with a great team every day."

THE ROPES

As in the interview process, *informal* is the operative word concerning orientation at SeamlessWeb. One first jobber explains, "SeamlessWeb is a small company that does not have a human resources department, so our 'orientation' was not an official outlined process, but rather a [series] of meetings and [observation experiences] that helped us to learn more about the logistics and operations of the company." Another adds, "The training process was just as informal as the interview process. There was no training manual, and there was no [set] schedule. It was a hands-on, learn-by-observing-the-pros, be-proactive-and-ask-lots-of-questions process." Employees report having to be proactive "to get questions answered." But, one notes, "being the type of person who [dislikes being] micromanaged, I enjoyed the freedom and the fact that they put the success and speed of the training program in my hands. The training program [foreshadowed] my position [in that it had] an abundance of freedom and the understanding that only my proactive efforts and motivation to excel would bring success; nothing would be handed to me."

DAY IN THE LIFE

A number of the first jobbers we spoke with began their SeamlessWeb careers performing data entry, customer service, database maintenance, filing, and receptionist duties. They tell us it was a good way to learn the business and find a place within it. They then moved on to take jobs in marketing and sales, where their days involved working directly with restaurants and corporate clients to build the business and publicize the SeamlessWeb brand. In a company this small, everyone's job is unique, and no individual's day-to-day routine looks anything like another's.

PEERS

First jobbers at this "young and energetic company" enjoy "a lot of after-hours contact with other employees," though "in some cases, people choose to keep their office and social lives separate." One employee observes, "A few times a month we tend to get together for drinks or activities outside of the office, some of us who happen to be closer friends, even [get togethers] on the weekends. We try to include everyone, including those from other departments and teams so that everyone can get to know [one another]. I think there is a level of cliquishness between some of the people who have been here longer and developed friendships when the company was smaller; but for the most part, everyone gets along both in and out of the office." The overall vibe is "friendly," and "there is a feeling of family because everyone is so close."

MOVING ON

Because SeamlessWeb is a small company with lots of growth potential, first jobbers aren't anxious to move on. Many realize that they are joining what could potentially soon be a big and booming business. Because of this, they may have opportunities for advancement that are relatively rare in the first-job world. Those who leave generally do so because they're not interested in the SW business itself; some leave to go to graduate school.

ATTRITION

The company reports that about 5 percent of first jobbers leave SeamlessWeb within twelve months of taking a job here.

BEST AND WORST

The company tells us "We have had many very successful entry-level employees. The most successful are those who started either after graduating college or even working part-time as data entry clerks while still attending school. People who started with SeamlessWeb five years ago in an entry-level capacity are now running or helping to manage areas of their departments."

And the least successful SW hire? "An employee came in and didn't want to take the time to learn the core requirements of the company. He just wanted to push ahead without having the proper foundation."

SEARS
Retail Management Development Program

THE BIG PICTURE

"Sears has everything!" That's what this venerable retailer claimed in one of its early slogans; after its merger with former competitor K-Mart, the assertion rings truer than ever. We've been assured that the company's well-regarded management training program will not change as a result of the K-Mart deal.

STATS

LOCATION(S) WHERE ENTRY-LEVEL EMPLOYEES WORK
Candidates select from six geographic regions that cover the U.S. In each region, multiple metro markets are available and select stores are identified for training locations.

AVERAGE NUMBER OF APPLICATIONS EACH YEAR
The company receives 1,200–1,500 applications per year.

AVERAGE NUMBER HIRED PER YEAR OVER THE LAST TEN YEARS
The company hires 150 entry-level employees each year.

ENTRY-LEVEL POSITION(S) AVAILABLE
Entry-level hires enter the Retail Management Development Program.

AVERAGE HOURS WORKED PER WEEK
New hires work forty to fifty hours per week.

AVERAGE STARTING SALARY
The starting salary is $36,000 per year, plus an annual target incentive.

BENEFITS OFFERED
Sears offers HMO and PPO plans. The company provides dental insurance, health care flex spending accounts, disability insurance, life insurance, business travel insurance, a 401(k) plan, Sears discounts, tuition reimbursement, education loans, daycare flex spending account, vacation, and flex time off.

CONTACT INFORMATION
Visit the company's website at www.sears.com/collegerecruit.

GETTING HIRED

Sears recruiters look for "demonstrated leadership skills and abilities, as well as a strong interest in the program and company" through a "structured candidate assessment process" that "utilizes both business representatives as well as human resources professionals." The company recruits on thirty-two core college campuses and also considers internal referrals and unsolicited candidates, who may apply via the Internet. One successful hire reports, "The first-round interview was held at my college campus. It was about forty-five minutes long. I was interviewed by a Sears rep sent by Chicago. She was absolutely pleasant and quite relaxed. The tone was very professional, and she focused on my abilities and skill sets rather then my limited job experience or my nontraditional major. I was e-mailed the following week to congratulate me on my interview and was invited to Chicago for the second and final round of interviews. I was allowed to pick the date of my trip. The interview day began at 6:00 A.M. We had a series of interviews for most of the morning as well as simulation activities. The day ended at 8:00 P.M. I was exhausted. It was a very impressive process. It made me want the job even more because I felt as though I was interviewing for something much larger." (Sears officials note that final interviews are typically scheduled from 7:00 A.M. to 4:00 P.M.)

MONEY AND PERKS

Retail Management Development Program trainees start at $36,000 per year and "are eligible for an annual incentive based on the following: Sears earnings per share and Full Line Store Balanced Scorecard (a metric combining customer, people, sales, and profit goals)." After twelve months, successful trainees are "promoted into an assistant store manager assignment" and receive a commensurate raise. Popular perks include the associate discount; one trainee points out, "This company is involved in many facets of retail, and in one way shape or form the discount for me has been very beneficial." Another notes, "Besides the discount, the best benefit from this program is the opportunity to run around with the high-level managers, both on the store and district level. As a result, as a new ASM, I am not intimidated by the district or regional staff because I [have] always worked with them and [am] familiar with their expectations."

THE ROPES

Orientation begins in Hoffman Estates, Illinois (a suburb of Chicago), where trainees are flown to attend a full-day session at a Sears training store. Here, trainees complete the requisite paperwork and benefits overview, then are trained in eLearning, an Internet-based training tool that preps trainees for upcoming rotations. Team-building activities take up much of the afternoon, along with an overview of the program, a career-planning workshop, and a Q-and-A session. Subsequent training occurs online and on the job, with a rotational system ensuring that trainees learn all aspects of the business ("We work in each department of the store for two weeks to a month," reports one participant). Most are "impressed by the depth of the training program offered by Sears. This was the longest training program available (among recruiting retailers), which I found attractive. To me, it meant that Sears would be investing time and money [in] me, thus giving me the information, tools, and background I would need to be successful in my first assignment."

DAY IN THE LIFE

The day-to-day life of management trainees varies with their rotational assignments, "shadowing experiences that include time in all selling and nonselling aspects of a Sears Full Line Store." Trainees also perform two special assignments "that will challenge their leadership skills. Each assignment will last three to four months and include goals in alignment with the Balance Scorecard." One trainee sums up her experience in the program this way: "My responsibilities were generally the same throughout the entire program. Phase one consisted of me shadowing all five assistant store managers. I worked with them, did their reports, conducted their walk-throughs, assisted with customer opportunities, etc. I essentially lived their lives for at least two weeks each. I then followed each of their leads (hourly managers/sub managers); I learned how they supported their ASM and how they contributed to the team as a whole. Phase two consisted of two special assignments. I assumed the role of a lead in both a hardlines and softlines position. I took ownership of specific departments and reported to a specific ASM."

PEERS

Trainees report that the size of their peer network depends greatly on their placement. Those in larger districts enjoy a large group of contemporaries. One trainee reports, "I instantly became friends with the other trainees and younger management staff in my district. We frequently meet for dinner or karaoke throughout the week." Those in smaller districts have relatively few peers in their own age group. A trainee from the hinterlands warns, "My advice for new trainees would be to really consider where you are asking to be assigned. Your area will become your new home. In the world of retail, most managers are older, with families, etc. Your social life is dependent on what you bring to the table, who your other trainees are, and where you ask to be assigned."

MOVING ON

Trainees who move on usually do so "for multiple reasons, but most revolve around career fit." Top motivators include "selecting a line of work other than retail," "returning to school," "moving to a competitor within the retail industry," and "personal reasons, including location issues." A typical trainee writes, "I think I will probably want to continue my education at some point and perhaps to go forward in higher level jobs in the company or I may take another route all together."

ATTRITION

Less than 10 percent of Sears Management Development trainees don't remain through the end of the first year. Those who do leave "talk about how they feel the work-life balance that Sears promotes is only for [the] corporate office. They complain about the hours and the crazy schedule." There were concerns in the past that trainees were not well connected to the company's suburban Chicago headquarters, but a change in corporate personnel has improved the situation. Nowadays, "trainees really have the potential to accelerate quickly if they work hard and are willing to demonstrate their capabilities."

BEST AND WORST

According to the company, "There are several high-potential leaders at Sears who began their careers in the Retail Management Development Program. Common keys to their success include [having] tremendous passion for the business, [being] highly results-driven, and [cultivating] expertise in performance management."

SHERWIN-WILLIAMS COMPANY
Management Trainee Program

THE BIG PICTURE

Sherwin-Williams, one of the nation's leading names in paint, painting supplies, wallpaper, and chemical coatings, offers college grads a thorough training program that transforms them from eager greenhorns into store managers in one brief, but intense, year.

STATS

LOCATION(S) WHERE ENTRY-LEVEL EMPLOYEES WORK

Sherwin-Williams has 2,700 stores throughout North America.

AVERAGE NUMBER HIRED PER YEAR OVER LAST TEN YEARS

The company hires between 450 and 500 people per year.

ENTRY-LEVEL POSITION(S) AVAILABLE

New hires work as management trainees.

AVERAGE HOURS WORKED PER WEEK

New hires work forty-four hours per week.

AVERAGE STARTING SALARY

New hires earn a base salary in the low- to mid-30s (depending on location), plus quarterly bonuses.

BENEFITS OFFERED

Sherwin-Williams offers various choices in company-paid health insurance (with small employee co-payments), dental insurance, and eye care. Additional benefits include a stock savings plan, a 401(k) plan with company match, company-paid pension plan, tuition aid, sickness and accident leave, paid holidays, and vacation.

CONTACT INFORMATION

Visit www.sherwin.com, click "Careers," and look for the map of the United States. Click on the part of the map that interests you, and the recruiter for that geography will be identified.

GETTING HIRED

With the job market as tight as it has been the past few years, candidates have been taking increasingly novel approaches to distinguishing themselves from their fellow candidates. One successful hire at Sherwin-Williams recalls, "I focused on my cover letter, knowing that whoever read it would continue to my resume if I conveyed intelligence, structure, and personality, which are vital in a sales position. I sent my resume to the headquarters, and it made its way to the human resources director, who was the first person to interview me. I sent a shoe wrapped nicely in a box with a note on top that read 'Thank you for letting me get my foot in the door.' Since the interview process can be nerve-wracking, the strong cover letter and the ice-breaking shoe helped me feel a little calmer and more confident." Once your foot is in the door, interviewing at Sherwin-Williams is a three-stage procedure. One who survived all three stages explains, "During my first interview with human resources, I felt the tone to be very professional but not too rigid. I was impressed that the interviewer was selling the company to me as much as I wanted to sell myself. He asked me questions about how I had handled situations in the past concerning customers and about setting and achieving goals and multitasking. His questions were all positive and directed toward my past work and school experiences. He explained to me the path I would take both with the interview process and upon being hired, as well as how the MTP (Management Training Program) worked. Following this interview I met with the district manager of the area where I would start, and finally, with the vice president of sales of the same division. The second interview had the same tone, but had more specific questions applicable to the job and the management training program. The third interview felt like more of a formality and a get-to-know the company interview. During this interview, I was officially offered the job."

Money and Perks

At Sherwin-Williams, "All employees receive annual merit increases, plus bonuses. At such time, a trainee is promoted to manager or representative (about one year after being hired), there is a substantial promotional increase, [and] bonus potential increases threefold." Start date and location can be negotiable, if the company has numerous openings at the time of hire. Salary is not negotiable. Most first jobbers agree that the best perks are "the paid vacation time and the 401(k)."

The Ropes

New management trainees spend their first six weeks on the job "in a training store learning the basics of the business. Trainees are provided with videos and literature to help familiarize them with benefits, policies, and procedures. The training store manager is specifically trained in training techniques and is compensated, in part, on the success of the trainees. It is the responsibility of the training store manager to orient the trainees, introduce them to employees and customers, and ensure that they are familiar with policies and procedures and are aware of the resources available to them as new employees. After six weeks in a training store, trainees participate in one week of classroom training at their division-training center. The third phase of training entails being assigned to a store as an assistant manager." One former trainee writes, "The entire orientation process lasted about six months. During this time I completed courses that helped with all aspects of the job, including product knowledge, quality control, financial reports, managing employees, and time management. I also worked in several different stores. This helped me get to know not only the people in my area, but also the market. The START (Store Training and Reference Tool) courses and books, floating around and working in different stores with different managers, and a week of training at the headquarters helped me to develop during the orientation process. One of the greatest things about this job is that you learn something every day. After six years, I still draw [on] things I learned during the first six months, and I continue to learn more every day."

DAY IN THE LIFE

A current management trainee tells us, "When I was first hired, my biggest responsibility was to focus on training, learning all I could about my own duties as an assistant manager as well as [about] my employees. I needed to know where the stock went and how to put it away, how to order, how to delegate tasks, and what tasks needed to be done; doing everything from mopping the floor to filling orders to helping customers find what they need[ed] for their project was included in a typical day; [and] understanding the paperwork and what needed to be done was important so that I could learn how to prioritize and manage my time on the job. Another great thing about this position is that there are not many 'typical' days. Every day is different with different tasks to complete and new things to learn." One former trainee who has since moved onto a management position notes, "At first, product knowledge is the toughest part of the job. However, over time your knowledge in products grows, and you then have to start learning your customers. You learn that each customer is completely different from the next. In this industry, you may see a person once a year or twice a day. The goal is to know what customers need no matter how often you see them." As time progresses, trainees "take over the tasks of the assistant manager. These tasks include making collection calls, fulfilling orders, staffing the store, and managing accounts payable."

PEERS

One Sherwin-Williams management trainee says, "[We] make lifelong friends during the management training program week [at division headquarters]. They are from different parts of the country, and we still keep in touch. I see them all once a year during the National Sales Meeting in Nashville, Tennessee." Once back at their jobs, however, they don't see other trainees regularly; one explains, "Since I was the only MTP in my district, I had very little exposure to other people [across] the country in my position. However, other employees throughout the district were very welcoming to me. I have had many opportunities to interact with other employees on a social basis as well as [for] business. The mix between the two has made my first six months very enjoyable." First jobbers tell us that Sherwin-Williams has a congenial work vibe; one notes, "Friends are easy to make at Sherwin-Williams. Each day it gets hectic and chaotic. By busting your butt and getting the job done, everyone is brought together as a team. My best friend works at Sherwin-Williams!"

MOVING ON

Sherwin-Williams carefully tracks former employees. Although the employee turnover rate is low (in the single digits), company officials tell us that out of all who leave, three-quarters of people leave for other job offers; about one in eight leave for personal reasons; and about one in ten leave for other reasons." Company representatives report that the vast majority of people leave to "start their own business, take a sales job in another industry, become a painting contractor, or go back to school." Those who stay say they like the fact that many different opportunities are available within the company. One writes, "Sherwin-Williams allows its employees to wear many different hats. If I wanted to get into the marketing side, I could choose to go to marketing. If I wanted to go into corporate management, I could have that opportunity. The fact is, with Sherwin-Williams you have the opportunities to grow into the position that [best fits] you."

ATTRITION

Some folks can't hack it in Sherwin-Williams' Management Trainee Program; one who could says, "I found, and still find, that those people who drop out of the program or are dissatisfied are not ready to work. Most people were expecting to put on a tie and sit behind a desk after college. I felt like my strong work ethic set me apart from them, and I enjoyed my success." The job is certainly demanding; as one trainee tells us, "I guess the most common complaint that I have heard is being frustrated about not being able to learn fast enough. What is interesting is that I have never heard anyone complain about the program itself, but only about their own ability or inability to learn the products."

BEST AND WORST

The most successful first jobber ever, Sherwin-Williams tells us, is "John Morikis, who entered the program in 1984 and is now president of our stores division, a more than $3 billion business."

Starcom
Media Associate

The Big Picture

Starcom is one of the giants of brand communications, an industry that offers services in media management, multicultural media, and internet and digital advertising. Clients include beer companies, consumer packaged goods, high-tech businesses, and just about every other business you can think of.

Stats

Location(s) Where Entry-level Employees Work

Entry-level employees work in Chicago, Illinois and Los Angeles, California.

Average Number of Applications Each Year

Starcom receives about 3,000 applications each year.

Average Number Hired Per Year over the Last Ten Years

Starcom hires about 100 entry-level employees each year.

Entry-level Position(s) Available

Entry-level employees are hired at the media associate level.

Average Hours Worked Per Week

New hires work forty to fifty hours per week.

Percentage of Entry-level Hires Still with Company After Three, Five, and Ten Years

Half of entry-level employees remain with the company after three years.

Average Starting Salary

Starting salaries range from $25,000–$30,000.

Benefits Offered

Medical, dental, and vision benefits are available to all employees. Additional benefits include tuition reimbursement, short-term disability, long-term disability, life insurance, fitness center memberships (very low cost), 401(k) participation immediately and company matching, employee assistance program, paid vacation, paid holidays, personal legal assistance (low cost, through vendor partner), paid time off for wedding leave, paternity leave, commuter spending account, health reimbursement account, and dependent care account.

Contact Information

Visit the company on the Web at www.smvgroup.com/careers.asp.

GETTING HIRED

Starcom recruiters seek hires with "strong verbal and written communication skills, strong math and analytical skills, and a passion for work in the media industry." Applications are accepted "either online or through campus visits. If there is a strong fit with the candidates' backgrounds and interests and our recruiting needs, they would be contacted to start the interview process." Interviews "focus on questions surrounding communication (both verbal and written), teamwork, relationship building, knowledge of and interest in the media industry, quantitative skills, critical thinking, problem solving, innovation, and creativity." One successful hire describes the process: "My first round of interviews was with five people from [my university], which was awesome because we already had a relationship established, and it made it a bit more comfortable. [It] was very casual. I was very comfortable, and we spent the majority of the time talking about my experiences and how they relate to a work environment. I was given ample opportunity to be myself and really sell myself through to the company. About a week after my first interview, I was then invited back for second round, which subsequently took place a month and a half later in Chicago. I, along with about 100 other students, came to Starcom for a day full of interviews. I had interviews with supervisors and media directors, none of whom I knew before. These interviews were a bit more tense, not as comfortable, and the questions were a little harder."

MONEY AND PERKS

First jobbers agree that starting salaries; are "not negotiable," but they appreciate what they get in return. Most are philosophical about the situation; one newbie writes, "That is how this industry is. We don't make much less than the industry standard; I just feel we may work more than the rest of the industry." In addition to gaining valuable career experience, newbies "are wined and dined by vendors, and your social calendar is constantly booked with sporting events or after-work parties/concerts/festivities." One worker writes, "On any given occasion, a vendor could take me out to sushi for lunch, out for a manicure, dinner/limo ride/ tickets to a Cubs game, or an invitation to a media party where we get to drink all night free while listening/ dancing to a band, singing karaoke, and eating a full-buffet dinner. These 'perks' are definitely icing on the cake." The company itself also provides "lots of perks. We celebrate our anniversary every year by having a party in the downstairs lobby, with bands, food, and lots of prizes. Also, every December, the company gets together for 'The Breakfast.' The entire day is filled with incredibly fun stuff, including drinking at bars and watching the executives perform skits."

THE ROPES

New hires at Starcom "participate in a twelve-week formal training program introducing them to the world of media. This program strongly differentiates us in the marketplace, is considered a competitive advantage, and is often a primary reason why candidates want to work here." One first jobber explains, "The first four weeks are called MMLS (Media Math Language and Systems). We spent three hours a day learning about media math, doing mock plans for fictitious products, [and] learning about all the different acronyms. Usually two hours of the day were devoted to presentations about the different investment groups or divisions within the agency, and one hour was devoted to an interactive class project. The last week of class was spent off-site at training centers, where we learned how to use specific computer programs. We had regular homework assignments and a take home final exam. The second half of the program is a nine-week training program called 'FBP: Fueling Brand Power.' In this class, our two daily two-hour sessions focus more on planning and targeting, and we complete one large group project that involves doing an entire media plan from start to finish."

DAY IN THE LIFE

"Every day is *very* different" for media associates at Starcom, the company's only entry-level position for media professionals. That's due in part to "an excellent rotational program where one can move from a specific department to another." The three main groups for associates are strategy groups, which "create and present media plans to clients" to meet their advertising needs; investment groups, which "invest client budgets with media vendors in the most effective and efficient way" and monitor advertising buys to ensure that they run as ordered; and specialty groups, which focus exclusively on "one medium or type of advertising," such as multicultural media, Internet marketing, out-of-home marketing, field marketing, international media, TV programming, or entertainment marketing. One media associate observes, "Some days will be absolutely crazy, while others are quite slow. I have never felt I couldn't get help from someone if I had too much to do, though. And if things are slow, I usually ask for an extra mini-project or volunteer for something that needs to get done in the group."

PEERS

Starcom "is full of young, vibrant, engaging people just like myself," making "the transition into the work environment easy because you are starting with people just like yourself who are just out of college and new to the work world." Accordingly, there is "a lot of camaraderie amongst first-jobbers. You grow very close to one another because you begin training together, you are in the same life-stage as one another, and you have similar life experiences. Many people get together after work for social events, shopping, drinks, and even intramural athletic teams."

MOVING ON

Those few who leave Starcom do so to "pursue advanced education on a full-time basis, professional careers outside of the media industry, opportunities at other media agencies, or for personal reasons." Company representatives note, "People who want to work in the media industry tend to stay here long-term."

ATTRITION

Only about 10 percent of Starcom newbies don't remain with the company through the end of the first year.

STARWOOD HOTELS AND RESORTS
Various Management Training and Other Entry-Level Positions

THE BIG PICTURE

Starwood Hotels and Resorts Worldwide, Inc., "one of the leading hotel and leisure companies in the world," is the proprietor of such world-famous facilities as St. Regis, the Luxury Collection, Sheraton, and Westin. Although a relative newcomer to the field, Starwood is a major player and has entry-level positions available in a broad range of areas, including the coveted and more competitive positions at corporate headquarters as well as on the front lines at Starwood's various hotels.

STATS

LOCATION(S) WHERE ENTRY-LEVEL EMPLOYEES WORK

Entry-level employees are hired to work almost anywhere. Starwood has more than 700 properties worldwide.

ENTRY-LEVEL POSITION(S) AVAILABLE

Line-level, supervisory, coordinator/administrative, assistant manager, and manager positions are available in the following departments: sales, accounting, guest services, catering/convention services, rooms, food and beverage, six sigma, and other corporate management positions in IT, legal, hotel management, real estate, and revenue management.

AVERAGE HOURS WORKED PER WEEK

People may work thirty-five, forty, and forty-seven and a half hours per week, depending on title, corporate/property, and union status.

AVERAGE STARTING SALARY

"[Salary] starts at $10 [per hour] for interns and goes up from there. [The] typical entry-level management [salary] is [from] $32,000–$36,000, depending on region and hotel. We have a very competitive compensation structure and continually compare our structure against our competitors and other industries."

BENEFITS OFFERED

Starwood offers all standard benefits, including medical, dental, and vision insurance. Additional benefits include paid vacation, discounted hotel rooms, tuition assistance, savings and retirement plans, business travel and accident insurance, [an] employee stock-purchase plan, long- and short-term disability insurance, [an] employee assistance program, adoption assistance, life insurance, and accidental death coverage.

Contact Information

Visit the website at www.starwoodcareer.com or e-mail collegerelations@starwoodhotels.com.

Getting Hired

"While Starwood has a centralized college relations program through which approximately thirty college graduates enter, college recruiting is not the primary way people join Starwood." For those seeking corporate jobs with Starwood, "a big plus is an early, demonstrated interest in the hotel and hospitality business through a hotel-school education—summer internships in hotels, resorts, and other customer-focused businesses." Hospitality, Starwood representatives note, "is very much a hands-on business, and we look for business professionals who also know how to work with customers, have a guest-service ethic, and know how to lead those who serve the guest." Because of the high demand for corporate jobs with Starwood, the company "only recruits for the small-management training and internship programs from a core group of ten hotel schools and, currently, two business schools. Students from other schools are encouraged to contact hotels local to their homes or schools to inquire about available internships [and entry-level positions] throughout the year." One successful hire reports, "I was explicit in my cover letter and stated that this was the job I wanted; it was my top choice, and if given an offer, I'd accept on the spot. I think this really helped my application." The hiring process for property positions is less formal; one accounts-payable employee who works at a hotel learned of the position through a college professor, sent her cover letter and resume, and underwent a "very laid-back, carefree" interview. No matter what position you're applying for, all respondents agree that your cover letter and resume are important.

Money and Perks

Starwood representatives advise, "The hospitality industry in general does not have the reputation for very high entry-level salaries, but, with time, it is known for great bonuses, the opportunity to work in different locations in the country (or world) throughout one's career, and the opportunity to be associated with a very old, yet also very exciting industry." The best fringe benefit, first jobbers here agree, are "the Starwood HotRates!!! Cheap five-star hotel rooms. I'd never be able to travel like this right out of college, but I stay at the top hotels in the world for next to nothing."

The Ropes

Participants in Starwood's corporate management training program go through a number of rotations, allowing them to learn all the different responsibilities within a certain area of the company. Company representatives explain, "The program is a twelve-week rotational training through all departments of the hotel with a concentration in one of three areas: food and beverage, rooms, or sales. At the completion of the program, each participant is placed in a position of responsibility at the same hotel where the management-training program was completed." The experience starts with "an informal orientation process. For me, it entailed one day of touring our hotels in New York, New York and a couple of days learning about how Starwood's systems work and what each group does within STARS [Starwood

Technology and Revenue Systems, the program in which this employee was enrolled]." The newbies we spoke with agree that "most of the real learning comes on the job." For positions at Starwood's properties, the orientation and training process is less prescribed and is specific to the position. For example, one such employee took classes on how her hotel "stands out from other [Starwood] properties." Another respondent took "classes pertaining to customer service and guest satisfaction, computer programs, [and] property management systems as well as brand standards."

DAY IN THE LIFE

Corporate management trainees agree that "the learning curve is pretty steep. You start right away on projects. A typical day includes some meetings, preparation for an upcoming presentation, and a dialogue with my boss around the issues that have come up and how we need to tackle them." Contact with Starwood higher-ups is fairly frequent; one employee in strategy explains, "We are always invited to meetings where we have done work to support the conclusions. We are encouraged to speak at meetings." Employees at Starwood properties seem less overwhelmed by their day-to-day tasks; for one employee in accounting, it is "pretty straight forward. I work from nine to five." A Whatever/Whenever agent—an aptly named position—agrees: "With each passing day, my resposibilities increase."

PEERS

The first jobbers we spoke with describe a pretty subdued peer network at Starwood. One person working at a hotel tells us, "We have special cocktail time within our property once [a] month; [this] allows us to interact with people from other departments, and we spend time together, like one hour, including lunch break. It all depends [on] what kind of event we go to, but generally three hours in a week." People at corporate headquarters tell us that "the groups here are pretty small. There's not really an after-work scene, since the main office is in White Plains and most of us live in the city. It becomes difficult to coordinate and motivate when we commute. But we get together for special events and whatnot."

MOVING ON

Starwood does not track data on former employees. People we spoke with still work at Starwood and plan to remain there. They tell us that those with complaints "sometimes have problems with their specific bosses" and "wish there would be a little more training at the beginning."

STATE FARM

Various Positions

THE BIG PICTURE

"Insurance and financial services are not glamorous professions, but they're stable, and both provide valuable services." It's the grown-up world in all its glory, and State Farm is one of the biggest players in the game.

STATS

LOCATION(S) WHERE ENTRY-LEVEL EMPLOYEES WORK

Entry-level hires work across the nation and in parts of Canada.

ENTRY-LEVEL POSITION(S) AVAILABLE

"State Farm has many positions that can be considered entry-level, but the most hiring activity occurs for positions in our claims and underwriting operations. In addition, we have a very large systems (information technology) department [in which] we hire many recent college graduates for entry-level positions."

AVERAGE HOURS WORKED PER WEEK

The hours vary widely by position.

AVERAGE STARTING SALARY

"Starting salaries can vary by the skill sets that a candidate brings to the position and by the geographical location of the job."

BENEFITS OFFERED

State Farm offers PPO and HMO plans, medical, dental insurance, and long-term disability. It also has a 401(k) program, employer-funded retirement plan, tuition reimbursement, professional education opportunities, Select-A-Gift (a holiday gift benefit), adoption assistance, LifeWorks (an employee assistance program), childcare assistance, and business casual dress.

CONTACT INFORMATION

"Visit the 'Careers' section on www.statefarm.com to submit your resume for a job or internship, to find out where we will be recruiting on campus, and to learn more about our benefits. Visit the 'Zone Offices' link in the 'About State Farm' section to find office addresses and phone numbers for the State Farm office nearest you."

Getting Hired

State Farm recruits on a number of college campuses; prospective employees may also search for job openings and post a resume via the Internet. Interviews are conducted in several stages. One successful applicant explains, "The tone of the first interview was professional, and it was directed with open-ended questions. Some of the questions that were presented are 'Tell me about yourself. Why do you want to work for State Farm?'" Those who clear this hurdle receive a second interview, generally with their prospective boss. One first jobber reports, "During the second interview, most of the questions asked were scenario questions, such as, 'What would you do if you had an angry policyholder?' or 'Describe a situation [in which] you resolved a conflict with a customer and what the outcome was.' When responding to those questions, I tried to answer them as clearly as possible and elaborate on the answer. When faced with a question of a situation I had never encountered, I was honest with the interviewer in saying that I had never been in such a situation, but I [also] answered the question hypothetically. Throughout both interviews, I showed confidence and advised both interviewers that I was in here for the long haul; I was interested in a career, not a position."

Money and Perks

First jobbers report that there's minimal room for salary negotiation from the outset. There are, however, opportunities to qualify for raises and incentives that can quickly increase one's earnings. Location is more negotiable, a benefit of the company's size and widespread presence. Newbies appreciate the generous benefits package, which includes "retirement [plans] and different paid absences [for such events] as personal family leave, doctor or dentist appointments, and sick leave among others." They also love the extracurriculars; one writes, "There are several clubs and sport groups that have been created for employees."

The Ropes

Training varies from job to job and from site to site at State Farm, with a few constants. New hires start with your standard orientation: They meet superiors, fill out paperwork, and learn about benefits, compensation, and corporate philosophy. The real training begins on the second day and continues for the first few months of an employee's tenure. One claims rep explains, "In training, we learned from the very basics of insurance terminology to the actual claim-handling process. We worked in a classroom setting, studying material on different subjects such as property and casualty, medical terms, auto inspections, legal concepts, etc.; we were then tested. We later learned to work the software used to handle claims. Later we learned hands-on by actually handling claims—the easier ones initially and progressing into the more complex ones, always with our trainer/boss by our side. The training lasted three full months. At the completion of those three months, we traveled to State Farm's headquarters offices in Bloomington, [Illinois], where we received two additional weeks of training. This trip made me connect with our home office and be even more proud of my company."

DAY IN THE LIFE

Daily life varies depending on the particular entry-level job. The four major entry-level positions are claim rep, which involves screening potential customers for risk level and working directly with State Farm agents; business analyst, which involves "serving as a liaison between business areas or the IT department"; and systems analyst, which focuses on the technical aspects of State Farm's business. Training in all areas is extensive, and first jobbers happily report that "State Farm promotes a good work-life balance. Employees are encouraged to be open about their workload and be honest if they are feeling overwhelmed. I have had to turn assignments down before because of my workload. I was never reprimanded when I had to do this."

PEERS

"The culture here is employee-oriented," first jobbers tell us, noting that "flexible work schedules are available, it is business casual dress, and surrounding stores and restaurants have discounts for State Farm employees. The list goes on." The peer network is strong, "and it doesn't only include the under-twenty-five and first-jobbers. Almost all come out to happy hours and other events."

MOVING ON

According to company data, "The top five reasons for departures from State Farm are 'another opportunity,' 'retirement,' 'employment agreement expired' (this is when someone is hired temporarily for a specified period of time), 'returned to school,' and 'no reason given.'" State Farm does not track first jobbers independently of other employees, but notes that "recent data shows that voluntary turnover at State Farm is lower than the industry average."

ATTRITION

"For the most part, people at State Farm are very happy and proud to work for the company," explains one first jobber, adding that "clear evidence of this is the longevity of most employees at State Farm. It is not unusual to see people [who] have been working for the company for thirty to thirty-five years. In my opinion, that says a lot." Those who bail out sometimes do so "because they do not like the current position they are in. I do not think that they are unhappy with the company itself." The same employee adds that "State Farm is an excellent company because they provide ways for employees to move within the company. If a person is unhappy with [his or her] current position, I believe that [he or she has] opportunities to improve on this if [he or she wants] to take action."

BEST AND WORST

State Farm tells us that "successful candidates vary in skills and competencies. We look for individuals who are good at what they do and want to continue to develop. In positions dealing directly with our policyholders, people who want to help others and care about providing quality service do the best. An interest in learning about our industry (insurance and financial services) is important as well." Poor employees demonstrate "an inability to be flexible and lack of desire to learn and grow."

State Street
Entry-level Accounting and Portfolio Administration

The Big Picture

State Street, a leader in the financial services industry, hires scores upon scores of college grads every year. The pay is relatively low, but the work is challenging, the learning opportunities numerous, and the chances for advancement even more so. A solid benefits package further sweetens the deal.

Stats

Location(s) Where Entry-level Employees Work

"State Street is a global organization, and we have entry-level opportunities at most of our twenty-five offices worldwide. The largest percentages are currently within our corporate headquarters in Boston, Massachusetts and its environs. Additionally, there are entry-level opportunities in our other State Street locations, including some of our European locations."

Average Number of Applications Each Year

State Street receives 3,000–4,000 applications each year.

Average Number Hired Per Year

State Street hires 1,000 entry-level employees each year.

Entry-level Position(s) Available

The majority of entry-level hires at State Street take positions as portfolio administrators, portfolio accountants, and mutual fund accountants. Other entry-level positions are also available in specialized areas across the organization.

Average Hours Worked Per Week

New hires work 36.25 hours per week, with some overtime.

Average starting salary

Entry-level employees earn salaries in the low $30,000s.

Benefits offered

State Street offers seven medical and two dental plans to choose from. Employees also receive vision care and may take advantage of flexible medical spending accounts. Additional benefits include life insurance, long-term disability, pre-tax transportation accounts, salary savings program, a 401(k) program, retirement plan, generous vacation, educational assistance, adoption assistance, and work/life programs.

Contact Information

Visit State Street on the Web at www.statestreet.com.

GETTING HIRED

State Street posts job openings on various posting websites worldwide, at colleges across the nation, and on its own website. Many of the first jobbers we contacted found their positions through these resources. The firm also "has a strong campus-recruiting program at a diverse population of schools across the nation" and "[gives] consideration to all applications, whether [they're] from a target school or outside of our current list of schools." Ideal candidates are "hard working, customer-focused, determined, engaging, creative team players with global knowledge, [who demonstrate] integrity and strong computer skills." Interviewers look for "an understanding of what the candidate knows about State Street and why he/she would be a [good] fit for the organization and the position. We also ask what the candidate is looking for in his/her next job to see if it fits what we look for here. We ask about skills and interests, as well as experience." One successful hire recounts her experiences: "I was contacted for a phone interview/screening approximately three weeks after I submitted my online application and cover letter. At that point I scheduled my interview, which took place in Quincy, Massachusetts. I had two interviews (with current managers), both of which involved a set group of questions. Most of the questions were stated in the following way: 'Tell me about a time where you. . . .' It was up to me to fit in as many of my own experiences and qualifications without going through my resume piece by piece. I tried not to talk about only my job experiences, but my leadership ones as well."

MONEY AND PERKS

"Salary is not negotiable" at State Street, fresh hires tell us; but there "can be some flexibility about start date." Entry-level employees are not eligible for bonuses, though they become eligible for them as they move up the hierarchy. They *are* eligible for performance-based pay raises, promotions, and overtime pay. Of the many perks offered, first jobbers praise the 401(k) package and the tuition reimbursement program; of the latter, one writes, "I am currently working on my MBA, and State Street recently created an alliance with Suffolk University so that they pay for my class upfront. I do not have to wait until the course is over to get reimbursed."

THE ROPES

New fund accountants, portfolio accountants, and portfolio administrators at State Street all undergo extensive "required training programs prior to going on the floor/to the business unit for [which] they are hired. The program is an overview of State Street: who we are in the industry and what our role is in the market." The program also gives new hires "a place to learn our proprietary system and understand both the basics of the job and how to apply these basics in a real life environment. It is also builds a foundation so [that] when the new hire is on the floor, he or she can much more easily adapt to the position." One portfolio administrator reports, "Training was a several weeks-long process. It was done in a classroom environment, and it included quizzes and homework. There was a great deal of group work; we also had many simulations in which we were able to work through typical requests/procedures ourselves. We were graded on our ability to meet deadlines and perform with accuracy."

Day in the Life

State Street hires the majority of its first jobbers in three positions: mutual fund accountant, portfolio accountant, and portfolio administrator. Accountants spend their days occupied with such "daily processing" chores as "reviewing ledger accounts, verifying financial statements, and delivering monthly pricing reports." As their expertise increases, their duties expand to include "auditing the work of coworkers, taking on *ad hoc* requests, taking on additional projects and reporting, and training new employees." Portfolio administrators are "responsible for the daily processing of all cash and securities transactions to a series of mutual fund accounts. This includes: forecasting cash flow to the client, monitoring the physical movement of securities purchased and sold, and posting all portfolio and shareholder activity onto State Street's mainframe accounting system. Weekly and monthly reporting is also required."

Peers

State Street hires lots of people fresh out of college. One first jobber explains, "That is one of the great things about this company when you are coming right out of college: There are a lot of young people working there, and it [presents] a great opportunity to make new friends. The nature of the job allows a lot of bonding. Everyone goes to lunch at the same time, and the entry-levels, the seniors, and some of the managers tend to stick together." The initial training program provides an instant common bond for those starting here. As time goes on workers enjoy "a definite after-hours scene, [though] it depends some on the office that you work out of. I think those located in Boston tend to go out after work a lot more than the Quincy workers."

Moving On

Those who are unhappy at State Street grumble about the relatively low starting salaries and heavy workloads. One first jobber acknowledges, "Many of State Street's competitors who have local offices pay better." What grousers fail to realize, according to their more sanguine peers, is that "this job is a great steppingstone to a successful future. State Street is a huge company with tons of room for growth, both professionally and monetarily. The career path at State Street is endless." One newbie writes, "State Street probably offers more opportunity to move up and expand your knowledge than our competitors do."

TARGET CORPORATION
Various Positions

THE BIG PICTURE

Although most of the country regards Target as "the new kid on the block"—especially in relation to its downscale rival Wal-Mart—this giant discount department store chain has been in existence since 1962. The company traces its roots back even further, to the Dayton Dry Goods Company, founded in 1903. Throughout its history, Target has earned a solid reputation both for contributing to its host communities and for creating a hospitable work environment for its employees.

STATS

LOCATION(S) WHERE ENTRY-LEVEL EMPLOYEES WORK

Corporate hires work in Minneapolis, Minnesota; the company has stores in many cities.

AVERAGE NUMBER HIRED PER YEAR OVER THE LAST TEN YEARS

Target employs more than 273,000 people in forty-seven states.

ENTRY-LEVEL POSITION(S) AVAILABLE

Target offers entry-level positions in all areas of the company.

BENEFITS OFFERED

"[Benefits include] dollar-for-dollar (up to 5 percent of your salary) matching of our 401(k); company discount at all stores; savings on prescriptions; and flexible work schedules. Target has specific benefits programs, but they share a focus on flexibility, family, and financial security."

CONTACT INFORMATION

Apply online at www.target.com.

GETTING HIRED

Target employees caution that "Target considers only resumes that are submitted to www.target.com and www.monster.com online; there's a Team-Member Referral program, but anyone referred to the company through a current employee still has to apply online." An exception is made for people who are recruited at campus events; students must submit resumes directly to the campus career center; you can learn more about these events at the Target website. The interview process "is the same style used by many other employers. First, there is a phone interview [conducted] by a human resources recruiter, then a formal interview with the human resources recruiter; afterward applicants have an interview with two of the people who would be managing [them], followed by an informal meeting with the national head of [their] department. The tone of the interviews are serious but friendly." One particular applicant "was asked job-related questions, such as 'Describe your past job experience. Why do you think you are right for this position?' Other questions that were also asked were geared toward finding out about my personality." One first jobber notes, "One thing about Target—the company places a very high value on education. No matter how well you do your job, if you don't have a college degree, you will only go so far in the company. Many people want to advance but can't because they didn't go to college. Although many entry-level jobs seem mundane to someone with a college degree, you have to start somewhere—and you'll move up if you stick it out, demonstrate a work ethic, and have a degree." Target seeks "a diverse workforce to reflect the communities we serve."

Money and Perks

Most of the terms of employment at Target are negotiable, first jobbers tell us; as in all such cases, the more you bring to the table—and the less competition there is for jobs (such as when the economy is strong)—the better chance you have of negotiating a higher starting salary. As employees move forward, "It's hard to get a pay increase at any time other than at annual reviews. We're reviewed twice a year—the annual is in March."

The Ropes

All Target employees start their tenure with the company with a half-day orientation class. One first jobber writes, entry-level employees find out "a lot about Target, what is acceptable (protocol, etc). A lot was geared toward harassment, benefits of Target, what they're trying to do to improve Target, and its history." In many areas of the company, subsequent training is handled by fellow employees on a "need to know" basis. One newbie explains, "My training was conducted by the three individuals [who] I work directly with. Since my position was open, they all helped to train me on the procedures, day-to-day activities, [and] all of the technical equipment that I would be working with." Some formal classes in technical areas, such as computers, are required of new workers in certain areas; these classes constitute part of the employee's formal work day.

Day in the Life

First jobbers work in all areas of the giant Target world. We spoke with first jobbers in many different departments doing a wide variety of jobs. All of them say that they quickly assumed important responsibilities and that they felt their managers and bosses offered them sufficient support to get their jobs done. According to company representatives, workers benefit from "a fun and challenging work environment," one that rewards "performance-driven risk takers."

PEERS

Of the entry-level employees in several different areas and functionalities at Target, all of them agree that at Target "people are really friendly. The company is full of young twenty-somethings." One writes, "We do things outside of work. We're going bowling tonight, for example." Another notes, "All of us get along and do happy hours regularly. Target has several touch football teams in the fall and baseball teams in the summer." Many do volunteer work together as well; one newbie reports, "Target does a *ton* for the community. I volunteer once a week at a local school, just reading to kids. There are always ways to get involved in the community, and that's been a good way to meet Target people who aren't in my department (and to get out of the office for awhile to do something helpful and fun)."

TEACH FOR AMERICA
Corps Member/Teacher

THE BIG PICTURE

Teach For America's mission is to build the movement to end education inequity. They recruit outstanding recent college graduates of all academic majors to commit two years to teach in urban and rural public schools and to become lifelong leaders in the effort to expand educational opportunity. If you're looking for an opportunity to make an immediate impact and assume a leadership role right after college, then Teach For America may be for you. As one Teach For America alum says, "I knew that this was going to be the toughest job I could imagine, but boy am I glad I did it. [It was the] best first job I could have hoped for."

STATS

LOCATION(S) WHERE ENTRY-LEVEL EMPLOYEES WORK

Teach For America members teach in twenty-two urban and rural areas where they are needed most: Atlanta, Georgia; Baltimore, Maryland; Bay Area, California; Charlotte, North Carolina; Chicago, Illinois; Houston, Texas; Las Vegas Valley, Nevada; Los Angeles, California; South Louisiana; Miami–Dade, Florida; Mississippi Delta; New Jersey; New Mexico/Navajo Reservation; Greater New Orleans, Louisiana; New York, New York; Eastern North Carolina; Philadelphia, Pennsylvania; Phoenix, Arizona; Rio Grande Valley, Texas; St. Louis, Missouri; South Dakota; and Washington, DC.

AVERAGE NUMBER OF APPLICATIONS EACH YEAR

The organization received 17,000 applications for the 2005 corps, and officials report that "over the last few years, applications for Teach For America have increased dramatically."

AVERAGE NUMBER HIRED PER YEAR OVER THE LAST TEN YEARS

Teach For America has an alumni force of more than 10,000 strong, in addition to the 3,500 corps members in the midst of their two-year commitments. The organization anticipates placing a corps of 2,800 new teachers in the fall of 2006.

ENTRY-LEVEL POSITION(S) AVAILABLE

New hires work as corps members/teachers (available to recent college graduates).

AVERAGE HOURS WORKED PER WEEK

"In addition to the [more than] forty hours a week [that] corps members spend [in the classroom], they spend extra hours on the weekend and at nighttime preparing lesson plans, tutoring students, and/or attending graduate school."

PERCENTAGE OF ENTRY-LEVEL HIRES STILL WITH THE ORGANIZATION AFTER THREE, FIVE, AND TEN YEARS

All Teach For America corps members become alumni after completing their two-year commitment. Sixty-three percent of alumni work or study full-time in education.

AVERAGE STARTING SALARY

Salary depends on the school district for which the corps member works. "Average salaries range from $25,000–$44,000, depending on the region."

BENEFITS OFFERED

Benefits also vary by region; "however, corps members generally receive the same health benefits and insurance as other beginning teachers." Additional benefits include summer training institute room and board paid for by Teach For America and financial aid packages that range from $1,000–$5,000, based on demonstrated need and the cost of living in an applicant's assigned region. "Teach For America is currently a member of AmeriCorps. Through this relationship, corps members are eligible to receive forbearance and interest payment on qualified student loans during their two-year commitments. Those who have not previously received AmeriCorps awards receive an education award of $4,725 at the end of each year of service. These benefits are contingent on membership renewal."

CONTACT INFORMATION

To learn more and apply to the corps, visit www.teachforamerica.org or e-mail admissions@teachforamerica.org. If you are interested in working on Teach For America's staff, e-mail staffing@teachforamerica.org.

GETTING HIRED

Teach For America accepts applications through its website, www.teachforamerica.org. Once the selection committee has reviewed the initial application, it "invites the most promising applicants to participate in a day-long interview, which includes a sample teaching lesson, a group discussion, and a personal interview." One corps member advises, "The interview process is intense and time consuming. Once you have been asked to interview with Teach For America, you are required to create a five-minute lesson [plan] that you must teach to fellow applicants; this lesson is subject to their questions and critiques. There are also many roundtable discussions during the day of your interview." The final interview is conducted one-on-one by a Teach For America staffer. One program participant recounts, "I have heard horror stories about people being grilled; this wasn't, however, my experience. The staff is looking for people who will ultimately persevere in difficult situations, and they want to make sure that each applicant will before supporting his or her application."

MONEY AND PERKS

Teach For America corps members "are paid directly by the school districts for which they work, [so] salaries and salary increases vary by school district." Corps members tell us that salary and start time were "not really negotiable. Maybe subject area [was]. Most folks knew this going in and were up for it." As for placement, "You are able to suggest where you would like to be placed in the country. Teach For America does consider your preferences. However, they must also adhere to the needs and requirements of the various districts." Fringe benefits are mostly nonmaterial and include "sleeping well at night knowing that you're making life a little more bearable for your students" and "the smile that the students would give me every morning as they greeted me, the gleam of understanding in a students' eyes when they 'get it,' the look of pride in parents' eyes when seeing their child's accomplishments, the energy and motivation in the classroom when all students are involved in their learning, the satisfaction of making difference in these children's lives—take your pick!"

THE ROPES

Training for Teach For America corps members is rigorous. One teacher writes, "We go through what is called 'institute,'" a five-week training held in several sites across the country. This intense training program is designed to create teachers out of recent college graduates. One newly-minted teacher praises, "It was a wonderful way to realize that we were all integral parts of a national corps and also a way to get a great deal of training in a relatively short amount of time." According to organization representatives, "A typical day of our training institute is full of activities designed to help corps members progress quickly as teachers. In the morning and early afternoons of the institute, corps members teach in a summer school program. In the afternoons and evenings, they participate in a full schedule of discussions, workshops, and other professional development activities with a faculty of exceptional corps members, alumni, and other experienced educators." The final stage of training is called "induction," during which "corps members learn about local, historical, social, and political dynamics that may have an impact on their students' academic experience and their schools' culture." As one Louisiana corps member explains, it means immersion in "Zydeco music, food, schools, students, teachers, neighborhoods, and parents of students."

DAY IN THE LIFE

Teach For America corps members are teachers; and like most teachers, they work long, difficult hours. Their responsibilities and tasks vary according to grade, subject, and students' level of ability. One Teach For America corps member described a typical day this way: "I would get to school at 6:30 A.M. to start school at 7:08 A.M. I would prepare my classroom during my off-hour first period for the day, organizing lesson materials and arranging the seats according to the activity. I would teach for the next five periods with a thirty-minute lunch break in between (eating with a coteacher and two faithful lunchtime students). During the seventh hour I would reorganize my room from the day's events, take a ten-minute break, and begin to prepare for the next day. I got into the habit of not leaving my classroom until all work was completed; I would be there late into the evening on many occasions." The goal is "to attain significant academic gains for students," a challenge even under the best of circumstances and doubly tough in the schools that typically hire corps members.

PEERS

"There is a great deal of camaraderie among [Teach For America corps members]," participants in the program tell us. "The support received from the corps member down the hall who taught the same students I did, my roommate, and corps neighbors was critical to my success." Another explains, "I met some of the most intelligent, passionate, innovative, socially conscious, motivated, empathetic, and just amazing people while in Teach For America. It was refreshing to find people [who] can talk about the state of education in our country on a Friday night and not feel like dorks!"

MOVING ON

Teach For America representatives report, "Approximately 60 percent of our alumni remain in education beyond their two-year commitment, while 40 percent go on to other fields such as law, business, medicine, and politics. Teach For America's Office of Career and Civic Opportunities works with organizations, government entities, and corporations to connect alumni with professional and civic opportunities. Additionally, we develop partnerships with graduate schools to offer benefits—ranging from fellowships, course credit, and waived application fees—to our alumni who are accepted into their programs." A typical graduate of the program said, "I fulfilled my commitment and discovered that my future was with education. I found I had a passion for teaching mathematics and was appalled with the number of teachers and students that I found had deep-rooted 'math phobia.' Thus, I just completed my master's of science in mathematics education and have started a PhD program in the hopes of becoming a professor. My intention is that in being a professor [I will help] future elementary teachers love to teach math."

ATTRITION

According to the organization, "Between 85 and 90 percent of Teach For America corps members complete their two-year commitment." The others leave because of personal circumstances or, according to one corps member, because "teaching can be tough and isn't for everyone. People tend to sometimes feel isolated and overwhelmed and not take full advantage of the network available to them." Another corps member adds, "Some of the locations and schools that Teach For America places corps members in are really difficult schools."

Teach in Virginia
Teacher

The Big Picture

Teach in Virginia (TIV) is one of many state- and city-wide programs across the country that "recruit candidates to teach in various K–12 positions." Teach in Virginia hires end up in one of more than "sixty partner school divisions throughout the Commonwealth of Virginia." The program "specifically recruits candidates in the critical need subject areas of math, science, and special education."

Stats

Location(s) Where Entry-level Employees Work

Entry-level employees teach in schools across the state of Virginia.

Average Number of Applications Each Year

Teach in Virginia receives 2,000 applications each year.

Average Number Hired Per Year

The program hires 110 teachers each year.

Entry-level Position(s) Available

Workers are hired as teachers.

Average Hours Worked Per Week

Teachers work fifty to sixty hours per week.

Average Starting Salary

"The starting salary for Teach in Virginia varies by partner school division and [by] their regional presence in the state. The average starting salary for a first-year teacher in our partner school divisions is $33,500 annually."

Benefits Offered

Teachers in the program enjoy a choice among a variety of health insurance and prescription drug plans. In addition, "many of our partner school divisions offer tuition reimbursement and [other such] opportunities for professional development."

CONTACT INFORMATION

Teach in Virginia
101 North 14th Street, 24th Floor
Richmond, VA 23219
Tel: 804-225-4544
Fax: 703-991-2622
E-mail: info@teachinvirginia.org
www.teachinvirginia.org

GETTING HIRED

Teach in Virginia "recruits at colleges and universities across Virginia and in the Southeast;" but program managers note that "students from all colleges and universities across the country are encouraged to apply to the program online." All applicants to the program "must submit one online application that includes a resume and personal statement explaining their interest in teaching." One successful hire reports, "I think the personal statement was an incredibly important part of the application." Applicants "indicate up to three regions of interest [within] the state on their applications. These are used to determine what partner school divisions will be able to view their materials once the applicant has been accepted into the program. Applicants are notified of their status within two weeks," typically by e-mail. If selected into the program, "applicants must register for state tests in order to be referred to partner school divisions. These school divisions then contact and interview candidates for their individual vacancies." The local schools "make all hiring decisions. Candidates are required to interview with human resources personnel and principals before receiving an offer from a school." The ideal candidate "has demonstrated excellence in previous academic endeavors and community involvement." TIV "does not require prior teaching experience, but we look for candidates who want to help strengthen hard-to-staff schools across Virginia. We want candidates who are committed to having a positive impact on student achievement."

MONEY AND PERKS

Salaries and benefits for Virginia teachers are determined by local school districts. The website notes, "Beginning salary will vary based on experience, the specific teaching placement, and the pay scale of the individual division. Starting salaries for our partner school divisions ranged from $26,000–$35,000 for the 2003–2004 school year; however, teachers may have the opportunity to earn more money depending on their level of education and experience. Moreover, some school divisions also offer teachers the ability to augment their salaries by teaching summer courses, coaching, and the like." Some school systems offer bonuses "for teaching in specific subject areas or schools." Raises "are awarded by partner school divisions annually. [These are] based on post-graduate coursework, additional subject certification, and years of experience in the classroom."

Among the best perks of the job: "Most partner school divisions offer tuition reimbursement opportunities for candidates who want to pursue further coursework. Many school divisions coordinate this coursework for candidates within their divisions for easy access." Also attractive to newly-minted college grads are the "many different opportunities for loan forgiveness or deferment [that are] available to teachers in low-income schools or in critical-shortage subject areas, as determined by the Virginia Department of Education."

THE ROPES

The organization does not run its own orientation program; rather, candidates are trained at the school-division level. It reports that "most school divisions have an additional orientation for first-year teachers. Divisions typically conduct their orientations in late August, and [orientation] usually lasts around two weeks. Candidates can expect professional development from the division level and a chance to get acclimated with trainings in their individual school." Unlicensed teachers have three years to complete mandatory professional training and earn a license; this process typically requires them to attend evening classes at an accredited teachers college.

DAY IN THE LIFE

TIV teachers must fulfill all of "the responsibilities of a classroom teacher." According to the TIV website, "There is no definition of a teacher's 'typical' day in any one of our schools or districts, but a general outline would be as follows: School days are roughly six to seven hours long. A typical schedule is 8:00 A.M. to 3:00 P.M., but there is some variation among schools. Teachers also spend a significant time outside of the classroom preparing lessons and grading schoolwork. A teacher's job is incredibly intense, regardless of his or her background or preparation; new teachers should be prepared to work long hours." To assist them in their demanding tasks, "Divisions are required to assign mentors to first-year teachers, and the assignment is typically based on subject and location. Candidates can expect to be assigned mentors within their schools who can help with the first-year transition. Divisions usually pick motivated, master teachers to help guide first-year teachers."

PEERS

Teach in Virginia attracts both recent college grads and more experienced adults who are exploring new careers.

BEST AND WORST

TIV "measures the success of teacher candidates [in terms of] the academic gains made by their students. Generally our most successful new teachers are ones who realize that they will not start off knowing everything and must constantly refine their skills to meet the changing needs of their students. One of our most successful teachers from last year had to completely adjust his approach to teaching after being hired in a magnet school that employed an open-classroom system. The environment was different than anything he had been prepared for; yet he took full advantage of the training seminars and mentor program offered by his school and became an active member of the school community. He created a website and newsletter to help parents become more aware and involved in the learning process and has sought out community volunteers to enhance several of his classroom activities."

Unsuccessful teachers are those who "see teaching as job from eight in the morning to three in the afternoon. When they encounter difficulty with a student, they do not proactively research alternative techniques, but rather teach only to the students that show interest. If they continue to experience difficulty with other students, they assume it is a consequence of the environment without making any attempt to alter the environment."

TeachGSU
Teacher

The Big Picture

TeachGSU, a "selective teacher certification program based at Grambling State University (GSU) in Grambling, Louisiana," offers aspiring teachers the opportunity "to pursue certification in the high-needs area of special education (grades one through twelve) or elementary education (grades one through five)." First jobbers here "choose to teach in one of our partner school districts, including Caddo Parish school district located in Shreveport, Louisiana."

Stats

Location(s) Where Entry-level Employees Work

Entry-level employees work in Northern Louisiana.

Average Number of Applications Each Year

TeachGSU receives about 115 applications each year.

Average Number Hired Per Year

TeachGSU hires about twenty-five new teachers each year.

Entry-level Position(s) Available

Workers are hired as teachers.

Average Hours Worked Per Week

Teachers work about fifty hours per week.

Average Starting Salary

Average starting salaries range from $27,700–$31,500.

Benefits Offered

"As employees of one of TeachGSU's partner school districts, participants are eligible for the same comprehensive benefits [that] all teachers receive; [these include] health and dental plans." Beyond those benefits, "accepted TeachGSU applicants are [also] eligible for signing bonuses with several of our school districts. Many school districts also will reimburse teachers for the costs of their coursework and the fees for the required exams. New teachers are also encouraged to apply for financial aid through the university."

Contact Information

Find job postings at: www.teachgsu.org. You may also contact the program office by phone at 318-274-2785 or by e-mail at teachgsu@gram.edu.

Getting Hired

Applicants to the TeachGSU program "must complete a program application and submit a resume, a personal statement, and four copies of official college transcripts. Applicants who submit a complete application will be notified within two weeks [after receipt] of their application status. If granted an interview, candidates come to the Grambling State University campus at a scheduled date and time. After the interview, candidates are notified of their status within two weeks. Selected candidates will be required to submit passing scores on the Praxis I and Praxis II tests before enrolling in summer coursework."

For the interview, the program "asks all applicants to prepare and teach a five-minute lesson on a topic of their choice. This helps us understand how the candidate conveys knowledge, puts together a coherent lesson, and delivers it to an audience. During the interview day, candidates also participate in a discussion group, [have] a thirty-minute personal interview, and prepare a written response." Ideal candidates "are ready to enter the classroom and succeed," though they "do not need previous education experience. We look for candidates with a strong record of achievement, dedication, and a desire to [have a positive] impact [on the] community's students."

Money and Perks

For TeachGSU teachers, all aspects of pay—salary, raises, and benefits—are determined by the employing school district. According to TeachGSU, "Bonuses (presented by the school district, not by the TeachGSU office) may be offered for teaching in specific subject areas or schools." Teachers tell us that the best perk of the job is "knowing that I am making a difference in a child's life."

The Ropes

The TeachGSU experience begins with a six-week session in June, during which teachers begin their certification coursework. During this period, "candidates are enrolled in GSU's College of Education. Candidates are divided into cohorts, either special education or elementary. The summer classes are incredibly demanding, but they prepare candidates to be excellent teachers. Courses typically run from 8:00 A.M. to 5:00 P.M. Participants are taught by experienced staff [who are] dedicated to positioning [them] for success." Training continues throughout the school year "through weekly meetings and visits by the teachers' supervisors." During the school year, teachers must also take courses leading toward permanent certification.

Day in the Life

TeachGSU instructors have the same responsibilities as do all full-time teachers in Louisiana. The organization informs us that "raising student achievement is the main responsibility [of] all selected participants. Our teachers are accountable to the principal and school district for executing all [of the] tasks needed to run an effective classroom." Teaching special education, as many TeachGSU teachers do, means "providing for the individual needs of each student;" this includes adhering to the student's Individualized Education Plan (IEP). According to the TeachGSU website, IEPs "are powerful tools for planning and managing student instruction, but they also involve extensive documentation. Paperwork is a constant across all special education positions and should be considered as you entertain working in this area."

TeachGSU teachers receive a temporary Practitioner Teacher License (renewable for a maximum of three years) that "stipulates that the individual must be enrolled in an alternative certification program, meet all program requirements, and be employed by a Louisiana school district in the area of certification being pursued." Thus, teachers must take classes toward their certification in the evenings. The organization cautions that "the first year of teaching is challenging for any new teacher, [and] participants should anticipate [expending] an intense effort, especially at the beginning of the year."

PEERS

TeachGSU teachers convene for a summer training program, an experience that not only provides invaluable preparation for the job, but also creates an instant network of peers. Teachers continue their certification training throughout the school year, so even though they may be assigned to different schools during the day, they still see one another regularly during evening classes. The organization explains, "Since our program recruits midcareer professionals as well as recent graduates, most participants are entering the classroom for the first time, and have the advantage of entering as a [member of a] cohort. The compact, intense nature of our program helps build lasting relationships [among] program participants." The result is a group of "great friends who help [one another] a lot" and "spend a lot of time together."

MOVING ON

TeachGSU first jobbers who decide to leave the program most often cite "personal reasons and challenges in the classroom." The program's goal is for teachers "to remain in the classroom far into the future."

BEST AND WORST

Administrators at TeachGSU explain that great teachers are "accountable for both themselves and their students. They seek out all available resources to ensure [that] their students are fully reaching their potential. They are not deterred by challenges, but [rather] accept them with a positive sense of perspective. A successful teacher has clear, demanding goals, and has a well-developed plan for achieving them. An excellent teacher also seeks feedback and employs this feedback to improve [personal] performance."

Poor teachers are those who "do not listen to feedback. They are consistently unprepared or under-prepared. They are unwilling to accept responsibility for their performance. They do not put forth an effort to establish meaningful relationships with their students. An unsuccessful teacher would not be flexible and does not see the potential in all students."

TeachPinellas
Teacher

The Big Picture

TeachPinellas "is a program of Pinellas County Schools" designed to hire teachers in high-need disciplines and at high-need schools. Participants "teach at the secondary level in shortage subject areas, such as special education, math, science, and English." The inaugural year of the program was 2005–2006.

Stats

Location(s) Where Entry-level Employees Work

Entry-level employees work in Pinellas County, Florida (the St. Petersburg/Clearwater area near Tampa Bay).

Average Number of Applications Each Year

The program receives 455 applications each year.

Average Number Hired Per Year

In the inaugural year, TeachPinellas sought to hire between thirty and sixty new teachers. In 2006–2007, its goal is to hire sixty to eighty new teachers.

Entry-level Position(s) Available

Workers are hired as teachers.

Average Hours Worked Per Week

Teachers work about fifty to sixty hours per week.

Average Starting Salary

The average base pay is $34,000; "other salary increases are made based on highest degree earned and years of experience."

Benefits Offered

Teachers have a choice of health insurance plans, as well as dental, prescription, and vision coverage that vest after sixty days of employment.

Additional benefits include a pension, 401(k) plan, and optional 403(b) plan. In addition, "participants are provided with a three- to five-week training free of cost. Upon completion [of the training], they are given a stipend of approximately $840."

TeachPinellas

301 4th Street, SW

Largo, FL 33770

Tel: 727-588-6259

Fax: 727-588-5174

E-Mail: info@teachpinellas.org.

www.TeachPinellas.org

GETTING HIRED

TeachPinellas "actively recruits at Florida colleges and universities" and also "accepts applications from all colleges and universities." Prospective teachers "must complete and submit an online application" that includes a resume and a personal statement. Candidates granted an interview can schedule that interview using an online scheduler. "After the interview, candidates will be notified of their status within two months. At this time, selected candidates will be supplied with an enrollment package." Acceptance is also contingent on passing two Florida Teacher Certification Tests: one in general knowledge and one in the relevant subject area.

One successful hire reports, "The tone of my interview was calm, and [it] flowed nicely. They asked me scenario questions specifically relating to my job as a teacher. Questions included, 'How would you handle an upset parent who comes in your classroom while you are teaching and is threatening you and saying that she thinks that you haven't been fair to her child?' Other questions included 'What are your strengths?' 'Describe an experience in your previous job that has been personally rewarding.' 'Describe a time when what you were doing wasn't working in your job. How did you handle the situation?' I waited two weeks and then I got an e-mail from my Teach Pinellas director, followed by a letter in the mail, stating that I had been selected for the Teach Pinellas Program. Shortly after returning my acceptance into the program, I was invited to an information/orientation [session]. The Teach Pinellas director welcomed all of us and gave us [the] textbooks that we would be using in our two-week Teach Pinellas Institute."

MONEY AND PERKS

"All raises and compensation issues for all teachers in the district are governed by the collective bargaining agreement in place between the district and the teachers union," TeachPinellas reports, noting that "in general, teachers are given raises based on years of experience." Teachers explain that "the job is negotiable in that you can select your placement if you are recommended by more than one school." Teachers "placed in a St. Petersburg school who are interested in living in the city of St. Petersburg are eligible for a grant of up to $14,000 for a down payment," and such teachers "must commit to teaching in St. Petersburg for five years." According to teachers, the best perk of the job is "seeing students progress in their work. The job is personally rewarding."

THE ROPES

TeachPinellas trains new teachers twice a year. One cohort of teachers starts training in June to begin teaching in August; a second cohort trains in November to begin teaching in January. Training "is led by a group of veteran teachers who focus on teaching strategies, behavior management, rules and procedures, lesson planning, and emphasizing diversity in the classroom. Whenever possible, teachers also have a school experience at which they observe a cooperating teacher as well as deliver instruction."

Subsequent training occurs at the district level; one special education teacher writes, "I was invited to our school district's week-long training, which [occurred] a week before school started. It was called 'Beach Camp.' During this week, I attended mandatory trainings in my subject area. I found this to be very informative. I also took training in classroom management and learning through movement, [a session led] by a veteran gym teacher. Additionally, I took two additional [reading and writing] trainings during pre-school. Teachers must also take courses leading toward permanent certification during the school year."

DAY IN THE LIFE

TeachPinellas newbies are entrusted with all of "the responsibilities of a classroom teacher: specifically, to ensure that all students are achieving at the desired levels for their grade and skill level and to complete any additional school requirements set by the principal or district (e.g., attending all staff meetings, participating in committees, preparing lesson plans)." A special education teacher writes, "My daily tasks include creating substitute plans, organizing my classroom, attending faculty and department meetings, creating weekly lesson plans, and creating rules, consequences, policies, and procedures for my classroom. In addition, I was assigned a certain number of students to my caseload. I sometimes feel overwhelmed and in over my head with the paperwork required for my students' IEPs (Individualized Education Plans). There never seems to be enough time in the day to do what I need to do." Fortunately, all new teachers in Pinellas county are assigned a mentor who "visits first-year teachers and focuses on providing the support they need to be successful in the classroom. For struggling teachers, Pinellas County Schools also offers a Professional Development Improvement Network (PDIN). The PDIN program provides additional mentors to those teachers who would benefit from short-term assistance and support."

PEERS

First-time teachers in Pinellas County tell us that their peers are "very thoughtful, very friendly, and very helpful. They would leave notes in my box to say 'Hello' and to wish me a nice day at school." There isn't much socializing (there isn't time!), though schedules grow more flexible and free time more abundant as the school year progresses.

Moving on

TeachPinellas is a relatively new and small program; to date, relatively few teachers have left it. Those who do leave, we're told, "cite personal reasons (e.g., moving from the city) as well as the challenges at their school placement." The program anticipates that its recruits "will become department and school leaders, seek out additional roles and responsibilities within their schools and the district, and may even apply to be school principals."

Best and Worst

Great teachers, according to the folks at TeachPinellas, are "resourceful" and "proactively seek out support and feedback." They "take steps toward building relationships with colleagues and the broader community" and "overcome challenges by tapping into resources, as well as [implementing] a variety of teaching strategies. They are focused on raising student achievement for all students."

Poor teachers are "rigid" and "unable to ask for help." They "do not provide students with meaningful work assignments, but rather hand out worksheets and 'busy work.'" They fail "to assess students properly in order to meet their individual needs," "do not plan adequately, do not take steps to improve instruction," and "do not focus on raising student achievement."

TEXAS TEACHING FELLOWS
Teaching Fellow

THE BIG PICTURE

Like many states, Texas has a relatively hard time recruiting teachers in mathematics, science, special education, and bilingual education. The mission of the Texas Teaching Fellows program is to address the shortage of teachers in these areas by attracting "the most talented and outstanding professionals from all walks of life" and getting them "to commit to teaching in the state's critical shortage subject areas." The organization's website points out that "teachers do need to have a record of university coursework focused on the subject area(s) [that] they would like to teach. Candidates interested in the areas of math and science should have academic backgrounds specifically in the areas of math and science, [however]. Candidates interested in teaching bilingual education, special education (at the elementary level), English as a second language, or elementary (limited positions) should have well-rounded academic backgrounds." This brand-new program had its inaugural year in 2005–2006.

STATS

LOCATION(S) WHERE ENTRY-LEVEL EMPLOYEES WORK

Teaching fellows work in Dallas, Texas.

AVERAGE NUMBER OF APPLICATIONS EACH YEAR

Texas Teaching Fellows receives 1,000 applications each year.

AVERAGE NUMBER HIRED PER YEAR

The program hires 100 employees each year.

ENTRY-LEVEL POSITION(S) AVAILABLE

This program seeks to hire teachers in "hard-to-staff content areas" (such as math, science, special education, and bilingual education).

AVERAGE HOURS WORKED PER WEEK

Teaching fellows work fifty-five hours per week.

AVERAGE STARTING SALARY

The average starting salary is $37,000. "Fellows teaching special education, math, bilingual education, and science can expect their salaries to either start at a higher level or be augmented by a stipend."

BENEFITS OFFERED

Teachers in the TTF program have a choice of health insurance plans, as well as dental, prescription, and vision coverage. Additional benefits include a pension, a 401(k) plan, and teacher certification earned at little/no charge.

Texas Teaching Fellows

2427 Carrick Street, Room 218

Farmers Branch, TX 75234

Tel: 972-968-4350

www.texasteachingfellows.org

GETTING HIRED

The Texas Teaching Fellows program "is designed for individuals without a background in education or previous education coursework." The program seeks "recent college graduates and career changers who can demonstrate leadership and achievement, analyze situations thoroughly and [then] generate effective strategies, and assume accountability for reaching outcomes despite obstacles."

To apply, "candidates must complete and submit an online application and attach a resume and personal statement describing why they want to become teachers, particularly in a high-needs content area. Applicants must also provide the program office with copies of official college transcripts. Applicants are notified within two weeks of their application status [about whether they have been granted an interview]. After the interview, candidates are notified of their selection status within two weeks." One fellow reports, "After being accepted into the program, I still had to interview with the school district and principals." Candidates must also pass state teacher tests before they start to teach.

MONEY AND PERKS

As in most states, teacher salaries in Texas are set by law; they are based on a formula that takes into account "years of experience, [level of] certification, content specializations, and level of education." Teachers may earn bonuses "when sponsoring an extracurricular activity or teaching in a specific content area." Opportunities to earn extra money by "tutoring in an after-school program or teaching during summer school" are also available. Fellows tell us that their favorite perks are "the summers off" and "doing what I love for a living."

THE ROPES

TTF is "a fast-track certification program, [and so] training and certification requirements are condensed into one year. All fellows begin their formal participation in the TTF program during a Summer Training Institute, which begins in late May. During the Institute, fellows participate in seven rigorous weeks of training [that focus] on two domains: classroom management and culture and instructional design and delivery. During the summer, fellows also participate in student-teaching under the watchful supervision of experienced summer-school teachers. District-specific orientation occurs once the fellow is hired and attends New Teacher Training prior to the beginning of the school year."

Once the school year begins, "Fellows continue their professional development by participating in content seminars. These seminars are conducted by experienced district teachers and equip fellows to translate their current content knowledge into high-quality lessons and instruction. Seminars are hosted two times per month and serve as a support mechanism for fellows."

DAY IN THE LIFE

Fellows have "all the responsibilities of a [traditional] classroom teacher." One special education teacher reports that "there is a lot of paperwork in the beginning of the year [as well as] lots of scheduling, planning, and testing. Eventually you get to teach." Another fellow warns, "There is not time to do everything my school wants me to do (update my website, plan good lessons, plan good learning goals, attend meetings/seminars, [and] other tidbits) [as well as] get ready for class each day. I [also] take home work to do (either grading tests/labs and/or lesson-planning)." Despite the demanding workload, many praise their positions for providing them with the opportunity to do worthwhile, rewarding work.

PEERS

Texas Teaching Fellows "are all different, but great in their own ways. We are all smart and capable." Fellows are willing to share insights and information; one writes, "Some of us have the same students and have helped [one another] out to understand those students. I have used ideas from other class lessons and in classroom management from other teachers." Outside the classroom, "there are some after-hours events [to which] everyone is always invited." One teacher reports, "We have gone to football games and dinners together. It has been nice to have those people around to vent and share!"

MOVING ON

Those who have left the Texas Teaching Fellows program to date "have cited personal reasons," the organization tells us. The program is too young to have accumulated significant data on former fellows. A program organizer notes, "We anticipate that those who leave classroom instruction will do so to further their careers in another educational capacity (e.g., [to become] principals, counselors, or specialists)."

BEST AND WORST

The most successful fellow to date, we're told, is "a gentleman who consistently models the characteristics of a successful employee and teacher. He proactively takes responsibility in his learning of new and [traditional] effective teaching strategies and [in] understanding the larger classroom concepts. He continually seeks out additional guidance through mentors, TTF staff, and his school colleagues to improve his teaching skills and abilities. A man of constant optimism, he fosters effective relationships with both his principals and his colleagues."

Among the least successful fellows was someone who "consistently remained inflexible and continually created negative relationships [with] students."

TGI Friday's
Manager and Assistant Manager

The Big Picture

TGI Friday's management-training program rotates future managers through all the hourly wage positions in one of its restaurants to teach them the ropes. It's a whirlwind tour that lasts a scant fourteen weeks, culminating in the trainee's ascension to the captain's chair. Graduates say it's a great way to learn the chain restaurant business quickly as well as an excellent means of getting ahead in parent company Carlson Restaurants (which also owns the Pickup Stix chain of Chinese eateries).

Stats

Location(s) Where Entry-level Employees Work

"We operate in forty-eight states, primarily east of the Rockies."

Average Number of Applications Each Year

"We review and receive over 500 applications a year for entry-level management jobs."

Average Number Hired Per Year over the Last Ten Years

TGI Friday's hires fifteen to twenty entry-level management trainees per year.

Entry-level Position(s) Available

New hires work as assistant managers and managers.

Average Hours Worked Per Week

New hires work fifty-five hours per week.

Average Starting Salary

New hires earn $38,000 per year.

Benefits Offered

"We offer several different medical, dental, and vision plans." Additional benefits include vacation, a 401(k) plan, purchased time off, long-term disability insurance, and a complimentary dining discount.

Contact Information

Visit TGI Fridays on the Web at www.fridays.com/hr/jobs.htm.

Getting Hired

TGI Friday's "visits specific colleges each semester to participate in career fairs, on-campus interviewing, and classroom presentations. Students from other colleges can apply online at www.fridays.com or send a resume to the college recruiter." The next step in the process is a personality-profile assessment; "If the result of the assessment fits our profile, then the candidate interviews with a general manager and spends time observing in a restaurant," company representatives tell us. "Finally, the candidate would interview with a director of operations. An applicant can be discontinued at any point during the interview process." Sound daunting? A successful applicant makes the experience sound a little less so. He writes, "I did not do anything specific to help me get an interview, but I did have some good experience. I was interviewed by the college recruiters over the phone and given personality tests. I was then interviewed by a few of the general managers from the local stores. After that I was interviewed by the regional manager. The interviews were all good; they asked me what I had done in the past, where I thought I would go with Friday's, what types of things I was looking to accomplish, and a lot of questions about my critical thinking skills. A few days later I was offered a position. From start to finish, the process took roughly two weeks."

MONEY AND PERKS

According to the trainees we spoke with, "start date, location, and salary are all negotiable" at TGI Friday's. One notes, "Everything that was explained to me during the interview process [captured] how [the process actually] happened. I was told once I completed the internship and made the move to management [that] all I would have to do was talk salary and location; no additional training would be necessary. I also did research at school [regarding] similar jobs and what students were offered in terms of jobs and salaries, and the offer seemed pretty high." Regarding raises, "each manager's compensation is assessed yearly through a performance evaluation compared with a salary range. Average raises are 4 percent." Asked which fringe benefits they most enjoyed, trainees responded, "Free meals during shift[s], being able to make [our] own schedule, and bonuses. If we hit pace dollars or pace percent or if we hit our sales goal, we get a certain percentage of money in return. It's done quarterly, and it's a great incentive to manage responsibly and to pay attention to what is going on around you at all times."

THE ROPES

The management training program at Friday's takes place over the course of a fourteen-week period during which a future manager "spends time in each hourly level position learning those specific jobs as well as shadowing a manager and ultimately performing management-level tasks." One graduate of the program explains, "I was trained on every hourly position, both 'front of the house' and 'back of the house,' and then learned all management functions and procedures. I learned about food cost, beverage cost, and the different parts of the income estimate. When I learned the hourly stations, I was trained by hourly employees, and when I trained on the management functions, the general manager as well as the rest of the management staff trained me." Besides familiarizing the manager with each worker's role in the restaurant, the training regimen yields another valuable benefit; one manager explains, "If the restaurant ever gets so busy that someone needs help, I am able to assist in any position we have!"

Day in the Life

Once the training period is over, management trainees drop the trainee designation and start managing. Here's how one describes her responsibilities: "I was placed in a high-volume store and given the bar as my department. Aside from the typical management duties of running a shift, I also have the responsibility of beverage cost. I have to ensure that we hit our budgeted weekly/monthly/yearly beverage cost percentages. I also have the ultimate responsibility for the bar staff—hiring, promoting, training, and developing their abilities to take care of the guests—and the overall cleanliness of the bar. On a typical day, I start out with a pre-shift meeting with my employees for the shift, letting them know our sales projections, sales contests, any additional expectations, and what I would like to see on our shift. I then spend a majority of my time out on the restaurant floor talking to guests and making rounds to ensure the shift is running clean and smooth. If necessary, I help out in the kitchen or at the door when needed, running sales reports on a frequent basis to help keep the staff positive and motivated. At the end of the shift, I am responsible for the collection of any monies and the closing of the daily computer reports and functions. I then check out the employees to ensure they closed everything down, and it all looks clean."

Peers

Sitting atop the hierarchy (or food chain, if you will) of a restaurant can be a lonely job; as one manager explains, "I don't have interaction with any first jobbers. Sometimes I hang out with other managers, but that is like once a month." Accordingly, "there are no after-hours social scenes. However, I do interact with my management team every single day. We communicate on a daily basis about the day-to-day operations of our job. I spend a lot of quality time with them at work. I don't spend much time outside of work with them. I would much rather go home and spend time with my family and my dogs. The only time I communicate with others outside of work is through voice-mail to keep lines of communication open amongst us."

Moving On

People leave Friday's for a variety of reasons; for some, it's "not what they expected," while for others the "work-life balance" doesn't suit their goals. Some people, according to company representatives, have "unrealistic expectations of life after college." Some head for other industries, while others seek work at restaurants that do not keep late hours (TGI Friday's stays open until 2:00 A.M., some trainees consider this a drawback).

Attrition

Friday's representatives tell us that "due to the interview and recruiting process, less than 5 percent of [their] first jobbers leave within twelve months."

Best and Worst

A great management trainee "is able to network and use their resources to better understand the business and the company, while successfully adjusting to the pace of the business." The worst, "besides the employees who are no longer part of the organization due to bad business/professional decisions," are "those who were unable to keep up with the pace of our business."

TURNER BROADCASTING SYSTEM
Various Positions

THE BIG PICTURE

Turner Broadcasting, also known as TBS Inc., is a Time Warner company whose networks include TBS, CNN, CNN Headline News, Cartoon Network, TNT, Turner South, and Turner Classic Movies. The company is a "magnet for college grads looking to break into the world of broadcasting, entertainment, or professional sports."

STATS

LOCATION(S) WHERE ENTRY-LEVEL EMPLOYEES WORK

New hires work primarily in Atlanta; positions are also available in Los Angeles, California; Washington, DC; Chicago, Illinois; and New York, New York.

ENTRY-LEVEL POSITION(S) AVAILABLE

New hires work in a variety of positions across the company. They "typically hold assistant and coordinator-level positions in production, programming, marketing, human resources, public relations, sales, and other departments within the Atlanta Braves organization. In addition, Turner has a variety of paid, entry-level trainee programs for recent graduates interested in the news (Video Journalist Program) and entertainment (T3) industry." Turner offers several innovative entry-level programs: the Video Journalist Program, Turner Trainee Team Program, and Atlanta Braves Trainee Program. The video journalist (VJ) position provides hands-on experience and training for newbies who aspire to work in the technical control room, do video editing, or work as editors. The Turner Trainee Team (T3) is designed for newbies who have a passion for the entertainment industry. The Atlanta Braves Trainee Program is specialized for those who hope to pursue careers in professional sports.

AVERAGE HOURS WORKED PER WEEK

New hires work more than forty hours per week.

AVERAGE NUMBER HIRED PER YEAR OVER THE LAST TEN YEARS

"Turner Temps hired more than 500 temps during 2004–2005 and placed more than 170 temps in permanent positions during that time. In 2005, more than 70 Turner temps found permanent placement within the company."

BENEFITS OFFERED

Turner offers a variety of medical, vision, and dental plans; life, accidental death, and dismemberment insurance; flex spending accounts for medical expenses and dependent care; disability; and same-sex domestic partner medical benefits. Additional benefits include transportation reimbursement; a 401(k) program;

on-site athletic club; stock purchase plan; tuition reimbursement and professional development; leaves of absence; a daycare center (Atlanta); and discounts on sporting events, theater, airfare, hotels, restaurants, etc.

CONTACT INFORMATION

Visit the website at www.turner.com/jobs.

GETTING HIRED

Many first jobbers at Turner get their foot in the door via Turner Temps, an "in-house temporary agency for all TBS divisions in Atlanta." One employee warns, "Even getting a temp job is a feat at Turner. For me, it required persistence. I sent my resume several times over a period of about six weeks. That was in 2000, right before the crash. Turner is a very popular company—especially in Atlanta and especially for college grads." Temping allows you to network throughout the company; it also keeps you at the center of the action, so you'll be among the first to know when a full-time job opens. Interviews at Turner, we're told, are "very casual. Generally they're looking to find out about your career path. They don't want somebody who will leave them quickly. People want you to commit at least a minimum of one year to their department. They weren't as interested in levels of experience as they were in general education and ability to pick up on things quickly."

MONEY AND PERKS

"[My starting date] was negotiable, and that was pretty much it," explains one Turner first jobber. "They have a base salary here. The only time I've heard it was different was when somebody moved from one entry-level position to another within the company. Other than that, what they offer is what you get." Perks are numerous, as they are at many entertainment companies, and include "free movies, sporting events, [and] discounts on a lot of [products from] vendors the company works with." There's also the more mundane— but extremely valuable—benefits such as the "401(k) that's one of the best there is"—the company matches 160 [percent], up to 4 [percent] of base salary—"a company-match nonprofit contribution program [up to $500], and free MARTA (Atlanta public transportation) passes." Employees also enjoy the on-site athletic club and professional development course offerings. A few people point out that "even with all the fringe benefits Turner offers, the best thing may be the environment with so many other young, creative types. [People meet] many who inspire [them]."

THE ROPES

"In television, it's very much [a matter of] on-the-job training," a production assistant at Turner tells us. "Most people get overeducated in school. Each company does things differently. And it's also a very welcoming environment. For instance, a lot of what you have to learn is just jargon, and they don't expect anyone to know it coming in." A production assistant notes, "I learned it by watching, asking lots of questions, and learning from mistakes. Coworkers would take me on edit sessions and through their daily schedule. I'd be shadowing them, and it worked well" largely because "the folks I shadowed were very helpful." Orientation here "takes most of the first day. It's an overview of the company: policies, human resources, benefits, that sort of thing. They were there to answer any questions we had."

DAY IN THE LIFE

First jobbers at Turner are generally assigned lots of grunt work, the type of jobs usually foisted off on the inexperienced (and temps, which is what many first jobbers at Turner start as). They "answer phones, write correspondence, type up calendars and schedules, answer mail and viewer phone calls, handle data entry, log library tapes, keep track of databases, run errands, check equipment orders, and get lunch for everyone." Employees who make a good impression on their bosses soon take on more responsibilities; one production assistant writes, "Over time I grew into actually scheduling originals, writing storylines for them, answering even more viewer mail, and helping to input the schedule for the entire network. I was included in more meetings about operations, scheduling, ratings, closed-captioning, and so forth, so I became more and more an important part of the day-to-day." The pace of work at Turner can be crazed or sluggish, depending on the time of year; one first jobber explains, "Television goes in cycles. If you're in reruns, you have downtime."

PEERS

"There is a ton of contact and camaraderie with other first jobbers" at Turner. One new hire writes, "It was like being on a college campus or something. I hung out with the other first jobbers not only at Turner South, but [also] at all the other networks in our building. I met a lot of people, and there was always time to chat and laugh. There were also happy hours and parties. I would joke that I couldn't go out in Atlanta without bumping into someone I knew from work." One production assistant sums up the experience, "I felt as though my peers were very much like myself, but different enough to make being friends with them interesting. I made most of my friends here."

MOVING ON

Just about everyone we spoke with at Turner moved up the corporate ladder. None of them have left, and none of them have any intention of leaving. While "some people complain that it's hard to advance and that they can't get what they want out of the job," our respondents felt that plenty of opportunities were available to go-getters. Those who leave the company often go to other broadcast networks.

UNITED TECHNOLOGIES CORPORATION
Entry-Level Engineering Jobs and Financial and IT Leadership Training Programs

THE BIG PICTURE

UTC is a heavy hitter, a $37 billion company with a product line that includes Carrier heating and cooling, Hamilton Sundstrand aerospace systems and industrial products, Otis Elevators, UTC Fire & Security systems, UTC Power fuel cells, Sikorsky helicopters, and Pratt & Whitney aircraft engines. Beyond the scores of entry-level engineering positions available at UTC, the company also has a Financial Leadership Program (FLP) and an IT Leadership Program (ITLP) that provide a two-year rotational training experiences to promising college grads in business and computer science.

STATS

LOCATION(S) WHERE ENTRY-LEVEL EMPLOYEES WORK

Entry-level employees work in Hartford, Connecticut; Farmington, Connecticut; and East Hartford, Connecticut.

AVERAGE NUMBER OF APPLICATIONS EACH YEAR

UTC receives 700–800 applications for entry-level positions each year.

AVERAGE NUMBER HIRED PER YEAR

UTC hires seventy-five to eighty entry-level employees each year.

ENTRY-LEVEL POSITION(S) AVAILABLE

The company has many engineering jobs; it also has a Financial Leadership Program (FLP) and an IT Leadership Program (ITLP).

AVERAGE HOURS WORKED PER WEEK

Entry-level employees work forty hours per week.

AVERAGE STARTING SALARY

Starting salaries are, HR officials note, "comparable by functional area with the NACE Senior Salary Survey."

BENEFITS OFFERED

UTC offers "medical and dental coverage," which are "available after thirty days of employment." Additionally, "employees build their own plans." Additional benefits include an Employee Scholar Program (100 percent payment of tuition and textbooks and time off to study); retirement plan; pension (available after one year, vested after five years); vision care discounts; and vendor discounts.

CONTACT INFORMATION

Prospective applicants are encouraged to visit UTC on the Web at www.utc.com/careers.

GETTING HIRED

UTC's offices are located near several major universities, and the company draws on these resources to populate a broad range of internships and co-op positions. A solid number of college graduates who ultimately take full-time jobs at UTC start in these positions. Others check job openings and submit their resumes online. The company does not generally conduct on-campus interviews; instead, it "encourages students to attend a variety of alternative activities that they participate in on campus (career fairs, sponsored workshops, student group events) as a means of engaging with our representatives. This allows us to consider a larger number of candidates than a typical campus interview schedule would allow. Only a few select programs schedule campus interviews." Those invited to a UTC business for an interview can expect "behavioral interviewing methods that give candidates the opportunity to share with us examples of past work/experiences that relate to our core competencies. We are trying to determine individuals' fit within our organization [and] learn about their backgrounds and what they would bring to UTC." One UTC engineer writes, "During my interview I was asked about my classes in specific areas, how I have worked with teams, and what area of engineering would I be most interested in working in. I received a call a couple of weeks later asking me to come to Pratt & Whitney's campus for another interview. Two managers from different disciplines interviewed me. Again, I was asked about my experiences with working in teams, my strengths and weaknesses, and the areas and/or disciplines [in which] I would be most interested in working. I also asked many questions about opportunities at Pratt & Whitney and [about] how Pratt & Whitney supports their employees to achieve their goals within the company. Knowing about the company and having questions is very important."

UTC recruits on targeted campuses for its IT and Financial Leadership Training programs, both of which accept applications online. The screening process for these is similar to the process outlined above for conventional hires.

MONEY AND PERKS

Job offers at UTC are "somewhat negotiable," in that "it is possible to have multiple offers from different divisions." Once an applicant settles on a position, though, salary and job definition are pretty much set; however, start time can be negotiable, according to some newbies we surveyed. Raises "occur yearly based upon the performance of the organization." Perks include "a great Employee Scholar Program that pays for your tuition, fees, and books for any graduate or undergraduate degree you want to pursue, regardless of your job function or responsibilities. They even give you paid time off from work to do homework or to work on projects that are school related, and [the company also] gives you a stock bonus when you complete your degree. So even though I had to work all day I was still able to continue my education and not at my own expense."

First jobbers also love "the opportunity to travel outside of the continental United States on business, [often] to visit suppliers and/or remote offices. There are a lot of travel opportunities in some departments and groups."

THE ROPES

"Specified orientation varies by business unit or program, though each employee is a part of the new employee orientation conducted by HR," UT officials tell us. One young engineer notes, "Orientation lasts for half a day. You meet other new hires, and then you go over the company history, organizational structure, and benefits packages available to you (healthcare, dental, life insurance, etc.). You also fill out any paperwork that was missing in your file. Afterward, your supervisor picks you up and takes to you to your work location."

Ongoing training includes "classes that specialize in job functions or programs you need to do your daily work, as well as generalized courses like the Seven Habits of Highly Effective People to help your professional proficiency."

DAY IN THE LIFE

The daily routines of UTC first jobbers vary tremendously, as the company brings college grads on in many different divisions and departments. Participants in the leadership programs perform rotations; finance trainees rotate departments every six months; and IT trainees rotate every nine months. Trainees in both finance and IT perform tasks that teach them skills in project management, business analysis, and decision-making.

PEERS

UTC is a sizable company, and accordingly, the experiences of new hires here vary greatly among the different divisions and departments. Some engineers report that they participate in "a New Hires Club, [in which] there are always events going on and opportunities to hang out after work and on the weekends. It also allows us to get to know [one another] and help those that are [even] newer than [we are]." One newbie writes, "Some of my coworkers are my old college buddies, [and] some are my friends from high school. We share similar interests, watch similar TV shows, hang out in similar locations after work. And even if we don't, I can still talk to anyone in my group about things outside of work." Others, however, experience less camaraderie on the job. One writes, "I'm the youngest person in the office, so I haven't made many friends at work [whom] I can connect with outside of work. Most of the people I work with (or for) have kids only a few years younger than I am."

Moving on

Those who leave United Technologies often do so "to pursue new opportunities" or "to relocate due to a change in family status." Some here "criticize their workload," complaining that "we need more bodies in the office to accomplish the work without putting such a workload strain on the employees." Still, most stick around here a long time, in part "because there is always plenty of room to grow within the various UTC companies. One could move up in levels or receive bonuses and/or awards for working hard on certain projects. One could also move from working in engineering to the [business] side of the companies. Since UTC also pays for their employees to continue their education, employees can develop and grow on the company dime."

Attrition

UTC reports that "We have a strong retention rate, in particular with our entry-level employees who converted (i.e., those who were previously interns (INROADS) or co-ops with us). For INROADS, the retention rate is 80 percent."

VH1
Various Positions

THE BIG PICTURE

"The wonderful thing about VH1 and a lot of cable networks is that they give young people a real hands-on chance to make television that wouldn't be afforded to them at a network," explains one first jobber, who adds, "They also, by nature, don't pay as well, but the work environment and experience you'll accrue there is worth it." There you have it; at VH1, you'll have the opportunity to learn—learn how to select, produce, and market programming to adult music fans—and learn how to live on a relatively tight budget.

STATS

LOCATION(S) WHERE ENTRY-LEVEL EMPLOYEES WORK

Entry-level hires work in New York, New York.

ENTRY-LEVEL POSITION(S) AVAILABLE

There are various positions available to entry-level hires.

AVERAGE HOURS WORKED PER WEEK

New hires work more than forty hours per week.

CONTACT INFORMATION

Visit https://jobhuntweb.viacom.com/jobhunt/main/jobhome.asp, click on the "Job Search" link, then highlight VH1 in the "Channels" column. There is also a "Jobs" link at the bottom of the screen at www.VH1.com.

GETTING HIRED

Persistence is key to success in broadcasting, our VH1 entry-level employee correspondents tell us. One writes, "In the film business, it's always said, 'It's all who you know.' Bull pucky! It's all [to whom] you extend your friendship, your support, and your best effort." I can't think of another profession where they don't care if you have two heads, dark green complexion, and no eyes. If you can do your job, they don't care about anything else. Where one went to school? No concern. Whom one is married to, it may get you a few doors opened, but if one isn't passionate and successful, out the door they go. It's all about the moment. Not yesterday or tomorrow, but what can you do *now*. I love that philosophy. Only *now* matters." Or maybe it *is* who you know; another of our correspondents writes, "I sent in my resume; my brother, who worked at VH1, passed it on; the interview was casual and comfortable. The head of www.VH1.com interviewed me, and he asked my familiarity with certain software." The company posts openings at the Viacom website; jobs at other Viacom broadcast companies can be browsed on the same site.

Money and Perks

"Nothing seemed too negotiable" in VH1's job offer to our first timers, and this makes sense; as one employee puts it, "Since there's no shortage of people who want to work in television, the moment you've put in your time at a place like VH1 and start applying for more lucrative network television jobs, there's dozens of hungry young kids ready to take your place. To this end, some [may] say that cable networks serve as kind of a bush league to the free-access networks." Another newbie adds, "In the beginning there was no negotiation for pay or when and where one worked. One had nothing to barter with, but after having experience one could negotiate all of the above." The best perks of working at VH1 are "the casual atmosphere" and "the parties. At the end of a show's season, there's always a party, and one gets to get crazy and hang with the creative pulse of the entertainment industry."

The Ropes

Orientation at VH1 "lasts about half a day. It mostly covers benefits information." After that, first jobbers often find themselves on their own. "It's the only way to learn," writes one assistant editor at the network. "I love being in over my head, and any chance I get I try to chew off way too much." To get up to speed, the editor "learned as much before and after work as I could. I asked coworkers for help when I couldn't figure [a] problem out. I learned [that] if one constantly asks for help, people tend to not give it; but if one attempts to go at it by oneself, people will . . . help out."

Day in the Life

First jobbers are scattered throughout VH1, performing all the various support jobs necessary to run a television channel. Those we spoke with logged and digitized video, edited rough cuts of programs, performed clerical duties, conducted research, and assisted the development of programming. All told us that those who asked for more responsibility were given it and that they were recognized and rewarded if they succeeded. One writes, "I would recommend that any recent college graduate get their start at MTV Networks [VH1's parent company]. You'll probably have as much responsibility at your level as you want, and as they often promote from within, you'll rise through the ranks with other people you'll see again later down the road. It's a great place to start in television production, especially for fans of pop culture." It also offers numerous opportunities "to make contacts and to try on a lot of different hats."

Peers

First jobbers at VH1 share the same ambitions and many of the same interests, so it's no surprise that many "make most of [their] friends at work. All of [them] are heading in the same direction: up." As one first jobber tells us, "There's definitely a strong bond between people working in show business. It comes from following dreams, and everybody understands you're going after the big prize because they're doing the same thing. And putting yourself out there like that brings everyone together." The company holds "after-hours parties for special occasions" and other similar events to "encourage camaraderie."

Moving On

VH1 first jobbers usually either move up the corporate ladder at Viacom, or they move on to other jobs in television.

WASHINGTON MUTUAL

PACE Program

THE BIG PICTURE

Through its rotational PACE management training program, Washington Mutual exposes entry-level employees to the various sales, management, and technical concepts required of a manager at one of the bank's financial centers. Call it a year-long financial boot camp, if you like; those who make it through will find their future prospects considerably brighter than those of typical entry-level employees.

STATS

LOCATION(S) WHERE ENTRY-LEVEL EMPLOYEES WORK

Entry-level hires work in Arizona, California, Florida, Georgia, Idaho, Nevada, New Jersey, New York, Oregon, Texas, Utah, and Washington.

AVERAGE NUMBER OF APPLICATIONS EACH YEAR

Washington Mutual receives approximately 600 applications each year.

AVERAGE NUMBER HIRED PER YEAR OVER THE LAST TEN YEARS

As a result of a change in the system used to track the PACE Program, this information is not available. Since 1986, approximately 700 trainees have graduated from the program.

ENTRY-LEVEL POSITION(S) AVAILABLE

Approximately 150 positions per year are available in the PACE program.

AVERAGE HOURS WORKED PER WEEK

New hires work forty hours per week.

AVERAGE STARTING SALARY

New hires earn from $2,200–$2,800 per month in the Northwest, Florida, and Texas; they earn from $2,400–$3,175 per month in California, New York, and New Jersey.

BENEFITS OFFERED

Trainees may be eligible to choose from three kinds of coverage options under the medical plan: no coverage, Preferred Provider Organization (PPO) options (known as the Washington Mutual plan), or Health Maintenance Organization (HMO) options in some areas. Additional benefits include dental coverage, supplemental life insurance, a 401(k) plan, pension plan, employee stock purchase plan, wellness center, transit subsidy, employee discounts, and flexible spending accounts.

Contact Information

Nancy Parker-Wright
Tel: 206-377-1395
www.wamu.com

Getting Hired

Trainees find the PACE program through a variety of channels. Some candidates are recruited, and others are referred by friends or relatives currently working for the company; some are even company employees themselves looking for advancement opportunities. Washington Mutual vets applicants through a multiple interview process; company officials explain, "There are typically three stages of interviews. The first interview is with a recruiter, the second is with the PACE manager, and the third is with the PACE manager and PACE graduates." Trainees tell us that interviewers "ask scenario questions that require open-ended answers. The interviewers were polite, smiled, and took notes (but asked to take notes beforehand, so I would not become nervous when I saw them writing)." Why such a rigorous interview regimen? "Since Washington Mutual is a sales-and-service culture, we focus on sales and customer service abilities," explains the company. Interviewing is the best way to gauge these skills. In addition to completing the interviews, PACE applicants must also submit a "descriptive paper of a real situation in which they used their leadership or sales abilities, explaining the situation and the outcome of their actions. The paper must be typed, double-spaced, and no longer than one page." They must also complete an employment application and provide references from previous employers.

Money and Perks

One trainee notes, "[Trainees] have to tighten their belts for the year of the PACE program. All of us look forward to the income potential that we have *after* graduation." Perks include "free financial advice, free accounts," and an invite to a "national meeting of all management trainees within the Banking and Financial Services Division, [at which trainees] have the opportunity to hear from top Washington Mutual leaders, learn key professional development strategies to prepare them for leadership roles at Washington Mutual, and meet and share experiences with other management trainees from across the country."

The Ropes

The PACE Program begins with "a two-day welcoming orientation [that] gives [new hires] all the details of the program and the expectations they [have] of all of [them]." One PACE trainee writes, "We were provided with well-organized materials that gave us all we needed to get started: contact numbers, how-to sheets, answers to frequently asked questions, and introductions to the current PACERS (six months ahead of us in the program) who were assigned to us as mentors. The orientation also included a lunch with regional and back office managers. It was a fantastic opportunity for us to begin building our network and 'getting our names out,' as well as [getting] a great feeling for the culture and leadership at Washington Mutual."

Day in the Life

According to trainees, the primary goal of the PACE program "is to familiarize you with all aspects of the financial center. There is a set curriculum with time spent as a teller, a new-accounts representative, [and a] consumer and residential lending [agent], and an internship phase where you act as an assistant manager. Each phase has a number of required training courses." As such, "over the course of the year, PACE trainees spend approximately sixty days in classes. The training is provided by an excellent internal training staff and covers everything from operational training for job functions to leadership development and strategic planning." Classwork is "scheduled to correspond with the phase of the program [that new hires are] in, allowing [them] each step of the way to combine 'book learning' and experience in the field." At every stage, "trainers are always available and willing to help and follow up, whether it be after class, by e-mail, or [by] coming to the financial center to help you one-on-one. Because PACERS end up wearing so many hats, there is no typical day; a trainee's schedule depends on the phase of the program he or she is in." Because of the variety of trainings, one trainee writes, "After only one year, I have been fully trained in teller operations, accounts, lending, insurance and annuity sales, and in the operation and management of a financial center. That is amazing to me!" Another employee says, "Trainees never feel overwhelmed but almost always feel like we're in over our heads—but in a good way. Every day is an exciting new challenge."

Peers

PACERS, as trainees call themselves, form "great networks and great friendships." One explains, "It seems as though we are a family. We depend on [one another] and use [one another] for support." However, "There is not a big after-hours social scene. If we gather after-hours, it is for volunteer projects, grabbing lunch together after a class, or having a dinner party or holiday celebration at someone's house. We enjoy [one another's] company, but most of us have families to get home to."

Moving on

All the trainees we spoke with hoped to remain with Washington Mutual when their program ended. "I'll stay as long as they'll have me!" writes a typical PACER. Company officials say, "Typically, trainees move into the role of assistant financial center manager and become eligible for incentive and a base salary." Some PACE graduates "have moved into numerous financial center manager positions, several regional manager positions, and even a group manager position." No wonder one trainee tells us that there's "lots of opportunity for promotion" at Washington Mutual.

WELLS FARGO
Management Trainee Programs

THE BIG PICTURE

There are about 150,000 jobs at Wells Fargo; this profile focuses on the approximately 120 positions available each year in the bank's professional development programs for recent college graduates. These programs offer project- or rotation-based training to provide broad-ranging exposure to the many facets of Wells Fargo's business; in this way, they allow first jobbers to select the career path best suited to their tastes and talents.

STATS

LOCATION(S) WHERE ENTRY-LEVEL EMPLOYEES WORK

"There are more than 300 potential locations available, though most positions are clustered around our primary cities of employment: San Francisco, California; Minneapolis, Minnesota; Phoenix, Arizona; and major cities in Texas."

AVERAGE NUMBER HIRED PER YEAR OVER THE LAST TEN YEARS

Wells Fargo HR officials note that they hire "on average, 120 team members per year" in their various professional development programs.

ENTRY-LEVEL POSITION(S) AVAILABLE

Professional development programs include the following: Audit Rotational Development Program (audit services), Business Banking Associate Program (business banking), Finance Associate Development Program (corporate finance), Information Technology Associate Program (internet services group), Leadership Development Program (technology and operations), Financial Analyst Program (wholesale banking), and Project Management Leadership Development Program (wholesale banking).

AVERAGE HOURS WORKED PER WEEK

"New hires work about forty to fifty hours per week, with the chance of having to work longer hours during a large project."

PERCENTAGE OF ENTRY-LEVEL HIRES STILL WITH THE COMPANY AFTER THREE, FIVE, AND TEN YEARS

After three, five, and ten years, the percentage of people who remain with the company are 99, 94, and 73, respectively.

AVERAGE STARTING SALARY

"Starting salaries vary by position, [and] they also vary by program depending on geographic location, prior work experience, market reference point for the function, etc. Overall, our programs ranged from $41,000–$65,000, plus bonus and benefits, in 2004."

BENEFITS OFFERED

Health care options vary by state, but Wells Fargo "offers comprehensive medical, dental, mental health, and vision plans. There are also a number of medical cash balance plans, etc., to help offset the cost of treatments. Benefits are available to all team members, spouses, domestic partners, and dependents." Additional benefits include "up to twenty-five days of paid time off per year and discounts on services and goods at nationwide vendors, etc. A matched 401(k) plan, tuition reimbursement, commuter benefits, financial product discounts, flexible spending accounts, a stock purchase plan, and disability/life insurance are all also available. It's worth noting that Wells Fargo is also recognized for its flexible work arrangements."

CONTACT INFORMATION

Students interested in applying should visit www.wellsfargo.com/jobs and select "Undergraduates," "Full-Time Opportunities," choose a program of interest and select "Express Interest."

GETTING HIRED

Wells Fargo interviews on many campuses each year and "reviews applications from hundreds of campuses nationwide. Wells Fargo hired students into these programs from approximately forty campuses this year." Applications are also accepted online. Wells Fargo seeks out team members "who share our core values." These include ethics, customer satisfaction, leadership and personal accountability, and diversity." "Interviews are conducted in two stages; the first is typically handled by a recruiter, and the second, by one or more managers." Wells Fargo advises prospective applicants "to be well versed on the company," as candidates who are "tend to be the strongest." "We make it easy by providing much of the information a candidate needs to know on our website." A few entry-level employees we spoke with noted that "some of the interviewing questions were pretty difficult; they were trying to get a feel how you handled yourself under pressure." One, for example, reports that questions he found "particularly hard (and thought-provoking) were: 'If you were a product, what would you be, how would you market yourself, and how much would you cost?' 'What would your enemy say about you?' and most memorably, to conclude the interview, 'What do you think I think of you based on this conversation?'" Another newbie who had "three interviews with senior executives and an on-the-spot presentation in one day" called her interview process "intense, exciting, and memorable."

MONEY AND PERKS

Raises "vary based on team member performance, potential relocations, etc." According to people we spoke with, location and start date are negotiable for some positions, while starting salary and bonuses are less likely to be open to discussion. According to HR officials, "salary reviews are conducted in conjunction with performance reviews on an annual basis." There may, however, be "exceptions to this, depending on start dates and individual business practices. Increases are dependent on individual performance [as well as] company performance." Although Wells Fargo offers generous benefits, many newbies focus on the intangible perks. "The best fringe benefit has been working with all of the great people in my group. They have made the work fun and exciting while also an educational experience," boasts one. "I've enjoyed becoming very involved in the community by attending numerous sporting events, shows, luncheons, etc. That's been the best perk," notes another.

THE ROPES

Every professional development hire next year will participate in Wells Fargo's Class of 2006 program, "a year-long corporate-level program focused on broadening their understanding of Wells Fargo—its businesses, values, and strategy—and helping them build their professional network at the peer and executive levels. The highlight of the year is a two-day forum in San Francisco, where participants are introduced to our chief executive officer and leadership team." Professional development programs also involve rotational training, supplemental classroom training "to build in-demand skill sets," and mentoring. One participant in the business banking services program writes, "I have received extensive training from many different avenues, including, but not limited to, my boss, classes, online tutorials, and my mentor. The training was on accounting, office applications, credit underwriting, treasury management, sales, and personal growth." While new hires appreciate the availability of resources, most note that the bulk of their training was "on-the-job, from the existing group of analysts of associates." One also notes having taken "a couple of accounting classes from the local city college [as a] supplement."

DAY IN THE LIFE

Profiles detailing a typical day in the life for most appear at the company's website. Still, one employee notes that he "never really had a typical day, but felt challenged on most assignments." The rotations that many newbies make provide "a good opportunity to try different job functions and see what would be a good fit." One explains that "we're sent out to all rotations to learn, to network, to seek out projects; it's a very developmental program. On the micro-level, I'm in charge of my own development [so I can] do the best job I can do while learning. With programs like this, it's less about productivity and more about development." Still, first jobbers warn that "some rotations will not be as exciting as others; this will vary on personal interests as well as assigned hosting managers. Many times the assignments can be overwhelming." As one trainee tells us, "There is such an incredible breadth of learning resources, such as online training, that there was no time to be bored. With the amount of work that is being done, if an individual has any initiative whatsoever, the management team is quick to respond, and you can often receive incredible opportunities merely by asking."

PEERS

Entry-level employees' peer network and social scene at Wells Fargo "is dependent on work location and rotation group." Newbies characterize their peers as "very smart and talented," "outgoing," and "very welcoming and willing to help out when aid is requested." That said, many work with only a few other new hires, so there isn't much of an after-hours scene. As one first jobber tells us, "Being straight out of college, I still enjoy all of the things that college kids do. Most of my coworkers are older and live a more domestic lifestyle than I do. But they are wonderful people, and I truly enjoy spending my days with them and spending nights and weekends with my friends." Trainees stay in touch through "numerous networking events" and "constant telephone contact." Additionally, "there are a number of events scheduled so that first jobbers can socialize;" most such events are "organized by [program] recruiters."

MOVING ON

Wells Fargo tracks information about where its trainees end up if they leave the bank, but informs us that "this information is gathered during exit interviews, which are confidential." None of the employees we spoke with offer any further insight on this subject, except to say that some leave to pursue MBAs. As the numbers above attest, most people stick around for at least three years, and with the depth and breadth of experience in financial services that they are likely to receive during their tenure, many will be well positioned for other jobs in the industry.

ATTRITION

Wells Fargo tells us that "there are usually no more than two program participants who drop out of a program in any given year. Generally, a dropout that early on has to do with an unusual or unexpected personal situation. We find that it's rarely a reflection of the program." Employees agree; one tells us, "Everyone that I have spoken with seems extremely satisfied with the job. All of us appreciate the amount of responsibility that we are given and have been able to maintain a good balance between our work and outside lives."

BEST AND WORST

"One of our recently retired executive vice presidents started with Wells Fargo as a proof operator, a person who visually verifies that cashed checks have accurate information, before being referred into one of our programs. At [the job from which he retired], he oversaw a business line that was responsible for approximately 30 percent of Wells Fargo's earnings, and [he] reported directly to our chief executive officer."

WILLIAM MORRIS AGENCY
Assistant and Trainee

THE BIG PICTURE

In operation for more than a century, William Morris Agency is the oldest and largest talent and literary agency in the world, and industry insiders consider it to be one of Hollywood's two most powerful agencies today. Its agents represent all "above the line" talent, including actors, writers, directors, producers, musicians, comedians, hosts, and a variety of companies (many entertainment entities and others seemingly unrelated to Hollywood) that have interests that can be furthered using the agency's extensive experience and connections in the industry. The three main departments in which assistants work are television, motion picture, and music (there's also a noteworthy consulting department in Beverly Hills, and a significant theater department in the New York office). Even though the pay could be better and the hours for assistants are many, "it's known as one of the best places to start, whether you want be an agent, producer, filmmaker, whatever. It's the graduate program in entertainment." Expect to work hard, earn little, get yelled at a lot . . . and love it.

STATS

LOCATION(S) WHERE ENTRY-LEVEL EMPLOYEES WORK

Entry-level hires work in Beverly Hills, California; New York, New York; Nashville, Tennessee; Miami, Florida; and London, England. The vast majority of entry-level employees start in Beverly Hills or New York.

ENTRY-LEVEL POSITION(S) AVAILABLE

New hires work as assistants or trainees.

AVERAGE HOURS WORKED PER WEEK

First jobbers work from forty to sixty hours per week.

AVERAGE STARTING SALARY

According to our respondents, the starting salary is not much. One new hire goes so far as to call it unlivable, but another says that if you can handle a humble lifestyle for a little while, you can even manage to save a little dough.

BENEFITS OFFERED

One first jobber writes, "I received a basic HMO-type medical plan, for which I had to pay a small monthly fee. I had the option of paying more for a far superior PPO plan, but the additional cost did not justify the benefits for most healthy twenty-somethings." Additional benefits include two weeks' vacation and paid sick leave.

CONTACT INFORMATION

www.wma.com/0/careers/wmacareers/

Beverly Hills

Human Resources

William Morris Agency, Inc.

One William Morris Place

Beverly Hills, CA 90212

Fax: 310-859-4205

New York City

Human Resources

William Morris Agency, Inc.

1325 Avenue of the Americas

New York, NY 10019

(The Beverly Hills office is the only one that accepts fax submissions.)

Nashville

Human Resources

William Morris Agency, Inc.

2100 West End Avenue, #1000

Nashville, TN 37203

GETTING HIRED

Competition for assistant and trainee positions is fierce. One first jobber notes, "There are two application processes—one for those who have industry connections and one for those who do not. The former almost always are offered interviews; the latter almost never are. I originally sent my resume directly to the human resources department, and I was fortunate to be offered an interview. (Incidentally, I was offered an interview only after I followed up with a phone call after faxing my resume, and I highly recommend that everybody do this.) I met with two people from the human resources department, and they seemed to have two primary concerns. First, they wanted to make sure I knew what I was getting myself into (low pay and high stress in a fast-paced environment). Second, they wanted to make it clear that I would have virtually no contact with celebrities. While I was waiting for them to get back to me with a job offer, I did my homework and found an alumna from my college who worked there. I faxed her my resume, and the next thing I knew, I had an interview with an agent she knew. That agent offered me a job, but he also introduced me to the gentleman who eventually became my boss."

MONEY AND PERKS

Like most highly desirable gateway jobs, entry-level offers at William Morris are essentially a take-it-or-leave-it affair. One assistant writes, "Most things were not negotiable. I had the option of starting the week after I was given the offer or the week after that. The salary was set, and I was expected to do what my boss told me to do." Assistants start at about $500 per week and can earn overtime; trainees earn about $400 per week and don't earn overtime pay, "[though] they surely work overtime hours." The perks are good; one first jobber reports, "Although people often work on the weekends, the work is often semi-enjoyable (reading scripts, attending social events, etc.) and does not require people to come into the office." Another plus is that "you can get into any party in Hollywood. You have access to anybody in entertainment." One trainee sums it up this way: "The perks are fun. The in-office desk is pretty tedious and can oftentimes be awful, but you will always have better stories than your friends. 'Yeah, I was hanging out with Martin Sheen. Yeah, I was hanging out in the skybox with DiCaprio.' It becomes a way of life. The glam wears off eventually, though, and it becomes a job. If you want to be an agent, you stay focused and stay at the agency."

THE ROPES

For assistants, "the orientation process is about a week long. Along with the other people starting that Monday, you attend computer-training sessions and a variety of meetings with people from human resources. When you're not in formal training, you're working alongside an experienced assistant on your new boss's desk." Training is "mostly trial and error, [though] sometimes your predecessor will spend a few days training you." One assistant explains, "Once I earned my boss's trust, he would often take me aside and give me mini-tutorials on different aspects of his job. Almost daily, we would have informal discussions about things I read in the trade papers, questions I had about the business, interests I had in my boss's phone conversations, etc. This was unusual, though; most agents don't make the time to become a formal mentor to their assistants." Trainees often start in the mailroom. One writes, "They threw you in there right away. Orientation and training comes in bits and pieces. You [do] an afternoon of computer training for two hours, then [you're] back in the mailroom. Then a day or two later you'd do phones for forty-five minutes, then back. It last[s] over a few weeks, but each specific session [is] very brief." A trainee adds, "You learn by doing, [by] getting in people's faces, and [by] asking if you can help them. The benefit of starting in the mailroom is that you get a chance to decide what area of the department you want to work in. Television, new media—you get a chance to decide, and you go and jockey for position, trying to get out of the mailroom and get a desk when it opens up. That's when you really start your formal training on how to become an agent. The mailroom is basically boot camp."

DAY IN THE LIFE

Assistants serve as agents' gophers. "I was little more than a glorified secretary when I began my job," writes one. Trainees do all the other grunt work at the agency, and in terms of sheer quantity, it usually well outweighs the assistants' responsibilities. Trainees traditionally have the inside track on opportunities to advance within the agency. One assistant explains, "More is often expected from trainees, but more is offered to them (in terms of future possibilities) as well. I think trainees have a slightly better chance of being promoted to agents—after all, they were handpicked from the start. It's a bit like honors classes in high school—it's not impossible to get into an Ivy League school without being in all the honors classes, but if you're playing the odds, you're going to bet on the kids in the honors classes." One trainee disagrees; he says, "It used to be that the only people that'd get promoted were the trainees. My class and those after me have found that you're no more likely to get promoted [as a trainee] than as an assistant. The only value is that you're able to pick your path. As an assistant, you have to go where the opportunity is." Regardless of their point of entry, successful first jobbers soon find themselves with growing responsibilities. One writes, "By the end of my first year, I was my boss's right-hand man. If he was unavailable, I might be asked to listen in on a phone call in his place. Experienced assistants will tell you that they do pretty much everything that their agents take credit for. Admittedly, this is an exaggeration, but only slightly so."

Peers

"There is a great deal of contact and camaraderie" among William Morris Agency's first jobbers, "but there is also a bit of competition, especially among trainees." One trainee agrees: "Some peers become your best friends, [and] some become your enemies. There's more competition in a mailroom between the trainees than any other job in Hollywood. You can't trust anyone. The desk will be opening up, and it won't be on the board. So oftentimes there'll be a couple people there, and you'll get screwed out of it if you're not on top of your game." The after-hours scene "is fairly large." Many people view after-hours socializing as part of the job. One trainee writes, "It's not a job where you punch in, punch out, and go home. I would get home on average at 11:00 P.M. [or] 11:30 P.M., and I'd be out till 4:00 A.M. sometimes. You should always have dinner or drinks to schmooze."

Moving on

"People who leave the agency find success at studios, production companies, management companies, publicity houses, other agencies, and as personal assistants to the stars. The list of possibilities is virtually endless." As one assistant puts it, "for every career in Hollywood, it's *the* best place to start and to learn quickly. They run Hollywood; they have all the information."

Attrition

Many of those who leave the agency do so because they grow disillusioned with the industry, while others decide that they would rather work in a different facet of the industry. Producing is a popular aspiration among people who leave these days, for example; and many who leave pursue creative executive positions at studios. Some "point out that the place is not especially friendly toward women and minorities. . . . People displeased with the Agency also argue that, due to the very low salaries for trainees, only applicants from wealthy backgrounds are able to remain on the trainee track long enough (usually four-plus years) to have a shot at being promoted to agent. And even then, your chances are quite slim." It's important to note, however, that in regard to these issues the William Morris Agency is not unique among talent agencies. The most powerful executives in the most powerful entertainment companies continue to be mostly white males these days. Also, the agency does seem to make an effort to hire significant numbers of women and minorities into entry-level positions; it's just that most of them tend to leave the agency before they are promoted to agent.

YMCA
Various Positions

THE BIG PICTURE

Working at the YMCA is a great way to get involved in a local community. Y's across the country offer child care, education, athletic training, youth counseling, and a host of other services, all in pursuit of a single mission: "to put Christian principles into practice through programs that build a healthy spirit, mind, and body for all." The YMCA needs young, enthusiastic employees to fulfill its mission.

STATS

LOCATION(S) WHERE ENTRY-LEVEL EMPLOYEES WORK

"There are [more than] 970 independent YMCAs in communities throughout the United States. Many of these independent nonprofit corporations have multiple locations in the same city or region. All totaled, there are more than 2,500 YMCA locations nationwide. In fact, YMCAs are collectively the largest nonprofit community service organization in the United States. In addition, there are YMCAs in more than 120 countries around the world."

AVERAGE NUMBER OF APPLICATIONS EACH YEAR

"Given the highly decentralized nature of the YMCA organization, this information is not available."

ENTRY-LEVEL POSITION(S) AVAILABLE

"The number of entry-level positions changes frequently, often on a day-to-day basis. Most professional-level employment opportunities are posted on the YMCA National Vacancy List, [which you can find] at www.ymca.net. Begin your search for a rewarding career," and look for openings by job title, city, state, salary, or keyword (e.g., "youth sports," "aquatics," "marketing").

AVERAGE HOURS WORKED PER WEEK

"Employment conditions for salaried staff are defined by the local YMCA."

PERCENTAGE OF ENTRY-LEVEL HIRES STILL WITH THE COMPANY AFTER THREE, FIVE, AND TEN YEARS

After three, five, and ten years, the percentage of people still with the company are 74, 33, and 18, respectively.

AVERAGE STARTING SALARY

"For [fiscal year] 2006, the YMCA recommends that local YMCAs hire entry-level staff at a minimum salary range of $27,000–$29,000, taking into consideration cost of living, cost of labor, and specific responsibilities of the position. Each local YMCA establishes compensation based on local market conditions and its own salary administration plan."

BENEFITS OFFERED

"Each local YMCA establishes a benefits package to meet the needs of its employees; [these] may include health care, disability, dental, and vacation. The National Y Employee Benefits Trust provides consultation and offers a menu of benefits for YMCAs to choose from." Additional benefits include "the YMCA Retirement Fund, Inc., [which] is a retirement plan created to meet the specific needs of YMCA staff. Most YMCAs in the United States participate in the YMCA Retirement Plan; retired Y professionals praise the retirement fund."

CONTACT INFORMATION

People interested in employment opportunities "should contact YMCA University at YMCA of the USA and request to speak with a leadership development or a human resources and talent management consultant (800-872-9622)." Also, check the YMCA national vacancy list at www.ymca.net.

GETTING HIRED

Local YMCAs are encouraged to post all available full-time salaried positions on the website; many hires we spoke with, however, tell us that they learned about their prospective jobs by word of mouth. "A college friend introduced me to the staff, [with whom] I immediately bonded. In conversation, the available position was mentioned," writes one. Another adds, "A relative told me about it, and I needed a job." The Y seeks candidates with "a passion for positively influencing the lives of others, a commitment to the mission of the YMCA, the ability to thrive in a fast-paced environment, a strong sense of customer service, a commitment to applying ethics and values in the workplace, and technical skills in a specific program area of not-for-profit administrative application." Many who work at the YMCA have extensive prior experience with the Y, most often as members but sometimes also as interns and volunteers. Here's how one successful hire (to a teen-programming position) describes the process by which he got his job: "My resume reflected my previous part-time employment, including certification I earned through the YMCA of the USA. I was interviewed by the senior program director and the executive director of the YMCA branch. For much of the interview we discussed my previous work with the YMCA and my involvement with teen leadership programming as a teen participant. We also discussed my vision and philosophy of teen programming. On my request, I sat in on a teen leadership club meeting. A week later, I was offered the job. We negotiated for about one week prior to my acceptance."

MONEY AND PERKS

The YMCA informs us that "entry-level candidates typically spend two to three years in their first YMCA positions (especially in situations related to program and membership services). Salary increases are usually merit-based, based on individual accomplishment of agreed-upon goals. As the skills and competencies of that job are mastered, higher-level jobs, with increased responsibility and increased remuneration are developed." Salaries are determined by "guidelines established on a national basis, which are then applied by local YMCAs taking into account local market conditions, cost of living, and cost of labor." Fringe benefits offered at one local YMCA include "being given three hours a week [of paid time] to enjoy the outdoors, exercise facilities, beaches, etc." The Y also provides "an extensive professional development and education program of certification courses offered throughout the country. There is a strong commitment to life-long learning. Additionally, most local YMCAs participate in the YMCA Retirement Fund."

THE ROPES

The YMCA is not a highly centralized organization, and local Ys have wide latitude in determining services, hiring, etc. The YMCA of the USA tells us that "each local association establishes its own orientation process," but also notes that "many utilize the YMCA of the USA's 'New Employee Orientation Tool,' a computer-based training module designed to provide new staff insight into the history and scope of the YMCA movement. Additional orientation to the local Y structure and specific job are generally part of the orientation process." Local Y employees have access to the national organization's "team of leadership development specialists, who are dispersed throughout the country and who have the responsibility for counseling and mentoring Y staff regarding career development issues." Formalized learning paths offer staff members guidance as they consider the education and experience required of the next level in the organization and plan for advancement. Most first jobbers we spoke with tell us that the Y offers training relevant to their job descriptions, often in relatively short training programs conducted in a classroom environment. A partnership with Cornell University's "eCornell" online education program allows YMCA of the USA to provide a broad range of eLearning training opportunities to all YMCA staff.

DAY IN THE LIFE

"The YMCA hires a workforce that has considerable diversity in job focus," the YMCA of the USA tells us. It also notes that "many new entrants are focused in program and membership positions. Others may be employed in administrative or business functions required to effectively operate a nonprofit organization." New hires usually benefit from mentors, as "supervisors typically work closely with new entrants to assist them in fully understanding their goals and responsibilities. Performance management systems are frequently utilized to create measurable goals and objectives."

PEERS

Entry-level employees are spread among the YMCA's 2,500 local centers, and they are often among a small number of similarly experienced peers. One writes, "It has been a year and a half since I started, and I am still the newest staff member. The other people who are first jobbers at this YMCA are older than I am." Even so, most "still spend time with a lot of the staff even though there is an age difference," and "the social scene is active. We gather once a week to go bowling, have game nights weekly, and get together to watch movies from time to time." They regard their coworkers as "some of the greatest people [they've] met so far in [their lives]."

Moving on

The YMCA's national office informs us that "there is no comprehensive data on the reasons that entry-level staff leave YMCA employment for other pursuits. The conventional wisdom is that there is no significant difference between the for-profit and not-for-profit sectors on this issue." Some of the workers we spoke with said they would consider leaving the Y if opportunities for advancement did not present themselves. Education and community service are sectors accommodating to former Y workers. It should be noted that many here are clearly satisfied with their jobs; about one in four YMCA employees has been with the organization for at least fifteen years. Apparently, it really is fun to stay at the YMCA.

Attrition

While no hard data exists, employees speculate that relatively low wages, long hours, and the frustration of trying to run projects on an ever-shrinking budget are the chief complaints of Y employees and the main reasons that they leave the Y to pursue other career opportunities.

Best and Worst

"[The best] are hundreds of senior-level staff at YMCAs . . . [who] moved into positions of increasing responsibility over time, including chief executive officers and senior leaders of YMCAs in communities in almost every state in the United States. It is not unusual to have staff members with more than twenty years of professional experience in the YMCA movement." The worst are "first-time employees who are hired without full appreciation of the organization. The work of the Y is demanding, requiring a desire to build strong kids, families, and communities. Those without a true passion for helping others may find the work unrewarding."

JOBS WITHOUT ORGANIZATIONS

CONGRESSIONAL STAFFER

THE BIG PICTURE

First jobbers hired to congressional staffs rarely get to do glamorous work; for the most part, they answer phones, respond to letters from constituents, and do all the other tasks their superiors are too busy to perform. However, they do get to enjoy a front row seat to America's legislative process. Opportunities for advancement abound for go-getters, a term that describes most people who land these jobs.

STATS

LOCATION(S) WHERE CONGRESSIONAL STAFFERS WORK

Entry-level employees work in Washington, DC and the "home offices" of members of Congress.

ENTRY-LEVEL POSITION(S) AVAILABLE

Congressional staffers work as staff assistants, correspondence assistants, and legislative assistants.

AVERAGE HOURS WORKED PER WEEK

Congressional staffers work forty hours per week.

AVERAGE STARTING SALARY

Employees earn from $25,000–$40,000 per year.

BENEFITS OFFERED

Federal employees receive excellent medical benefits. They also receive a handsome array of additional benefits. Learn more about them at www.usajobs.opm.gov/EI61.asp.

CONTACT INFORMATION

You can find available assistant jobs in both houses of Congress and for both major parties at www.hillzoo.com/jobs.htm.

GETTING HIRED

Congressional staff positions are determined by individual members of Congress, and each follows a different hiring process. In all cases, however, the same basic rules apply. First, submit your resume with a letter demonstrating your passion for politics and your commitment to the congressperson's agenda. Second, be persistent; make a follow-up call, and, if no positions are available at the time you apply, continue calling every so often to see whether a position has opened up. One staffer explains, "I followed up regularly after submitting my resume and after my first interview. After that, I had second- and third-round interviews with several members of the staff. The interviews were all fairly casual, and we primarily talked about my political interests and academic focus. After three interviews for a legislative assistant position, I was told (and was well aware) that I didn't have enough Hill experience to be a legislative assistant; they offered me a staff assistant position instead. I was very pleased with this, as I had no expectations to get the legislative assistant job given that I had never worked or even interned on the Hill before. The staff assistant position was a perfect entry into the field." Many successful hires present a resume "with lots of political internships."

MONEY AND PERKS

Congressional staffers don't make a whole lot of money. In fact, most employees would agree that "Hill staffers, with the exception of committee directors and chiefs of staff, make abysmal salaries that are incredibly difficult to live on in Washington, DC." According to one staffer, the allure of this job lies not in the financial rewards but rather in the "exposure to a variety of issues that I knew little or nothing about before I started; the relationships with other offices and outside groups; and the education in lawmaking and the political process from the inside out." As another staffer explains, "When I took this job, I cared about only one thing—getting onto the Hill—so salary never mattered. Also, I had always counted on my talents to move me out of an entry-level position as fast as I could negotiate it, so I figured that if I didn't like my work, I could change things."

THE ROPES

For most congressional staffers, orientation is a brief meet-and-greet around the office; training occurs on the job. "There was no formal orientation process," cautions one staffer, "but I suppose the first month was probably an ongoing orientation for me." In many cases, first jobbers replace a staffer who is moving up to a more responsible position in the same office, and that person provides all the necessary training. One staff assistant recalls, "I was trained by the legislative correspondent, who held the staff assistant position before me. I was also trained by the office manager because she and I would be doing administrative work together. I was trained on the phones, the mail system, the coding system, and the office computer programs." Those who have previously interned on the Hill explain that they already know most of what is required of them, since their jobs are "extremely similar to [their] internships."

DAY IN THE LIFE

Most entry-level positions are for staff assistants who "do mostly grunt work, albeit work that needs to be done so the office runs smoothly and others can get more important work done." On a typical day, a staff assistant "answers phones, sorts the congressperson's public e-mail account, does the daily news clips, sorts and codes the mail twice a day, gives tours of the Capitol, and assists the legislative staff whenever they ask." Some work on the staffs of individual members of Congress; others serve all the party members on a particular committee. For most staffers, the next step up is to the position of legislative assistant, where they "work on various issue areas for a congressperson or committee, write letters, review legislation, and attend meetings throughout the day."

PEERS

A common passion for politics and access to the thriving and legendary nightlife of Capitol Hill make for "a great after-hours social scene." Because "most staffers have families and children at home," the social scene generally includes only the youngest staffers. One staffer writes, "There is a lot of camaraderie among the younger staff in the office and with other offices, and we are constantly interacting at work and often outside of work as well."

MOVING ON

Entry-level staff jobs pay poorly and involve a lot of grunt work, so first jobbers try to move on to staff jobs with better salaries and more responsibilities as quickly as possible. Some people use the contacts they've made through work to find other positions in the government, while others return to school or use the experience to launch a career in elective politics (see "Best and Worst" below).

ATTRITION

Low pay is the chief complaint among congressional staffers. As one explains, "There are certainly those who are much less fortunate than us young Hill staffers, but for the amount of work that we do, the responsibility that we carry, and the education that we all have under our belts, the pay should be an embarrassment to the federal government. My friends make at least $10,000 [a year] more than [I do], even those working in nonprofits. But the best part about it—and this is why we all put up with the terrible pay— is that it looks good on any political resume. People know the sacrifice that's involved with these positions, even if they don't work in DC."

BEST AND WORST

The best workers include many former congressional staffers who currently serve in Congress (such as John Breaux, Hillary Rodham Clinton, Tom Daschle, Mitch McConnell, and Trent Lott). The crown unquestionably belongs to Lyndon B. Johnson, who went to Washington as a legislative assistant in 1932 and eventually served as a United States representative, senator, vice president, and finally president in 1963. Johnson passed more legislation through a single Congress than any president before or since.

Legal Assistant (aka Paralegal)

The Big Picture

The job of a legal assistant "is definitely not an exciting one;" its challenges usually result from the amount of work required rather than the ability level necessary to do the work. It is, however, a great way "to experience law before you actually decide to go to law school. Most assistants work for a year or two and then decide that either they want to be lawyers and go to law school or switch careers." It's also an important gateway job; many law schools expect prospective students to have put in time at a law firm typing, photocopying, proofreading, and getting yelled at for things that aren't their fault.

Stats

Location(s) Where Legal Assistants Work

Legal assistants work anywhere that law is practiced (most often available in large firms).

Average Hours Worked Per Week

Legal assistants work from forty to eighty hours per week.

Average Starting Salary

In 2000, the median salary for paralegals nationwide was about $35,000 per year.

Benefits Offered

Benefits vary according to the firm.

Contact Information

Send a resume and cover letter to every law firm in your area; follow up on each with a phone call, unless specifically instructed not to by the firm's website.

Getting Hired

Some paralegals find their jobs by mass mailing their resumes; others use contacts: either friends who are already at firms, professors, or mentors, who can help influence the hiring process. Interning at a law firm while still in college can be very helpful in leading to a paralegal job after graduation, many of our respondents tell us. They say that when crafting an application, "the secret is to talk to people to find out what the job is like—its responsibilities, the personality traits that fit it best—and then tailor your resume and cover letter accordingly." Pay careful attention to the type of law practiced by the firms to which you apply, as "most firms hire certain types of personalities and skill sets for litigation paralegals and corporate paralegals; litigation paralegals tend to be more outgoing and less business-oriented. Corporate paralegals are often economics, finance, and accounting majors, who often go to law school, but are considering business school as well." In all instances, remember that "law firms always want to hear that you're good at multitasking, have no objection to working overtime—a lot if it—can function within a hierarchical environment, and can shoulder your share of less than glamorous tasks. So a successful applicant would describe in a cover letter how his or her previous job experiences and activities in college helped develop these skills."

MONEY AND PERKS

Paralegal salaries are "normally nonnegotiable because the prestigious firms have someone just as qualified lined up right behind you who would be more than happy not to give them problems by trying to negotiate the salary. The base salary should be between $31,000 and $35,000, with most firms leaning toward $35,000." Many paralegals earn substantially more in overtime pay; one explains, "Most of these places give you enough work that if you want to earn twice your salary in overtime, you can." Among the perks most paralegals enjoy are "car rides home and the free meals. That said, after about the first month, you don't really view it [as] a benefit anymore. Most firms allow you to bill dinner and a cab ride home if you're working past 8:00 P.M. And, when you work seventy-hour weeks, you pretty much think you're entitled to these things. And you are."

THE ROPES

Every law firm is different, of course, and each firm handles orientation and training its own way. In general, larger firms have formal orientation and training programs; smaller firms "wing it," since they may not hire new paralegals every year. For most paralegals, training covers "the basics of litigation and procedure, basics of document productions, basics of preparing for a trial, services within the firm, and firm policies," as well as "learning the different software programs and how to do legal research on Lexis-Nexis and Westlaw." A typical legal assistant at a smaller firm reports, "They sort of threw me right into it, which made me learn everything very quickly. I loved it, though. I like constantly being challenged, and to help me learn about law and civil procedure, the two partners let me participate in everything they did, from client conferences to drafting to billing, everything. I had a lot of responsibility and also a lot of support from them to make sure I did things correctly."

DAY IN THE LIFE

"The work I do is definitely grunt work, but someone has to do it. I'm sure that I could be fired today and replaced with someone tomorrow, and there would be no effect on the company," writes one paralegal, neatly summing up what all of them tell us. Another notes, "I am always bored, always. There are some scraps of interesting work that get thrown my way, but 99 percent of the time, I'm performing tasks that a third grader could do: making sure copies match the originals, making copies, assembling binders, [and] indexing documents." The job does offer some real rewards, legal assistants concede; one explains, "It's not that you don't learn anything as a paralegal at a large firm. But you reach a plateau within two or three months, and then there's not much else to learn. You can always learn more if you want to take the initiative—read the briefs and filings of the cases you're on, ask the attorneys questions. And it's not that most legal assistants don't want to do that. It's just that there's no time, and it's not what you're there to do."

And the job can even be interesting, occasionally, as when you're "doing a lot of legal research, tracking down records and documents from a million different places (which is fun—almost like detective work), putting together files for individual clients, and drafting and filing documents with the court or other agency, if applicable." Even so, paralegal work isn't for everyone. "The hours can be very long, and the work can be very boring and tedious. I truly hope that people know what they're getting themselves into. I had one friend who started as a paralegal at a law firm and quit after three days because he hated the hours. This job's really for those interested in pursuing a legal career. And, if you can tolerate the long hours, the overtime pay is great."

Peers

At large firms, the peer network among legal assistants is typically strong. That's a good thing because these folks spend plenty of time with one another. According one legal assistant, "Hands down, the best part about my job is my relationship with other legal assistants [who] I work with. All of us are between twenty-one and twenty-five years old; we spend a lot if time with [one another] having to survive the same tedious work; and all of us become really good friends as a result. We go out after work for drinks often (maybe one night during the week) and often on the weekends and for special occasions. Some of the best friends I've ever made have been at the firm, and I couldn't think of a more ideal segue from college into the corporate world than getting to work with fifty twenty-somethings." At the smaller firms, "There are only a few legal assistants who are the same age as [your typical legal assistant]. Some of the first-year associates are also friendly. Everyone seems to get along, but we tend not to spend time together outside of work." One paralegal at a small firm writes, "There were no other first jobbers, nor was there an after-hours scene. There were five people working there, and I was about thirty years younger than the next person closest to my age."

Moving on

It's rare to find a legal assistant who isn't gunning for law school one or two years down the line. Working as an attorney's lackey is a means to that goal, which means few drop out, despite the negative aspects of the job. Many of those people who quit do so when they realize that a life in law is not for them; they either return to school to seek an unrelated degree or move on to unrelated careers.

Attrition

Legal assistants are largely aspiring lawyers, and they are driven by that goal. Few quit, though fewer enjoy the job; most will also tell you, however, that "there's more to this job than its negative aspects. It does teach you to learn how to work with difficult people, and the work forces you to be extremely focused. This type of position also looks great on a resume for law school or graduate school."

Best and Worst

Most lawyers have at one time worked as legal assistants, meaning that the best and worst to emerge from their ranks can be found among today's political leaders, judges, attorneys, and a host of others in a myriad of professions.

MODEL

THE BIG PICTURE

Modeling can be "really fun, but it can also very challenging." It can be pretty lucrative as well, but it can also be incredibly frustrating; as one model tells us, "It's very hit-or-miss. Clients definitely know exactly what they are looking for, so if you aren't that, it isn't your fault. Just keep going on to the next casting until someone wants you." If you've got the temperament to deal with the ups and downs of freelance work and " [a] very superficial [industry that] requires a strong-minded person who is naturally very thin," you may want to consider a career in the world of runways and photo shoots.

STATS

LOCATION(S) WHERE MODELS WORK

Models work in major cities, especially New York, Los Angeles, Chicago, Miami, Dallas, Atlanta, and Seattle.

AVERAGE STARTING SALARY

Because of the freelance nature of this job, models can earn anywhere from minimum wage to a veritable fortune.

BENEFITS OFFERED

Typically, models do not receive benefits because they are independent contractors responsible for their own insurance. If you're successful, though, the benefits include travel opportunities, lavish parties, and socializing with the rich and famous. If you're not successful, there are no benefits.

CONTACT INFORMATION

There is no contact information, but you should have photographs taken of you, send them to every modeling agency, follow up with phone calls, and attend open calls.

GETTING HIRED

You don't need to be stunningly gorgeous to get a job as a model. "I've seen girls who don't look particularly amazing without makeup; it's all about being transformed into something different," writes one model. But it certainly can't hurt in an industry that's "completely based on looks. It's sad, but you have to realize it is all an image. You aren't being rejected because you aren't nice or smart; it's just [based] on what people want to look at, at that time." There are many different ways of getting into the business; as one model puts it, "The modeling industry, at entry-level, only requires one to be confident enough to pursue the position." Some people take modeling classes, which are "pointless, but they brought me to a place where I knew about the business of it and how it worked," explains one model. Other new models circulate photographs to modeling agencies, attend open calls, and enter contests. Some models are even discovered while minding their own business, just like in the movies.

MONEY AND PERKS

In modeling, "There is no guarantee of work or pay. Payment fluctuates from job to job, though there are certain understandings—lingerie shots pay more than regular clothing [shots], longer jobs are paid by the day and not the hour, etc. Notice of auditions or work is often last minute—a day or an hour in advance— and can interfere with other work." In many markets, rates are good when you work, running from $100 an hour for catalog shoots to four figures a day working a runway. Be forewarned, though, that even working models consider themselves lucky "to work once or twice a month—but there's a lot of small, local work out there." Models enjoy "the many opportunities to travel and make significant [money] with little work involved," as well as "meeting interesting people, learning fashion and makeup tricks, and occasionally getting gifts or clothes. And the after-parties are great."

THE ROPES

"The orientation process is basically the same as the application process" for models; it's "a thirty-minute meeting and a 'we'll call you.'" An agent can help you learn about the business; one model explains, "I met a lot of agents and development people from [my agency's] New York office. They taught us how to work the runway. A man actually did; a man in high heels. He was huge, and I wish I remembered his name. I owe him a lot." Models can also "learn things from stylists, makeup artists, hair stylists, other models, designers, photographers, and people running fashion shows. You pick it up as you go along." One model explains that ultimately, "you really have to figure it out for yourself. It's all experience. You can tell when girls have worked before, and I always try [to] help out the new girls. I don't know as much as some, but there are a few basic things that you have to know or you will get completely lost."

DAY IN THE LIFE

One model we spoke with says, "There is no 'typical day' in modeling. You may do nothing. You may have castings and fittings, then a shoot, and then have to run to your agency to meet with someone. It can get pretty hectic. I am supposed to stay good looking, though; that's my real job. I have to be nice to clients and be prompt and quiet and really pay attention to what people are telling me to do. And I have to stand up straight. That part's hard. I'm too tall to stand up straight." At first, the unpredictability of the work schedule, the frantic pace during busy periods, and the unrelenting pressure to stay thin can be extremely wearing, but "over time, you get more used to it and better able to meet expectations as expediently as possible. You get used to chatting blithely with makeup and walking around half-naked in slippers and then going back to the real world." People who deal best with modeling are those who don't take themselves too seriously; as one model puts it, "Looking pretty isn't important. Selling clothes, shoes, and makeup is important to the people who profit from it, but my job isn't to look pretty and run a business or save the planet or cure cancer. It's such a silly business, and so much money goes into and comes out of it, it's unbelievable. I enjoy doing it, and fashion is important in some ways, and someone has to do it, so I may as well." The job certainly has its own rewards and not just monetarily. One of our respondents sums it up: "Being a model has a lot of negative connotations, but the confidence gained through your career can put you in a place, mentally, that you wouldn't have been in if you hadn't explored that opportunity, thus giving you the opportunity to explore other career possibilities that you may not have ever considered."

Peers

Because models are often in competition with one another for jobs, modeling is not a profession that typically breeds deep, long-lasting peer relationships. As one model explains, "My peers are often smart, cool, well read, well traveled, and very fashion savvy. They're usually liberal and good at chit-chat. That said, they're also often shallow and competitive. I haven't made many friends, but I've enjoyed hanging out during assignments—you're thrown together with these people you have little in common with [except for] a certain look, and you make do." Another adds, "Most models think about their appearance too much, and all they talk about is modeling, which is annoying. Work is work, and fun is fun."

Moving on

All the models we spoke with knew exactly when it would be time for them to move on; one says, "If I leave, it will be because I am old and overweight and not so cute anymore or if I had another job that I liked more. It's not really up to me. When I stop getting work, I guess my modeling career is over." Another agrees, "If and when I have a child or my body changes, I will no longer be as marketable. I'm not terribly concerned with doing this for the long-term. It's a fun experience while it lasts, and I'm open to doing it for as long as I can find work without much sacrifice."

Attrition

Modeling is not for everyone. You have to have thick—but also smooth and beautiful—skin to deal with "the rejection involved when trying to get a job, the criticism of your weight," and "the pressures—to have whiter teeth, to take more inches off your hips, to refrain from playing sports that [may] bulk up your thighs, to avoid pasta, all the stereotypes—which are ridiculous." Those who can't cut it eventually give up, as do many who are chronically underemployed.

Best and Worst

The worst model ever was a fictional character; his name was Chris Peterson (professional name "Sparkles"), played by Chris Elliott in the short-lived television series *Get a Life*.

PERSONAL ASSISTANT
TO SOMEONE FAMOUS

THE BIG PICTURE

Celebrities write books, direct movies, star on television shows, and run giant corporations, so they are left with very little time to make dinner reservations, shop for birthday gifts, pick up the dry cleaning, and answer the telephone. That's where a personal assistant comes in. It's a great job for people who want a glimpse at how the truly fabulous live. It's also a great way to break into glamour professions because of the many of the contacts you make—not the dry cleaner, necessarily, but many of the others—will be invaluable.

STATS

LOCATION(S) WHERE PERSONAL ASSISTANTS WORK

Personal assistants tend to work in New York, New York; Los Angeles, California; Vail, Colorado. Basically, wherever the rich, beautiful, and famous people dwell.

AVERAGE HOURS WORKED PER WEEK

Personal assistants work from forty to eighty hours per week.

CONTACT INFORMATION

Although some agencies may find places for personal assistants to work, individuals usually find these jobs through word of mouth.

GETTING HIRED

One personal assistant describes the hiring process: "A friend of mine told me that the celebrity was in need of an assistant and thought I'd be the perfect candidate for the job. I figured 'Why not? It could be fun.'" What follows may be the most nerve-wracking interview in the job world, [because] it almost invariably involves meeting with the celebrity. One assistant to a pop singer explains, "I was first interviewed by the vice president in X's production company, then by X. The vice president asked general questions to make sure I was not an aspiring singer/actress who would try to compete against X. X asked questions about home and personal management. Her old assistant sat behind her, waving at me—'Not to worry' about any of her questions [because] I would be hired. X loved that I was a writer because she liked creative people on board." It's an odd business from beginning to end, so it should come as no surprise that there's no conventional way to learn you've actually landed the job. One assistant writes, "I figured that I didn't get the job, and then out of the blue, X's business manager called me and invited me to a lunch at a corner deli, just an average place, and it was there that I met X for the first time—over a very casual and fun lunch. It was a couple [of] days later that the business manager called me and began to have me do things—make some calls, pick up laundry, etc., and I realized that I had been hired."

MONEY AND PERKS

Most assistants are drawn to the job by the glamour of celebrity, not by the promise of cash. As one explains, "I was too naïve at that point to know [that I should negotiate my starting salary]. It could've been negotiable, but it was so exciting to be offered the job that I didn't ask." Asked to name the fringe benefits of their job, assistants list "free travel and life experience" and "the opportunity to know an American legend on a personal basis." For a personal assistant to a major fashion designer, the major perk was "the clothes, hands down. We had the best wardrobes in town. I hate shopping now. It was definitely the best."

THE ROPES

"The orientation of the job was 'Hi, I'm X.' *GO*," is the way one assistant describes how her job started. This is typical of nearly all the assistants we spoke with. The fortunate assistants get to learn from their predecessors; one assistant to a movie star writes, "The old assistant and her house sitter filled me in on a thing or two: her likes and dislikes, shopping lists, petty cash, her family, her charity work, and clothing/costume donations." The learning curve is steep and can include such subjects as "the type of dry cleaning that had to be done, the airline tickets, or the fact that X had no clue how to handle money and that I had to give him only certain amounts at a time because he would just go through it like it was water." The best experience for the job, most assistants would agree, is to have worked in jobs commonly associated to teenagers who work for spare cash: "I had worked in the entertainment industry most of my adult life, and I knew about the 'babysitting' that usually goes on, so I wasn't surprised that this is in fact what I was called on to do," explains one assistant. Asked what they wish they'd known going into the job, assistants answered, "I didn't realize how much of my life I'd have to give up. They told me I'd be in from 8:30 A.M. to 5:00 A.M. It didn't happen like that at all. I wish I'd spoken to other celebrity assistants."

DAY IN THE LIFE

For a personal assistant, "No two days are ever the same." There are the standard chores—"setting up X's calendar, getting his clothes and bags ready, getting him food, responding to fan mail, getting him personal things to fulfill his habits, and anything that would make his life more comfortable"—and then there are the unexpected extras. One assistant writes, "Often I would have to get in a cab and run after X if he lost his cell phone (which happened nearly every week) or forgot where he was going. In addition, I had to handle all calls from his manager, lawyer, ex-wives, college-age children, etc. Just managing his life." For some, this winds up being "too much info. This job is perfect for someone who wants to be on the 'inside' of a celebrity's personal life because you will know *everything*. I saw my boss naked, saw her break down in tears, watched her fight with her husband. It was all too much for me." For others, however, getting up close and personal with a celebrity is a revelation: "I have met celebrities, and I learned that they are just like you and me—they have a normal side to them in addition to this larger-than-life cachet," writes an actor's assistant. Most people concede that much of what they do is grunt work, but they consider it *important* grunt work. "I felt that in helping him, I was letting the world know of his talent, and the joy that he has brought to the world is immeasurable," explains one assistant.

PEERS

Some famous people have more than one assistant working at a time, and assistants to such celebrities do enjoy a certain amount of camaraderie with their peers. "The assistants were together twenty-four hours a day, in-office and socially. One is still my best friend. She'd only been there four months, but we hit it off," reports one assistant. Most, however, work solo; one offers, "I had absolutely no contact with any other assistants working with other celebrities—I had contact with the celebrity's manager and lawyer, etc., but that was just business, nothing social." Some assistants do manage to become pretty close with the celebrities they work for; "X taught me about life and what people are really like. He was a good friend," writes an assistant to a comedian.

MOVING ON

Personal assistants—especially good ones—can make amazing contacts in their boss' industry, and these can often lead to better jobs. One assistant moved to a network position. Another used her experience in the fashion industry to establish herself as a fashion publicist. An assistant to a movie actress landed an agent and is currently writing screenplays in Hollywood.

ATTRITION

It's often difficult to be anyone's personal assistant because the job typically requires a volatile combination of extreme intimacy and extreme subservience. "Everything when you work for a celeb is based on them. If they're in a good mood, you are. If they're in a bad mood, you are," explains one assistant. Add into the mix the general weirdness of a celebrity's life and the eccentric personality traits of most celebrities, and you know why some folks don't last long in this job. As one lucky assistant tells us, "I have heard and read folks say that many celebrities are just overgrown children and that they are selfish, difficult, and outrageously impossible to work for. I was just blessed with working with a neat human being who also happens to be a household name."

INDEXES

ALPHABETICAL INDEX

JOBS WITHIN ORGANIZATIONS

JOBS WITHOUT ORGANIZATIONS

INDEX BY INDUSTRY

ACCOUNTING

ADVERTISING

AEROSPACE

ASSISTED LIVING

BEER

BIG MACHINERY

CHEMICALS

COMMUNITY SERVICE/NONPROFIT

CONSULTING

CONSUMER PRODUCTS

DOT-COM

EDUCATION/FOR-PROFIT

EDUCATION/INTERNATIONAL

EDUCATION/NONPROFIT

ENERGY

ENVIRONMENTAL ACTIVISM/NONPROFIT

FINANCIAL

TALENT AGENCY

TECHNOLOGY

TECHNOLOGY/DEFENSE

THEATER

ABOUT THE AUTHORS

Ron Lieber is a consumer reporter for the "Personal Journal" section of the *Wall Street Journal*. In past jobs, he's written about career issues for *Fast Company* and contributed to the cover package for *Fortune Magazine's* first list of the 100 Best Companies to Work For. His first book, *Taking Time Off,* encourages students to take a year off before or during college. The book, coauthored with Colin Hall, was a *New York Times* bestseller in 1996 and is now available in an updated edition from The Princeton Review. His second book, *Upstart Start-Ups,* is about young entrepreneurs. He lives in Brooklyn with his wife, Jodi Kantor, who edits the Sunday Arts & Leisure section for the *New York Times.*

Tom Meltzer is a freelance writer who has taught and written materials for The Princeton Review for eighteen years. He is the author of eight books covering such diverse subjects as United States history, government and politics, mathematics, and the arts, and he is a contributing editor to both *The Best Colleges* and *The Best Business Schools* guidebooks series. Tom is also a professional musician and songwriter who performed for many years with the band 5 Chinese Brothers. He attended Columbia University, where he earned a bachelor's degree in English, and currently lives in Durham, North Carolina, with his wife, Lisa, and their two dogs, Daisy and Lebowski.

Lower your monthly student loan payments by
up to 51%

Call The Graduate Loan Center to find out how

Federal student loan consolidation is a free, government-backed program created to save you money. Call now and you can:

- **Lower your monthly payments by up to 51%**
- **Make just one payment each month**
- **Choose your own repayment plan**

Call right now and you can lock in the lowest fixed interest rates in history.

The Graduate Loan Center **Call 1-866-581-4GLC**
(5 8 1 - 4 4 5 2)

The Graduate Loan Center

MANAGE STUDENT LOAN DEBT LIKE A PRO

The day finally came. It was the moment you had been waiting for. The past four years melded into one huge blur of quirky professors and impossible exams. All of the seemingly endless headaches and the occasional heartaches that you experienced throughout your college career became part of an expansive collage of scrapbook memories. The day you thought would never come not only arrived, but now it's a distant memory.

Now that graduation has passed, it is time for you to face the "real" world and do things that you thought could never be accomplished. Many exciting journeys lay ahead such as getting your first job and moving away from home. However, combined with these exciting journeys, there are some pretty big obstacles like buying a home and paying off your student loans.

Many people find it exceptionally difficult, if not impossible, to pay their college tuition without taking out loans. Fortunately, the United States Federal Government recognized this problem several years ago and developed a program that helps ease the pain of repaying student loan debt.

In 1965, the Federal Government passed *The Higher Education Act*. This legislation was passed to strengthen the educational resources of our colleges and universities. It provides financial assistance to students who are enrolled in postsecondary and higher education programs; thereby encouraging more students to pursue their college dreams.

Average college tuition increases have outpaced the growth in personal and family income over the past two decades. For this reason, the need for private and federal aid has increased dramatically. As school has become more expensive to attend, students and parents have been required to increase the amount they need to borrow to finance their education. Consequently, the loan amount that students and parents have to pay on a monthly basis has also increased.

In order to ease the financial burden on student and parent borrowers, Congress passed the *Consolidation Loan Program* under the *Higher Education Act in 1986*. Through this program, student loan borrowers are able to benefit by combining all of their existing variable rate federal loans into one new loan, locking in a low fixed interest rate for the life of the loan and extending the term in which they need to repay the loan. By consolidating, in some cases, borrowers can lower their monthly payments by up to 51%.

The Federal Consolidation Loan Program

The Federal Consolidation Loan Program is a unique program offered by the Federal Government that provides student loan borrowers with the following benefits:

- Borrowers can lower monthly loan payments up to 51%.

- Borrowers have the ability to lock in a low fixed interest rate for the life of the loan.

- All existing federal loans are combined into one new loan, requiring you to make only one payment per month.

- All existing deferment options are maintained and there are no prepayment penalties. (Deferment is the postponement of payment on student loans. While in deferment, all subsidized loans will accrue zero interest).

- There are several types of payment plans to choose from. In some cases you can take up to 30 years to repay and you can change the plan annually without any penalties.

- Additional borrower benefits may be offered by the lender to reduce the interest rate even more substantially

- Borrowers can apply with no application fees or credit checks required.

The eligibility guidelines for this program are very simple. In order to be eligible for a consolidation loan:

- The borrower's loans must be in their repayment (including deferment and forbearance) or grace period.

- The borrower must not be in default on their loans.

- The borrower must have at least $10,000 in total outstanding loans. This minimum balance may vary, depending on the lender

Qualifying Loans Under the Federal Consolidation Loan Program:

Several types of student loans are eligible for consolidation, including:

- Federal Family Education Loan Program (FFELP)
  - o   Federal Subsidized and Unsubsidized Stafford Loans
  - o   Federal PLUS Loans
  - o   Federal Consolidation Loans
- Direct Loan Program
  - o   Direct Subsidized and Unsubsidized Stafford Loans
  - o   Direct PLUS loans
  - o   Direct Consolidation Loans
- Perkins Loan Program
  - o   Federal Perkins Loans
- Health Profession Student Loans (HPSL)

- Federal Education Assistance Loans (HEAL)

- Federal Nursing Student Loans (NSL)

The Six Month Grace Period = Opportunity for Big Savings

Most borrowers know that they do not have to start paying off student loans until six months after graduation. This six month period is called the 'Grace Period'. Recent graduates are awarded time to start planning for their future before they are required to make payments on their student loan debt.

Contrary to popular belief, the grace period is actually the best time to begin repaying student loans. During the grace period, student loan interest rates are actually over half of a percent lower than when the borrower is required to make payments six months later.

If student loans are consolidated while they are in their grace period, a borrower may be able to enjoy up to 51% additional savings each month on their loan payments. Depending on the total amount due on the borrower's loans, this savings could translate to hundreds of extra dollars in the borrower's pocket each month..

Student Loan Interest Rates

Not all student loan borrowers have - or lock-in - the same interest rate when they take advantage of the Federal Family Education Loan (FFEL) Consolidation Program. This is not due to the borrower's personal credit or the lender selected, but rather, it's due to rules mandated by the government. A borrower's interest rate is determined by several factors. For each of the following Stafford loan scenarios, we are at very low interest rates.

- Originated after 07/98 in grace period or any type of deferment—4.70%

- Originated before 07/98 in grace period or any type of deferment—5.50%

- Originated after 07/98 in repayment or forbearance—5.30%

- Originated before 07/98 in repayment or forbearance—6.10%

FFELP Consolidation is a federal program. The actual interest rate is determined by a set of rules defined by the U.S. Department of Education. The interest rate is determined by taking the weighted average of all of the loans being consolidated and rounding up to the nearest 1/8th of a point. This new interest rate is fixed, rather than variable, and locked-in for the life of the loan. For this reason, the maximum increase of 1/8th of a point, or 0.1249%, is minimal. And, this is the only cost associated with consolidation.

As of July 1, 2004, interest rates on Federal Stafford Loans, the most common type of education loan, have dropped to nearly their lowest point in years. The interest rate is 4.70% in school, grace or deferment status and 5.30% for loans in repayment. Parent PLUS loans have a rate of 6.10%. Rates are adjusted on July 1 of each year based on the final auction of the 91-Day T-Bill for loans disbursed after 7/1/98. The PLUS loan interest rate is equal to the weekly average of the one-year constant maturity Treasury yield for the last calendar week ending on or before June 26 of each year.

www.gradloancenter.com   *1-866-581-4GLC*

Many mailings and advertisements from consolidation lenders promote the lowest possible interest rates and favorable borrower benefits. It is standard practice for companies to offer a 0.25% interest rate reduction for making automatic payments from a checking account. Many lenders also offer a 1% interest rate reduction once a certain number of on-time payments have been received. The actual interest rate is mandated by the federal government and is the same for all companies.

Repayment Options

The Federal Consolidation Loan Program allows borrowers to get the best payoff terms without imposing penalties for early re-payment. All Stafford loans are initially based on a ten-year payoff plan and the borrower is able to opt for a non-payment status such as deferment or forbearance when experiencing a cash flow problem. Many borrowers want lower monthly payments and may choose to have the payoff term on their loans extended. Switching to a longer-term payoff plan provides an immediate increase in short-term cash flow. Since there is no pre-payment penalty in the program, a borrower can make aggressive payments toward the principal at any time.

Most lenders do not require a borrower to accept the extended terms associated with repayment plans. At the borrower's request, the servicer of his/her consolidation can adjust the payment plan to a ten-year payoff schedule. Borrowers are initially set up on the following terms based upon the balance of their Consolidation Loan:

Total Loan Balances	Maximum Repayment Period
$10,000 to $19,999	15 years
$20,000 to $39,999	20 years
$40,000 to $59,999	25 years
$60,000 or more	30 years

A borrower may choose among four types of repayment plans:

- **Level Repayment**
  The level repayment plan, which is by far the most common method selected, provides for a fixed monthly payment throughout the life of your loan..Many borrowers choose this plan because they like the security and simplicity of a fixed monthly payment. But, more important, the level repayment plan usually is the least expensive in terms of total interest charges. The latter plans cost more because they slow down the repayment of the principal.

- **Graduated Repayment**

  The Graduated Repayment Plan offers more affordable payments throughout the early years of repayment and increases gradually over the remaining period of the loan.. The payments increase no more than 4% every couple of years. The loan is repaid in the same timeframe as the Level Repayment program, but the total interest costs are slightly higher. The purpose of this payment plan is to provide the borrower with more disposable income immediately upon beginning repayment.

- **Extended Repayment**

  This plan allows the borrower to repay their Federal Consolidation Loans over a 25-year period under a level or graduated repayment schedule. In order to qualify for this plan, the oldest Federal Stafford (subsidized and unsubsidized), Federal PLUS and/or Federal Consolidation Loan must have been disbursed on or after October 7, 1998. In addition, the combined outstanding balance on all eligible loans must be between $30,000 and $40,000.

- **Income-sensitive repayment**

  The income-sensitive plan is targeted to those borrowers who have considerable financial difficulty. Under this plan, monthly payments rise and fall on an annual basis and are tied to the borrower's income. This is the most flexible plan, but it also could prove to be the most expensive in the long run. It's also important to note that the borrower must reapply for the plan annually.

Thirty years is the maximum length for a loan unless a borrower takes out another federal loan. For those who qualify, a new federal loan allows a borrower to consolidate again with new payment terms. While extending the repayment term may increase the overall amount of interest paid over the life of the loan, those who have higher interest debt often find the longer payoff schedule to be acceptable.

In addition to the choice of plans, the borrower can switch from one repayment plan to another once a year. There's no additional cost or penalty, but not everyone qualifies for this service.

Making the Right Decision

Now that all of the benefits of the Federal Consolidation Loan Program have been explained in their entirety, it is up to you, the borrower, to make the final decision. Find the company that offers the best explanation of terms, or find the one with the best incentives. Remember, the actual interest rate is the same everywhere. The decision simply becomes a matter of personal choice. So what are you waiting for? Consolidate your student loans today and save money tomorrow!

The Graduate Loan Center, based in Chicago, Illinois, helps borrowers manage paying for the high cost of education by offering the Federal Consolidation Loan Program and Private Loan Programs. The Graduate Loan Center works with some of the nation's leading financial institutions, which combined have consolidated well over $1 Billion in student loans. Call today to speak with one of our specially trained Financial Aid Advisors.

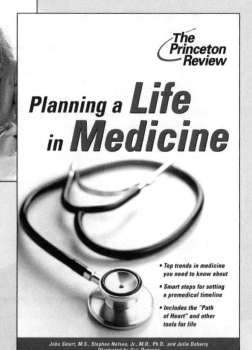